THE DEVELOPMENT OF
MARRIAGE AND KINSHIP

CLASSICS IN ANTHROPOLOGY

Paul Bohannan, Editor

THE DEVELOPMENT
OF
MARRIAGE AND KINSHIP

By C. STANILAND WAKE

Edited with an Introduction
by
RODNEY NEEDHAM

THE UNIVERSITY OF CHICAGO PRESS / CHICAGO & LONDON

Originally published by George Redway, London, 1889

Library of Congress Catalog Card Number: 66-20596

THE UNIVERSITY OF CHICAGO PRESS, CHICAGO & LONDON
The University of Toronto Press, Toronto 5, Canada

EDITOR'S INTRODUCTION

"Who knows whether the best of men be known?
or whether there be not more remarkable persons forgot . . . ?"
—Thomas Browne

I

It is scarcely problematical whether a book may be described as a classic, meaning by this term a work of generally conceded excellence, when it made no memorable impact at the time of publication, exercised no discernible influence on the subsequent course of the discipline to which it was intended to contribute, and is now, seventy-seven years after its appearance, almost totally unknown. Yet these are the circumstances of the present work, by Charles Staniland Wake, which is now brought out again, for an audience of social anthropologists, in a series of "Classics in Anthropology."

The Development of Marriage and Kinship was originally published in 1889, in London.[1] It appears to have been almost entirely neglected, as indeed were the generality of Wake's publications. Otis Mason, in *Woman's Share in Primitive Culture*,[2] published six years later, made three incidental references to Wake, including two (one on wife purchase, the other on four-section systems) specifically to the present monograph,[3] and she also included many quotations from sources as cited in it. Elsie Clews Parsons, in 1906, singled out points[4]

---

[1] Pp. xii, 484. George Redway, York Street, Covent Garden.
[2] Otis Tufton Mason, *Woman's Share in Primitive Culture* (London, 1895).
[3] Pp. 213, 215, 220.
[4] Elsie Clews Parsons, *The Family* (New York, 1906), pp. 147, 175, 201, 257, 285, 307.

in four of Wake's papers published in the *Journal of the Anthropological Institute,* though she made no use of the work in which the arguments in question found their culmination. This appears to be the sum of near-contemporaneous advantage taken of Wake's writings by other anthropologists, and it is to be found only marginally in works which themselves have enjoyed no sustained renown.

Thereafter, Wake's views received not even this degree of notice. Hartland, in his *Primitive Paternity,*[5] might well have been expected to refer to Wake's arguments on this topic, but he did not. Lord Avebury, who as Sir John Lubbock had repeatedly been expressly controverted in Wake's monograph, published a book on marriage and other matters with the explicit subtitle *An Answer to Critics*[6] in which he made many references to Morgan, McLennan, Fison, and Howitt, yet none to the critic who had offered him such precise and resoluble points of argument. In 1921, Westermarck did indeed refer to Wake's book in his history of marriage,[7] but then only in a solitary bid for support in his contention that there was a feeling of sexual indifference among those who lived closely together as housemates; and this, as it happened, was an unevidenced assumption merely adopted by Wake, not the conclusion to one of the trenchant arguments which were more characteristic of him.

More recently, Wake's arguments have passed largely unused, and his very existence uncommemorated, even by anthropologists to whose special concerns these historical facts are least might have been thought relevant. Although by no means an inconsiderable figure in the anthropological world of his day, Wake received no notice in, for example, Lowie's *History of Ethnological Theory.*[8] Radcliffe-

[5] Edwin Sydney Hartland, *Primitive Paternity,* 2 vols. (London, 1910).

[6] Lord Avebury, *Marriage, Totemism and Religion: An Answer to Critics* (London, 1911).

[7] Edward Westermarck, *The History of Human Marriage,* 5th ed., 3 vols. (London, 1921), II, 193, n. 1.

[8] Robert H. Lowie, *The History of Ethnological Theory* (New York, 1937).

Brown, in his retrospective and comparative paper, "The Study of Kinship Systems," made a particular point of agreeing with the long-neglected views of Starcke[9] (whose book was published in an English translation in 1889, the same year as Wake's), but made no mention of Wake. Later, even Murdock's *Social Structure*,[10] which is far superior to the latter essay as a work of reference on the history of the study of kinship, includes no reference to Wake's *Development* or to any of his numerous papers in this field.

It is true that Wake has not been absolutely neglected, for Tax, in a short historical survey of the study of social organization,[11] has devoted a footnote to certain of his papers, Elkin has more recently mentioned the present monograph in an examination of work done on the study of Australian aboriginal societies,[12] and Burrow has briefly considered his place in Victorian anthropological thought,[13] but it could hardly be said that these notices constitute any substantial claim to modern recognition. It may be, too, that appreciative acknowledgments of Wake's abilities lie undiscovered in still dustier pages than those of his book, but in that case their authors must be in an even more obscure situation than Wake himself.

In the common acceptance of the word, therefore, the present volume clearly is not a classic. It will be argued, nevertheless, that it is a work of classical merits, and it is on this count that it has been thought worth the labor of revival. But before expatiating on the

[9] A. R. Radcliffe-Brown, "The Study of Kinship Systems," *Journal of the Royal Anthropological Institute*, 71 (1941) : 1–18 (see p. 5).

[10] George Peter Murdock, *Social Structure* (New York, 1949).

[11] Sol Tax, "From Lafitau to Radcliffe-Brown: A Short History of the Study of Social Organization," *in*: Fred Eggan (ed.), *Social Anthropology of North American Indian Tribes*, 2d ed. (Chicago, 1955), pp. 445–81 (see p. 464 n. 36).

[12] A. P. Elkin, "The Development of Scientific Knowledge of the Aborigines," *in*: Helen Sheils (ed.), *Australian Aboriginal Studies* (Melbourne, 1963), pp. 3–28 (see p. 17).

[13] J. W. Burrow, "Evolution and Anthropology in the 1860's: The Anthropological Society of London, 1863–71," *Victorian Studies*, 7 (1963) : 137–54 (see p. 151).

virtues of the book, it will be well, since so little prior knowledge can be taken for granted, to say something about Wake himself.

II

Charles Staniland Wake was born on March 22, 1835, in Kingston-on-Hull, England, and he died on June 21, 1910, in Chicago. Between these dates there is little, apart from the offices he held and the papers and books he published (see the appended bibliography), that can securely be reported about the manner and course of his life. He was a "man of unusually retiring and unassuming character" who "rarely figured conspicuously in public";[14] and a few years before he died, moreover, his papers were lost by fire.[15] For a man who died only fifty-six years ago, he has left remarkably few personal memorials.

He was educated at Hull College, a private school which closed in 1852, about the time that Wake probably left it. He was admitted a solicitor in Easter Term, 1858, and practiced in London. Nothing can be related at present about his other occupations until 1863, when he became a member of the Anthropological Society of London, which was formed in that year by secessionists from the Ethnological Society of London. It was in the same year that he published his first paper, "The Relation of Man to the Inferior Forms of Animal Life," in the *Anthropological Review,* the organ of the Society. In 1868 he published his first book, *Chapters on Man,* and in the succeeding years he brought out a series of papers on a variety of anthropological topics. In 1870 or 1871 he gave up his London practice, perhaps partly for reasons having to do with developments in the London anthropological community. He must by this time have attained some prominence in the Anthropological Society, for he was one of its delegates to the meeting of the British Association for the Advancement of Science in 1870. When, also, the Society amalgamated with the Ethnological Society in 1871, in the formation of the Anthropological Institute of

[14] Obituary by F. S. [presumably Frederick Starr], *American Anthropologist,* 12 (1910) : 343–4.

[15] He alludes to this incident in his pamphlet *Vorlex Philosophy* (1907), p. 3.

Great Britain and Ireland, he was one of the signatories to the report of the amalgamation, and he was appointed first director of the Institute.[16] There followed, however, certain rapid and rather curious moves, of a character which led Richard Burton so far as to speak of "sharp practice,"[17] and the effect of which was that nearly all the officers of the Institute who had previously been members of the Anthropological Society alone (some were members of both societies) were relieved of their posts and replaced by former members of the Ethnological Society.[18] Wake was one of the casualties and in 1872 found himself supplanted as Director. In this year he became a partner in a firm of solicitors at Hull. He then joined a number of members who in 1873 broke away from the Institute and founded the London Anthropological Society, of which he was elected a vice-president (the other being Richard Burton). But after less than three years the new society failed, for want of financial support, and in 1875 Wake was again a member of the Anthropological Institute.[19]

From 1876 onward he practiced in the Hull firm of solicitors, Owst-Atkinson and Wake (later Atkinson, Wake and Daly), of which he was a partner until 1889. His profession in 1882 was given in a local directory as "commissioner for oaths and solicitor." He was an active member of the Hull Literary and Philosophical Society and was at one time president of the Hull Subscription Library, to which he was the first Honorary Solicitor. Neither his profession nor the distance from London diverted him, however, from an increasingly industrious application to anthropology and to the affairs of the Anthropological Institute. He was a member of Council of the Institute for the years 1878–82 and again in 1885, and until he gave up his practice in England he produced an impressive flow of books and articles.

[16] *Journal of the Anthropological Institute*, 1 (1872): appendix, xxxvi.

[17] *Anthropologia*, 1 (1873–75): 2.

[18] See *Journal of the Anthropological Institute*, 1 (1872): xxxvi–vii; 2 (1873): 442.

[19] See "List of Members of the Anthropological Institute of Great Britain and Ireland," July, 1875.

An unexpected indication of his sociological leanings appeared in his contributions to *Ancient Symbol Worship* (1874), in which, writing on "The Influence of the Phallic Idea in the Religions of Antiquity," he asserted that the "phallic superstition is founded essentially in the family idea." His ingenious reasoning of this position was that "the father of the family is venerated as the generator; this authority is founded altogether on the act and consequences of generation. We thus see the fundamental importance, as well as the phallic origin, of the family idea."[20] In *The Evolution of Morality* (1878), he attempted to show "how far the doctrine of 'Evolution' is applicable to the field of morals."[21] Something of its Victorian flavor can be seen in the "Five Stages of Mental Progress," outlined in the second volume, according to which the Selfish Phase is represented by the Australian aborigines, the Wilful Phase by the American Indians, the Emotional Phase by the Africans, and the Empirical Phase by the Turanians, i.e., Asians. It is of more specific, if minor, interest here that he refers to Morgan's *Systems of Consanguinity and Affinity* as a "very valuable work."[22] The book also includes early hints of Wake's developing sociological interests, for example, in his observations on the solidary effects of "tribal initiation" and its connection with the rule of descent.[23] From this point onward, sociological topics increasingly occupied him, although in 1882 he gave another substantial demonstration of his polymathic interests, in *The Origin and Significance of the Great Pyramid,* which was designed primarily to refute a current contention that the pyramid had been

[20] "Influence of the Phallic Idea in the Religions of Antiquity" (1874), pp. 34, 35.

[21] I, v.

[22] I, 364. He was already critical of Morgan's scheme, however (cf. "Marriage among Primitive Peoples" [1873]). In what is apparently the only printed reference to Wake made by Morgan the latter alludes rather tartly to his denial, in a paper delivered in 1878, of the existence of the "consanguine family" (Introduction to L. Fison and A. W. Howitt, *Kamilaroi and Kurnai* (Melbourne, 1880), p. 4 n. (cf. "The Origin of the Classificatory System of Relationships" [1879]).

[23] I, 437.

constructed under divine inspiration (rather as Morgan had taken his scheme as evidence of "the plan of the Supreme Intelligence"). Wake concluded that "the builders of the Great Pyramid intended to perpetuate certain scientific ideas, and, moreover, that they had a religious motive in its erection. There is little doubt, indeed, that it is a monument of Sabaism—the worship of the heavenly host, which had a wide extension in the ancient world, and with which 'Serpent worship' was intimately connected."[24] This last interest, in turn, was embodied in *Serpent-Worship and other Essays* (1888), in which he collected a number of his papers on phallism, serpent worship, sacred prostitution, etc. The volume also included, however, essays on marriage among primitive peoples (in which he made some refutation of Morgan), marriage by capture, and the development of the family. These papers had already been published some years earlier, in anthropological periodicals, but this was Wake's first venture in presenting sociological investigations in a book intended for the general public. His work on such matters culminated in *The Development of Marriage and Kinship* (1889), in which his previous arguments were ethnographically far extended and greatly developed. We shall return below to a close consideration of this work.

By this time Wake had formed some American connections, for in 1889 he published his first article in the *American Antiquarian*, transferring his attention, with typically decisive energy, to a consideration of "The Distribution of American Totems." Not long thereafter, it appears, he emigrated to the United States. This move probably took place in late 1889 or the beginning of 1890, for his lecture to the Brooklyn Ethical Association (Wake 1890), of which he was not yet a member, seems to have been delivered early in the latter year. By January 1892, at any rate, he was established in Chicago, and in 1894 he was so firmly connected with anthropological affairs there that he edited the *Memoirs* of the International Congress of Anthropology. In 1895 he is reported to have joined the staff of the Field Columbian Museum (later the Field Museum of Natural History),

[24] *The Origin and Significance of the Great Pyramid*, pp. iii–iv.

though a local directory published two years later gave his occupation as "journalist." He was formally appointed to a position in the Field Museum on February 1, 1898, as a "preparator and clerk" in the Department of Anthropology, where he remained until his death, in lonely poverty, in 1910.

During his years in Chicago Wake contributed a series of articles to the *American Antiquarian,* of which he was an associate editor, the majority of these being concerned with the American Indians. For many years he also worked on a treatise on "vortex philosophy," but at some time in the early years of this century the 600-page manuscript, together with all his other papers, was accidentally burnt. Wake laconically reported that ten years' work on his philosophical system had thus been lost. A hint as to its nature appeared in a few pages privately printed under the title *The Geometry of Science* (1904), and more ample indications were supplied in a summary of the argument comprising the thirty-five pages of *Vortex Philosophy* (1907). This work, which had been salvaged from the fire, was intended to be a "study and application" of the theory of evolution, and was acknowledgedly inspired by Hegel and by Herbert Spencer. Something of its style can be gauged from the first proposition: "The totality of nature is a vast vortex . . . everything in nature is vortical in operation."[25] It contains nothing directly on society or sociology, and appears to have been Wake's last publication.

Wake is reported to have been "well known and greatly esteemed and respected by a large circle of neighbours and friends,"[26] and yet his death seems to have made as little stir as any event in his life. There appeared, so far as can be discovered, only one obituary notice, that in the *American Anthropologist.* The Royal Anthropological Institute, of which Wake had been first Director, which he had served as a member of Council, and with which he had been constantly associated over a period of some twenty years, found it fitting to misspell his name (as "R. S. Wake") in a list of deceased members and to report, as its epitome of his life, merely that he had been "a

[25] P. 11.
[26] See the Obituary (1910).

member of the Anthropological Institute from its commencement, having joined the Anthropological Society in 1863."[27] The *American Antiquarian* was still featuring Wake on its opening page, as one of its "regular contributors," in June, 1911, one year after his death.

None of Wake's papers can be found to have survived, the institution for which he worked and the societies of which he was a member can tell nothing of him, and it has not even proved possible to find any portrait or other representation from which it might be learned what he looked like. In spite of the relative recency of his time, Wake is indeed a man who can be known only through his published works.[28] In these he shows himself to have been a man of very wide erudition, with a scholarly command of a variety of disparate subjects, and an unrelenting determination to further general enlightenment. It might be held that in such respects, as in his energetic investigations and prolific writings, he was nothing out of the way in the company of our formidable Victorian predecessors, but even in such a period— and certainly by the standards of the anthropological world today—he evidently possessed uncommonly respectable gifts. As the present work will show, he had a clear and independent mind, he was pertinacious in his pursuit of ideas, and he had an admirable capacity for hard work. He was not only capable of mastering a very wide range of evidence in a particular field, and of adducing it tellingly at apt points in a long but coherent argument, but he also had the crucial ability to strike right to the fundamentals of an issue, seeking the principles behind the tangled and refractory welter of various facts. Though always temperate and measured in his arguments, he was agreeably unimpressed by authority or status, and he clearly suffered no qualms in opposing his views to those of the most renowned figures of the day. In some respects he was inevitably swayed by the intellectual prejudices of his time, but in his writings he entirely abstains

---

[27] Report of Council for the year 1911, *Journal of the Royal Anthropological Institute,* 42 (1912) : 3–4.

[28] In the nature of the case this conclusion has no final certainty, but is implicitly an appeal for any information on Wake's life, character, or appearance.

from the insufferable assumption of moral superiority—and lacks completely the concomitant pomposity—of many of his contemporaries. Throughout his work he conveys the impression of a straight, vigorous, and imaginative thinker, a man of genuinely scholarly temper. These virtues may be appreciated by a careful examination of the present volume, the work which for a social anthropologist constitutes Wake's most considerable achievement.

III

The Development of Marriage and Kinship was published when Wake was fifty-four and at the height of his powers; but it is not an easy book to assess or to profit from without a fair knowledge of the assumptions, the modes of argument, and the state of empirical research of the period. It is, moreover, a professional and technical piece of work, and must appear such even to social anthropologists of today who have acquired some special competence in the matters with which it deals. It requires far more preparation, therefore, than can feasibly be attempted in an editorial note, and little can be done on this score beyond recommending that at least the relevant works by McLennan, Morgan, and Robertson Smith be perused before any serious appreciation of Wake's views is made.[29] McLennan and Morgan are the chief figures whose arguments Wake sets out to disprove, and for us are principal theorists of the period; Robertson Smith's *Kinship and Marriage in Early Arabia* deserves this particular notice because, in addition to its prominence in certain parts of Wake's monograph, it is such a striking example of the deep influence of a theoretical scheme (namely, McLennan's) on the opinions of an unchallenged scholar working in his own field of evidence.

Wake's book, for all its large merits, is also perhaps stylistically a little foreign to readers of today, and lacks in general a distinctive mode of exposition such as makes a return to certain Victorian authors a special pleasure. It is indeed always clear and well ordered, but it

[29] J. W. Burrow, *Evolution and Society: A Study in Victorian Social Theory* (Cambridge, 1966) will be found a most useful contribution to an understanding of the period.

has not the contentious verve of McLennan, the limpidity and fluency of Robertson Smith, or the direct plainness of Tylor. What is attractive in Wake's book is not so much his workmanlike style as the operations and terms of his thought. This also, however, is made a little difficult for us, initially because of two features: the evolutionary cast of the general argument, and the degree of conjecture.

The book's title, after all, has to do with "development," and its conclusion is expressly that "mankind has progressed upwards from a state of group-marriage, through polyandry and polygyny, to . . . monandry."[30] Even to concede that these phrasings are typical signs of an intellectual influence which Wake could hardly have escaped may not much reduce the obstacles which they may place in the way of a sympathetic apprehension of the argument. Yet they are not in fact characteristic of the work, and they need not be entertained in order to appreciate its virtues. A good indication of this is to be had in the word "phase," which is used very frequently throughout the argument. It is a word which may well convince the reader that Wake had an inveterate predisposition to an evolutionary case, and precisely in a sphere (the institutions of marriage and kinship) where hard experience has most given reason to distrust such hypotheses. We must profit, however, from the ambiguity of the word, which as well as "state or stage of change or development" also means "aspect"; and if "phase" is construed as "type" (to effect a slight further extension) it will be found that Wake's method of argument often accords far better with modern synchronic persuasions than may at first appear. Thus when he writes of "the possible phases which permanent marital engagements may assume,"[31] he means the types of union possible; when he refers to Australian marriage systems as "the simplest phase" of group marriage,[32] he has in view a logical, not a chronological, scale; and when he speaks of variations in the rule of descent "in combination with different phases of marriage,"[33] he is concerned,

[30] P. 467.
[31] P. 98.
[32] P. 99.
[33] P. xii.

as will be seen, essentially with the question of the structural concomitance of rules of descent with types of marriage. This is not always so, of course, and it is true that on occasion he uses the term in a sense which is quite clearly evolutionary, as when he writes of "the earliest phase of polyandry,"[34] but in general it will be found an aid to Wake's correct meaning if, whenever the word "phase" is encountered, the construction "type" is kept in mind. It is a question, incidentally, how far Wake himself kept the distinct connotations of "phase" separate in his own thought, but it is not a decisive matter. He seems, indeed, very much to prefigure Rivers (antedating him by twenty and more years) in his theoretical waverings between an evolutionary idiom proper to his time and a relational analysis in which he glimpses answers of the precision and fertility he seeks. The very word "phase" is at once a shackle and an instrument in his endeavours to master problems which we also recognise as significant.

The other feature which may hinder communication, the conjectural element, is less ambiguous and more readily dealt with. We may not be able to subscribe easily to any of the hypothetical schemes or processes of development propounded by the Victorians (and not only by them), but one thing which is quite certain is that there is no escape from conjecture. The extremest conjectures will inevitably propose themselves, even if only to be hastily battened down, in the most pragmatic mind. Nor is there any good reason, for that matter, why we should abstain from even the wildest or most tenuous conjectures, so long as we know what we are doing and do not commit ourselves to any of them without proper grounds. Conjecture may be more or less coherent, more or less plausible, and more or less well founded in reliable fact; and if there is to be conjecture on the development of marriage and kinship (as there certainly will be, whatever the scientific state of social anthropology), then it is better, on all these scores, that a social anthropologist should make it. We still suffer in this regard from the stunting effects of Radcliffe-Brown's sterile scientism and his castigations of "conjectural history." Yet what a folly it would be to blockade the mind, or to prune the exploratory tendrils of even the most weedlike growths of speculative thought. It is difficult enough

[34] P. 134.

to think at all, let alone think imaginatively, without subjecting the intellect to a ukase which would blight any conjecture. It requires imagination and erudition, of course, to pursue interesting conjecture, a circumstance which should make one look particularly hard at the authority of anyone who would extirpate this faculty, and it is one of the lessons of Wake's argument, in this connection, that he demonstrates a kind and degree of responsible conjecture. Another lesson is that, by tacking across the border between undemonstrable developments and empirical correlations, he induces us to be as skeptical of its inviolability as we ought to be of any dogmatic injunction to cleave to only one method of understanding and to abjure all others.

The character of the evidence available to Wake also calls for comment, for it too is characteristic of a period. We are now so accustomed to professional ethnography, and so confident in our reliance upon the reports of social anthropologists such as Evans-Pritchard, Louis Dumont, or Victor Turner, that it requires a special effort to appreciate the lesser quality of most Victorian narrations and to imagine the circumstances of the investigations on which they were based. No ethnographic report is final, admittedly, or can be expected to respond fully or exactly to all subsequent theoretical inquiries, but we may be thankful that we are not limited today, as Wake so commonly was, to such sources of evidence as *At Home with the Patagonians* or *Tent Life in Siberia*. Wake cannot at all be held responsible for the character of the information he employed, and he clearly took pains to discover the more scholarly and responsible works of his time, but much of his evidence cannot be accepted precisely as it stands. His book is therefore less of value as a repository of facts relating to certain topics, but claims respect even more obviously as a demonstration of argument.

IV

The development of Wake's argument is well ordered, but it deals with too many issues to make it feasible to survey them in a comprehensive fashion. We may therefore best try to isolate certain features of his thought and pick out only a few examples of his treatment of problems.

His beginning is typical, in that his opening lines go straight to what he thinks are the fundamental principles of social life: the instinct of self-preservation and the sexual instinct. The sexual instinct, under different aspects, is at the basis of marriage and kinship; it is subject, however, to social constraints and to natural restraints instinctive to the individual. These are the factors which are to be taken into account in conjecturing the life of primeval man, and which are to be traced through the history of institutions. Wake is careful to speak of marriage "in its widest sense," without begging the question by any more precise definition, and he characterizes the social restraints as those arising from the claims of "parents or others to have an interest in, or a right of control over the conduct of, the females, or bearers of offspring, belonging to their family group."[35] He thus scrupulously employs as neutral a vocabulary as he well may. We might dispute the natural restraints which he posits, or be dubious that the social aggregate in question should be described as a "family" group, but these are matters for particular argument. They do not affect the merit of his evident determination to get to the roots of social life, and to do so by purging his vocabulary of prejudicial terms. Contrast this approach with that of Morgan, whose entire argument is couched in terms of "savage," "barbarian," and "civilized," who writes of the "inferiority of savage man in the mental and moral scale, undeveloped, inexperienced, and held down by his low animal appetites and passions,"[36] and who judges an Australian section system (of all possible objects of moral opprobrium) to be "nearly as objectionable" as the "special abomination" of brother and sister marriage.[37]

Wake's entirely unemotive assessment of social facts, and the socio-

[35] Pp. 1–3.

[36] L. H. Morgan, *Ancient Society* (1877), p. 41. Morgan is not speaking here only of imagined brutish predecessors of historical man, but he refers also to "the present condition of tribes of savages in a low state of development, left in isolated sections of the earth as monuments of the past" (p. 42). Cf. Morgan's introduction to Fison and Howitt, *Kamilaroi and Kurnai* (1880), p. 12: "The thoughts of a savage are feeble in degree, and limited in range," his intelligence is "infantile."

[37] *Ancient Society*, p. 58.

logical temper of his thought, are well illustrated in his observations on the *areoi* of the Society Islands. Ellis had described them as "a sort of strolling players, and privileged libertines . . . spreading a moral contagion throughout society." Upon examining the evidence, however, Wake by contrast concludes that they were "a military class bound to celibacy, but forming illicit connections, which were allowed so long as no children sprung from them."[38] He continues, in the same sociological vein, to compare the *areoi* with the Nair, the Cossacks, and the Templar order of Christian knights, a procedure more likely to yield understanding than is Ellis's expression of moral revulsion.

It is initially this calm appraisal of the evidence which allows Wake to undermine the hypotheses of primitive promiscuity, on which both McLennan and Morgan founded their evolutionary schemes, the consanguine family of Morgan, the supposed historical change from matriliny to patriliny, and many other notions propounded by these and other authoritative writers. He does so not only by a rational attention to the facts, but also by adducing comparative material from all over the world and from any period of history, and in this too he distinguishes himself from McLennan and Morgan. Although it is true that, as Evans-Pritchard has pointed out, McLennan adhered to the thesis that social institutions are functionally interdependent,[39] he did so in a search for general laws of social development, and he selected his evidence piecemeal. Morgan was on safer and more restricted ground in trying to establish an Asiatic origin for the American Indians, and he was more systematic in his reliance on complete terminologies of relationship, but in his arguments he was still interested in reconstructing history, and in that alone.[40] Wake, however, in spite of his intention to show the "development" of marriage and

---

[38] Pp. 139–40.

[39] E. E. Evans-Pritchard, *Social Anthropology* (London, 1951), p. 34.

[40] Sol Tax, "From Lafitau to Radcliffe-Brown" (1955), p. 460; Fred Eggan, "Lewis H. Morgan in Kinship Perspective," *in*: Gertrude E. Dole and Robert L. Carneiro (eds.), *Essays in the Science of Culture* (New York, 1960), pp. 179–201 (see p. 195).

kinship, is essentially a structuralist: he is interested in principles of order rather than in items of custom, and in sociological correlations rather than in historical sequences. When he examines ethnographical evidence, he does not interpret it by reference to institutions the characteristics of which are supposedly already known, such as "marriage by capture" or even plain "marriage," but relies instead on far more abstract and general jural features. An admirable instance of this procedure is to be seen in his proposition: "The authority of a man over his wife or daughter consists largely in his permitting or restraining sexual conduct on their part."[41] This premise relates directly to his postulation of the sexual instinct as one of the two forces on which social life is based, and is not only a sign of Wake's style of thought but in itself contributes considerably to the clarity of his arguments. Similarly, when dealing with rules of descent he does not start from some a priori or conventional definition of descent, but considers more directly what is really at issue. He argues, in effect, that rules of descent are concerned with the transmission of rights from one generation to the next, and takes as his premise the generalization that the "primitive test of kinship was the right to the children born of the sexual union," so that his problem is then more usefully and neutrally defined as "to ascertain the principles which govern the right to the offspring of marriage."[42] His very use of the word principles is revealing, as displaying a capacity to achieve systematic understanding with the aid of analytical notions, or of general features of social life, more abstract and more manipulable than are such quasi-substantial institutions as "matriarchy" or "communal marriage."

With the above considerations in mind, let us take up the chief features of Wake's arguments on certain prominent topics. Perhaps the most obvious one to begin with is that of "marriage by capture."

McLennan's *Primitive Marriage,* it will be recalled, is subtitled "An Inquiry into the Origin of the Form of Capture in Marriage Ceremonies," and this custom clearly had to be dealt with thoroughly

[41] P. 56.
[42] Pp. 268–69.

in Wake's attempt to show that McLennan's hypotheses were "fundamentally erroneous." McLennan's chief arguments were that after a primal stage of promiscuity the first rule of descent was matrilineal; the men of the social groups in this early stage of culture practiced female infanticide, because braves and hunters were more useful than women, thus depriving themselves of marriageable women through the "thoughtlessness and improvidence of men during the childish stage of the human mind"; they were therefore compelled to seek wives elsewhere, but since a uniform state of hostility prevailed between the groups it was necessary to capture them; with the development of civilization, and the foundation of new social laws and more pacific political ties, the practice of actual capture diminished to the point at which it remained no more than a survival, or "symbol," testifying to man's rude past, while the established custom of marrying outside the group persisted as "exogamy."

Wake brings up a battery of critical shafts against McLennan's position. Capture, he argues, is not necessarily due to a scarcity of women (as, indeed, McLennan at one point recognizes), however this scarcity may be brought about; and the persistence of exogamy, in societies suffering no such scarcity, proves that this marriage rule must have had a different origin. Nor is it probable that a prejudice against marriage with women of the same stock was ever produced by the practice of forcible marriage, let alone that exogamy should have so arisen; for captive women are commonly held in low esteem, and their children are of low status. Where an inferior status is not assigned to captives, forcible marriage is in any case subject to the law of exogamy, as in certain Australian societies. There is thus no necessary connection between the capture of women and exogamy, and at the utmost "the practice of obtaining wives from the outside *by force,* would have led to a similar usage *by consent,* without there being any prohibition of marriage within the group, unless this already existed alongside of the original practice." In fact, the connection between exogamy and marriage by capture is "accidental." McLennan's scheme is defective, moreover, in that the rule of descent associated with marriage by capture could not have been, as he claims, matrilineal; for the capturers would not have recognized any authority of a woman's kinsfolk over her children, and these children would hence have been regarded as belonging to the father's group. The rule of patrilineal descent would thus have been established, contrary to the order in McLennan's scheme, while wife-capture subsisted.

Closer examination of the evidence, furthermore, leads Wake to raise still more objections. There is plentiful evidence throughout history for the capture of women as slaves or for childbearing, in which cases the capture is without the consent of the woman herself or of her relatives. But this is not the same thing as symbolic capture, and there is no necessary connection between the two institutions. Even more, Wake claims, they are further distinguished in that forcible abduction is correlated (but not necessarily, or on historical grounds) with matriliny, whereas ceremonial capture is correlated with patriliny. In the case of ceremonial capture the will of the bride-elect is a very important consideration, and she has the opportunity to escape from the proposed alliance if she objects to it. Not only this, but there is commonly a prearrangement with the relatives of the girl who is to be ceremonially captured, which makes it even more improbable that the ceremony should be merely an imitation of an ancient practice of abduction, especially since the symbolic capture is essential to the validity of the marriage. What, then, is the meaning of the ceremony? Wake abjures the kind of reconstruction favoured by McLennan and by Morgan, and offers instead what is ultimately a sociological explanation. The ceremony of capture expresses the "objection of the clan to part with one of its members," as the resistance of the bride is a formal expression of her unwillingness to leave her natal family.[43] The ceremony has to do also with "the change which

---

[43] This is the view which Radcliffe-Brown was to express, sixty-one years later, in writing that: "the loss of a person who has been a member of the group, a breach of the family solidarity . . . is very frequently given symbolic expression in the simulated hostility between the two bodies of kin at the marriage ceremony, or by the pretence of taking the bride by force" (Introduction to A. R. Radcliffe-Brown and Daryll Forde (eds.), *African Systems of Kinship and Marriage* [London, 1950], p. 49.)

. . . takes place in the position of the bride," and is "intended to denote that her family and clan have ceased to have any claims to her or her offspring."[44] The sham conflict is evidence of the consent of the bride's friends to her marriage and its consequences, and constitutes a public announcement of the marriage. Wake rounds off his case with a consideration of bridegroom-capture among the matrilineal Garo, a custom which he cogently claims as a strong argument in support of his interpretation of the ceremony, "seeing that there is no evidence of the former general abduction of men for husbands." The Garo ceremony is thus not a reflection of an earlier practice of genuine abduction, and there is no more reason to think that such an explanation is correct in the case of bride-capture. Not only this, but bridegroom-capture is seen to be practiced in a matrilineal system, i.e., the very type in which, on the contrary, according to McLennan, it was originally the bride who was captured. Ceremonial marriage by capture, Wake concludes, is thus a public ratification of "the contract of marriage," and acceptance of its jural consequences. We shall return briefly to this topic below, but for the present we may well be satisfied that this barrage of systematic criticism[45] has effectively leveled McLennan's construction.

A related issue which may also be singled out is the explanation of polyandry. McLennan, it will be remembered, maintained that primitive men killed their female infants because women were less capable than men of self-support and of contributing to the common good; the practice of female infanticide "led at once to polyandry within the tribe, and the capturing of women from without." Polyandry, he thought, was regularly practiced, or had certainly been practiced, very widely throughout the world, and had formerly prevailed over a still

---

[44] Radcliffe-Brown writes: "The proper interpretation of these customs is that they are symbolic expressions of the recognition of the structural change that is brought about by the marriage" (*African Systems of Kinship and Marriage,* p. 50).

[45] Below, pp. 64, 65, 67, 411, 415, 417, 427, 431–34; cf. "Marriage by Capture" (1873). On the Garo practice, see Robbins Burling, *Rengsanggri: Family and Kinship in a Garo Village* (Philadelphia, 1963), pp. 83–6, 117.

vaster area. "Its origin can only be ascribed to a scarcity of women as
compared to men." Morgan did not pay it such attention, but he
included "Polyandria" as the twelfth stage in his scheme of social
evolution, placing it after "the patriarchal family" and before "the
rise of property and the settlement of lineal succession to estates."

Wake deals at length with polyandry, discussing its real incidence,
its forms, and its connection with different rules of descent and of
marital residence.[46] We may best, for brevity, extract certain main
points from his argument. He finds evidence that in Tibet polyandry
was superseded by polygyny where the people were much in contact
with Hindus or Muslims, and he therefore argues that scarcity of
women was not the cause of polyandry. One report, indeed, has it
that there was even a large surplus of women in Tibet who were
provided for in nunneries. Among the Dapla, moreover, polygyny was
practiced by the rich while polandry was practiced by the poor. Wake
therefore argues, taking up an observation made by Wilson, that
Tibetan polyandry "arises not from a scarcity of women but from
the pressure of population." Polyandry limits population growth, for
the evident reason that a woman with a number of husbands can produce no more children than if she were married to only one. Where
the means of subsistence are difficult and scarce, it provides an effective check on numbers.

A report from the Toda suggests nevertheless that there may in fact
be some connection between polyandry and a scarcity of females
brought about by infanticide, but Wake well argues that because
polyandry and female infanticide are now associated it by no means
follows that they have always been associated. The Tibetans do not
kill their female children, and yet they still practice polyandry; the
object of the custom is "to keep down population, and . . . its real
reason is 'poverty'." By comparison of Tibetan practices with those
of the Rajput, the Jat, and the Arabs, Wake then argues that it is
poverty which is actually the constant and determinative factor; polyandry, he maintains, is the result of poverty, even where this is not
always associated with infanticide and scarcity of women. "Poverty

[46] Chap. 5.

is, indeed, the real parent of (a) female infanticide and (b) scarcity of females, as well as of polyandry, and as (a) and (b) are not necessarily associated with polyandry, they cannot be the original causes of it."[47]

Wake thus arrives at a position resting on a correlation which Prince Peter, in his comparative study of polyandry, was to state seventy-four years later in the proposition that: "Polyandry is initially due . . . to the fact that certain peoples find themselves living in a difficult and insecure natural environment which imposes upon them a strenuous economic and social organization."[48] The terms are not the same, and Wake and Prince Peter certainly draw very different inferences from the correlation which they independently establish; but the lesson for our present purpose (as in our general estimation of the work of which this case is a part) lies not so much in the substantive correctness of Wake's conclusion as in his method of explaining social facts. What he does, namely, is to examine the evidence carefully and in context, then isolate significant institutional features, and finally seek correlations in an attempt to establish which features are independent variables and which are constants. He is applying, in other words, the method of concomitant variations, which Durkheim was to proclaim six years later as "l'instrument par excellence des recherches sociologiques."[49]

Wake approaches Durkheim more particularly in his analysis, to

[47] Pp. 154, 155, 158, 178. There is, incidentally, no confirmation of the report of polyandry among the "Dapla" (Dafla) in Christoph von Fürer-Haimendorf, *The Apa Tanis and their Neighbours* (London, 1962). The wealthy do practice polygyny, with high bridewealth, but the Dafla attitude to wives and to the sexual conduct of women seems scarcely consonant with polyandry (pp. 92–8).

[48] H. R. H. Prince Peter of Greece and Denmark, *A Study of Polyandry* (The Hague, 1963), p. 568. With reference to Morgan's sequence of institutions, it deserves notice that Prince Peter maintains that polyandry is conditional upon "a developed sense of property and of the husbanding of resources" (p. 570), a conclusion directly the reverse of Morgan's.

[49] Emile Durkheim, *Les Règles de la méthode sociologique* (Paris, 1895; 10th ed., 1947), p. 131.

take one final example, of four-section systems, a favorite topic of
the period.[50] Two cardinal apprehensions underlie Wake's argument.
The first is that there is a necessary distinction to be drawn between
"relationship" and "kinship." The former of these terms, he states,
is "wider than the latter, as two persons may be related to each other,
and yet not be of the same kin. Systems of kinship have reference to
the particular, and not to the general, relationship of persons to each
other."[51] Theoretically, "Kinship, as distinguished from mere relationship, must be restricted . . . to one line of descent,"[52] and, as a
matter of ethnographic fact, "descent in either the male or the female
line is usually preferred for the purpose of tracing kinship. . . ."[53]
This may be contrasted with McLennan's supposition that in a patrilineal system "the sons of sisters or of brother and sister were no relations," and that in a matrilineal system "the nephew—a sister's

---

[50] It is an odd comment on the progress of the subject that whereas
four-section systems were familiar subjects of discussion for educated
Victorian gentlemen, they are now commonly regarded as posing
dauntingly technical problems in which only social anthropologists,
and those specialized in the study of them, may reasonably be expected
to take an informed interest.

It is an odder, and more dejecting, matter that although such systems were fairly well described in the last century, and in spite of the
fact that their rationale was brilliantly analyzed by Durkheim in 1898,
there is still no scholarly or theoretically satisfying examination of
this type of society.

[51] P. 254; cf. p. 267.

[52] P. 268.

[53] Pp. 294–95; cf. "Marriage among Primitive Peoples" (1873), p.
206; "The Origin of the Classificatory System of Relationships"
(1879), p. 164. Lévi-Strauss attributes to J. R. Swanton ("The Social
Organization of American Tribes," *American Anthropologist*, 7
[1905] : 663–73), a generation later, the insight that "même dans les
tribus en apparence les plus unilatérales, l'autre lignée n'était jamais
complètement ignorée" (*Les Structures élémentaires de la parenté*
[Paris, 1949] p. 134). Cf. M. Fortes ("The Structure of Unilineal
Descent Groups," *American Anthropologist*, 15 [1953] : 17–41) on
"complementary filiation" (pp. 33–4).

child—is a relation of [Ego], but his son is none at all."[54] Wake's second premise is the recognition that within one system rights may be differentially associated with descent traced through one parent and with relationship traced through the other.[55] Though apparently modest enough, these two connected notions really mark a very considerable advance. They constitute a break away from McLennan's and Morgan's view of paternal and maternal connections as two entirely distinct and mutually exclusive criteria of organization, and consequently away from the imagined necessity to arrange matriliny and patriliny in an evolutionary sequence.[56]

From this point of understanding Wake can readily grasp the importance of Fison's observation, concerning the Kamilaroi, that certain relatives in Australian section systems are affines rather than cognates; they are "fathers-in-law and mothers-in-law, rather than uncles and aunts, sons-in-law and daughters-in-law rather than nephews and nieces."[57] The report is indeed Fison's, and he deserves great credit for it, since it is an interpretation of quite capital theoretical importance. Wake, however, has a distinct claim to our respect in this regard because, in the first place, he saw that it was so important. If this should be thought no great feat, it may be taken into account that it was not until 1953 that a systematic application of this idea to a terminology of symmetric alliance was effected, magisterially and independently, by Louis Dumont in his paper "The Dravidian Kinship Terminology as an Expression of Marriage."[58] Wake writes,

---

[54] J. F. McLennan, *Primitive Marriage* (Edinburgh, 1865), p. 237. In fairness to McLennan, it must be remarked that he qualifies one such assertion by saying that in an agnatic system children by the same mother but different fathers are not relations "to any legal effect" (p. 236), but this is not a distinction which he maintains.

[55] E.g., p. 278.

[56] Pp. 386–87.

[57] Pp. 335–36; cf. Fison and Howitt, *Kamilaroi and Kurnai* (1880), p. 76.

[58] *Man*, 53 : 35–9, art. 54. "My mother's brother is essentially my father's affine"; "It is this [affinal] alliance as an enduring institution that is embedded in the terminology, that provides it with its funda-

further, that "the term 'cousin' . . . practically points out the group of individuals to which a man stands in the marital relation, or from which he must obtain a wife" ;[59] that is, just as Dumont is doing when he writes (though in more exact terms) that "Ego's 'cross cousins' are essentially Ego's affines,"[60] he is defining a system of prescriptive alliance.

He takes an additional step, and one which is remarkable for its time, especially in comparison with the procedures of McLennan and of Morgan, when he isolates the principles of order at work in a four-section system. The rule of descent is matrilineal, although the Kamilaroi ban on marriage with the father's sister's daughter shows that relationship on the father's side is nevertheless recognized. By contrast with the matrilineal Iroquois, who are matrilocal, the Australian practice is, however, that the wife goes to reside with her husband's family and the son remains in his father s horde.[61] In Levi-Strauss's terms, therefore, the Iroquois have a harmonic regime, whereas the Australian aborigines in question have a dysharmonic regime.[62] This means that in the latter case persons related by matri-

---

mental and characteristic opposition'' (pp. 37, 38). If the comment be admitted here, it was Radcliffe-Brown's confessed inability to understand Dumont's formal analysis (*ibid.*, p. 112, art. 169) which was the immediate occasion of a regretful observation that he ''never really grasped the necessity to view a kinship terminology as a form of classification'' (Introduction to E. Durkheim and M. Mauss, *Primitive Classification* [Chicago, 1963], p. xxxv n. 2). This failure is displayed especially in his questions about the positions of the father's brother and the mother's sister, and in his observation on the Kariera category *nuba* (cf. Dumont, *Man*, 53 : 143, art. 224), from which the conclusion must be, sadly, that he seems not to have arrived at an intrinsic comprehension of the principles of Kariera social classification (cf. A. R. Brown, ''Three Tribes of Western Australia,'' *Journal of the Royal Anthropological Institute*, 43 [1913] : 143–94).

[59] P. 336.

[60] L. Dumont, *Man*, 53 (1953) : 38.

[61] Pp. 125, 301, 337.

[62] C. Lévi-Strauss, *Les Structures élémentaires de la parenté* (Paris, 1949), pp. 270–5.

lineal descent will be dispersed among local groups based on patrilineal inheritance of territorial rights. The connection between such scattered matrilineal relatives is accompanied by certain rights and duties, particularly relating to marriage (they are forbidden to intermarry among themselves), and it is a useful effect of totemism that it makes known with certainty who these persons are. Wake's general conception of a four-section system, then, is that it consists effectively of two intermarrying groups with matrilineal descent, but recognizing relationship through the father for certain purposes, especially the perpetuation of the local organization; marriage is prescribed with certain members ("cousins") of a class (section) of terminological affines, this class being one of four into which the entire membership of the society is divided; the classes are grouped into pairs, but children never take the class name of either parent, and "every family passes, therefore, through each of the classes in the course of four generations."[63]

Now it is true that the individual pieces of information come from Howitt and from Fison, and that McLennan also touched on the integrative effects of matrilineal totemism, but Wake has composed the evidence into a strikingly modern-looking system of social facts, entirely unaffected by the evolutionary glosses of the former writers. His interpretation is so close to Durkheim's classical formulation[64] that it is a sharp disappointment to have to concede that he fell just short of it. His own suggestion is that the postulated original moieties were divided into four sections, and that the latter were "intended, not so much to alter or limit the range within which marital connections were possible, as to point out more distinctly what persons stood together in the relation of class parents and children, and, therefore, could not intermarry."[65] There is some force in this also, but not

---

[63] Pp. 326, 124–25, 335, 333.

[64] E. Durkheim, "La Prohibition de l'inceste et ses origines," *L'Année sociologique*, 1 (1898): 1–70 (see pp. 18–21). The most economical explication, in modern terms, is that a four-section system is a dysharmonic two-section system.

[65] P. 111.

the definitive articulation of principles of order which Durkheim was to discern nine years later. Nevertheless, we see a clear indication of his analytical approach in his comparison of matrilineal North American tribes with the Australian aborigines, in which he makes a resemblance by reference to "perpetual succession through males, combined with descent through females."[66] We have only to revert to McLennan or Morgan, to Fison or Robertson Smith, in order to appreciate that, unlike these writers, Wake is adducing, not moralistic characterizations or evolutionary conjectures or historical connections, but a correlation of purely sociological criteria.

This is a feature of his thought which may be seen in his examination of a range of other matters, of which the following is a partial list: the distinction between matriliny and the supremacy of women; marriage as a contract between groups of individuals; alliance groups as not nearly so large in practice as in theory, and quite consistent with individual rights; the importance of marital residence in analysis, and its "political effects" in practice; the relative independence of marital residence and rule of descent; the correlation of systematic polygyny with patriliny; the purely contingent connection between "wife purchase" and polygyny; the position of women as not necessarily improved by matriliny or impaired by polygyny; the coexistence of individual marriage together with "group marriage," polyandry, or polygyny; the significance of ghost marriage; the compossibility of either patriliny or matriliny with any type of marriage; the correlation between matriliny and absence of bridewealth; the correlation between matriliny and matrilocal polyandry, and between patriliny and patrilocal polyandry; that while patriliny may replace matriliny, it appears that the converse never takes place; that a gens or totemic group (lineal descent group) may include physically unrelated members; the congruence of section names with relationship categories; that the Turanian and Ganowanian "classifications" differ only in the rule of descent, from which it follows that there is no necessity that

---

[66] P. 303. It would be too much, of course, to expect Wake to go into the fundamental question of why these two factors do not produce a four-section system among the Iroquois.

the patriliny of Turanian systems should be less original than the matriliny of the Ganowanian; that either patriliny or matriliny may originate from a cognatic situation; that patrilineal and matrilineal systems, far from being genetically linked, may have had "independent origins under special social conditions"; the distinction between the levirate and wife-inheritance; that cognatic reckoning of relationship reduces the range of marriage prohibitions, and operates by reference to degree rather than to category.

When we consider these terms, ideas, and propositions (some of which can be traced to earlier formulations in articles dating back to 1873), together with the relational style of analysis which characterizes them, it is hard to associate Wake with McLennan, Lubbock, Morgan, or Robertson Smith. In such respects, it may rather be claimed, he is intellectually far more of a kind with Durkheim and the later members of the *Année sociologique* school. In his analytical capacity, as displayed in this book, it may well be said that Wake was a man ahead of his time. This may partly account for the contemporary neglect of his work, while in later years, when the kind of approach to social facts of which he had given this early evidence had become established in the universities, his writings were eclipsed by more prominent and professional investigations. But certainly he was a worthy precursor of theoretical developments which not until decades later were to be distinguished as social anthropology.

V

We must be careful, naturally, not to overrate Wake. It cannot be held against him that he arrived at wrong or disputable conclusions for lack of suitable evidence, but in some of his ideas he was still very similar to more typical writers of the period,[67] and expectably enough he made a number of argumentative mistakes, some of which were of serious effect for his general position. One instance is to be seen in his assertion that "the true cause [of systematic monandry] must be

---

[67] E.g., "If Africa is not the birthplace of polygyny, then it must be sought in Western Asia" (p. 191).

sought in the development of a sense of self-respect,"[68] in which he not only seeks a distant cause of a social institution in a hypothetical moral sentiment, but moralistically argues backwards from Victorian convictions about the right and true form of marriage. Another example is his axiomatic insistence that marriage prohibitions can be explained by reference to "the feeling that persons closely related by blood ought not to intermarry,"[69] a feeling which he makes into a principle of explanation under the name of a supposed "fraternal instinct."[70] There are not many such fallacies, but they are there and should not be glossed over.

Another ground on which his achievement might be depreciated is the extent to which he draws upon or repeats the work of others. For example, the useful observation that bridewealth secures rights in the children of the marriage[71] was preceded by Robertson Smith's conclusion that in Arabia what a husband purchases is the right to have children by a certain woman and "to have these children belong to his own kin."[72] The point that exogamy and endogamy are not opposite conditions of society, as McLennan had thought, but that social divisions could be at once exogamous in one context and endogamous in another,[73] was similarly preceded by Morgan's argument to the same effect.[74] The cohesive value of totemic affiliation in a dysharmonic system[75] was earlier argued for by McLennan,[76] and although Wake

[68] P. 251.

[69] P. 55; cf. pp. 33, 255.

[70] Huth, referring to earlier papers of Wake's (1879; 1880a), had already commented that "Mr. C. S. Wake ascribes no other cause to the limits on intermarriage than a desire on the part of savages to avoid incest" (Alfred Henry Huth, *The Marriage of Near Kin*, 2d ed. [London, 1887], p. 20.)

[71] P. 270.

[72] W. Robertson Smith, *Kinship and Marriage in Early Arabia* (London, 1885; new ed., 1903), p. 130.

[73] P. 101, n. 1.

[74] Lewis H. Morgan, *Ancient Society* (London, 1877), p. 514.

[75] Pp. 325–26.

[76] J. F. McLennan, *The Patriarchal Theory* (London, 1885), p. 227.

had previously argued decisively that patrilateral relatives were recognized in a matrilineal system the crucial and full distinction between kinship and relationship was more due to Fison.[77]

In other instances, Wake was either forestalled by work with which he was unacquainted or did not take sufficient advantage of publications with which he was familiar. For example, when he published his book, Wilken had already advanced reasons to deny that female infanticide would lead to a scarcity of women, thus attacking McLennan's theory in a different quarter. Wilken's points were that there are naturally more women than men in a population, that more boys than girls die in infancy, and that men are exposed to far more dangers to life than are women. The real problem for primitive societies, he argued, was that of a surplus of women, and he thereupon rejected McLennan's argument that female infanticide was the cause of exogamy. Moreover, Wilken contended, while female infanticide in one tribe would have caused a scarcity of women in that tribe, the same practice in other tribes would have caused a similar scarcity among them also and would have made exogamy impossible as a means to redress the scarcity in the first. As for marriage by capture, he rejected the idea that ceremonial capture was merely a survival of actual abduction, since the relatives of the bride play such an important part that the proceeding appears to take place entirely with their consent.[78] Spencer, too, had made numerous cogent criticisms of McLennan's scheme,[79] not all of which were taken up by Wake.

There remains—to take one further particular matter—an issue of fundamental and continuing importance in social anthropology

[77] "The Origin of the Classificatory System of Relationships" (1879), p. 164; L. Fison and A. W. Howitt, *Kamilaroi and Kurnai* (1880), pp. 76, 119–27.

[78] G. A. Wilken, "Over de primitieve Vormen van het Huwelijk en den Oorsprong van het Gezin," *De Indische Gids*, 2 (1880) : 601–64; 3 (1881) : 232–83 (see pp. 614–5); "Het Matriarchaat bij de oude Arabieren," *ibid.*, 6 (1884) : 90–132 (p. 123); cf. "Huwelijken tusschen Bloedverwanten," *De Gids*, 54 (1890) : 478–521 (pp. 505–7).

[79] Herbert Spencer, *The Principles of Sociology*, 3 vols. (London, 1876–96), I, 648.

which Wake might well have gone into more thoroughly. This is the
question of the significance of relationship terms. McLennan argued
that a major mistake on Morgan's part was "to have so lightly assumed
the [classificatory] system to be a system of blood-ties." Morgan's
tables, he contended, showed "that 'son' and 'daughter,' in the classificatory system, do not mean son or daughter 'begotten by' or 'born to';
that 'brother' and 'sister' are terms which do not imply connection by
descent from the same mother or father; and that 'mother' does not
mean the bearing mother." His own position was, in a famous passage:
"What duties or rights are affected by the 'relationships' comprised
in the classificatory system? Absolutely none. They are barren of
consequences, except indeed as comprising a code of courtesies and
ceremonial addresses in social intercourse. . . . The classificatory system is a system of mutual salutations merely. . . ."[80] Wake reports
that he does not find it necessary to consider this position, and declares simply that "we cannot doubt that the relationships of the
classificatory system are real, and that it has a very intimate connection with the rules of marriage and descent."[81]

This is a just enough conclusion, but it does not resolve the real
point at issue between McLennan and Morgan. This point was well
brought out by Donald McLennan, brother of J. F. McLennan, in an
editorial note in the second edition of *Studies in Ancient History*. He
showed there that according to Lafitau and many other observers the
classificatory terms were used as terms of address, that everybody
used them "whether addressing relatives or not," and that they did
not carry any implication of blood relationship. Among the Iroquois
they were in fact used "to indicate the respect due from the speaker
to the age and station of the person spoken of." After adducing numerous supporting instances from the Iroquois ethnography, he concluded
that "Mr. Morgan was wrong in supposing that the classificatory
terms were only used between relations, and to denote blood-relation-

[80] J. F. McLennan, *Studies in Ancient History*, edited by D. McLennan (London, 1876), pp. 361–2, 366 (new ed., London, 1886), pp. 269–
70, 273.
[81] P. 342. Cf. W. H. R. Rivers, *Kinship and Social Organisation*
(London, 1914), pp. 6–8, 17.

ship.''[82] This is indeed a crucial issue, which Morgan never came to terms with, and which still recurs today in academic disputes about "kinship" and biology.[83] McLennan, in spite of his polemical over-reaction in asserting that no rights and duties were involved, was making a point of the first theoretical importance. Wake, although he concluded as early as 1873 that "We shall find in . . . the obligations of clanship the key to the classificatory system of relationships,''[84]

---

[82] *Studies in Ancient History* (new ed., 1886), pp. 306, 308; cf. pp. 309–15.

[83] A particularly effective example of the persistence of erroneous preconceptions on this score, since it compounds antique fallacies from both Morgan and McLennan, is to be seen in the assumptions of one philosopher that "kinship" can be defined in terms of biological connections, and that in the construction of an ideal descent terminology a matrilineal rule should more conveniently be adopted "in view of the fact that it is harder for an individual to be ignorant of the identity of his mother than of his father" (E. Gellner, "Ideal Language and Kinship Structure," *Philosophy of Science,* 24 [1957], 235–42).

Yet these positions were effectively invalidated, more than half a century before, by two scholars of more continued renown than McLennan, let alone Wake. The former point was demolished by Durkheim in 1898 (*L'Année sociologique,* 1:306–19), when he demonstrated that consanguinity is neither a necessary nor a sufficient condition for the recognition of kinship (pp. 316–7) : "all kinship is social; for it consists essentially of jural and moral relationships sanctioned by society. It is a social tie or it is nothing. There can be only one kinship, namely that which is recognized as such by society" (pp. 318–9). The latter point was made untenable by Van Gennep in 1906, when he contended that the rule of descent is not determined by the certainty of parentage from the mother, or uncertainty from the father, but that such an argument can be assessed only in the light of indigenous theories of conception, which are contingent and largely uninvestigated; among certain Australians, for example, "from the fact that the mother bears the child it does not follow . . . that she conceived it; she appears to them as no more than a temporary receptacle" (Arnold Van Gennep, *Mythes et légendes d'Australie* [Paris, 1906], pp. xxvi–vii).

[84] "Marriage among Primitive Peoples" (1873), p. 203.

shows himself less than usually percipient in not following up D. McLennan's demonstration that, by various criteria distinct from biological connections, classificatory relationship terms denote social status.

In the year before the publication of Wake's monograph, however, these points had already been taken up by Starcke, in *Die Primitieve Familie*.[85] In the English edition, published in 1889, Starcke acutely observed that: "The value of [McLennan's] suggestions consists in his emphatic assertion that nomenclature is in no way founded on the facts of procreation, and that its development is due to the altogether formal principle of reciprocity." And, on the actual significance of relationship terms: "The nomenclature was in every respect the faithful reflection of the juridical relations which arose between the nearest kinsfolk of each tribe. Individuals who were, according to the legal point of view, on the same level with the speaker, received the same designation."[86] The latter formulation contains, in the word "nearest," a dangerous implication of an "extension" theory of classificatory terms,[87] but the analytical standpoint is of notable theoretical and historical interest. Radcliffe-Brown has remarked that it would be "interesting to consider why it is that Starcke has had so few followers and Morgan so many,"[88] a question which is closely similar to that

---

[85] C. N. Starcke, *Die primitieve Familie in ihrer Entstehung und Entwicklung*, Leipzig, 1888.

[86] C. N. Starcke, *The Primitive Family* (London, 1889), pp. 186–7, 207. These propositions, together with D. McLennan's explanatory observations, hardly support the suggestion that McLennan's attack on Morgan was "sufficiently convincing to keep the subject of kinship terminology from its proper sphere for many years" (Sol Tax, "From Lafitau to Radcliffe-Brown" [1955], p. 456, cf. p. 464).

[87] Perhaps adopted from D. McLennan, who distinguishes between "the nucleus in which the terms originated and the circle throughout which they were commonly used" (*Studies in Ancient History* [new ed., 1886], p. 310).

[88] A. R. Radcliffe-Brown, "The Study of Kinship Systems," *Journal of the Royal Anthropological Institute*, 71 (1941): 1–18 (see p. 5).

concerning Wake's near-oblivion. More important, the two men were of somewhat similar styles of mind also. Starcke was perhaps in some respects even a little in advance of Wake, for he relied more on the relationship terminologies provided by Morgan, and he seems to have appreciated more clearly what their precise sociological value might be.[89] An example of this is the generalization that societies which have "a single designation for the mother's brother and all his descendants follow the male line,"[90] i.e., the correct proposition that the "Omaha" feature (MB = MBS) is associated with patriliny. In such respects both Wake and Starcke were to be technically far outstripped by Kohler, in his intensive and diagrammatic analyses of various types of relationship terminologies,[91] but in more essential regards it is they who may be recognized as inaugurating, probably under the influence of Herbert Spencer and thus of Comte,[92] the era of sociological analysis which was to be decisively opened by Durkheim.

In rounding off our assessment of Wake's position in the development of social anthropology (see Tables 1 and 2), we should pay some attention to the little that is known about the circumstances of his life. Like Bachofen, Maine, McLennan, Morgan, and Kohler, he was a lawyer, if of a humbler sort, not a gentleman of means like Lubbock or an academic like Fustel de Coulanges or Tylor or Robertson Smith.

---

[89] On the supposed historical value of terminologies, he writes that a jural explanation of the kind he suggests "diminishes the significance of nomenclatures as a contribution to the means of historical research to such an extent that it ceases to possess the interest which would entitle us to dwell further on the subject" (1889, p. 207).

[90] 1889, p. 195.

[91] J. Kohler, *Zur Urgeschichte der Ehe: Totemismus, Gruppenehe, Mutterrecht* (Stuttgart, 1897). Cf. the review by E. Durkheim, *L'Année sociologique*, 1 (1898), 306–19; W. H. R. Rivers, *Kinship and Social Organisation* (London, 1914), p. 19.

[92] Wake was evidently acquainted directly with Comte's writings also, for as early as 1873 he quoted him at length and respectfully referred to him as "one whose teaching on [the position of women], as on all other subjects, demands the most thoughtful consideration" ("The Social Condition of Woman" [1873], p. 85.)

TABLE 1

PRINCIPAL WORKS OF THE PERIOD

1861	J. J. Bachofen. *Das Mutterrecht.* Stuttgart.
1861	H. S. Maine. *Ancient Law.* London.
1864	N. D. Fustel de Coulanges. *La Cité antique.* Paris.
1865	J. F. McLennan. *Primitive Marriage.* Edinburgh.
1870	J. Lubbock. *The Origin of Civilisation.* London.
1871	L. H. Morgan. *Systems of Consanguinity and Affinity of the Human Family.* Washington, D.C.
1871	E. B. Tylor. *Primitive Culture.* London.
1871	C. R. Darwin. *The Descent of Man.* London.
1876	J. F. McLennan. *Studies in Ancient History.* London.
1876–96	H. Spencer. *The Principles of Sociology.* London.
1877	L. H. Morgan. *Ancient Society.* New York.
1878	E. B. Tylor. *Researches into the Early History of Mankind.* London.
1880	L. Fison and A. W. Howitt. *Kamilaroi and Kurnai.* Melbourne.
1885	J. F. McLennan. *The Patriarchal Theory.* London.
1885	W. Robertson Smith. *Kinship and Marriage in Early Arabia.* London.
1888	C. N. Starcke. *Die Primitieve Familie in ihrer Entstehung und Entwicklung.* Leipzig. (English edition: *The Primitive Family,* London, 1889.)
1889	C. S. Wake. *The Development of Marriage and Kinship.* London.
1895	E. Durkheim. *Les Reglès de la méthode sociologique.* Paris.
1896	J. F. McLennan. *Studies in Ancient History: Second Series.* London.
1897	J. Kohler. *Zur Urgeschichte der Ehe.* Stuttgart.
1898	E. Durkheim (ed.). *L'Année sociologique,* Vol. I. Paris.

He had not the opportunities, either, which Morgan had to make direct inquiries among American Indians or other peoples in whose institutions he was interested, and he was not resident for years, as were Fison and Howitt, within reach of Australian aborigines and in easy communication with correspondents among them. It seems unlikely that Morgan would ever have made his immense contribution to knowledge if he had not first been able to ask questions of the Seneca and the Ojibwa, and Fison and Howitt could never have written their remarkable book (much neglected since) except for the circumstances of their occupations. Lacking their ethnographical advantages, Wake also lacked the scholarly advantages possessed by academic researchers. Robertson Smith did not have an undistracted life, but he was a professor, and pursued his investigations in an environment especially

TABLE 2

Comparative Table of Life Spans

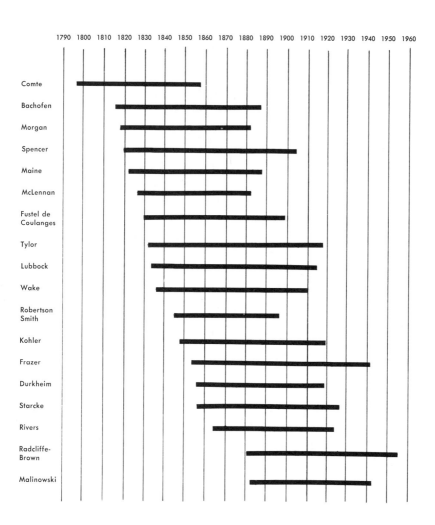

designed for the advancement of learning. Durkheim, in conclusion, presents a new contrast, for he was not only an academic but he devoted his life to the establishment of the discipline to which Wake had made his amateur and necessarily intermittent contributions. Against this background the quality and volume of the latter's work attract an especially sympathetic and admiring regard. Let us recall, moreover, that the aim of *The Development of Marriage and Kinship* was to demonstrate that the disparate hypotheses of McLennan and of Morgan were both fundamentally erroneous.[93] He thus undertook an extensive and important task, and the large degree of success which he achieved amply deserves recognition. If either McLennan or Morgan is worth reading today, Wake certainly is too. More than all this, he displayed a disciplined imagination, a flair for relational analysis, and a method of posing and tackling problems which earn him a secure place in the history of social anthropology.

While we make such posthumous amends as we may, finally, and as we scan Wake's bibliography and contemplate his life's work in the furtherance of understanding, we shall do well to ponder the extent to which a man of this caliber was forgotten and his arguments ignored. No electronic devices, lavish grants, or jet flights to learned conferences, no academic dignities, grandiose research programs, or textbook surveys of work done by others will preserve any of us from the fate of Charles Staniland Wake—and who can think himself to compare so well, by the true standards of scholarship, that posterity will find him as much deserving of ideological resuscitation?

VI

The editing of this book has been guided by the principle that the greater one's respect for an author the less one will tamper with what he decided he wanted to say, or with how he wished to express it.

---

[93] Perhaps it should be explained that these were more robust days, when it was not considered offensive to all the academic proprieties, and to carry personal imputations besides, to use terms of logic such as "mistaken" or "fallacious" or "unsound" in theoretical debate.

There are indeed *longueurs* in Wake's monograph, particularly in chapter 7, but the work as a whole is so well constructed, and the order of topics so consequentially taken up, that no excisions have been made. Similarly, the original diagrams and text figures have been retained, not just because they are original but also because the effort to adjust one's thoughts to them is an historical aid to participation in the author's conception of the problems. A very few editorial footnotes have been appended where they seemed of some particular interest. Minor corrections of names and spelling have been made in the footnotes—but not in the body of the text, which has not been reset.

The chief editorial labor connected with the text has been the preparation of the bibliography of sources used by Wake. None of his titles is complete by modern standards, and they have all been made conventionally full; some are mistaken, and these have been corrected. "Mariner," for example, is a very brief indication to *An Account of the Natives of the Tonga Islands;* and if *"Wanderings in West Africa"* was clear enough to members of the London Anthropological Society, who knew very well that it was written by their vice-president, Richard Burton, it may be less so to a modern reader, who may not know in any case that the work in question has only "A F.R.G.S." on the title page instead of the author's name. Presumably, too, there will be readers of this edition who will be relieved not to have to cast about for a reference under plain "Smith," with no initials, no date, no place, and (exceptionally, for Wake) a wrong title. Wake is normally scrupulous about specifying the editions he uses, and when he does not do so they have usually been ascertained. In a few instances he cites a standard work which went into a number of editions (e.g., Gibbon), without stating which one he is employing, and in such cases the date of the first edition is given, with the consequence that the page references are uncertain. The sources, finally, have been brought together in a consolidated bibliography at the back.

For the most part it has not been thought feasible or necessary to check the references, but wherever they have been looked up they have proved correct. The index has been considerably augmented, particularly in analytical respects, but still includes Wake's own headings.

A number of persons have assisted in a long and generally fruitless search for biographical information on Wake, and also in the matter of references. The following are especially thanked for their kind help: Mr. George H. Davis, Mr. R. F. Drewery, Miss Margaret E. Kenna, Dr. W. C. Sturtevant and Mr. E. Leland Webber. The preparation of this edition would have been far more difficult without the magnificent resources of the Bodleian Library and the friendly efficiency of its staff. Dr. P. G. Riviere has been so good as to read the introduction in draft and to offer comments which are gratefully acknowledged.

R. N.

University of Oxford

A BIBLIOGRAPHY OF
CHARLES STANILAND WAKE

1863   "The Relation of Man to the Inferior Forms of Animal Life."
        Anthropological Review 1 : 365–73. London.

1867   "On the Antiquity of Man and Comparative Geology." *Anthropological Review, 5, Journal of the Anthropological Society of London,* cv–cxi, cxiii–cxvii.

1868a   *Chapters on Man, with the Outlines of a Science of Comparative Psychology.* London : Trübner.

1868b   "On the Psychological Unity of Mankind." [Abstract.] *Anthropological Review, 6, Journal of the Anthropological Society of London,* clxviii–clxix.

1869   "On Language as a Test of Race." [In collaboration with R. S. Charnock; abstract.] *Anthropological Review, 7, Journal of the Anthropological Society of London,* xxxviii–xxxix.

1870a   "The Race Elements of the Madecasses." *Anthropological Review, 8, Journal of the Anthropological Society of London,* xxix–lv.

1870b   "The Aim and Scope of Anthropology." *Journal of Anthropology* 1, No. 1 : 1–18.

1870c   "The Influence of the Phallic Idea in the Religions of Antiquity." *Journal of Anthropology* 1, No. 2 : 97–105, 199–227.

1870d   "Report of the Delegates from the Anthropological Society of London to the British Association for the Advancement of Science Meeting, 1870. Liverpool." *Journal of Anthropology, 1, Journal of the Anthropological Society of London,* iii–vi.

1870e   "Tribal Affinities among the Australian Aborigines." *Journal of Anthropology, 1, Journal of the Anthropological Society of London,* xiii–xxxi.

1870*f* "The Psychological Unity of Mankind." *Memoirs read before the Anthropological Society of London* 3 : 134–47.

1871   "The Physical Characters of the Australian Aborigines." *Journal of Anthropology* 1, No. 3 : 259–61.

1872*a* "The Mental Characteristics of Primitive Man, as Exemplified by the Australian Aborigines." *Journal of the Anthropological Institute* 1 : 74–84.

1872*b* "Report on Anthropology at the Meeting of the British Association for the Advancement of Science for 1871, at Edinburgh." *Journal of the Anthropological Institute* 1 : 268–74.

1872*c* "The Adamites." *Journal of the Anthropological Institute* 1 : 363–74.

1873*a* "Marriage by Capture." *Anthropologia* 1 : 73–77. London.

1873*b* "The Social Condition of Woman as Affected by 'Civilisation'." *Anthropologia* 1 : 78–86.

1873*c* "Sacred Prostitution." *Anthropologia* 1 : 156–64.

1873*d* "Marriage among Primitive Peoples." *Anthropologia* 1 : 197–207.

1873*e* Review : *Organic Philosophy*, Vol. III, by Hugh Doherty. *Journal of the Anthropological Institute* 2 : 133–34.

1873*f* Review : *Etude sur les races indigènes d'Australie*, by Paul Topinard. *Journal of the Anthropological Institute* 2 : 307–9.

1873*g* "Man and the Ape." *Journal of the Anthropological Institute* 2 : 315–28.

1873*h* "The Origin of Serpent-Worship." *Journal of the Anthropological Institute* 2 : 373–86.

1873*i* "The Hamath Inscriptions." *Journal of the Anthropological Institute* 2 : 446–47.

1874*a* "Influence of the Phallic Idea in the Religions of Antiquity." *Ancient Symbol Worship*, by Hodder M. Westropp and C. Staniland Wake, with an introduction, additional notes, and an appendix by Alexander Wilder (pp. 33–78). New York : J. W. Bouton ; London : Trübner.

1874*b* "Spiritism among Uncultured Peoples Compared with Modern Spiritualism." *Anthropologia* 1 : 459–64.

1875*a* "Cannibalism." *Anthropologia* 1 : 571–78.

1875*b* "The Origin of the Moral Idea." *Anthropologia* 1: Supplement, cvii–cxii.

1878 *The Evolution of Morality, Being a History of the Development of Moral Culture.* 2 vols. London: Trübner.

1879 "The Origin of the Classificatory System of Relationships Used Among Primitive Peoples." *Journal of the Anthropological Institute* 8: 144–79.

1880*a* "The Primitive Human Family." *Journal of the Anthropological Institute* 9: 3–19.

1880*b* "The Classification of the Races of Mankind." Paper read before the Hull Literary Club, October 18, 1880. Printed for private circulation.

1881*a* "Notes on the Polynesian Race." *Journal of the Anthropological Institute* 10: 109–22.

1881*b* Review: *Contributions to the History of the Development of the Human Race,* by Lazarus Geiger. *Journal of the Anthropological Institute* 10: 366–70.

1882*a* *The Origin and Significance of the Great Pyramid.* London: Reeves & Turner.

1882*b* "Notes on the Origin of the Malagasy." *Journal of the Anthropological Institute* 11: 21–31.

1882*c* "On Non-Mussulman Arabs." *Journal of the Anthropological Institute* 11: 355.

1882*d* "Notes on the Origin of the Malagasy." *Antananarivo Annual and Madagascar Magazine* 2, No. 6: 103–13.

1883*a* "The Papûans and the Polynesians." *Journal of the Anthropological Institute* 12: 197–220.

1883*b* Review: *Rivers of Life,* by J. G. R. Forlong. *Journal of the Anthropological Institute* 12: 568–73.

1884 "The Nature and Origin of Group Marriage." *Journal of the Anthropological Institute* 13: 151–61.

1886 "Les Cambodgiens et leur origine." *Revue d'anthropologie* 3d Series, 1: 204–25.

1888*a* *Serpent-Worship and other Essays, with a Chapter on Totemism.* London: George Redway.

1888*b* "The Primitive Human Horde." *Journal of the Anthropological Institute* 17: 276–82.

1889a *The Development of Marriage and Kinship.* London: George Redway.

1889b Letter: "The Primitive Human Horde." *Journal of the Anthropological Institute* 18 : 99.

1889c "The Distribution of American Totems." *American Antiquarian* 11 : 354–58.

1890 "Growth of the Marriage Relation." *Sociology, Popular Lectures and Discussions before the Brooklyn Ethical Association* (pp. 69–87). Boston: James H. West.

1891 "The Chichimecas." *American Antiquarian* 13 : 229–33.

1894a *Memoirs of the International Congress of Anthropology, Chicago.* Edited by C. Staniland Wake. Chicago.

1894b "The Suastika and Allied Symbols." *American Antiquarian* 16 : 41–43.

1894c "Migrations of the Algonkins." *American Antiquarian* 16 : 127–39.

1896 "Musical Tone and Colour." *Music* 2, No. 2.

1898 "The Musical Octave." *Music* 15 : 25–34. Chicago.

1901 "Language as a Test of Race." *American Antiquarian* 23 : 379–84.

1902 "The Beard as a Test for the Classification of Races." *American Antiquarian* 24 : 43–45.

1903a "Notes on the Indian Origin of the Polynesian Islanders." *American Antiquarian* 25 : 44–48.

1903b "The Peopling of Asia and America Compared." *American Antiquarian* 25 : 101–7.

1903c "The Kauravas of the Hindu Puranas." *American Antiquarian* 25 : 175–77.

1904a "Legends of the American Indians." *American Antiquarian* 26 : 23–28.

1904b "American Origins." *American Antiquarian* 26 : 105–15.

1904c "Nihancan, the White Man." *American Antiquarian* 26 : 225–31.

1904d "The Navaho Origin Legend." *American Antiquarian* 26 : 265–71.

1904e "The Mayas of Central America." *American Antiquarian* 26 : 361–63.

1904f   *The Geometry of Science.* Privately printed. Chicago.

1905a   "Mythology of the Plains Indians." *American Antiquarian* 27 : 9–16.

1905b   "Mythology of the Plains Indians, II : Nature Deities." *American Antiquarian* 27 : 73–80.

1905c   "Asiatic Ideas among the American Indians, Part I." *American Antiquarian* 27 : 153–61.

1905d   "Asiatic Ideas among the American Indians, Part II." *American Antiquarian* 27 : 189–96.

1905e   "Mythology of the Plains Indians, III : Terrestrial Objects." *American Antiquarian* 27 : 323–28.

1906a   "Mythology of the Plains Indians, IV : Magical Animals." *American Antiquarian* 28 : 205–11.

1906b   "Indian Original of the Polynesians." *Science of Man* 8 : 11.

1907a   "Cambodia and Yucatan." *American Antiquarian* 29 : 244–48.

1907b   "The Classification of Mankind." *American Antiquarian* 29 : 347–54.

1907c   *Vortex Philosophy: The Geometry of Science.* Published by the author. Chicago.

PREFACE.

In the preface to "The Evolution of Morality," published in 1878, reasons were given for dealing only incidentally in that work with sexual morality. The justification for the course then pursued is to be found in the present volume, which could not then have been written; although the second edition of Dr J. F. M'Lennan's "Primitive Marriage" had appeared in 1876, with certain additions, under the title of "Studies in Ancient History," and in 1877 had been published Dr Lewis H. Morgan's "Ancient Society," which severely criticised Dr M'Lennan's views. It was not until the appearance, in 1880, of the result of the enquiries made by the Rev. Lorimer Fison and Mr A. W. Howitt into the system of marriage and relationship in use among the aborigines of Australia, under the title of "Kamilaroi and Kurnai," that a serious attempt to deal with the whole subject of sexual morality was possible. Such an attempt is made by the present work, during the preparation of which I have had the advantage of corresponding with Mr Fison, with reference to the Australian system, and I have to thank him and Mr Howitt for their ready consent to my making use of information received from them. If Dr J. F. M'Lennan had lived, however, this work might not have appeared. In the year 1877 I had some discussion with him relative to the Australian marriage system, and in one

of his letters he wrote : "Since I saw you the subject
has acquired fresh importance in my opinion, and I
mean to work at it." Subsequently he wrote that he
had been hard at work, and had been making progress.
It appears from Mr D. M'Lennan's preface to "The
Patriarchal Theory," published since his brother's
death, that Dr M'Lennan had collected materials for
"a general work on the structure of the earliest
human societies." This work would have been of the
utmost importance, and it is to be hoped that it will
not be wholly lost to science. In its absence I may
be allowed to bring forward the result of my own
enquiries, which go over much the same ground as
Dr M'Lennan's, although probably he would have
rejected many of my conclusions as differing from his
own. I have the less hesitation in doing so, as the
subjects treated of in the present volume have engaged
my attention for many years past, and as the conviction has been forced upon me that the hypotheses of
Dr M'Lennan and Dr Morgan, differing so widely
from each other as they do, are both fundamentally
erroneous.

CONTENTS

INTRODUCTION.

IT was stated, when treating, in "The Evolution of Morality," of the altruistic sentiments, that the active virtues, while having a certain objective analogy to, differ essentially both in nature and in aim from, the actions required by the merely passive duties. The latter are founded on the right which every man has to the possession and enjoyment of his own property ; whereas, benevolent actions are not founded on any such right, although their practical effect is to confirm it after it has been acquired. In fact, the object of such actions is, "instead of abstaining from interference with a man's possessions, to aid in preserving them, and this in the largest sense, as including body and mind, material and immaterial." Both the passive and the active virtues are seen thus to have relation to others, and at first sight it appears as though sexual conduct, except in the case of adultery, was not within the sphere of morals, seeing that it is not concerned with the possessory rights of others. The difficulty is removed, however, when it is shown that morality has two sides, the objective and the subjective. There would be no moral "law" in the absence of the *wrong to another*, or interference with possessory rights, which is at the base of the objective phase of morality, but the subjective result is not less important. This appears from the consideration of actions as wrong (criminal) in relation to their consequences to others, and wrong (sinful) in their effect on the individuals performing them. Actions may have the former quality without partaking of the latter. Criminality has relation to society, while sinfulness has reference to the moral nature of the individual. Thus the criminality of murder, stealing, and adultery consists in the interference by these actions with the social rights of others; their sinfulness depending on their tendency to injuriously affect the moral nature of the criminal. It is only when this tendency becomes the predominant motive for the prohibition of such actions that they are thought to be sinful. At this stage the social injury assumes, from the moral standpoint, a secondary place, as a mere incident of a depraved moral condition; and it is now only that sexual conduct, except where actual injury to others is occasioned by it, can strictly be treated as wrong either objectively or subjectively. The moral wrong of sensuality is thus seen to be subjective rather than objective, and the fact that such conduct may be sinful without being criminal, shows that the element of injury to others is not always essential to the idea of moral obligation. It shows, in fact, that the ultimate foundation of the moral nature of all actions is duty, not towards others, but towards self, and therefore that *this* is the primary motive to right action, and not duty towards one's fellow-men, which is strictly a secondary motive. The true ground of morality is to be found in the being of man, as part of the universal whole of nature, although his relationship to mankind at large, as well as to the members of the animal kingdom, gives rise to special obligations. Or, as it may be stated, morality is based, so far as concerns the passive virtues, on man's duty to himself as an offshoot of the Universal Existence, and as to the active virtues, on his duty to others as members of the human brotherhood. The distinction between these two classes of virtues is, however, purely objective. Subjectively they have a common basis in the nature of man, and therefore they must both be traced to the Universal Existence, of which mankind forms part. The active, no less than the passive, virtues spring from the condition of moral purity which characterises those whose being is in perfect harmony with the Organic Whole. The spring and source of all moral conduct should be, therefore, the perfection of one's own being, and seen in this light, sexual conduct is not less subject to the law of morality than a life of passive virtue, or the practice of benevolence and the cultivation of the altruistic sentiments.

Moreover, although sexual conduct may not be in itself objectively wrong, it may be criminal when it infringes the regulations of society. The family is the result of the sexual union of individuals, and as it forms the unit of society as now constituted among the most cultured human races, whatever may have been the case in the past, the constitution of society itself depends largely on the relation between the sexes. In treating of the development of the law of marriage, it is necessary, therefore, in the first place, to show what was the sexual condition of primeval man ; that is, whether during the earliest period of man's history there was a recognised law of marriage, or whether the sexes lived together in a state of promiscuity. The idea of law implies restraint on free action, but the restraint may not necessarily have been imposed by man on man ; as it may have been implanted in man's nature, whether he sprang from an inferior form of animal life, or was derived from a superior source. In whatever manner it originated, that restraint gave form to the law of marriage, the nature of which has to be considered and its developments described. In pursuing the enquiry it will be found that the doctrine of kinship is intimately connected with that of marriage, the consideration of which will lead therefore to that of the primitive rule of descent and its variations, as existing in combination with different phases of marriage, and the system of relationships by which that rule is accompanied.

MARRIAGE AND KINSHIP.

CHAPTER I.

PRIMEVAL MAN.

SOCIETY is based on two instincts which are as powerful in their operation in the animal kingdom as with
mankind—the instinct of self-preservation, and the
sexual instinct. The activity of the instinct of self-
preservation may be said to affect the form or "mode"
of society, giving rise to the idea of law, or the regulations under which society endures ; while the sexual
instinct is concerned with the existence of the individuals who make up the social group. Without the
latter the race could not be perpetuated, and it would
come to an end, and society with it, as soon as the
individuals of the race ceased to exist. The sexual
instinct is thus equally fundamental with that of
self-preservation, and it is no less general. Every
individual, male or female, at a certain age, becomes
cognisant of the former just as truly, although not at
so early a period, as he or she shows the influence of
the latter. Those instincts have another feature in
common. That of self-preservation has two phases :
the subjective and the objective, of which the one
relates to the agent, while the other concerns the
action which is at the base of moral law. In like
manner the sexual instinct has a subjective and an

objective phase, the former of which concerns the
individual, and the latter the result of his activity.
In both cases, moreover, the instinct has *subjectively*
a double relation—that to the individual acting, and
that to the individual affected by the action. Here,
however, the analogy ceases, for the objective phase
of the sexual instinct, unlike that of the instinct of
self-preservation, cannot, except where force is an
element, come into existence without the consent,
and, indeed, co-operation of the individuals immediately concerned ; which is, indeed, no less
necessary to the subjective phase of that instinct
if it is to exhibit its proper activity.

The subjective phase of the sexual instinct concerns
the individuals whose co-action is thus seen to be
required, and its outward expression is the union
of the sexes in "marriage," using this term in its
widest sense. In like manner the objective phase of
the sexual instinct has relation to the result of this
union, and may be said to affect the offspring of
marriage. The birth of offspring gives rise to feelings
in the minds of its parents so active and so general
as to be regarded as constituting a secondary instinct.
This is usually referred to as the maternal instinct,
but it would be more properly termed the *parental
instinct,* as it is common to both parents ; although
it is generally more strongly developed with the
mother, owing to her closer connection with the
child as its nourisher or nurse both before and after
its birth. The intimate association between mother
and child is of great practical importance from the
fact that, as we shall see, the rules of kinship, as
distinguished from simple relationship, are in the
first instance usually connected with that special asso-

ciation, although not necessarily so. The maternal, or rather parental, instinct has thus relation to offspring, and through it the objective phase of the sexual instinct may be said to be at the foundation of the idea of *kinship;* as the subjective phase of that instinct is at the base of the law of *marriage.*

As the sexual instinct is so fundamental and general, its expression in action must be regarded as necessary and proper. Like that of the instinct of self-preservation, however, the activity must be controlled, otherwise much evil would ensue both to individuals and to society at large. A condition of absolute promiscuity between the sexes would be highly objectionable, as well on individual as on social grounds ; but it must have existed at one period, and probably would have continued to exist, unless the action of the sexual instinct was subjected to restraining influences. As a fact, such influences have operated from a very early date among all the races of mankind. Their nature will be fully considered in a future chapter ; but it may be stated here generally, that they consist, *first,* of *social restraints* arising from the claim of parents or others to have an interest in, or a right of control over the conduct of, the females, or bearers of offspring, belonging to their family group ; and, *secondly,* of *natural restraints* arising from the feeling, which, from its universality, may almost be termed the *fraternal instinct,* that persons closely related by blood ought not to form sexual alliances. Whether or not the restraints on promiscuity have operated from the earliest ages, so as to have always limited the range within which the formation of such alliances was allowable, is a question which we are not now able to determine with certainty.

We may, however, determine whether it is probable
that mankind has passed through a prolonged stage of
promiscuity. In the next chapter we shall consider
certain supposed evidences of this condition, and we
will now see what may be supposed to have been the
sexual arrangements of primeval man, judging from
the conduct of the members of the animal kingdom
the nearest to him in physical organisation, and from
what we know of the ideas of savages on the subject
of " marriage."

On the first point we have the authority of Darwin,
who states [1] that so far as the habits of existing quadrumana are known, the males of some species are
monogamous, but live during only a part of the year
with the females, as with the orang ; while several
kinds of monkeys in India and America, which are
strictly monogamous, associate all the year round with
their wives. The gorilla and several of the American
species of monkeys are polygamous, and each family
lives separate. Darwin thinks it probable, however,
that the families inhabiting the same district are to
some extent social, as the chimpanzee is occasionally
met with in large bands. Such is the case also with
several species of baboons, of which several males,
each with his own females, live together in a body.
To these examples may be added that of the bald-
headed *Nscheègo Mbouvé* of Western Africa, which
builds shelters on the branches of trees. This curious
man-like ape appears to be monogamous, the male and
the female, however, sleeping under different shelters
placed on neighbouring trees.[2] The soko of East

[1] Darwin 1871, II, 361.
[2] Duncan 1876–82, I, 30.

Central Equatorial Africa is also monogamous, but it lives in communities of about ten. Dr Livingstone states that an intruder from another camp is beaten off with fists and loud yells, and if one male tries to seize the female of another he is caught by the others, who all unite in beating and biting him.[1]

The conclusion arrived at by Darwin is, that " from what we know of the jealousy of all male quadrupeds, armed, as many often are, with special weapons for battling with their rivals, promiscuous intercourse in a state of nature is extremely improbable."

What, then, is the opinion formed by that distinguished writer as to the sexual habits of primeval man ? After referring to the evidence adduced by Mr Morgan, Dr M'Lennan, and Sir John Lubbock, which evidence will be considered in the next chapter, he remarks, " it seems certain that the habit of marriage has been gradually developed, and that almost promiscuous intercourse was once extremely common throughout the world." This guarded statement is, however, rather the expression of the views of other writers than the independent opinion of Darwin, who, after referring to the habits of the quadrumana, goes on to say, "it is extremely improbable that primeval men and women lived promiscuously together." He adds that, "judging from the social habits of man as he now exists, and from most savages being polygamists, the most probable view is that primeval man aboriginally lived in small communities, each with as many wives as he could support and maintain, whom he would have jealously guarded against all other men. Or he may have lived with several wives by himself, like the

[1] *Ibid.*, I, 49.

gorilla." In another place[1] Darwin says, " Whether savages who now enter into some form of marriage, either polygamous or monogamous, have retained this habit from primeval times, or whether they have returned to some form of marriage, after passing through a stage of promiscuous intercourse, I will not pretend to conjecture." He does, however, again express his opinion as to man's earliest sexual condition. He says,[2] " Turning to primeval times, when men had only doubtfully attained the rank of manhood, they would probably have lived, as already stated, either as polygamists or temporarily as monogamists. Their intercourse, judging from analogy, would not then have been promiscuous. . . . They would have been governed more by their instinct, and even less by their reason, than are savages at the present day. They would not at that period have partially lost one of the strongest of all instincts common to all the lower animals, namely, the love of their young offspring; and consequently they would not have practised infanticide. There would have been no artificial scarcity of women, and polyandry would not have been followed; there would have been no early betrothals; women would not have been valued as mere slaves; both sexes, if the females as well as the males were permitted to exert any choice, would have chosen their partners, not for mental charms, or property, or social position, but almost solely from external appearance. All the adults would have married or paired, and all the offspring, as far as that was possible, would have been reared."

The great naturalist states these conclusions in connection with the subject of sexual selection, but they are equally applicable to the questions discussed

---

[1] *Ibid.*, II, 363.　　　　　　[2] *Ibid.*, II, 367.

in the present work. They are especially important
as confirming the opinion that promiscuity was not
the necessary starting-point in man's social progress.
Darwin's conclusions are based on the assumption that
mankind originally consisted of more than one pair. It
is possible, however, that the human race had its Adam
and Eve, in which case it is evident that the race
must in the second generation have been perpetuated
by the intermarriage of brother and sister or parent
and child, or a general intermarriage. The distinction
made by the Hebrew book of Genesis (vi. 1) between
the " sons of God " and the " daughters of men," and
the use of certain expressions, would seem, however, to
show that the author of that book believed in the
existence of a non-Adamic race, from among whom the
sons of Adam may have taken wives. In this case
there would not have been either promiscuity or consanguineous marriage. It is different, however, with
the case of Lot and his daughters (Gen. xix.) ; as the
language used by the latter shows a belief that they
and their father were the only persons then living on
the earth. The reason given by the daughters for their
conduct might be regarded as a sufficient justification
for them from a natural standpoint, but it is remarkable that the writer of the narrative, who knew of the
existence of other peoples, does not condemn it. This
is no evidence, however, that he really approved of the
action of Lot's daughters, and we may indeed suppose
that the explanation of it was an addition of his own
to account for conduct which could be justified only on
the plea of necessity. Possibly, moreover, the whole
story may have been introduced for the purpose of providing a male parent for the sons which Lot's daughters
bore, or, what is still more probable, of tracing the

lineage of the Moabites and Ammonites to a Semitic source. Jesse, the father of David, was the son of Obed, whose mother Ruth was a Moabite. The teachings of Genesis on the subject of marriage are, as we shall see when treating of monogamy, entirely opposed to incestuous or promiscuous union, and nothing, therefore, can be inferred from the story of Lot and his daughters as to the general views entertained at that period on the subject of marriage.

That there may have been in the earliest ages of man's history a short period of barbarism, in which the intercourse between the sexes was unrestrained by any law of marriage, is of course possible. Probably, as female chastity before marriage is even now but slightly regarded among many uncultured peoples, all or any sexual alliances were allowable, so long as they were not opposed to any individual or general feeling of propriety. The existence of such a feeling, or rather that of an idea of impropriety, in relation to sexual alliances, is, however, the point to be considered, and it is advisable, therefore, to see whether it can have been influential with primeval man. The idea of impropriety may be due to the activity of a natural feeling, or it may arise from a feeling that the rights of the individual are being wrongfully interfered with.

The opinion held as to the existence or otherwise in the mind of primeval man of a notion of the impropriety of sexual conduct between persons near of kin will probably depend on the view entertained as to the origin of mankind. If the human race was gradually developed from an ape-like creature without the introduction at any stage of his development of a higher principle of being, or the evolution of a faculty of reflection, there may have been at first no recognition even of the fact of blood relationship. This is the real ground of the opinions held by Mr Morgan and other writers as to the existence of promiscuity with primeval man. Dr M'Lennan says[1] expressly, " The earliest human groups can have had no idea of kinship . . . . At the root of kinship is a physical fact, which could be discerned only through observation and reflection,—a fact, therefore, which must for a time have been overlooked." He adds, " No advocate of innate ideas, we should imagine, will maintain their existence on a subject so concrete as relationship by blood." Nevertheless, and although man may have been at one time without the idea of kinship, he may even then have had such a " feeling of kindred " as would have prevented persons near of kin forming sexual alliances. The objection to marriage between blood relations must originally have been founded on feeling, although it has become established by all powerful custom. Dr M'Lennan does not deny that a feeling of kindred may have always existed. He says, indeed, that a group of kindred in the rudest stage of ignorance were " chiefly held together by the feeling of kindred." Whether this feeling was innate, or was gradually developed, or whether it arose from a perception of the physical fact on which kinship depends, it must have acquired great strength at an early period of man's social progress. Kinship through the mother is usually supposed to have been first recognised, but even if this view is not correct, the children of the same mother would know from her conduct towards them and from their general surroundings, that they were more nearly connected with each other than with the children

[1] McLennan 1876, p. 121.

of other women. It may be affirmed, therefore, that the feeling of kindred would be active at a very early period as the result of the perception of maternal relationship, the more so if the filial and fraternal affections are instinctive in the human kind, as Dr M'Lennan admits is possible.[1]

The opinion that primeval man recognised the impropriety of sexual alliances between persons near of kin, say between parent and child, or children of the same mother, is consistent with the view that the mental faculties of primeval man were not so undeveloped as some writers maintain. Mankind may not have been simply descended, as Darwin states,[2] from " a hairy quadruped, furnished with a tail and pointed ears," which would be classed by a naturalist amongst the quadrumana, " as surely as would the common and still more ancient progenitor of the Old and the New World monkeys." He thinks that the hairy progenitor of mankind would " probably deserve to rank as man," but there is no reason why he should do so unless he had some special characteristics to distinguish him from the ape-like creatures to which he was allied. No one will now deride when he reads Dr Darwin's declaration[3] that he would " as soon be descended from that heroic little monkey, who braved his dreaded enemy in order to save the life of his keeper ; or from that old baboon, who, descending from the mountains, carried away in triumph his young comrade from a crowd of astonished dogs—as from a savage who delights to torture his enemies, offers up bloody sacrifices, practises infanticide without remorse, treats his wives like slaves, knows no decency, and is haunted by the grossest superstitions." At the same time, the

[1] *Ibid.*, p. 121.　　　　　　　　[2] Darwin 1871, II, 389.
[3] *Ibid.*, II, 404.

progenitor of mankind may have been truly man without being of the savage nature here depicted. His very position as " man " required that he should have a higher mental development than the apes.[1] As a fact, the savages referred to by Darwin hold in the greatest abhorrence sexual alliances between persons near of kin, and this shows them to be superior, in some respects at all events, to the monkeys with whom they are compared. That fact is of great importance, not only as being an argument in support of the opinion that, in very early times, if not in the earliest, man entertained similar views on that subject, but also owing to its influence over the development of the law of marriage.

Whatever conclusion may be arrived at as to the intellectual condition of mankind in the earlier ages, the sexual conduct of the quadrumana, even of the man-like apes, can hardly be taken as a perfect test of what human behaviour must have been at that period. Therefore the fact that when the young male gorillas grow up, the strongest will drive away the others and establish himself as the head of the community, furnishes no evidence that primeval man did likewise or allowed incestuous unions. The probability is, judging from the habits of present savages, and the strength of the fraternal instinct, which then, as now, would be influential to prevent marriages between brothers and sisters by the same mother, that the children of one maternal group would form sexual alliances with the children of some other group, and not among themselves. If by any means the grown-up females exceeded the males in number, a

[1] For the author's views on this subject, see Wake 1868; 1873.

system of polygyny would doubtless spring up, and the same would be the case if one man wished and was able to appropriate to himself several females. In this case, however, some men would be without wives, unless they could join with the more fortunate individuals, when polyandry might be established. It is probable that the instinct of self-preservation, combined with the action of the sexual instinct, which has to do with the preservation of the race, would have led men originally to dwell together in groups, where each man would have one or more wives, according to the number of females; and that if a man interfered with the females of another, he would be treated in the same manner as the soko is dealt with for such conduct. At the same time, it is possible that, under the pressure of special circumstances, the primeval polygyny or monogamy might give place to a system in which a group of men possessed their wives in common, and this change might take place consistently with the natural restraints on promiscuity, which are supposed to have been established at so early a date as to have become almost instinctive. Such a system has, indeed, been developed among the Australian aborigines, and probably it originated as a means of satisfying the sexual wants of man's lower nature in a very early stage of human progress, when man was driven by want of food to wander far from home. In this primitive form of marriage, possibly all the males of a generation in one group were considered as entitled to form sexual alliances with all the females in the same generation of another group, and *vice versâ*, resulting in the development of an elaborate system of polygamy such as has undoubtedly existed widely among the more uncultured races from a very early period. Group-marriage is not promiscuity, however, and it may be well to refer to the opinion of the Rev. Lorimer Fison, the discoverer of that institution, expressed in his valuable work on the usages of the Australian aborigines in connection with marriage and relationship. After stating[1] that the Australian system " is based upon communal marriage[2] between permitted groups," Mr Fison adds, " Although strong evidence seems to point further still to a more ancient undivided commune, this has never yet been found, and I know of no record of which we can positively affirm that it describes such a commune, and that the writer of it was a fully qualified witness in the case." Mr Fison is prepared to accept the view expressed by Mr Morgan, that if the undivided commune ever existed, the most likely method by which it would begin its advance to a better system of marriage, would be a " reformatory movement," and this because it would be a step in advance so difficult for men in the depth of savagery to take, that, if all the tribes of men started from the same level, the impulse " would be impossible in the first instance, and must have been derived from a higher power." As I shall now proceed to show, however, there is no real evidence of the former existence of such a social condition as that intended by the " undivided commune," and there is therefore no occasion to call in the aid of a supernatural power to enable mankind to get beyond it.

[1] Fison and Howitt 1880, p. 160.

[2] It is a pity that Mr. Fison uses this phrase, as it has been employed by earlier writers to denote absolute promiscuity.

CHAPTER II.

IT is evident that, on any assumption as to the origin
of man except that which supposes him to have been
" created " in the " Divine image," no absolute certainty can be arrived at as to his earliest sexual condition. Whatever conclusion may be formed on this
subject it must be purely hypothetical, and at best
one hypothesis can only be declared to be more probable than another. A consideration of the phenomena
observable among existing races of mankind has led
certain writers to suppose that in the earliest phase of
human society marriage did not exist in any form.
Bachofen asserts [1] that the Amazonism which resulted
in the Mother-Right of the ancient world, was due to
the revolt of woman against the degraded condition of
lawless *hetairism*, which previously had been universal
among mankind, a condition in which men had a community of wives and openly lived together like gregari-
ous animals. Dr M'Lennan arrives at much the same
conclusion as to man's primitive social state. He
affirms [2] that " the earliest human groups can have had
no idea of kinship," and that these groups " would
hold their women, like their other goods, in common,"
which he rightly terms a *general promiscuity*. Dr

---

[1] Bachofen 1861, pp. xxiv, 10.
[2] McLennan 1876, pp. 121, 135.

Morgan declares [1] that the earlier stage of man's social condition was one of promiscuous intercourse between the sexes, in which he "could scarcely be distinguished from the mute animals by whom he was surrounded. Ignorant of marriage, and living probably in a horde, he was not only a savage, but possessed a feeble intellect and a feeble moral sense." Sir John Lubbock adopts the conclusions arrived at by Bachofen, M'Lennan, and Morgan, and assumes [2] that the *communal marriage* system, "where all the men and women in a small community were regarded as equally married to one another," represents "the primitive and earliest social condition of man." It is not remarkable that Mr Herbert Spencer comes to much the same conclusion. He does not think that promiscuity in the relation of the sexes existed in an unqualified form. [3] Mr Spencer affirms, indeed, that monogamy must have preceded polygamy, although to account for the development of a system of kinship in the female line, he supposes there to have been a considerable extension of promiscuity accompanied by monogamous connections of a limited duration, and the birth of a larger number of children to unknown fathers than to known fathers. He admits, however, that paternity is now generally recognised, when he states [4] that where the system of female kinship subsists, "male parentage is habitually known though disregarded," a statement which nevertheless is not correct, as will hereafter appear.

Let us see on what evidence it is asserted that man-

[1] Morgan 1877, p. 500.
[2] Lubbock 1875, p. 90.
[3] Spencer 1876–96, I, 662.
[4] *Ibid.*, I, 667.

kind has passed through a stage of sexual promiscuity. The argument of Bachofen is based on the existence among certain peoples of the ancient world of practices which he thinks point to a still earlier condition of *hetairism*, in which men had a community of wives. This he supposes to be a law of nature, the infraction of which in individual marriage was required by the Earth Goddess, Demeter, to be expiated by a temporary promiscuity. Dr M'Lennan well objects[1] to this "fanciful" notion, that "the facts connected with the history of religion give no countenance to the supposition that men in the stage of savagery had thought out for themselves any divinity of the type of Aphrodite, whom Bachofen chiefly contemplates in connection with Hetairism." This subject will be referred to again when considering the question of sexual hospitality. It will suffice, therefore, to remark here that the facts are capable of a totally different interpretation from that which they receive at the hands of Bachofen. He affirms,[2] indeed, that Amazonism "divides with Hetairism the character of universality," but this universality cannot be proved, and even if it could be established, there is no necessary connection between the two classes of phenomena. There is, moreover, no evidence that the "mother-right" to which Amazonism is supposed to have given birth was ever recognised by all races. There is strong reason for believing that the practice of tracing kinship in the female line was very widely observed from a very early period, but this is very different from the establishment of the supremacy of women. Where this was found it was due to the development of the gentile institution, and the female kinship which

[1] McLennan 1876, p. 434.   [2] Bachofen 1861, p. xvii.

accompanied it, and on which, indeed, that institution was founded, had as little connection with a revolt of women against the degradation of hetairism as with such a social condition. As a lawless hetairism did not necessarily precede mother-right, so it is not requisite, as Bachofen affirms, that the "dominion of paternity" should be preceded by mother-right. That this was often the case is true, but, as will be shown when considering the origin of *kinship through females only*, it is none the less true that the idea of paternity is fully recognised by all races, however uncultured, whilst the idea that the father is the real parent of his child is almost equally general. Where, therefore, mother-right preceded father-right it was based, not so much on maternity, as on certain social ideas with which woman herself had only a secondary concern.

Whilst Bachofen infers the former existence of a condition of promiscuity from certain practices which he interprets as *expiation* for individual marriage, Dr M'Lennan infers a similar condition of society from the existence of a primitive phase of marriage. Dr M'Lennan's argument is as follows :—(a) relationship through females is the most ancient system of kinship ; (b) in nearly every case where relics of this system are to be found, traces of polyandry also remain ; (c) polyandry is merely a modification of promiscuous intercourse between the sexes, and, therefore, as all races were at first polyandrous, promiscuity must originally have been universal. As to the first link (a) in this chain of reasoning, it may be objected that although kinship appears to have been at one time very generally traced preferably through females, it is a mistake to suppose, as Dr M'Lennan does,[1] that relationship through the father was not recognised. This point has already been referred to, and it will hereafter be shown that the recognition of paternity is quite consistent, not only with the Australian system of consanguinity, but also with the Malayan and allied systems, though kinship through females may be preferred for tracing the line of descent. Dr Morgan, who considers[2] that prior to the gentile organisation, descent in the female line was superior to kinship through males, and was the "principal basis on which the lower tribal groups were organised," affirms nevertheless that the body of facts treated in "Primitive Marriage" have "little or no relation to that condition of mankind which existed prior to the gentile organisation." This bears on Dr M'Lennan's second hypothesis (b), the constant association between kinship through females and polyandry. He supposes[3] promiscuity to have caused kinship to be traced through mothers only, and to have produced the ruder form of polyandry as exhibited among the Nairs of Malabar, in which the husbands are not relations. From this form of polyandry, the less rude phase in which the husbands are brothers, prevalent in Tibet, is supposed to have been developed by the aid of kinship through females only. Wherever this was established, Dr M'Lennan infers[4] (c) that "the unions of the sexes were originally promiscuous or polyandrous." The objections to this reasoning are—(1) kinship through females only did not originate in such a sexual condition as here supposed; (2) Tibetan polyandry is not necessarily connected with that phase of kinship, even

---

[1] McLennan 1876, pp. 124ff. [2] Morgan 1877, p. 516.
[3] McLennan 1876, p. 138. [4] *Ibid.*, p. 167.

through a ruder type of polyandry; and (3) whatever may have been the origin of polyandry, it is not promiscuity or immediately derived from it. The arguments in support of these conclusions will be given in subsequent chapters. On the third point, however, may be cited here Mr Fison's opinion [1] with reference to certain social phenomena among imported labourers in Fiji, that they furnish "more than one startling proof that this seeming polyandry is neither true polyandry nor mere prostitution, but only *group* marriage in difficulties."

Let us now see what Dr Morgan says as to primitive promiscuity. In answer to the question whether any evidence exists of that early social condition, he remarks [2] that "the consanguine family and the Malayan system of consanguinity presuppose antecedent promiscuity." This was, however, limited to the period when mankind were frugivorous and within their primitive habitat, and ceased when they "became fishermen and commenced their spread over the earth in dependence upon food artificially acquired. Consanguine groups would then form, with intermarriage in the group as a necessity, resulting in the formation of consanguine families." It is added that the consanguine family "recognised promiscuity within defined limits, and those not the narrowest, and it points through its organism to a worse condition against which it interposed a shield. Between the consanguine family and the horde living in promiscuity, the step, though a long one, does not require an intermediate condition." Mr Morgan refers to certain tribes of savages and barbarians known to the Greeks and Romans, who are represented as living

---

[1] Fison and Howitt 1880, p. 145.   [2] Morgan 1877, p. 501.

in promiscuity, but he rightly concludes that the
perpetuation of such a people from the infancy of mankind would have been impossible, and he affirms that
the cases usually cited as examples of this practice may
be better explained as arising under the *punaluan*
family, found among the Hawaiians, of which we shall
speak further on.

Dr Morgan's argument is simply that "promiscuity
may be deduced theoretically as a necessary condition
antecedent to the consanguine family." But what
proof does he furnish of the existence of this family
itself? Practically none. Dr Morgan admits that
" as the first and most ancient form of the institution, it has ceased to exist even among the lowest
tribes of savages." He adds, however, that the Malayan system "defines the relationships which would
exist in a consanguine family, and it demands the
existence of such a family to account for its own
existence." Notwithstanding the assertion that this
family has ceased to exist, Dr Morgan elsewhere[1]
affirms that there is evidence of its having existed
among the Hawaiians. The fact which is supposed
to supply this evidence is that when American
missionaries first settled in the Sandwich Islands,
the monogamian family was unknown, and instead
they found the *punaluan* family, "with own brothers
and sisters not entirely excluded, in which the males
were living in polygamy and the females in polyandry." If it could be shown that among these
islanders marriages between brothers and sisters
were general, or that they were relics of a former
general practice, the fact would be of essential service
to Dr Morgan's argument. The American writer

[1] *Ibid.*, p. 415.

cites the testimony of the Rev. Hiram Bingham, that among the Hawaiians "brothers and sisters married without reproach," and he quotes the same authority for the statement that *Wakea*, the eponymous ancestor of the Hawaiians, married his eldest daughter.[1] The value of the inference drawn from Mr Bingham's statements is materially lessened by his observation that the union of brother and sister in the highest ranks became "fashionable." This evidently refers to a comparatively recent date, but the practice probably originated in the custom mentioned by Mr Jarves, according to which the highest chief was obliged to marry the woman next in rank to himself, whatever their relationship.[2] The object of this custom is explained by Admiral Wilkes, who states that such marriages were entered into by the king for the purpose of preventing competition to the throne;[3] which agrees with the remark of the Rev. William Ellis,[4] that among the higher ranks marriage was conducted on principles of political expediency. Admiral Wilkes says, nevertheless, that in other cases brother and sister marriages were "contrary to the customs, habits, and feelings of the people,"

[1] This story, found in the later versions of the Wakea legends, is shown by Judge Fornander not to have been fully accepted in more ancient times (Fornander 1878, I, 205).

[2] Jarves 1843, p. 80.

[3] The meaning of this will be understood when it is known that with the Hawaiians rank descended chiefly through females (Jarves 1843, p. 84; cf. Mariner 1817, II, 84, 96).

[4] Ellis 1832–34, IV, 435. It may be inferred from the prohibition of brother and sister marriages by the code of laws promulgated under the influence of the missionaries in the Society Islands, that such marriages were not unknown there (Ellis 1832–34, III, p. 181).

although in the decayed state of Hawaiian society [1]
it is not improbable that the lower chiefs sometimes
imitated the conduct of their sovereign. A similar
custom is mentioned by the Rev. James Sibree [2] as
existing among the Sakalaves of Madagascar, and he
gives a similar explanation of it. Marriages between
a brother and a sister were usually made "because of
the difficulty sometimes occurring of finding a wife of
equal rank with the chief or king. There was also
often a jealousy of any claimant to the supreme power
arising from the brother of the chief being of course
older than the chief's own children." Mr Sibree
states, however, that such marriages were preceded
by a ceremony of lustration and reciting prayers, "as
if there was a fear that such unnatural marriages
would call down upon the parties the anger of the
Supreme Being."

Dr Morgan thinks, further, that the former existence
of the consanguine family among the Sandwich Islanders
is proved by the custom which allowed two or more
brothers with their wives, or two or more sisters with
their husbands, to live together in common. Such an
association constituted the *punaluan* family, which Dr
Morgan supposes to have been formed out of the consanguine family. Brothers had ceased, [3] says the American writer, to marry their own sisters; and, "after
the gentile organisation had worked upon society
its complete results, their collateral sisters as well.
But in the interval they shared their remaining wives
in common. In like manner, sisters ceased marrying
their own brothers, and, after a long period of time,

[1] Wilkes 1849, IV, 30, 32, 45.
[2] Sibree 1880, p. 42.
[3] Morgan 1877, p. 428.

their collateral brothers ; but they shared their remaining wives in common." This is Dr Morgan's interpretation of the phenomena in question, but the *punaluan* group can, as will be shown hereafter, be accounted for satisfactorily without assuming the prior existence of the consanguine family. The relationships in that group depend merely on several brothers having their wives, or several sisters their husbands, in common, and there is no reason why this fact should, as Dr Morgan assumes, presuppose the intermarriage at an earlier period of brothers and sisters, and communism in their sexual relations. It is evident on consideration that the two customs are quite distinct, and that while the former is perfectly consistent with the general rule as to marriage founded on the incapacity of such a relation being established between persons bearing the same family or clan name, the latter is utterly opposed to it. There is nothing in the early rules of marriage opposed to the primitive custom of a man marrying several women, whether sisters or not, of a different clan from his own, and we shall see that such a custom is, indeed, not at all uncommon.

The peoples among whom the *punaluan* family was found in operation fully recognised the importance of blood-relationship, and it is extremely improbable, therefore, that they allowed, except under very special circumstances, marriages between brothers and sisters of the whole blood, that is, children bearing the same family name. It is very different, however, where a man and woman, although having the same father, are born of different mothers. In this case the ideas which are at the foundation of the classificatory system would not operate to render unlawful a union between the persons thus related. In accordance with this fact we shall find that marriage between half-brothers and half-sisters has been customary among peoples of all degrees of civilisation. This practice is, according to the first principles of the classificatory system, perfectly innocent, and like the *punaluan* custom of intermixed polygamous and polyandrous marriage, furnishes absolutely no evidence of the prior existence of marriage between brothers and sisters of the whole blood.[1] If this conclusion is correct, the Malayan system of consanguinity and affinity, instead of furnishing, as Dr Morgan asserts, conclusive proof of the prior existence of the consanguine family, may have an entirely different meaning. In a subsequent chapter it will be shown, not only that the *punaluan* family, or rather the group-marriage on which it is based, will give all the relationships of that system without the need of consanguineous marriages, but that the regulations of marriage among the peoples having the Malayan system have the effect of preventing, if they were not actually intended to prevent, marriages between persons near of kin. If this can be established, there will be no occasion for the consanguine family, and Dr Morgan's inference that it was preceded by a condition of promiscuity will fall to the ground.

The explanation above furnished of the incestuous marriages of the Polynesians will probably apply also to certain social facts referred to by Dr M'Lennan in

---

[1] In Cambodia, kings and princes often marry their half-sisters, aunts, or first cousins, which is excused because they are regarded as having the divine essence. Public opinion would not, however, permit them to marry a sister of the full blood, or even, at the same time, a woman and her daughter. The ancient law was very severe against incest. (Moura 1882–83, I, 335.)

connection with the Persians. He affirms,[1] as a familiar
fact, that in Persia there was anciently general incestuous promiscuity, and that its inhabitants " not only
allowed the union of brother and sister of the full
blood, but even of mother and son and father and
daughter." Such " a total absence of restrictions on
marriage," Dr M'Lennan thinks can only be explained
as those of " savage hordes, that somehow (probably
owing to their practice of polygamy) never became monogamous, and so never attained to the idea of incest."
The Medes are assumed to have been in the same case,
as they practised polygamy, and, according to Xanthus,
had no law of incest, and freely exchanged their wives.
In Sparta the Tibetan form of polyandry is said to
have been practised, as evidenced by the statement of
Polybius, that the brothers of a house often had one
wife between them. In the legends of the house of
Priam are instances of brothers succeeding to their
brothers' widows, the facts mentioned being thought
by Dr M'Lennan to prove the existence of promiscuity
and polygamy among the peoples referred to. It
cannot be denied that, assuming them to be true, those
facts show " promiscuity in its highest polyandric
form," as found among the Tibetans, and therefore
they must support Dr M'Lennan's conclusions, if his
theory is correct. According to this theory, the higher
or Tibetan polyandry is an advance from a lower, or
Nair, form, which is supposed to be always associated
with the system of kinship through females only.[2] This
reasoning fails, however, if it can be shown, as will
hereafter appear, that Tibetan polyandry is merely a
form of group-marriage or *punalua*, and not an advance

[1] McLennan 1876, pp. 269ff.
[2] *Ibid.*, p. 167.

from a lower phase of polyandry, and that the tracing
of descent in the female line was not evidence of any
earlier practice of promiscuity. If it was so, however,
there would be no evidence of this social condition
among the early Greeks and allied peoples. The
practice by them of polyandry would really be proof
that they had not any system of kinship through
females only; as, so far from the Tibetan form of
polyandry being based on this system, it is always
associated with descent in the male line.[1] Dr M'Lennan refers, however, to the Attic law, which allowed
a man to marry a sister by the same father, but not
by the same mother, as evidence that originally there
must have been kinship through the mother only, if
the Greeks were really exogamous. At the same time
he points out the existence in the Attic laws of a
provision identical with that in the Hindoo code of
Menu " for the interference of an authorised ' Sapinda '
to discharge the duties of the Levir when the Levir
was incapable." If the former provision is evidence
of female kinship, the latter must be evidence of male
kinship; but probably all that can be inferred is that
" proximity of blood or consanguinity was not, with
some few exceptions, a bar to marriage," although
direct lineal descent was so.[2] If Solon permitted marriage between a brother and a sister of the same father,
Lycurgus, on the contrary, forbade such marriages to
the Spartans, and allowed marriage with an uterine

---

[1] Dr. McLennan says: "With polyandry of the Tibetan
type, wherever it was long and generally established, kinship
through males must have been introduced" (*ibid.*, p. 157).
As a fact, there is no evidence that it ever existed without
male kinship.

[2] W. Smith 1842, art. "Marriage (Greeks)."

sister.[1] Brother and sister marriages appear, however, to have been regarded with abhorrence.[2]

The real explanation of the social phenomena referred to by Dr M'Lennan is very different from that which he supplies. So far from these phenomena being evidence of a condition of promiscuity having anciently prevailed in many Greek settlements, they were of comparatively late origin under special conditions, and were superimposed on an earlier system of marriage which may have been developed out of polyandry, but which appears to have been based on the union of individuals. The case of Œdipus and his mother Epicaste, referred to by Dr M'Lennan in a footnote,[3] no doubt shows the horror entertained by Homer of unions between persons so near in blood ; but surely the fact that, when Œdipus and Episcaste found out they were mother and child, the former tore out his eyes and the latter killed herself in despair, is evidence also that such marriages were contrary to the received ideas of the age. Moreover, the incestuous unions of the Medes and Persians cannot, from the very circumstances of the case, have been of ancient origin. Brother and sister marriages have usually had for their object the securing perfect purity of blood, or a superiority of blood where rank passed through females. These ideas could not have originated, however, at a time when, as is supposed by Dr M'Lennan, promis-

[1] Philo, *De specialibus legibus.* Lycurgus is said by Herodotus to have brought his institutions from Crete, and judging from the fact that, with the later Cretans, daughters were not so well treated as sons in the division of inheritances, they probably had kinship through males. The statement that the Cretans permitted marriage between brothers and sisters has been sufficiently confuted. (Daremberg and Saglio 1886, p. 1567.)

[2] Becker 1845, II, 448.   [3] McLennan 1876, p. 261.

cuity was general, and they could only have done so
under the influence of the "caste" prejudices of a
much later age.

According to Herodotus, indeed, the Persians were
not accustomed to intermarry with their sisters before
the reign of Cambyses, the son of Cyrus.   He says[1] :—
" Cambyses became enamoured of one of his sisters,
and then being desirous of making her his wife,
because he proposed doing what was not customary,
he summoned the royal judges, and asked them if
there was any law permitting one who wished to
marry his sister.   The royal judges . . . gave an
answer that was both just and safe ; saying that they
could find no law permitting a brother to marry his
sister, but had discovered another law which permitted
the King of Persia to do whatever he pleased."   It
appears also that Smerdu, the pretended brother of
Cambyses, was married to his supposed sister Atossa,
but this was only because he succeeded to the wives of
Cambyses, who had himself incestuously married that
princess.[2]   Lafitau observes[3] very properly that such
cases as these " evidently bear the mark of corruption
and novelty;" and he well suggests that, when it is
said the Parthian kings were allowed to marry their
mothers, it may mean only women of the "mother"
class, that is, their aunts.   It is said in one of the
Fragments of Berosus[4] that Zoroaster corrupted the
sanctity of marriage, in teaching men the abominable
mysteries of the Magi and to consult demons, authorising them by discourse and example the debauchery
which aroused the anger of God and brought on the

[1] Herodotus 1849, III, 31.   [2] Ibid., III, 68.
[3] Lafitau 1724, I, 553–54.
[4] Bk. III ; Lafitau 1724, I, 552.

Deluge. Not only did he, according to that writer, introduce plurality of wives, but he said boldly that they could form unions with any person, without any regard to nearness of blood, a mother with her son, and a brother with his sister; conduct which led to his being given the name Chemesuenus, that is, infamous, lewd. Notwithstanding the statement of Berosus, there is no proof that the Zoroaster in question allowed such marriages. They are, in fact, contrary to the genius of his teaching. It was the commentators of Zoroaster who, says M. Fontane,[1] "at a later date, thought right to authorise unions between persons too nearly related, which was a subject of great scandal for Saint Chrysostom, to whom Beausobre replies, freeing Zoroaster of all blame." That those who countenanced incestuous marriages claimed the sanction of the Iranian prophet for them is probable, but they were undoubtedly introduced long after his era, and a sufficient explanation of them is given by Dr M'Lennan himself, when he says [2] that such unions were in some cases required for the production of persons qualified for religious offices. The motive here was to obtain purity of blood, and the same idea, no doubt, led to the sister marriages of the Incas of Peru; although such alliances were excused on the ground that as the Sun, from whom they claimed descent, had married his sister the Moon, and had united in

[1] Fontane 1881b, p. 109. Dārāb Dastur Sanjānā, the translator of Dr. W. Geiger's *Civilisation of the Eastern Irānians in Ancient Times* (1885), which affirms that the Avesta describes the marriage of relations as "a meritorious and pious act," declares that there is no single instance in the Avesta which "can suggest the idea that amongst the Avesta nation there ever was a marriage contracted between brother and sister" (Geiger 1885, p. 66, note).

[2] McLennan 1876, p. 270.

marriage his two first children, it was necessary that
the same course should be followed in the persons of
the eldest children of the king.   The Peruvians said,
moreover, that, as the kingdom should be inherited
through both parents, it was not permitted to mix the
blood of the Sun with that of men, and hence the
eldest son, who inherited the kingdom, espoused his
nearest female kinsman of the blood royal, of whatever
degree of relationship to him she might be.[1] Marriages
between brothers and sisters appear to have been
practised by the ancient Egyptians, through extreme
indolence, as Mr Fontane says,[2] but probably the
persons who formed such alliances were not related by
the whole blood.

The answer to the argument for the prevalence of
promiscuity on the ground of marriages between full
brothers and sisters, is that either all the peoples mentioned in connection with the custom were too highly
civilised in other respects to have derived that practice
from an age of barbarism, or such marriages are of too
modern a date to be of service.   No doubt consanguineous marriages have been practised among many
peoples, but it has always been with a special object,[3]
and the practice is therefore opposed to the general
rule, which, as will be shown in the next chapter, is
almost universally recognised that persons very near
of kin cannot intermarry.   Even marriages between

[1] Lasso de la Vega 1715, I, 353. [For an excellent modern
account of Inca law, see Sally Falk Moore, *Power and Property in Inca Peru* (New York: Columbia University Press,
1958), especially, with regard to incest, pp. 74, 75, 134, 169.
—R.N.]   [2] Fontane 1882, p. 365.

[3] The practice of marrying in the family among the Greeks
was apparently intended to prevent the loss of family property. At Athens if a man died intestate and without male
children, his heiress was compelled to marry her nearest

brothers and sisters of the half-blood were not generally practised. The Australian tribes do not as a rule permit such marriages, and when they are allowed, it is only where descent is reckoned through the mother.[1] In this case the brother and sister are not considered so nearly related as to prevent their intermarriage. This explains the occurrence of such marriages among the Hebrews,[2] although in Leviticus (ch. xviii. v. 9) marriage with a half-sister is forbidden, whether the relationship is through the same father or the same mother.

We will now examine the grounds on which Sir John Lubbock assumes the existence, in the early ages of mankind, of a system of communal marriage. At the close of his chapter on Marriage and Relationship, he affirms[3] that " children were not in the earliest times regarded as related equally to their father and their mother, but that the natural progress of ideas is, first, that a child is related to his tribe generally ; secondly, to his mother, and not to his father ; thirdly, to his father, and not to his mother ; lastly, and lastly only, that he is related to both." Now, what is the evidence furnished in support of the first of these conclusions, or of the opinion that the lowest races of men live, or did live, in a state of communal marriage, that is " where all the men and women in a small community were regarded as equally married to one another " ?[4] Sir John Lubbock states[5] that such evidence is strong, and, indeed, his facts are so abundant

kinsman not in the ascending line. (W. Smith 1842, art. "Marriage [Greeks]."）

[1] Fison and Howitt 1880, p. 115.

[2] McLennan 1876, p. 175 ; cf. the case of Ammon and Tamar (II Sam. 13).

[3] Lubbock 1875, p. 149.

[4] *Ibid.*, p. 91.   [5] *Ibid.*, p. 82.

that suspicion is aroused as to their relevancy. A
little examination shows that Darwin viewed the
evidence too favourably when he said[1] that, although
the facts cited show that the licentiousness of many
savages is astonishingly great, yet " more evidence is
requisite before we fully admit that their intercourse
is absolutely promiscuous." The facts, such as they
are, have been carefully classified by Dr M'Lennan,[2]
who was induced to do so because " the evidence adduced of ancient communism in women" is so slight.
He divides the facts cited into two categories, the
first of which comprises the cases where promiscuity
is expressly ascribed to particular peoples, and the
second, the cases in which it is inferred from certain
customs which are supposed to be acts of expiation
for marriage. In the former we find the Bushmen, or
more properly the Bosjesmans, of South Africa, the
Chinese before Fohi, and the Greeks before Cecrops ;
the Massagetæ, the Auses, and the Garamantes of
Herodotus and Strabo ; the Peruvians before the
Incas, the natives of California, and the Queen Charlotte Islanders, all of whom are said to be, or have
been, without " marriage." Of these cases we may dismiss those of the Chinese, the Greeks, and the peoples
referred to by the Greek historians, as too vague for the
purposes of the present argument. As to the Bosjesmans, the statement is at least doubtful. Mr Kitchener,
as quoted by the Rev. Robert Moffat,[3] says expressly
that the men have several wives, and although Professor Lichtenstein states that the family tie is not
sanctioned by any law or regulation, and the wife is

---

[1] Darwin 1871, II, 358.   [2] McLennan 1876, p. 430.
[3] Moffat 1842, p. 57 ; see also Spencer 1875, div. I, pt. 2, A.

not indissolubly united to the husband, he adds that, besides the love for their common children, habit makes them inseparable companions, showing that he refers rather to the form than to the fact of marriage. The Bosjesmans were probably little worse than the Hottentots, who would not hesitate to give up either wives or daughters for tobacco, but who would avenge in a deadly manner the affront if strangers interfered with their wives without permission.[1] As to the ancient Peruvians, although some of them are accused by Garcillasso de la Vega of conduct approaching promiscuity, yet he expressly says[2] that the most dissolute women were the most sought after in marriage. As to the natives of California, it is true that Mr Bancroft, in his " Native Races of the Pacific States," affirms that they hold feasts at which promiscuous intercourse is practised, but there is nothing to show that the practice is not exceptional. Similar cases of sexual excesses will be noticed later on in relation to other peoples, among whom a system of marriage is fully developed. There remain only the natives of Queen Charlotte's Islands, and the evidence of their promiscuity is far from satisfactory. Mr Poole certainly says that the institution of marriage is altogether unknown[3] among them, but from the context it is evident that he means the monogamic marriage of civilisation. He adds that the females cohabit " almost promiscuously with their own tribe, although rarely with' other tribes," and he mentions an instance of

[1] Wake 1878, I, 205.
[2] Lasso de la Vega 1869–71, I, pp. 58, 169.
[3] Poole 1872, p. 312.

some of the women going to Victoria to "earn blan-
kets" by prostitution. One of the women, however,
is described as having a "husband," and Mr Poole
speaks elsewhere[1] of the daughter of a chief having a
charm which would protect her and her kin from
drowning at sea ; so that if "individual marriage" is
not known among those natives, a kind of group
marriage is fully recognised.[2]

The evidence supplied by the cases referred to by
Sir John Lubbock in support of the theory of expiation for individual marriage is equally weak, in its
bearing at least on promiscuity. Of those cases, five
relate, says Dr M'Lennan,[3] to phallic worship among
peoples far advanced from the primitive state, but that
assertion must be taken, as I shall show hereafter, with
some qualification. With them it is necessary to
connect the cases relating to the lending of wives and
the respect shown anciently to courtesans, a subject of
great importance.[4] The case of the Lydians, with reference to whom Herodotus says the daughters of the
common people were prostitutes before marriage, seems
also to belong to the category which Dr M'Lennan
connects with phallic worship. It has as little bearing
on the question of primitive promiscuity as the habits
of the Thranans, of whom Herodotus expressly says[5]

[1] *Ibid.*, p. 311.

[2] Sir John Lubbock refers to the custom of adoption among
primitive peoples as being due to the prevalence of social
conditions arising out of communal marriage (1875, p. 88).
The reverse of this is nearer the truth, as the binding nature
of adoption proves how fully recognized is the force of the
blood-tie which it imitates.

[3] McLennan 1876, p. 440.

[4] It will be considered in the next chapter in connection
with sacred prostitution.   [5] Bk. V, 586.

that, although no watch was kept over their maidens, they kept strict watch on their wives. With the exception of that of the Santhals, to which reference will be made later on, the only remaining cases of promiscuity referred to by Sir John Lubbock are those in which all the guests at a marriage are allowed the *jus primæ noctis*, and as to these Dr M'Lennan affirms[1] that " they are not cases of privilege granted to the men of the husband's tribe." If this were correct, they would be evidence of limited promiscuity under special conditions, but the assertion is criticised by the Rev. Lorimer Fison,[2] who thinks that Sir John Lubbock's theory as to " expiation for marriage" is the true one ." so far as it goes." The term *expiation for marriage* originated with Bachofen, and was applied by him, as already mentioned,[3] to the temporary prostitution required as a sacrifice to the Earth Goddess Demeter. As used in connection with the conduct of the bridesmen or clansmen of the bridegroom, it is said that individual marriage was an infringement of the communal marriage rights, the existence of which are supposed to be evidenced by the so-called Acts of Expiation. Whatever truth there may be in this notion of " expiation " as a religious act, or in relation to the bridegroom's totemic-group, there is none in connection with the tribe, the group to which a child is supposed to have been related generally before he was related to either of his parents. Sir John Lubbock appears to make no distinction[4] between the " tribe " and the " clan," or totem group, a mistake which vitiates his whole argu-

---

[1] McLennan 1876, p. 442.
[2] Fison and Howitt 1880, p. 151.   [3] Above, p. 16.
[4] Dr. McLennan does not sufficiently distinguish between the tribe and the clan. See Morgan 1877, p. 511.

ment. The facts cited as showing "expiation" relate to the smaller group and not to the tribe. He has fallen into the same mistake when treating of the development of relationships, inasmuch as he affirms[1] that relationship is at first a matter, not of blood, but of tribal organization, and that " the connection of individuals *inter se*, their duties to one another, their rights and the descent of their property, are all regulated more by the relation to the tribe than by that to the family," where for tribe should be read clan, or totem-group, the male members of which are, as Mr Fison shows, the only persons who can claim expiation for " special marriage."

It was stated before that Mr Fison regards Sir John Lubbock's theory of expiation for marriage as true " so far as it goes," and it is necessary to consider certain customs found among the Australian aborigines which relate to that subject and have a bearing on the question of promiscuity. Mr Fison refers[2] to a practice which he thinks furnishes strong evidence that " communal marriage " formerly prevailed among the ancestors of the Kurnai of Gippsland, and he regards it as a case of " expiation for marriage," and as being required before the " communal " right, that is, the right of the tribe to all its female members, can be got rid of. He speaks also of the " remarkable significance of the fact recorded by Mr Howitt, that when a woman elopes from her husband, she becomes for the time being the common property of her pursuers if they can catch her. By her own act she has severed the tie which, binding her to her husband, guarded her against the old communal right, and forthwith that right asserts itself."

[1] Lubbock 1875, p. 190.
[2] Fison and Howitt 1880, p. 310; cf. p. 202 n.

Now, it may be objected that the enforcement of this so-called "communal" *right* is in reality part of the punishment of the woman for her elopement. It is referred to [1] by Mr Howitt as one of the penalties by which a woman's fidelity to her husband is enforced, and Mr Fison himself, in mentioning a similar practice among the Fijians, speaks of it as a punishment which was inflicted openly in the public square of the town. Probably the idea of a reward to the captors was added, but the predominant idea would have relation to the offence. Even if we have in the case mentioned the assertion of a right, it is not "communal" in the sense intended by Sir John Lubbock by that term when he speaks of "communal marriage." This with him means general promiscuity, whereas Mr Fison uses the word "commune" as equivalent to a limited group. This is shown by the statement [2] that the Kurnai practice supplies precisely those conditions which Dr M'Lennan required as necessary to make evidence of "expiation for marriage" of value :—" The privileged persons should be of the bridegroom's group only, and the cases should be incapable of no simpler explanation." It is evident from Mr Fison's observation elsewhere,[3] that the men who exercise the "communal" right must belong to the husband's group, and therefore they stand in the same social relation to her as her husband himself. Mr Howitt does not say as much. Indeed, he states that "all the neighbouring men might turn out and seek for" the eloping woman; but we may judge by analogy that it must be so. When speaking of a similar subject, Mr Howitt refers[4]

[1] *Ibid.*, p. 205. [2] *Ibid.*, p. 152.
[3] *Ibid.*, p. 153. Mr. Fison here says that the fugitive wife becomes the common property of her pursuers, "these pursuers being of her husband's kindred." [4] *Ibid*, p. 346.

to facts which prove that among the Australians "marriage by capture was only permitted when the captor and the captive were of some classes which might legally intermarry." Among one tribe it is said that the female war captive was at first common to the men present at her capture, and then only became the property of her captor if she were of a class from which he might take a wife.

The so-called "expiation for marriage" itself is a simpler question, for here undoubtedly the men who assert the marital right belong to the husband's family group. Mr Fison says expressly,[1] "The group of men who can claim expiation for 'special marriage' is no longer the whole tribe, but the group of tribal brothers[2] who have a common right to the group of females to which the woman belongs." Sir John Lubbock's notion that the whole tribe could at one time claim expiation is not supported by evidence, and Mr Fison's admission[3] that "the ascertained facts go no further than to a community already divided into exogamous clans, with group marriage between them," shows that it has not been found among the Australians. Even if it could be shown that the practice of absolute promiscuity as a propitiatory measure is sometimes allowed, this fact could not be taken as evidence of the former existence of a condition of society such as that described by the term "communal marriage" used in its widest sense. It might prove that under special

[1] *Ibid.*, p. 155.
[2] This view is confirmed by Mr. Fison's statement in a private letter to me with reference to infant betrothal, that it is intended to put the *tapu* on a girl as early as possible, but that in some tribes all the husband's "group" friends consumate the marriage before he does. [3] *Ibid.*, p. 160.

circumstances all marital restrictions were suspended, but not that at one time they did not exist.

We have probably a case analogous to " expiation " in the licence which among certain peoples is claimed on the happening of particular important events. Thus, formerly, in the Sandwich Islands, on the death of a chief, " the whole neighbourhood," says Ellis,[1] " exhibited a scene of confusion, wickedness, and cruelty, seldom witnessed even in the most barbarous society. The people ran to and fro without their clothes, appearing and acting more like demons than human beings ; every vice was practised, and almost every species of crime perpetrated. Houses were burnt, property plundered, even murder sometimes committed, and the gratification of every base and savage feeling sought without restraint." The death of a chief appeared to be regarded as loosening the bonds of society, or rather as allowing each individual to give full play to his passions. There may be in such conduct something of an expiation, or of an offering to the dead, but probably the chief idea in operation was freedom from restraint. Thus, among the Hovas of Madagascar on the birth of a child in the royal family complete sexual licence was allowed. On one occasion, according to the Rev. William Ellis,[2] " the town, by reason of the scenes which the streets and lanes almost everywhere exhibited, appeared to be one vast brothel." Such a period was described by a term which denoted that death could not be then inflicted for any offence. Among the hill tribes of India licentious conduct takes place at religious or funeral festivals, and the same thing would seem to have been usual with some of the

[1] Ellis 1832–34, II, 177.   [2] Ellis 1838, I, 150.

peoples of ancient Peru.   The removal of the restraints
of authority are thus expressed, and in like manner,
during the Areoi festivals of the Tahitiians, the restrictions of the tabu were removed from females for the
benefit of a particular class,[1] the result being no doubt
much the same as the licentiousness of the Australians
on the occasions referred to by Mr Fison.   The idea of
removal of restraint is strikingly shown in the fact mentioned by Mr David Forbes, that among the Aymaras
of Peru, the explanation of the excesses committed
on Good Friday is that anything could be done on
that day, as *God was then dead.*   Mr Forbes was told
that instances are known where Aymaras have on Good
Friday " violated their own daughters in presence of
their mothers," and his informant assured him that as
God was then dead it would be no sin![2]

Mr Fison, in his " Notes on Fijian Burial Customs,"
gives much the same explanation of similar practices.
He says,[3] that in many widely separated parts of the
Fijian group, " a custom prevails which is found in
Central Africa[4] also, and elsewhere.   For some days
after the decease of a ruling chief, if his death be
known to the people, the wildest anarchy prevails.
The 'subject tribes' rush into the chief town, kill pigs
and fowls, snatch any property they can lay their
hands on, set fire to houses, and play all manner of
mischievous pranks, the townsfolk offering no resistance."   To prevent this practice, the death of the
chief is carefully concealed by the persons who have

[1] Ellis 1832–34, I, 247.
[2] Forbes 1870, p. 228.
[3] Fison 1881, p. 140.
[4] Bosman refers to a similar custom as prevalent among the
natives of the Slave Coast of Guinea (1721, p. 345).

had special charge of him for a period varying from four to ten days. The explanation of this custom given by Mr Fison is that not until decomposition may be supposed to have made considerable progress, "is the dead man fairly done with, and his authority handed over to his successor. The dead hand can no longer wield the sceptre, but it has not relinquished its grasp ; and the old communal idea asserts itself now that the power which kept it down is in abeyance. Hence the interval of anarchy if the death be not concealed." It might be objected, that as the "subject tribes" are the culprits, the idea which reveals itself is merely that the controlling authority having ceased the old independence can be temporarily reasserted. Other instances given by Mr Fison seem to prove, however, that there is the assertion of a "communal right." But this explanation will not be sufficient for the excesses which take place during purely religious or tribal festivals, which have nothing to do with the death of a chief or other person. Thus, during the Yam Custom of the Ashantees, which is held in the early part of September at the maturity of that vegetable, no notice is taken of theft, assault, or intrigue, and the grossest licence then prevails, everyone abandoning himself to his passions. Men, women, and children all get drunk together.[1] The Maya nations of Central America, who also indulged much in drink during many of their festivals, are said to have permitted women of any condition to abandon themselves

---

[1] Bowdich 1819, pp. 274, 278. During the coronation ceremony of the late Czar of Russia, riots occurred in St. Petersburg through the drunken excesses of the lower classes, who considered themselves allowed to do anything on such occasions (Reuter's telegram in daily papers).

to the embrace of whomsoever they pleased during a certain annual festival.[1] These appear to be cases of pure licence having, however, some relation to the season and the object of the festival, but there is nothing to show that absolute promiscuity was ever practised. Nor is there any evidence that the "indiscriminate sexual intercourse" asserted[2] to prevail occasionally among the New Mexican tribes went so far as to permit such intercourse between persons near of kin, and it is probably only a special exhibition of the ordinary debauchery to which those tribes appear to have been addicted. In the cases where it can be affirmed that the restraints on promiscuity have been relaxed for the purpose of appeasing the anger of an offended spirit, it must be questioned, until further evidence to the contrary is adduced, whether the so-called promiscuity extends to members of a common group. Possibly it may include individuals, such as father and daughter, who appear not, owing to the child following its mother, to come within the original class restrictions, as with the Aymaras; but such conduct must in any case be regarded as exceptional, and not as evidence of the former existence of a condition of society in which it was the rule, or even generally practised.

It may be objected, that the fact of the removal of the restraints of authority being attended by the outbreak of sexual excesses, justifies the inference that prior to the formation of such restraints similar conduct was the rule. This conclusion may be thought to be supported by such a fact[3] as that the phrase " to live

[1] Bancroft 1875, II, 676.   [2] Ibid., I, 566.
[3] Mentioned by the Rev. Lorimer Fison in his communication to me.

like the Tui Kamba "—the males of Thakombau's clan —is used by the Fijians as a proverbial saying, meaning incestuous intercourse. This practice is evidently restricted among the Fijians to the chiefs, and it may be argued that they are above the regulations of marriage, as they are the incarnations of the chiefs who made the regulations. This idea does not, however, supply a sufficient sanction for the practice. The natural restraints on promiscuity are so widely spread and so deeply ingrained into the social economy of all uncultured peoples, that they must have originated at a very early period in human history. It is not to be supposed, therefore, that the chiefs of any existing race can claim to represent the originators of those restraints, nor is it probable that a right of exemption from their operation has been handed down from primitive ages to the present time. Undoubtedly, the practice of the Tui Kamba is either an example of the privileges which the members of a caste often acquire or claim for themselves, or a means of perpetuating unmixed a strain of blood which it is desired for some reason or other to retain in a condition of purity.

This chapter cannot be brought to a close before examining the arguments used by Mr A. W. Howitt, the coadjutor of the Rev. Lorimer Fison in their investigation of the curious institutions found among the Australian aborigines, in support of the original existence of his "undivided commune," in which "there was probably more or less promiscuous cohabitation, at least between those of the contemporaneous generation."[1] Such an examination need not be at great

[1] Fison and Howitt 1880, p. 365; cf. Howitt 1883, pp. 496ff.

length, as the *Undivided Commune* is taken by Mr
Howitt as equivalent to the *Consanguine family,
Hetairism,* or *Communal Marriage,* of preceding
writers.   The objections to the existence of these
conditions of society are equally applicable to the
undivided commune.   Mr Howitt supposes that with
this state of society there existed also marriage by
capture, in which the female captives were incorporated into the commune, it being perpetuated in the
exogamous segmented communes of the Australian
system.   He states[1] that the evidence suggests that
" exogamy was the natural consequence of the segmentation of an original commune into two intermarrying
communes, and the institution thereby of two class
divisions embracing both."   From this it would seem
that Mr Howitt assumes the existence of the undivided
commune to explain that of exogamy, and if therefore
this custom can be otherwise satisfactorily accounted
for, the assumption may be dispensed with.   That its
existence can be otherwise explained will be shown
when dealing with the subject in the next chapter.
It may be remarked here, however, that, as exogamy
is the universal rule of the Australian class system,
in accounting for this system probably the origin of
exogamy will also be explained, a proposition which
agrees with that of Mr Howitt, although he would
give a different origin for the Australian classes from
that hereafter assigned for them.   In reality, there is
no evidence of the former existence of the " undivided
commune," now or before the establishment of the
Australian system.   Mr Fison's opinion[2] that the ascertained facts go no further than to a community already

---

[1] Fison and Howitt 1880, p. 360.
[2] See above, p. 38.

divided into exogamous clans, with group marriage between them, has already been quoted, and there is no occasion to suppose that it ever went any further, notwithstanding the supposed evidences of promiscuity which have been referred to as existing among the Australian aborigines. It is probable, indeed, that Mr Howitt himself would not now insist on the undivided commune. In a paper communicated to the Smithsonian Institute, he says,[1] " I doubt whether, even under an ' undivided commune,' there could have been anything more than a limited promiscuity, excepting when the whole community occasionally reunited. The general conditions of savage life on the Australian continent would not permit an entire undivided commune to remain united for any length of time in the same locality." He refers to a practice of the Dieri or Dieyerie tribe, settled near Cooper's Creek in Central Australia, as showing, in a modified form, what might take place ; but even with that tribe the sexual intercourse of persons who are considered too nearly related " is forbidden under all circumstances " under the penalty of death. It is true that the Kunandaburi, a tribe allied to the Dieri, are said[2] not to observe any such restriction on the occasion of the marriage of a betrothed girl, but Mr Howitt adds that it is an extreme and exceptional extension of the *jus primœ noctis* as to which he would obtain but little information, and we may doubt whether the right is so extensive as to include the father or brother of the bride. In any event, it is too exceptional a case to prove the existence of absolute promiscuity, and still less to establish the former prevalence of such a state of

[1] Howitt 1885, p. 807n.
[2] *Ibid.*, p. 804.

things among the Australian aborigines generally.
The Kunandaburi are in some respects slightly behind
the Dieri, but both are, according to Mr Howitt, at
the commencement of the " long progressive series "
formed by all the tribes dealt with by him ; so that it
is very improbable that while even " casual amours "
between persons who are forbidden to each other by
nearness of kinship or otherwise are regarded by the
latter tribe with the " utmost abhorrence" and punished
with death, absolute promiscuity should be allowed by
the former.

In connection with this subject, reference should be
made to a curious legend which the Dieri relate to
account for the origin of the sub-division of the tribe
into families, as it is thought to furnish indirect evidence of the former existence of the *undivided
commune* among the Australians.   The legend, as
given by Mr Gason,[1] is as follows :—" After the creation (as previously related) fathers, mothers, sisters,
and brothers, and others of the closest kin intermarried
promiscuously, until the evil effects of these alliances
becoming manifest, a council of the chiefs was assembled
to consider in what way they might be averted, the
result of their deliberations being a petition to the
Moora Moora,[2] in answer to which he ordered that the
tribe should be divided into branches, and distinguished
one from the other by different names, after objects
animate and inanimate, such as dogs, mice, emu, rain,
iguana, and so forth, the members of any such branch
not to intermarry, but with permission for one branch

[1] Gason 1879, p. 260.
[2] The Moora Moora are the deceased ancestors of the tribe
(Howitt 1883, p. 498).

to mingle with another. Thus the son of a dog might not marry the daughter of a dog, but either might form an alliance with a mouse, an emu, a rat, or other family." Mr Gason states that this custom is still observed, and that the first question asked of a stranger is, " What Murdoo ? " namely, " Of what family are you ? " Mr Morgan was much struck with the bearing of this legend on his hypothesis, and he accepted it as giving to his *consanguine family* " a basis of probability." He says [1] that the legend has more weight than mere negative assertion, and that it is " a plain statement of facts as they appear to the native mind familiar with their present, and to some extent with their anterior condition." If the consanguine family has no other basis of probability its foundation must be very weak, as a little consideration shows that the story, which is no doubt a genuine native legend, as similar ones appear to be current among other tribes,[2] cannot have the value assigned to it. It might be said with equal truth that the native legend of the creation has a basis of probability. In it, equally with the other legend, we have " a plain statement of facts, as they appeared to the native mind." Mr Gason relates the creation legend as follows [3] :—" In the beginning, say the Dieyerie, the Mooramoora (Good Spirit) made a number of small black lizards (these are still to be met with under dry bark), and being pleased with them he promised they should have power over all creeping things. The Mooramoora then divided their feet into toes and fingers, and placing his forefinger on the centre of the

[1] Fison and Howitt 1880, p. 4.   [2] Howitt 1883, p. 498.
[3] Gason 1879, p. 260.

face, created a nose, and so in like manner afterwards eyes, mouth, and ears. The Spirit then placed one of them in a standing position, which it could not, however, retain, whereupon the Deity cut off the tail, and the lizard walked erect. They were then made male and female, so as to perpetuate the race." Mr Gason adds that men, women, or children do not vary in the slightest degree in this account of the creation, which is as true to them as the Murdoo legend. These stories are, indeed, closely connected, and as one gives the idea of the origin of man entertained by the Dieri, the other gives their notion of the origin of the change from the social system which they received from their lizard ancestor to that which they now possess, and which they can account for only by supposing the intervention of the Good Spirit. Whether the Murdoo legend applies to the Dieri only, or to the whole Australian race, it really proves nothing as to their early social condition. At the utmost it shows only how the ingenious native mind [1] explains the origin of the division of the tribes into branches having different family names ; a division which, if it had an immediate relation to the question of marriage, may have been, and probably was, intended to prevent consanguineous connections, by furnishing an easy test of kinship when the tribe had become so numerous or widespread that kinship could not otherwise be determined without difficulty. Mr Fison, who believes the Murdoo legend to be genuine,[2] says that

[1] Mr. Howitt remarks that the lower savages do perceive such questions as the marriage of near relations, "and discuss them freely among themselves, the women taking an active part in the discussion" (1885, p. 815n.).

[2] Fison and Howitt 1880, p. 26.

" divisions similar to those which it mentions are found throughout the length and breadth of the Australian continent, as well as in many other parts of the world, and that from these divisions, with their inter-sexual arrangements, flows the entire system of kinship called the Turanian " by Mr Morgan. This fact in itself throws doubt on the value of the legend, seeing that it is very improbable the Australians, among all the peoples having the Turanian system of kinship, would have alone preserved a remembrance of the cause of the division into classes or gentes. This must have taken place some thousands of years ago, and it is very questionable whether a primitive legend could have been handed down among savages for so long a period, even if the ancestral mind was able to formulate it at so early a period as that at which it must have originated. To the suggestion that the legend and the promiscuous conduct observed on certain occasions mutually support each other, it may be replied that their agreement proves nothing more than that they are traceable to a common mental source. Man in the low social condition of the Australian aborigines, with whom the gratification of the sexual instinct is regarded as equally imperative with that of the instinct of self-preservation, may, under the influence of superstitious dread, temporarily give way to sexual conduct which, although at other times considered grossly improper, then becomes praiseworthy. This consideration is sufficient to explain the sexual excesses of the Australian aborigines, without supposing them to be degraded from the social condition of their ancestors, or requiring them to have advanced from a primitive condition of promiscuity.

In conclusion, the warning given by Sir Henry
Maine should be heeded by those who seek to infer
from the practice of modern tribes the existence of
social depravity among the early races of mankind.
That learned writer, while admitting that many of the
phenomena of barbarism adverted to by Sir John
Lubbock and Dr M'Lennan are found in India, says,[1]
"The usages appealed to are the usages of certain
tribes or races, sometimes called aboriginal, which
have been driven into the accessible recesses of the
widely extended mountain country on the north-east
of India by the double pressure of Indian and Chinese
civilisation, or which took refuge in the hilly regions
of Central and Southern India from the conquest of
Brahminical invaders, whether or not of Aryan descent.
Many of these wild tribes have now for many years
been under British observation, and have indeed been
administered by British officers. The evidence, therefore, of their usages and ideas which is or may be
forthcoming, is very superior indeed to the slippery
testimony concerning savages which is gathered by
travellers' tales. It is not my intention in the present
lectures to examine the Indian evidence anew, but,
now that we know what interest attaches to it, I
venture to suggest that this evidence should be carefully re-examined on the spot. Much which I have
personally heard in India bears out the caution which
I gave as to the reserve with which all speculations
on the antiquity of human usage should be received.
Practices represented as of immemorial antiquity, and
universally characteristic of the infancy of mankind,
have been described to me as having been for the
first time resorted to in our own days through the

[1] Maine 1871, p. 16.

mere pressure of external circumstances or novel temptations."

To these remarks I would add that the interpretation usually put upon such practices may not be correct. Mr Rowney says,[1] in relation to the wild tribes of India : "Among several races we see private morals so carefully watched over that the unmarried youths of both sexes are kept apart at night, not only from each other, but even from the married members of their own families, lest there should be any lapse of virtue within the family circle itself ; but we read in the same breath of such beastly customs as the *Bandana* among the Santháls, and the promiscuous intercourse of the sexes in various other shapes among many of the other tribes." The only other particular case of such a condition of licence mentioned by Mr Rowney is that of the Booteáhs, of whom it is said,[2] "the marriage tie is so loose that chastity is quite unknown amongst them. . . . Polyandry prevails among them, . . . but even the very slight restriction implied by the institution is not observed. The intercourse between the sexes is, in fact, promiscuous." In corroboration of this remark it is stated that on the death of a Booteáh his property goes to the Deb or Dhurm Rajah, and not to the children, "it being impossible to determine whose children they are." That this is the real reason why a man's property is thus appropriated is very questionable, but at least the licence allowed to the women appears not to be greater than among other polyandrist tribes of the same territory,[3] and is not evidence of "promiscuity" in the proper sense of this term. The same may be said of the

[1] Rowney 1882, p. 215.   [2] *Ibid.*, p. 142.
[3] *Ibid.*, pp. 129, 159, 163.

Santhal *Bandana*, which is a festival lasting six days, "when all the candidates for matrimony, male and female, are assembled together and permitted to have promiscuous intercourse with each other, each lover selecting his future wife after the termination of this general carnival."[1]   It may be doubted whether this mode of courtship is in practice much worse than the "bundling" system, which is known to races of a much higher culture, and which was not unusual in some portions of the British Islands not long ago.[2] The Santhal love-matches usually terminate in happy marriages, and although polygamy is permitted it is seldom practised.

There is, in fact, nothing in the present experience of mankind to authorise the view that it has passed through a stage of sexual promiscuity, although the phenomenal phases of marriage are varied and sometimes of an eccentric character.   Reference has already been made to Darwin's opinion, that "promiscuous intercourse in a state of nature is extremely improbable," it certainly not taking place among the quadrumana.   If it is wanting among the lower animals, much less can it be asserted of primitive man, who is supposed to inherit and improve on their experiences. That the union between man and woman was not that of individual marriage, is probable, and possibly it may have not endured for life.   Much would depend on whether it bore fruit.   Even in the present day, divorce, or the marrying of a second wife, is often justified by the absence of offspring, and the permanence of the sexual union in the early ages would doubtless depend in a great measure on the same condition.

[1] *Ibid.*, p. 76.
[2] Wake 1878, I, Index.

So far from there being evidence of the existence in primeval times of such a human horde as Dr M'Lennan's hypothesis requires, the facts tend rather to prove that the earliest human groups consisted of a number of individuals, or of family units, bound together by the ties of kinship.[1]

[1] Wake 1888*b*, p. 276.

CHAPTER III.

THE way has now been cleared for ascertaining the ideas which governed the development of the sexual relations among the earliest races of mankind. If the intercourse between the sexes was not one of absolute promiscuity, it must have been affected by certain rules and regulations, which it will be necessary to identify. This cannot be done unless it is remembered that to the savage mind the promptings of the sexual instinct are as imperative as those of the instinct of self-preservation. It has already been pointed out[1] that the subjective phase of the sexual instinct would, unless restrained, result in a condition of promiscuity, and possibly at first its operation, like that of the instinct of self-preservation, may have been subject to very slight control. We have seen reason to believe, however, that the activity of the sexual instinct was not allowed to go unchecked, and the "restraints on promiscuity" show their effect in the primitive law of marriage. These restraints have been divided into, 1st, *social restraints*, those arising from the claim of parents or others to have an interest in, or a right to control the conduct of, the females belonging to their family group ; and 2ndly, *natural restraints*, those arising from the feeling that persons closely related by blood ought not to intermarry. The operation of the

[1] p. 3.

social restraints must gradually have led to the formation of a rule of conduct, the observance of which would be stringently enforced. The social regulation thus established would probably be seldom infringed within any particular group. When mankind became separated into several groups or hordes, " capture" by one horde from another might gradually become established as a means of obtaining women, but this is not likely to have taken place to any great extent unless the females of any particular horde were by some means reduced in number below its requirements. The " capture" would be regarded by the members of the group to which the captives belonged as an infringement of their rights requiring strict retaliation, and therefore it would be seldom resorted to so long as the neighbouring hordes remained friendly and women could be obtained by other means.

The regulations springing from the operation of *natural* restraints were no less stringent. Experience proves that the sexual passion is much less easily aroused into activity between persons who grow up together from childhood than between other individuals. Thus, among uncivilised peoples, the closest friendship may be established between brothers and sisters without any reference to sexual feeling. This fact is quite independent of any idea of special relationship between brothers and sisters, although we cannot doubt that from the very earliest times the offspring of the same mother would be looked upon as nearer of kin to each other than to other children, even though they all had the same father. Every woman would consider herself as standing in a special relation to her own offspring, and they would regard themselves as being specially related to each other. This would give rise to a feeling of fraternity, which might almost be described as instinctive, and which would tend still further to hinder the formation of sexual connections between members of such a group. At the same time such connections would be formed without hesitation between the members of different maternal groups. Considering the opinion held by most savages as to the special relation between a man and his children, proving that the idea of paternity is fully recognised, we cannot doubt that the male head would be precluded from consorting with the young females of the group. There would, indeed, gradually be formed a paternal instinct which would itself oppose such connections, although it would not at first be so influential as the maternal phase of the parental instinct, which, as being the more intimately concerned with offspring, is the more influential in the formation of the idea of kinship.

It results from what has been just said that all sexual conduct was primitively regarded as right and proper which was not opposed to any social regulation or to any natural restraint. We have here the *law of marriage*, which, however its terms may vary, is always the same in principle. It is evident that the rights which a man or a group of persons may have over his or their female companions may be enlarged or lessened from time to time. The authority of a man over his wife or daughter consists largely in his permitting or restraining sexual conduct on their part, such conduct being under the control of the female, so long as she does not infringe the rights obtained by her husband or father, or the group to which they respectively belong. So also the natural restraints may vary from time to time. The group of kindred between whom sexual connections are not permitted may be enlarged so as to embrace all or any of the persons who are allied by blood, whether on the paternal or maternal side, and however distant may be the link of connection between them. What we have now to do is to show the operation of that law of marriage, and to trace its development from its most simple expression.

In considering the restraints on promiscuity which give form to the law of marriage in its earliest phase, we will first deal with those which have been described as *natural*. These have relation primarily to the family group, composed of a mother and her offspring, which ultimately developes into the larger group to which, under varying conditions, the name of *gens* or *totem* may be applied. That family group is the real social unit, and its maternal head is chiefly concerned with the internal concerns of the household, its male head being engaged more especially with its external affairs. Nor is this external authority based merely on the possessory rights which a man has over the members of the family group. It presupposes the recognition of his paternal relationship to the woman's offspring. If it could be established that from primeval times kinship has been universally traced through the mother it would furnish no real evidence that paternity was uncertain. As will be shown hereafter, the systems of relationship which are established among the uncivilised races of mankind who prefer female kinship, are consistent with the recognition of relationship through the father also, and in fact fully recognise it. It is true Mr Morgan affirms that " the maternity of children was ascertain-

able with certainty, while there paternity was not ";
adding, " but they did not reject kinship through
males because of uncertainty, but gave the benefit of
the doubt to a number of persons—probable fathers
being placed in the category of real fathers, probable
brothers in that of real brothers, and probable sons in
that of real sons." The notion of the uncertainty of
paternity is required by Mr Morgan's special views,
but there is little evidence of it in fact. It is equally
essential to the theory maintained by Dr M'Lennan,
the basis of which is the assumption, already shown to
be incorrect, that mankind has passed through a stage
of promiscuity, that is, in which women were not
appropriated to particular men.

The very early origin of the natural restraints on
promiscuity is evidenced by the strong objection entertained by peoples of even a very low degree of culture
to the intermarriage of persons near of kin. Reference to this point was made in the last chapter,[1] but it
is necessary to consider it now more in detail. The
cases in which peoples of varying degrees of culture
are positively known to forbid marriages between persons near of kin are too numerous to be fully specified
here.[2] It will be sufficient to quote as examples the
ideas on that subject of some of the lowest races of
mankind. Thus, the Bosjesmans of South Africa do
not permit marriages between brother and sister or
parent and child,[3] while the related Hottentots forbid

---

[1] Above, pp. 43ff.

[2] Many instances are given by Dr. E. B. Tylor (1865, chap.
10) and by Sir John Lubbock (1875, pp. 126ff.).

[3] Spencer 1876, p. 6; Barrow 1806, I, 276.

such alliances between first or second cousins, and punish all persons who act contrary to this custom.[1] Mr E. H. Man affirms,[2] as to the Andaman Islanders, that "in all the relations of life the question of propinquity is, in their eyes, of paramount importance, and marriage is only permissible between those who are known to be not even distantly connected, except by wedlock, with each other." He adds,[3] "although great freedom is allowed between the sexes before marriage, it is strictly confined to those not related by blood." The same remark may be made in relation to the aborigines of Australia, whose ideas on the subject of consanguineous marriages are well expressed in the Dieri legend, mentioned in the preceding chapter,[4] and are embodied, as we shall see, in their system of marriage and kinship. The objection to such marital alliances was general among the natives of America when discovered by Europeans. Mr Morgan, who mentions this fact,[5] supposes that "the structure and principles of the organisation (into gentes) tended to create a prejudice against the marriage of consanguinei." Unfortunately for this opinion, the gens was united by the bond of kin, and one of its fundamental regulations was the obligation not to marry into the gens,[6] an obligation which merely continued the primitive restriction which prohibited marriage between persons

---

[1] Kolben 1731, p. 156.   [2] Man 1883, p. 126.

[3] *Ibid.*, p. 135.   [4] Above, p. 46.

[5] 1877, p. 458. Some of the South American tribes (Letourneau 1876, p. 323), and the Aleuts (Reclus 1885, p. 77), appear to be exceptions, but probably it will be found that persons of kin in the female line are not permitted to marry.

[6] Morgan 1877, pp. 69ff.

near of kin. The Hawaiians are thought by Mr
Morgan[1] to show in some of their marriage customs
the former prevalence of consanguine marriages, but,
according to Admiral Wilkes, such alliances were
purely exceptional, and "contrary to the customs,
habits, and feelings of the people." This agrees with
what the Rev. George Turner states[2] in relation to
the Samoans, whose "list of what they deem improper
marriages would almost compare with the 'Table of
Kindred and Affinity.'" The Malagasy do not permit
marriages between brothers and sisters of different
mothers, but collateral branches on the male side are
permitted to intermarry in most cases, "on the observance of a slight but prescribed ceremony, which is
supposed to remove the impediment or disqualification
arising out of consanguinity."[3] According to the
Rev. James Sibree,[4] marriages between the children of
brothers are exceedingly common, and are looked upon
as the most proper kind of connection, as keeping
property in the family. He adds that marriage between brothers' and sisters' children is allowable, as
mentioned by Mr Ellis, on the performance of a slight
ceremony, but that between sisters' children, where
they have the same mother, it is regarded with horror
as incest. Again, the Malays of Sumatra forbid the
intermarriage of persons within a certain degree of
consanguinity, although the guilt is often expiated by
a ceremony,[5] as with the Malagasy. Finally, the

---

[1] See above, chap. 2, p. 21.
[2] Turner 1861, p. 185.
[3] Ellis 1838, I, 164.
[4] Sibree 1880, p. 39.
[5] Marsden 1811, p. 241. The *Dyaks* prohibit the intermarriage of first cousins, and of an aunt or uncle with a nephew
or niece (Brooke 1866, II, 336).

early Arabs, who appear to have been very lax in their sexual conduct, did not form consanguineous alliances. Professor Robertson Smith remarks [1] that "whatever the origin of bars to marriage, they certainly are early associated with the feeling that it is indecent for house-mates to intermarry." It may be safely affirmed that the dislike, based on such a feeling, to consanguineous marriages, is universal. The only exceptions to the rule are the brother and sister marriages, permitted for special reasons by the Hawaiians and some other peoples, referred to in the preceding chapter. It is true that the Veddahs of Ceylon and the New Caledonians are mentioned by Mr Herbert Spencer [2] as allowing consanguineous marriages. As to the Veddahs, it is stated on the authority of Mr Bailey, [3] that formerly it was the practice for a man to marry his younger sister. When, however, we find it asserted that the practice " is alluded to as a matter of course, without the smallest repugnance," we shall be justified in hesitating before accepting Mr Bailey's statement as absolutely correct. This hesitation will be increased when we know that the relationship of a " younger sister " with uncultured peoples often includes collateral sisters or cousins, as it does with the Tamil branch, [4] and probably with other branches of the Dravidian race, to which the Veddahs are allied. As to the New Caledonians, the Rev. George Turner affirms [5] that " no laws of consanguinity are observed in their marriages ; the nearest relatives unite." If

[1] Robertson Smith 1885, p. 170.
[2] Spencer 1874.
[3] Bailey 1863, pp. 294–95.
[4] Morgan 1877, pp. 447ff.
[5] G. Turner 1861, p. 424.

this statement is to be taken absolutely, the fact mentioned must be purely exceptional, seeing that among allied peoples consanguineous marriages are prohibited.[1] In reality, however, the near relatives who can intermarry are those on the paternal side only,[2] in which the New Caledonians agree with the Malagasy and other peoples.

That marriages between persons near of kin, according to the received ideas as to kinship, are not allowed among races of a low degree of culture, is evidenced by the marriage regulations in force among such peoples, which strictly prohibit such alliances. This fact was pointed out in connection with the Australian aborigines by the Rev. Wm. Ridley, and it is confirmed by the Rev. Lorimer Fison, who, when referring to the fact that marriage is forbidden within every division of a tribe, says[3] that this rule prohibits the marriage of all kinsfolk nearer than first cousins. He adds, " Nay, more, it excludes even those first cousins, according to our system, who are the children of father's brothers or of mother's sisters. It allows no union which is prohibited by our law, and it bars marriage between many persons whom we do not reckon to be in anywise akin." Mr Morgan[4] expresses his surprise at the vigour and persistence with which those marriage restrictions were enforced by savages whose " usages and customs exhibit the lowest possible views of the relations of the sexes." It is not to be wondered at,

---

[1] Mr. Bonwick states that with the Tasmanians such a connection would be illicit and incestuous (1870, p. 62).

[2] E. Foley, quoted by Letourneau (1876, p. 314).

[3] Fison and Howitt 1880, p. 118.   [4] *Ibid.*, p. 12.

therefore, that peoples of a higher social culture are equally strict in their marriage regulations. The rule which forbids the members of a gens to marry within the gens embodies the same ideas, and this prejudice against the marriage of consanguinei must have dated from the very origin of the gens. As I long since maintained,[1] the Australian classification of relations is " based on marriage customs having for their object the exclusion of near blood relations." This opinion is confirmed by Mr Howitt, who affirms[2] that the division of the community into classes and divisions was intended to prevent marriage between near relations, and that the fraternal relationship between a large group of contemporaries " not only prevents their being any intermarriage between them, but even a casual amour is regarded with abhorrence."

The opinion expressed above as to the fundamental nature of the feeling against marriage between persons near of kin is confirmed by the wide prevalence of *exogamy*. The custom to which this word refers is an expression of such a feeling, as shown by its definition,[3] " prohibited marriage within the tribe or group." Dr M'Lennan, to whom the word exogamy is due, traces[4] the custom to the practice of infanticide, which is supposed to have caused a scarcity of females within the tribe, and led to the capture of females from other tribes to supply the demand for wives. This usage is said to have established in course of time " a prejudice among the tribes observing it . . . . against marrying women of their own stock"; which

[1] Wake 1879, p. 30.
[2] Howitt 1885, pp. 815, 817.
[3] McLennan 1876, p. 41.   [4] *Ibid.*, p. 111.

prejudice began in a state of society having kinship through females and not through males, if, indeed, blood-relationship had then come to be recognised.[1] Exogamy is thus supposed to be almost coeval with the beginning of human society itself; and rightly so when we consider that it had relation then to a small group of kin, and not to the enlarged group represented by the gens or clan. But Dr M'Lennan's conclusions as to the origin of exogamy cannot be sustained. That the practice of stealing, forcibly or otherwise, women from neighbouring tribes is now very widely spread, cannot be denied, and probably it was in past ages more general than at present. Yet the capture of women for wives is not necessarily due to the scarcity of women. It may be so, no doubt, but women and children have always been regarded by savage tribes as lawful prey, and whatever the cause of quarrel which led to war between neighbouring peoples, the women and children of the conquered were always, if they could be reached, carried off by the conquerors. This practice was, indeed, almost universal in former times, and it may be exemplified by the conduct of the Israelites, who when they warred against the Midianites, slew every male, but "took captive the women of Midian and their little ones." [2] There is nothing to show that in this case there was any scarcity of women among the Israelites, such as is supposed by Dr M'Lennan's theory to be the "general cause" from which exogamy originated.[3]

[1] *Ibid.*, p. 112; cf. McLennan 1885, p. viii.
[2] Num. 31 : 7, 9, and see 17, 18.
[3] McLennan 1885, p. viii.

The persistence of exogamy proves that it had a different origin from that assigned for it by Dr M'Lennan. There is nothing to support his assumption that a prejudice against marrying women of the same stock was ever produced by the practice of forcible marriage. Moreover, from what we know of the conditions of savage life, it is very improbable that such a practice could have given rise to exogamy. The low estimate in which captives are held by the lower races would preclude such a view. Mr Walter Carew states that among the hill tribes of Fiji, " to call a person ' a child of a captive ' is a very great insult, even though the mother were of high rank." This agrees with Mr Sproat's observation in relation to the Ahts of British Columbia, that " the idea of slavery connected with capture is so common, that a free-born Aht would hesitate to marry a woman taken in war, whatever her rank had been in her own tribe." [1] But where an inferior position is not assigned to captives, forcible marriage would seem always to be subject to the law of exogamy; which, as already mentioned in connection with the question of *expiation for marriage,* " regulates the disposal of women who are taken from other tribes, or captured in war," [2] showing that the prejudice against marrying persons belonging to the same stock was antecedent to, or at least coeval with, forcible marriage.

We may justly conclude, therefore, that there is no necessary connection between the capture of women and exogamy, although this may sometimes be accompanied by force. Such a connection would require that, *because,* when the women of a tribe were few,

---

[1] Quoted by Fison (Fison and Howitt 1880, p. 143).

[2] Fison and Howitt 1880, pp. 65ff., 344.

men obtained their wives from their neighbours by
force, and therefore against their neighbours' will, they
should, when women are not scarce, necessarily, and
by consent, take their wives from among another
tribe. The necessity may be present in both cases;
but, while in the one case it arises from a scarcity
of women, in the other it depends on a prejudice
against intermarriage among the members of a common
group. Nor can it justly be argued that one necessity,
or rather the acting on it, would give rise to the feeling which led to the other. The two things are totally
distinct, and at the utmost the practice of obtaining
wives from the outside *by force*, would have led to
a similar usage *by consent*, without there being any
prohibition of marriage within the group, unless this
already existed alongside of the original practice.
We must presume, however, on Dr M'Lennan's theory,
that if there was no scarcity of women there would
be no capture, and *pari passu* the capture of women
from abroad would be co-extensive with their scarcity
at home. It is possible that, under special circumstances, all the female children in a tribe may be
destroyed, but such a practice could never have been
general, as otherwise mankind must have died out.
Nor is it probable that it was ever very common, and
we are justified in assuming that, in the absence of
such a prohibitory law as exogamy, some men in any
particular tribe would have wives of their own group,
and that when the scarcity of women came to an end,
the capture of women for wives, and with it marriage
out of the tribal group, would gradually also cease.

As a fact, however, the law of exogamy has retained
its binding force under all circumstances, and whatever
the condition of society. The presumption is, there-

fore, that the connection between exogamy, or the prejudice which leads to marriage outside the group, and capture of wives is accidental. It is true that what is termed *ceremonial capture* in marriage is intimately associated with exogamy, but, as I shall show in a subsequent chapter, it is totally different from forcible marriage, and has relation rather to the woman's offspring than to herself. On the other hand, exogamy can exist quite independently of marriage by force, and probably has often existed among peoples who did not capture wives, although they may have had kinship through females only, as Dr M'Lennan's theory supposes. In reality, *exogamy* is merely, as pointed out by Mr Morgan,[1] the rule that *intermarriage in the gens is prohibited*, and kinship through females is only the further rule of the gens (in its earliest form) that descent is limited to the female line. The latter point furnishes a strong argument against Dr M'Lennan. The rule of limiting descent to the female line arose partly from the close connection seen to subsist between a woman and her offspring, and partly from the retention of the latter within the power of the mother's family group. It would be impossible, however, for that rule to have originated while men captured their wives, as they would not recognise any authority of a woman's kinsfolk over her children, and these children would be regarded as belonging to their father's family group. Male kinship would thus be established while wife-capture subsisted, and it is very improbable that it would ever be displaced by female kinship, even though the practice of obtaining wives by force was replaced by pure exogamy.

[1] 1877, p. 511.

The American writer just referred to, Mr Morgan, affirms that the rule which prohibits intermarriage in the gens is intended to exclude brothers and sisters from the marriage relation, while permitting brothers to intermarry with each other's wives in a group, and sisters with each other's husbands in a group.[1] Reasons were adduced in the last chapter[2] for doubting the existence at any time of the consanguineous marriages this explanation requires, and it will be seen hereafter that the group relations referred to were not based on such marriages. It is true that in the primitive Australian system, all the divisions, gentes as well as classes, of the tribes are strictly exogamous,[3] and that the evidence supplied by that system is thought to " suggest that exogamy was the natural consequence of the segmentation of an original commune into two intermarrying communes, and the institution thereby of class divisions embracing both." If such an undivided commune existed, it was, says Mr Howitt,[4] " probably endogamous. The two resulting communes were exogamous as to each segment, but endogamous as to the whole." According to this view the division into classes gave rise to exogamy.

This explanation of the origin of exogamy is ingenious, but it assumes the prior existence of the undivided commune in which men and women lived in a state of promiscuity, and it must fail therefore if, as I have endeavoured to establish,[5] such a social state never existed. Nor is it really necessary to account for the custom in question. The regulation which forbids marriage within the gens was no doubt a rule

[1] *Ibid.*, p. 74.   [2] Above, p. 58.
[3] Fison and Howitt, 1880, p. 63.   [4] *Ibid.*, p. 360.
[5] See chap. 2.

of an earlier family group, which is identified by the further regulation that descent is to be traced in the female line. The earlier group consists, therefore, of the descendants of a common female ancestor, who, being forbidden to marry among themselves, must form alliances with the members of another and similar group. We have here the reason why exogamy is so intimately associated with descent in the female line, of which the prejudice against marriage between persons near of kin is a natural result. Usually, owing to the co-operation of the rule that children belong to their mother's gens, and the practice of women going to live among their husband's kin, a tribe consists of several gentes ; in which case, although the gentes are exogamous among themselves, the tribe itself is endogamous, seeing that its members have no occasion to marry outside of the tribe. But if by any means the gentes separate and form distinct tribes, pure exogamy would be absolutely necessary, unless the old marriage restrictions were entirely altered, and of such a change it is doubtful whether an authentic case could be supplied.

Dr M'Lennan affirms[1] that "wherever capture, or the form of capture, prevails, or has prevailed, there prevails or has prevailed exogamy," and yet, as we have seen, the latter has no necessary connection with capture, whatever relation it may have to the form of capture, which is a totally distinct custom. Moreover, so far from its being true that exogamy could not have originated "in any innate or primary feeling against marriage with kinsfolk,"[2] it is not only always associated with, but it is in fact the expression of such a feeling. It is objected, however, that exogamy could

[1] 1876, p. 110.　　　　　　　[2] *Ibid.*, p. 112.

not have originated in the intention to prevent the intermarriage of persons nearly related by blood, as this object is not effected by the rule in question. Thus, Mr Andrew Lang observes,[1] " where the family name goes by the male side, marriages between cousins are permitted, as in India and China. . . . But if the family name goes by the female side, marriages between half-brothers and half-sisters are permitted, as in ancient Athens and among the Hebrews of Abraham's times." The answer to that objection is that the law of exogamy does *not* fail of its purpose, for it excludes from intermarriage all the persons who are regarded as near of *kin*. It does not matter that at one time or in one locality the only relations recognised for the purpose of marriage prohibitions are those on the mother's side, while in another locality or at another time such relations are recognised only on the father's side. It would not be possible in small isolated communities to exclude from intermarriage all persons related through both parents, as such a rule would be tantamount to prohibiting marriage altogether. It is necessary in such cases, therefore, to make such a restriction absolute on one side only, although as a fact persons very closely related by blood on either side are usually prohibited from marrying together.[2]

The reasoning employed by Dr M'Lennan to prove the necessary connection between exogamy and marriage by capture, is equally applicable in support of such a connection subsisting between exogamy and a prejudice against marriage between persons near of kin.

[1] Lang 1884, p. 256.

[2] This is so among the Australian aborigines, whose restrictions on marriage are most complex. See Howitt 1885, p. 820.

The reasoning has much more force in the latter case than in the former; as Dr M'Lennan makes no distinction between simple capture or forcible marriage and ceremonial capture on marriage, a distinction which is most important in this relation. If we substitute the words " having an abhorrence of consanguineous marriages " for " a system of capture, or the form of capture," or words to the same effect, his argument[1] may be paraphrased as follows :—" If the existence of exogamous tribes [having an abhorrence of consanguineous marriages] should be established in a reasonable number of cases, it would be a legitimate inference that exogamy has prevailed wherever we find [an abhorrence of consanguineous marriages] existing. . . . The conditions requisite for this inference have been amply established, so that we may conclude that wherever [an abhorrence of consanguineous marriages] prevails, or has prevailed, there prevails, or has prevailed, exogamy. Conversely, we may say that, wherever exogamy can be found, we may confidently expect to find, after due investigation, at least traces of [an abhorrence of consanguineous marriages]. . . . It might be plausibly maintained, upon the facts already known to us, that the principle of exogamy has in fact prevailed, and the [abhorrence of consanguineous marriages] in fact been [entertained] at a certain stage among every race of mankind." Dr M'Lennan infers the former universal practice of wife capture from the fact that he has traced it " among tribes scattered over a large portion of the globe." The abhorrence of consanguineous marriages can be shown to be general among primitive peoples, however uncultured these may be, and exogamy can be most rationally explained as

[1] 1876, p. 109.

marriage out of the gens, clan, or group of kindred, arising from that feeling of abhorrence rather than from the practice of wife-capture or forcible marriage. Dr M'Lennan suggests [1] that an extensive practice of polyandry might prevent the rise of exogamy, but there is no evidence that it ever did so, and in fact the evidence conclusively points the other way, as will be shown when treating of polyandry and descent in the male line.

It is argued,[2] however, that "man must originally have been free of any prejudice against marriage between relations," and that "from this primitive indifference they may have advanced, some to endogamy, some to exogamy." Here Dr M'Lennan assumes the very point in question—indifference to the intermarriage of persons near of kin. If the existence of endogamy as a primitive institution could be established, the explanation given for the origin of exogamy would find some support. By the former, marriage out of the tribe is supposed to be forbidden and punished, the word "tribe" being here used in the sense of a group of persons of the same blood, or feigning themselves to be so.[3] That such a custom as this now exists or ever existed may, however, be much doubted. There may be tribes consisting of several gens, clans, or family groups which do not allow marriage outside the tribe, but they are not necessarily endogamous; as the members of one gens, clan, or family group may intermarry with those of another such group belonging to the same tribe in strict accordance with the principle

[1] McLennan 1885, p. 242; 1876, p. 169n.
[2] McLennan 1876, p. 116.
[3] *Ibid.*, p. 115.

of exogamy. Mr Fison very properly remarks [1] that if we could find an endogamous tribe without having exogamous divisions within it, " we should find what has been diligently sought for in vain for the last thirty years and more."

Dr M'Lennan, nevertheless, remarks that "the separate endogamous tribes are nearly as numerous, and they are in some respects as rude as the separate exogamous tribes." He refers [2] to the Mantchu Tartars as prohibiting marriages between persons *whose family names are different,* and states that the existence of such tribes is " of great weight in favour of endogamy as a primitive type of organisation." It is a pity no authority is given for that fact ; as, considering the customs of the Chinese in relation to marriage, and the restrictions on the intermarriage of consanguinei shown by the Turanian system of relationships, it is impossible to regard it as correct in the sense intended. [3] Dr M'Lennan also states that the Koch, Bodo, Ho, and Dhumal are " forbidden to marry except to members of their own tribes or kiels." The existence among those tribes of certain customs, such as female kinship and "marriage by capture," will lead us to believe that, although they may be endogamous so far as the tribe is concerned, yet that they are exogamous so far as regards the family or clan. The same objection no doubt applies to the cases of endogamy given in Sir John Lubbock's work. [4]

[1] Fison and Howitt 1880, p. 143.
[2] McLennan 1876, p. 116.
[3] Among the Mongols and Tartars, who have male kinship, a man might marry two own sisters, and even his father's wives after his decease, except his own mother, but he was not permitted to marry his own sister or aunt (Pétis de la Croix 1722, p. 364).   [4] 1875, pp. 136ff.

Dr M'Lennan lays down the principle that on kinship becoming agnatic, the members of a caste, formed by a feeling of superiority to other tribes and independence of them as regards marriage, feign themselves to be all descended from a common ancestor, and thus become endogamous." It is evident, however, from Dr M'Lennan's own testimony that such a caste is not truly endogamous. He remarks[1] that "nearly all the Indian castes, from the highest to the lowest, are divided into Gotrams or families, and that marriage is prohibited between persons of the same Gotram, who, according to the rule of Menu, are shown by their common name to be of the same original stock." This is an example of pure exogamy, and the mere fact of members of the caste intermarrying proves nothing in favour of endogamy. Dr M'Lennan also refers[2] to the Bedouin Arabs as an endogamous race. It is very doubtful, however, whether they are so in the proper sense of the term. Prof. Robertson Smith affirms[3] that "there is ample evidence that there was no law of endogamy among the Arabs at and before the time of Mohammed." That they were originally exogamous may be incapable of direct proof, although Prof. Smith infers from their having totemism and female kinship that they were so, and he thinks traces of exogamy are to be met with among them.[4]

Before leaving the subject of exogamy, reference should be made to the question of infanticide, which is the starting point of Dr M'Lennan's argument. According to his theory, the capture of women which resulted in exogamy was due to the scarcity

[1] McLennan 1876, p. 203.   [2] *Ibid.*, p. 207.
[3] Robertson Smith 1885, p. 60.   [4] *Ibid.*, pp. 184, 225, 311.

of women caused by the practice of infanticide. It
has been shown, however, that exogamy does not
depend on wife capture, therefore it is a matter of
little importance in this relation whether or not the
latter is traceable to the practice of infanticide. It is
not of much moment either to inquire, as Dr M'Lennan
appears to have done since the publication of his
" Studies,"[1] into " the prevalence of infanticide and
kindred practices" in relation to " the system of kindred
with which they are associated." If it could be shown
that infanticide is especially prevalent among peoples
having kinship through females only, or given to capture women for wives, it would not be evidence that
those practices had anything to do with the origin of
exogamy. In a future chapter, indeed, evidence will
be furnished that ceremonial capture in marriage is
found almost entirely among peoples tracing descent
preferably in the male line. Men may be driven to
capture wives through the scarcity of women, but the
connection between such scarcity, or the infanticide
to which it may be due, and exogamy is purely
accidental where it exists at all.

The importance of infanticide as a social factor
among the lower races of mankind may easily be exaggerated. The practice may, as Dr M'Lennan states,[2]
indicate "how slight the strength of blood-ties was in
primitive times," but it does little more. Whatever its
origin—and probably it is usually traceable to some
form of poverty, or to the inability of the mother to
rear her children, or her unwillingness to do so, especially in the case of females, under the conditions of life

[1] McLennan 1885, p. ix.
[2] McLennan 1876, p. 113.

to which women are subject among savages [1]—there is
no evidence that infanticide commonly creates so great
a scarcity of females for wives as to necessitate their
capture from neighbouring peoples as a general custom.
Dr M'Lennan ascribes the supposed prevalence of
female infanticide to the fact that, for various reasons,
daughters are a source of weakness.   Mr Fison has
shown,[2] however, that those reasons have not any force
as regards the lower races, and that instead of women
being an encumbrance, the contrary is true.   Mr Fison
points out, moreover, that a very powerful motive for
female infanticide—that among tribes who have descent
through the father, a " woman can transmit neither the
family name nor the family estate "—does not exist
among most savages, as descent is traced in the
female line.   To this argument may be added the fact
that when girls have an exchangeable value, that is,
where wife purchase is practised, they are, under ordinary conditions, as likely to be carefully reared as boys,
even among tribes who trace descent in the male line.

Sir John Lubbock accepts [3] the view that infanticide
is very prevalent among savages, but he denies that it
is the cause of exogamy.   At the same time, he agrees
with Dr M'Lennan in his view of the origin of the
prejudice against marrying women of their own stock
entertained by savages.   It is true that Sir John Lubbock supposes this prejudice to have arisen from *usage*,
that is, *the practice* of obtaining wives by capture,

[1] On this point see Darwin (1871, II, 363) ; Wake (1878, I,
419ff.). For an interesting note on infanticide among the
early Arabs, see Prof. Robertson Smith (1885, pp. 279ff.).

[2] Fison and Howitt 1880, p. 136, and see p. 358, where Mr.
Howitt expresses similar views.

[3] 1875, p. 125.

which he wrongly terms exogamy, while Dr M'Lennan speaks of it as *usage induced by necessity*, that is, the scarcity of women caused by infanticide. Moreover, the former, somewhat inconsistently with his views as to its origin, affirms [1] that " exogamy afforded little protection against the marriage of relatives," and that " where an objection to the intermarriage of relatives existed, exogamy was unnecessary ; where it did not exist, exogamy, if this view was correct, could not arise." It is not apparent at first sight what is meant by " exogamy," on which this dilemma turns. On consideration, however, it is evident that the term is used as almost synonymous with " marriage by capture." Sir John Lubbock supposes [2] communal marriage to have been superseded by individual marriage founded on capture, leading to exogamy, which means merely that the general custom of marrying out of the tribe (group) took the place of the individual practice of capturing women not members of the group. Here there is no reference to consanguinity, and Sir John Lubbock's argument, which is directed against Mr Morgan's view that exogamy was " a reformatory movement to break up the inter-marriage of blood relations," appears to be that, if consanguineous marriages were objected to by the tribe, communal marriage, that is, promiscuity, could not have existed, and therefore marriage by capture or exogamy would be unnecessary, as there would be individual wives within the group for all its male members ; while, on the other hand, if there was no objection to consanguineous marriages, then exogamy could not have arisen, as it afforded little protection against the marriage of relatives. The latter state-

[1] McLennan 1876, p. 123. [2] *Ibid.*, p. 95.

ment is, however, incorrect, as the marriages between half brothers and sisters referred to by Sir John Lubbock are not generally permitted by even the Australian aborigines, and where they are practised they are not regarded as consanguineous marriages.

We have now to consider the *law of marriage* so far as it is affected by *social restrictions*, or the restraints on promiscuity due to the acquisition of certain rights by an individual or individuals over the person of a female. These rights may control woman's actions before or after marriage, which is in itself one of the most important restraints on promiscuity. With many peoples it is customary for the parents of a girl to betroth her in marriage at a very early age. This is usual even among the Bosjesmans, and the girl removes to her husband's hut a few years afterwards. If she is not betrothed, her own inclination has to be consulted before she can be given in marriage. The custom of betrothal is prevalent also with the Australian aborigines. One of the chief causes which, according to Mr Howitt,[1] has led to the introduction of individual marriage among that race is the monopoly of women by the older men of the tribe. The perpetuation of this monopoly is encouraged " by those interested in it having sisters or daughters to exchange with each other for wives, and is aided by the custom of betrothal when girls are even mere infants." Mr Howitt adds that this custom occurs all over Australia, in tribes "which stand low down as regards other tribes in social development." Early betrothal was practised by the Tasmanians, and is

---

[1] Fison and Howitt 1880, p. 354. Mr. Fison states that betrothal is intended to put the *tapu* of a husband on a girl as early as possible. See above.

common to most of the Islanders of the West Pacific, and to many of the tribes of Southern Africa, and the Coast and Inland negroes.[1] We learn from Lafitau [2] that with many of the American tribes early betrothal was customary. Where it is largely practised we shall expect to find the unmarried women generally chaste, and such appears to be the case. It is so also where, although betrothals are not customary, early marriages are usual. This applies to many of the aboriginal tribes of India, especially those belonging to the Dravidian stock, who endeavour to ensure chastity among the young by providing a general dormitory for the unmarried men, and sometimes also for the unmarried women. In some cases the young people are allowed much freedom of intercourse. Colonel Dalton says,[3] indeed, that most of the Hill-tribes appear to have found it necessary "to promote marriage by stimulating intercourse between the sexes at particular seasons of the year." Thus, with some of the Abor tribes of Assam, at a particular season of the year, the single marriageable people of a village spend several days and nights together in one large building, after which they pair off and marry.[4] So, during the *Mágh Parab* of the Kolarian Hos, a festival held when the granaries are full, parents never attempt to exercise any restraint, and the utmost liberty is given to the girls, who sometimes pair off with the young men of a neighbouring village, and absent themselves for several weeks.[5] These adven-

[1] See Mr. Herbert Spencer's *Descriptive Sociology, passim.*
[2] 1724, I, 560.
[3] 1872, cited in Wake 1878, I, 130.
[4] Wake 1878, I, 149.
[5] *Ibid.*, I, 137.

tures generally end in marriage, as appears from what
takes place among the Santhals on similar occasions.[1]

Where betrothal is not the usual practice, one or
both of the parents have generally, among the lower
races, the right of disposing of females in marriage.
Thus, with the Australian aborigines, even where
descent is in the female line, a woman's actual husband, or *Noa*, claims to dispose of her daughters in
marriage, although they may not be in reality his
own children.[2] In the absence of the father, a brother
would seem to have the same authority. Where the
gentile organisation has been developed with descent
in the female line, as among many of the North
American tribes, the maternal uncle sometimes has
influence over the marriages of his sister's daughters,
and probably participates in the marriage presents.[3]
Lafitau expressly affirms,[4] however, that children
belong to the mother, and that the matrons of the
girl's family arrange her marriage, although with her
consent. Among the Caribs of South America the
maternal uncle is said to have a right over the
daughter of his sister from the moment of her birth,
and regards her as his future wife. Lafitau, who
mentions [5] this fact, suggests that by "sister" is meant
"cousin," in accordance with the classificatory system which exists among the American peoples, and
which the French writer appears to have been the first
to describe. Nevertheless, the right does not enable
the Carib to actually marry his niece or cousin, as

[1] Above, p. 51.
[2] Howitt 1885, p. 813.
[3] Morgan 1871, p. 158.
[4] Lafitau 1724, I, 563ff.
[5] 1724, I, 557.

it may be, without the consent of the girl and her parents. Originally the gens, clan, or tribe may have interfered in marriage arrangement, but this does not appear to be a common case. According to Mr Howitt,[1] a woman sometimes becomes the Noa of a man " by direction of the Great Council as a reward for some meritorious act on his part." He says also[2] that with the Kurnai tribe of Gippsland, among whom the class organisation, so far as marriage is concerned, is extinct, the local organisation has assumed authority over marriage, and in this respect stands to the children *in loco parentis*.

It is, perhaps, not surprising that where, as we have seen,[3] was the case with the Thracians, maidens are left entirely free, while the conduct of wives is strictly watched, to this strictness often being added hardship and cruel treatment, girls occasionally prefer to remain single. On the other hand, where strict watch is kept on the movements of unmarried women, the probability is that marriage is welcomed as a relief. In either case, marriage is regarded as giving the husband, or where any form of group-marriage prevails, the husbands, the sole right to the favours of the woman, or, at least, the right to decide to whom they shall be accorded. There will be occasion in a later chapter to refer to the condition of woman among the lower races of mankind, and it will suffice here to say that they are usually considered as a kind of property. The power of the father or husband over the person of his wife or daughter, combined with the view entertained by most peoples as to the naturalness of sexual conduct,

[1] 1885, p. 807.   [2] *Ibid.*, p. 809.
[3] Above, p. 34.

explains the wide-spread practice of what may be termed *sexual hospitality*. Sir John Lubbock refers to various cases of wife-lending, but he is in error when he explains them as relics of a condition of promiscuity. After stating[1] that among savage tribes the omission to provide a guest with a temporary wife would be regarded as inhospitable, he adds, " The practice, moreover, seems to recognise the existence of a right inherent in every member of the community, and to visitors, as temporary members ; which, in the case of the latter, could not be abrogated by arrangements made before their arrival, and, consequently, without their concurrence." This statement, although not very clear, probably means that the right to sexual hospitality could not be taken away without the consent of the guest. A little consideration shows, however, that the guest's consent is concerned with the having, rather than the not having, of the temporary wife or concubine. We are told[2] that the negroes of West Africa expect the European traveller " to patronise their wives and daughters, and these unconscious followers of Lycurgus and Cato feel hurt, as if dishonoured, by his refusal to gratify them. The custom is very prevalent along this coast. At Gaboon, perhaps it reaches the acme ; there a man will in one breath offer the choice between his wife, sister, and daughter. The women, of course, do as they are bid by the men, and they consider all familiarity with a white man as a high honour."

This would seem to give support to the supposition

[1] 1875, p. 119.
[2] Burton 1863, II, 24; cf. Wake 1878, I, 164.

that such a sexual connection establishes a kind of relationship, as affirmed by Bruce [1] of a similar custom among the Gallas of Abyssinia. From the prevalence of the custom among uncultured peoples generally, it is evident that it is regarded simply as a form of hospitality which the guest is supposed to desire, and which the host would expect under similar circumstances. With the natives of Virginia it was usual, when one chief visited another by night, " to set a woman fresh painted red with pocones and oil, to be his bedfellow." Probably the law of hospitality, which among some of the tribes of South America required the women to paint themselves afresh when a stranger arrived at a dwelling, had the same origin. The practice is not restricted to savage tribes, as is shown by the case of the inhabitants of Kamul, or Hamil, in Central Asia. The Venetian traveller Marco Polo says,[2] " If a foreigner comes to the house of one of these people to lodge, the host is delighted, and desires his wife to put herself entirely at the guest's disposal, whilst he himself gets out of the way, and comes back no more until the stranger shall have taken his departure. The guest may stay and enjoy the wife's society as long as he lists, whilst the husband has no shame in the matter, but, indeed, considers it an honour." The practice of sexual hospitality at Hamil, as well as in Fezzan, has been ascribed [3] to mercenary motives, both of these places

---

[1] Bruce 1813, V, 470.
[2] Wake 1878, I, 277, where other instances are referred to.
[3] Peschel 1876, p. 221.

being touched by caravans. The motive is, however, much the same in all such cases, as hospitality of the same kind is expected in return when the opportunity offers.

Among the aborigines of Australia the practice of sexual hospitality is sometimes connected with the system of group-marriage. Owing to the monopoly of women enjoyed by the older men of the tribes, the younger ones occasionally have to go without wives, but on certain occasions the old communal (group) rights revive in their favour, or rather, says Mr Howitt,[1] are granted them, and the same thing occurs for the benefit of friendly natives visiting the tribe. Not only have the Dieri tribes of Cooper's Creek that practice, but " in their gesture-language there is a particular sign — a folding of the hands — which signifies this custom, and may either mean a request or an offer, according as it is used by the guest or by the host." The system of " accessory spouses," which forms a special feature of Australian group-marriage, is intimately connected with the idea of sexual hospitality ; as shown by Mr Howitt's statement[2] that the proper husband of a woman will seldom refuse to accommodate temporarily the " accessory spouse," as he is liable to be refused himself under similar circumstances, although he will more freely lend his accessory spouse than his wife. We shall have occasion again to refer to this subject when treating of group marriage. The Kurnai of Gippsland compare favourably with other Australian tribes in this respect, as with them a wife is always expected to be faithful to her husband, and he never lends her to a friend or guest.

[1] Fison and Howitt 1880, p. 354.
[2] 1885, p. 807.

The custom of sexual hospitality supplies a much better explanation of certain facts connected with ancient society than that furnished by Sir John Lubbock, who remarks[1] in relation to the respect shown to courtesans at Athens and elsewhere, that these were originally fellow-countrywomen and relations, while the special wives were captives and slaves. This appears to be directly contrary to the fact, as at Athens—and such was the case also at Rome—no citizen could form a legal marriage engagement with a foreign woman. The noted Aspasia was a native of Miletus, and it is not improbable that the *heteræ* generally were at first foreign women of superior intellectual attainments, who, by the fortune of war or other means, found themselves in Greece, and not being permitted to marry Greeks, became the "companions" of those who sought their society.[2] Afterwards, no doubt, the class included many native-born women who, of a mental calibre above their position, preferred being a "mistress," with the freedom of such a status, to the more honourable condition of wife with its social disadvantages. The real secret of the matter is stated by Mr Grote, who says,[3] "Among the Heteræ in Greece were included all the most engaging and accomplished women; for in Grecian matrimony it was considered becoming and advantageous that the bride should be young and vigorous, and that as a wife she should neither see nor know anything beyond the administration of her own feminine apartments and household." Nor is there any evidence that the

[1] 1875, pp. 120, 122.
[2] The subject is more fully discussed in Wake (1878, II, 112).
[3] Grote 1865, III, 544.

wives of the Greeks of the earliest or heroic period, whatever may be said of their concubines, were either captives or slaves.

Not only, however, did the *heteræ* of antiquity furnish the citizens with "good friends," as they were called, but they supplied others, from mercenary motive no doubt, with the sexual hospitality which among the lower races is part of the ordinary entertainment accorded to a guest. We have here the key to the curious system of simple prostitution practised among so many of the civilised nations of antiquity, as still in India, and which Sir John Lubbock wrongly regards as furnishing evidence of a former state of promiscuity.[1] Marco Polo refers to a people living to the west of Tibet, among whom the women who had received the most favours from the other sex were sought after the most eagerly in marriage. He adds that mothers brought their marriageable daughters to strangers to enjoy their company during their stay, and that this prostitution to strangers was thought to be acceptable to idols.[2] Here there was probably the same mixture of motives as that which led the women of Cyprus who devoted themselves to the Great Goddess to walk about the shores of the island to attract the attention of the strangers who disembarked. In the earliest phase of what may be called sacred prostitution it was not every man who was entitled to enjoy its privileges. The Babylonian women, who were compelled to make

---

[1] 1875, pp. 116ff.

[2] Intercourse with the temple girls of southern India is not considered dishonourable, and Dr. Shortt affirms that it is even approved of by a man's wife and family, in consequence of its connection with their religion (Shortt 1870, p. 193).

a sacrifice of their persons once in their lives, submitted
to the embraces of strangers only.[1]   In Armenia and
Syria also strangers alone were entitled to ask for
sexual hospitality in the temple enclosures.   M. Pierre
Dufour, in offering an explanation of the fact that the
native inhabitants were so impressed with a worship
in which their women had " all the benefit of the
mysteries of Venus," observes [2] that the worship of this
goddess " was in some sort stationary for the women,
nomadic for the men, seeing that the latter could visit
in turn the different fetes and temples of the goddess,
profiting everywhere in these sensual pilgrimages by
the advantages reserved to guests and strangers."   No
doubt the custom referred to was also closely connected with the feeling so strong in the female mind,
especially in the East, where barrenness is often a
sufficient reason for divorce, that marriage should be
followed 'by child-bearing.   That its fundamental
principle, however, has been correctly assigned above
is confirmed by the observation of Eusebius that the
Phenicians prostituted their daughters to strangers
for the greater glory of hospitality.   The goddess of
fecundity and good fortune was bound to furnish this
hospitality to the pilgrims to her temple, and this she
was enabled to do by the piety of her votaries, who
sacrificed their own virginity at her shrine or dedicated
their daughters or other females to her service, for a
longer or shorter period.

We have here a much more reasonable explanation
of the phenomena in question than that of Bachofen,
who supposes that a temporary promiscuity was

_____

[1] See the paper on "Sacred Prostitution" in Wake 1888a,
(p. 158).
[2] Dufour 1851–61, I, 42.

required by the Earth Goddess as a sacrifice to
expiate the infraction in marriage of the law of
nature, according to which woman is an *Acca
Laurentia*.[1] Even if, as M. Giraud-Teulon says,[2] the
origin of the dowry is to be traced to the gain which
the bride anciently obtained by her prostitution before
marriage, the supplying of the marriage portion.by her
family being necessary to destroy heterism at its
source, this is not inconsistent with the views above
expressed. The fact would prove only that society
had passed from the stage where the wife was thought
so necessary for certain purposes that the husband was
prepared to give a price for her, to a stage where a
wife was regarded rather as an encumbrance, to be
accepted only if she brought a proper compensation.
In any case, however, the heterism referred to is no
evidence of promiscuity. Every woman was within
her natural right in receiving men before marriage, so
long as she did not infringe the rights of others, or the
restraints of consanguinity, in so doing. Where her
conduct was under the sanction of the goddess no disgrace could attach to it, a fact which, however difficult
for us to appreciate, would be understood by a people
like the Japanese, who regard prostitution for the purpose of supporting a parent as an act of filial piety
and deserving of all praise.[3] The receiving of a pecu-
niary or other return for the favours granted has no
actual relation to the question of morality. What we

---

[1] Acca Laurentia is "the mother of the Lares," the person-
ification of the fruitful earth, where are deposited the seeds
of the dead, and of the life which springs from her bosom
(Daremberg and Saglio 1877, p. 15).

[2] Giraud-Teulon 1867, p. 12n.

[3] Mitford 1871, I, 57, 67.

consider immoral may not be so in the eyes of those who look upon sexual conduct from the natural standpoint, so long as the natural or social restraints are not disregarded. The removal of the latter by the consent of the persons interested, is evidence of the existence of such restrictions, and where that consent is given, conduct however licentious according to our ideas may be, and is among the lower races, treated as unobjectionable.

These considerations account for the fact that temporary sexual alliances are looked upon among many of the lower races with a very lenient eye. The only restraint, beyond the natural one arising from consanguinity, placed on the conduct of the male is that he shall not interfere with the females over whom other men have special rights, at least without the consent of the latter; and so long as the proper consent is given, or if there is no one entitled to object, equal freedom is allowed on the part of the female.[1] Thus, among the Kafirs, the birth of a child before marriage brings no disgrace on the mother, so long as her paramour pays a fine to her father, whose consent is thus acquired, if the pair do not marry. According to Mr Kay numbers of children may often be seen outside the kraals of the chiefs, where they are kept for purposes of prostitution.[2] In Ashantee prostitutes were at one time numerous, the reason being that if a

[1] In a private communication Mr. Fison states that in many Australian tribes "the young people of 'permitted groups' may make such temporary arrangements as they please, until the *tapu* of a husband comes upon a girl. Thereafter intercourse with her is an infringement of the principles of right. She belongs to her husband." Hence the value of infant betrothal, which operates like marriage to put on the *tapu*.

[2] Kay 1833, pp. 157, 187.

girl refused to marry as her father wished, he, instead
of seeking to control her conduct, immediately dis-
claimed liability for her support and protection, and
thus abandoned, the girl could resort only to prostitution. The fetish women, who are frequently vowed to
the fetish before their birth, appear to be recognised
prostitutes both before and after their marriage.[1] In
these and in many other cases which could be cited,[2]
those who delivered themselves to the modified promiscuity of prostitution had received the express or
implied assent of those who were entitled to restrain
them. Such conduct would not be necessary where no
right was infringed. One of the most potent causes of
prostitution among the lower races is to be sought
not so much in licentiousness, as in the loss by its
victims of those on whom they are dependent for
support. In speaking of the natives of Virginia, the
old traveller, Captain Smith, says,[3] "They have harlots
and honest women, the harlots never marry, and are
widows." Widows and cast off wives among such
peoples would seem almost to be necessarily doomed
to a life of prostitution. Such is the case with many
of the Polynesian Islanders. Mr Pritchard states[4]
that in the Samoan Islands there are attached to the
native *fale-tele*, or free hotels, certain women who are
at the service of the travellers. These women are
generally the cast off wives of young chiefs, who may
have as many wives as they please, and put them
away as they think fit. According to custom, the

[1] Bowdich 1819, pp. 264, 302.
[2] Reference may be made to Letourneau 1876.
[3] J. Smith 1661 (Pinkerton, XIII, 245).
[4] Pritchard 1865, p. 324.

wife of a chief cannot become the wife of another man, and if she is cast off, " her only resource is to attach herself to the *fale-tele,* where, though still claimed by the husband who has cast her off, she may become the convenience of travellers, but not a settled wife." In India the members of the *vashee,* or prostitute · class, are chiefly women who have left their husbands and gone astray after marriage, or young widows, where they do not belong to the recognised caste of dancing girls attached to the Pagodas. [1] Among many races when widows are allowed the privilege of freely marrying again, it is only after they have done severe penance for the loss of their husbands.

The case of a woman who is freed from interference by the death of her husband or otherwise, is analogous to that of the unmarried girl whose parents do not exercise control over her inclinations. In the one case there is no person to object, and in the other the only persons who could object give at least a tacit consent to conduct which is perfectly legitimate according to their ideas, when it does not interfere with the social rights of others, or the natural restraints arising from consanguinity. The existence of these notions has an important bearing on the systematic prostitution and other forms of irregular intercourse between the sexes, usual among the more highly civilised races, which are, however, of a more immoral tendency than similar conduct among uncultured peoples ; seeing that with the former it is opposed to the general conscience, while with the latter it is consistent with the primitive

[1] See a curious paper on the bayadère of southern India by Shortt (1870).

law of marriage recognised by them. Moreover, it must not be supposed that female chastity before marriage at least, is disregarded by all the lower races.[1] Unchastity is indeed sometimes looked upon as an offence against the deity, for which the whole tribe is liable to punishment. Among the Malays of Sumatra, if a man seduces a girl he is compelled not only to compensate her father for the loss thus sustained, but to pay a fine for removing the stain from the earth.[2] This fact furnishes a happy commentary on Bachofen's theory that the Earth Goddess required her votaries to sacrifice their virginity as a penalty for desiring to escape from a condition of promiscuity. It is for a very different reason that some Eastern sects submit their females to that indignity. M. Rémusat relates,[3] on the authority of a Chinese traveller, that in Cambodia, on a day in each year fixed by a public functionary, the parents of the marriageable girls engaged the services of a priest for the performance of the ceremony of *Tchin-than*, or " défloration légale et religieuse." The priest received rich presents for the performance of this service, without which no girl could marry. That such a custom as this may have been known to the members of a religious sect in Cambodia is possible, as the Bhattias of Western India are said to consider themselves honoured by the cohabitation of their wives or daughters with the maharajas, who are regarded by their Vaishnáva followers as in-

[1] A curious chapter could be written on the means employed to preserve female chastity, and the evidence of it required on marriage. See Deut. 22 : 13–21.

[2] Marsden 1811, p. 262; cf. Wake 1878, I, 389.

[3] Rémusat 1829, quoted by Letourneau (1876, p. 338).

carnations of deity.[1] At the same time, no reference is made to such a practice by M. Moura in his elaborate account of the manners of the Cambodians, although he states that when a girl reaches the age of puberty the event is celebrated by prayers offered by the priests, and by a great feast, to which the parents invite their relations and friends, after which the young woman is kept in confinement during a prolonged period.[2] The Chinese story must therefore be regarded with suspicion ; but if true, it is consistent with the fact, that among primitive peoples any sexual conduct is allowable so long as it does not interfere with the rights of others, or is not opposed to the restrictions arising from blood relationship. This is the idea which is embodied in the primitive law of marriage, the special developments of which have now to be considered.

[1] *The Maharajas* (1861). The Vaishnavas are accused of practising promiscuous intercourse in their *Ras Mandalis*, or love feasts (p. 24).

[2] Moura 1882–83, I, 377.

CHAPTER IV.

GROUP MARRIAGE.

In the preceding chapters, after showing the probability that in primeval times mankind dwelt in small groups, in which each man lived with one or more wives, an examination was made of the grounds on which it has been asserted that the earliest social condition of mankind was one of promiscuity. The evidence in support of this opinion was seen to be of a very unsatisfactory nature, and the " law of marriage " was found to provide certain checks on promiscuity, although it regarded all sexual conduct permissible which did not infringe the *natural restraints* connected with consanguinity, or the *social restraints* based on the possessory rights of the man or kindred group, to which for the time being the woman belonged. The prejudice universally entertained by uncultured peoples against the intermarriage of persons regarded by them as *near of kin* does not apply to associations between persons not so related. So long as the rights possessed or acquired by others, or the social regulations of the community are not interfered with, sexual alliances may be entered into in any form between those belonging to the latter class of persons. We may expect therefore to meet with various developments of the marriage law among the lower races, in accordance with the changing requirements of savage life, and the natural and social conditions to which different peoples are subjected.

It is evident from what has already been said, that the term "marriage" is not intended to apply merely to permanent associations between the sexes. It refers primarily rather to that which is the object of the sexual act on which marriage is based, the getting of children, than to the contract of marriage itself. Temporary associations with that object are, therefore, not excluded from its operation, and they are as much subject to the natural and social restraints on promiscuity as permanent alliances. So long as those restraints are observed, however, temporary marital arrangements are as permissible by natural law as permanent ones. It is not necessary to refer at large to the temporary "marriages" occasionally to be met with among the lower races of mankind. According to Sir Edward Belcher,[1] we have a case in point in the Andamanese, among whom it is said to be customary for a man and woman to remain together until their child is weaned, and then to separate and each seek a new partner. Mr E. H. Man has shown, however, that this is a great libel on Andamanese character.[2] A form of temporary marriage is in use among the Hassaniych Arabs of Nubia, referred to by Dr Oscar Peschel,[3] among whom married women have free disposal of themselves every fourth day. Probably this arrangement has the same object as the Roman custom which allowed a wife to break the *usus* of the year. According to early Roman law, a man and woman could contract marriage by living together for a whole year, after which the wife became part of her husband's *familia*, with

[1] Belcher 1867, p. 45.
[2] Man 1883, p. 135.
[3] Peschel 1876, p. 221.

all the disabilities of this condition. If the woman absented herself for three nights during the year she retained her own *familia,* or rather continued to belong to that of her father, but she obtained the position of matron, which freed her from subjection to him.[1] A woman breaking the *usus* of the year thus occupied a position of considerable freedom, which was ultimately so greatly abused that the practice was finally abolished. The Hassaniych custom appears to have been at one time not uncommon among the Arabs, who gave the name of *nikâh al mot'a* to such temporary alliances, and it is still recognised by the Persian Mohammedans.[2] Prof. Robertson Smith refers to a tradition showing that *mot'a* marriages were sometimes allowed by Mohammed, who said, " If a man and a woman agree together, their fellowship shall be for three nights ; then if they choose to go on they may do so, or if they prefer it they may give up their relations." The meaning of this evidently is that, if the parties chose to go on, a regular marriage was constituted, in like manner as a Roman marriage by *usus* was established if the woman did not absent herself from her husband for three nights during the year. Prof. Smith remarks, that although the characteristic work of *mot'a* marriage is that the contract specifies how long the marriage is to last, yet that " the real difference between *mot'a* marriages and such as Mohammedan law deems regular, lies not in the temporary character of the union, but in the fact that in the one case both spouses have the right of divorce, while in the latter only the husband has it.

[1] W. Smith 1842, art. "Marriage."
[2] Robertson Smith 1885, p. 57.

It should be noted that the temporary marital engagements of the early Arabs, no less than the permanent ones, were subject to the common natural and social restraints on promiscuity. The woman did not leave her home, and hence her kin were not required to give up any right they might have over her or her offspring. Such being the case, it was not considered necessary that they should be parties to the *mot'a* engagement, which, says Prof. Smith,[1] was a purely personal contract, founded on consent between a man and a woman. It is none the less true that the woman's kin consented to it by implication, so that it was not opposed to any social restraints, although when descent came to be traced in the male line, *mot'a* marriage was condemned as the "sister of harlotry," because the offspring which it gave was reckoned to the tribe of the mother, and not to that of the father. There is no doubt, moreover, that the temporary marriages of the Arabs were subject to the natural restrictions recognised in relation to the permanent ones. Descent was traced in the female line, and although, as might be assumed, there appears to have been no bar to marriage in the male line, the formation of such an engagement was forbidden to persons standing to each other in a nearer relationship than cousins, on the mother's side.[2] According to Prof. Smith,[3] a grosser custom was in use among the early Arabs than *sadica* marriage with female kinship, in which "women did not live in absolute promiscuity, but had, for a time at least, one recognised husband." He states that in various parts of Arabia a quite unregulated poly-

[1] *Ibid.*, p. 68. [2] *Ibid.*, p. 163ff.
[3] *Ibid.*, p. 174. *Sadica* marriage is marriage without subjection, and therefore answers to the *mot'a* contract.

andry was common, and that "fornication" was "the resource of the poor after their betters had a more orderly marriage system." Although that practice was fully established before the time of Mohammed, it cannot have been the most ancient custom. It appears[1] to have been due to the fact that the price asked for a wife under the name of *mahr* was often so high that many men could not afford a wife, in which case, "intolerant of celibacy as all Arabs are," they actually "took refuge in what the prophet called *zinâ*, fornication." The payment of the *mahr*, or marriage price, by the husband to the bride's kin,[2] by which she passed under the dominion of her husband, is supposed to be of comparatively late origin, and was preceded by the custom which forbids a woman to leave her own tribe. The recognised practice of "fornication" must, therefore, have arisen when this *beena*[3] marriage was becoming disused. Prof. Smith says, indeed, that *zinâ*, before Islam, was only a kind of Nair-polyandry, in which the number of husbands was not defined, on the ground that "there was no trace of illegitimacy attached to the child of a harlot, even after male kinship and paternity was fully recognised."

Having referred thus briefly to temporary sexual associations, let us see what are the possible phases which permanent marital engagements may assume under the influence of the conditions which affect the operation of the marriage law. In the *first* place, it may be observed that the formation of the marriage relation need not be restricted to two individuals. So long as the natural and social restraints are duly

---

[1] *Ibid.*, p. 128.　　　　　　　　　　[2] *Ibid.*, p. 78.

[3] In which the husband goes to settle in his wife's village. See below.

regarded, any number of persons may be thus associated, and instead of marriage being a contract between
individuals, it may subsist between *groups* of individuals. Thus, assuming that a tribe is divided
socially into two groups, all the males of each division
collectively may stand in the sexual relation to all
the females collectively of the other division, each
group consisting of persons related among themselves
by blood through descent from a common ancestor.
We have here the simplest phase of *group marriage*, that of 'the Australian aborigines, (1) in which
theoretically[1] all the males of one group may cohabit
with any of the females of the other group; or one
or several males may associate permanently with one
or more females, the other males having power to cohabit temporarily with such females. It is not necessary that all the members of each group should be
related among themselves. One group may be composed of persons of the same kindred, and the other
of persons not thus related. This is the form of
group marriage practised by the Hawaiians, and known
as (2) *punalua*. This is distinguished by its simplicity
from the complex group marriage, or what might
almost be termed "hereditary punalua" of the Australians. Simple *punalua* has a double phase, (*a*)
where several brothers (own or tribal) have their
wives in common, and (*b*) where several sisters (own
or tribal) have their husbands in common. *Secondly,*
the number of members of either of the intermarrying
groups may be reduced, so that either group may
associate with a single individual. Thus, where (1)
a group of men is married to a single female, we have

[1] In general, however, only the individuals of the same
generation thus intermarry.

(*a*) the form of *polyandry* in which several kinsmen have a wife in common, and (*b*) that in which the husbands are strangers in blood. Again (2), with a group of females married to a single male, we have (*a*) the form of *polygyny* in which the wives are kinswomen, and (*b*) that in which the wives are strangers in blood, giving the patriarchal family. If the number of men in the one group, or the number of women in the other group, are reduced to a single individual, we have *monandry*, which, indeed, can exist alongside of any of the phases of group marriage.

The theoretical group marriage of the Australian aborigines is the most simple possible phase which permanent marriage could assume under the influence of the conditions affecting the operation of the marriage law. The Rev. Lorimer Fison, who first described that system, says that marriage is of group with group, and that the relationships connected with it are of group with group, and not of individuals. He affirms[1] that " it is the group alone that is regarded ; the individual is ignored ; he is not looked upon as a perfect entity. He has no existence save as a part of a group, which in its entirety is the perfect entity." Elsewhere[2] he says, " The idea of marriage under the classificatory system of kinship is founded on the rights neither of the woman nor of the man. It is founded on the rights of the tribe, or rather of the classes into which the tribe is divided. Class marriage is not a contract entered into by two parties. It is a natural state into which both parties are born." Theoretically, therefore, all the men of each of the related groups, which originally would be the two

[1] Fison and Howitt 1880, p. 57.   [2] *Ibid.*, p. 127.

primary classes,[1] are married to all the women of the group to which they do not belong. There are, however, various restrictions on that theoretical right, arising partly from the fact that, as we shall see hereafter, in many tribes each of the primary classes is divided into two sub-classes, each of these divisions being moreover made up of one or more groups of another nature, to which the name of *totems* has been applied. Each of the larger and smaller divisions of the tribe has a name, which is common to all the individuals belonging to it, and "all the members of such a group are held to be parents and children, or brothers and sisters, as the relative ages of the individuals may determine."[2] Notwithstanding this group relationship, it will be found that in practice the marital groups are not nearly so large as they are in theory, and that they are quite consistent with the exercise by individuals of a special right which, under favourable conditions, may entirely override that of the group.

However wide may be the operation of the Australian marriage system, it is from its very nature subject to the restraints on promiscuity arising from the rights of others. Only the members of a special group are married to or can enter into the marriage relation with the members of another group, whether the groups thus related be large or small. Australian marriage is no less subject to the natural restraints arising from consanguinity. This is evident from the fact that the Australian class divisions are exogamous, and from Mr

[1] As these two primary intermarrying classes were originally divisions of a tribal group, this would be endogamous in one sense and exogamous in another.

[2] Howitt 1885, p. 800.

Howitt's suggestion that the original division into classes was a reformatory movement intended to prevent the marriage of brother and sister (own and tribal), which, if Dr Morgan's hypothesis of a consanguine family is correct, must have taken place in an undivided commune.[1] The origin ascribed by Dr Morgan to the Australian class system will be considered further on, but it has already been shown that there is no evidence of the existence of such a stage of social progress as that represented by the consanguine family. This view is consistent with all we know of the class division, which is a group of persons who are forbidden to intermarry because, being of a common blood, they are own or collateral brothers and sisters. It is the fact of kinship which binds persons together in a class, the kinship itself depending on descent from a common ancestor. As the Australians, for the purposes of descent, at first preferred to trace kinship through the mother, the actual or theoretical common ancestor must have been a female. In the class, therefore, we have a body of kinsfolk tracing their descent from a common female ancestor, and forbidden to intermarry among themselves. This answers, not to the supposititious archaic gens of Morgan, which allowed intermarriage between all persons except *own* brothers and sisters, but to the actual gens, one of the obligations imposed on the members of which is not to inter-

---

[1] There is no ground for the assumption that the existence of two intermarrying classes presupposes an original whole —that is, an undivided commune. It might as reasonably be said that two intermarrying groups, consisting of the children of different mothers, must have had a common female ancestor whose children intermarried among themselves. The use of the terms "divided" and "undivided" is misleading. They imply a beginning for what may have always existed.

marry among themselves. As the class has the natural restraint on promiscuity arising from kinship, it is evident that to permit of marriage at all the Australians must originally have had more than one class. Many of their tribes have now four classes, but that they had at first only two intermarrying classes was supposed by Mr Fison, and the truth of this supposition appears to be established by later inquiries. Mr Howitt states [1] that the two primary classes are distinguished by native names for Eaglehawk and Crow over a large part of South-Eastern Australia, showing that they were totemic divisions. This is a confirmation of the opinion that the class answers to the gens, the totem being the symbol of the latter as it is of the former, and therefore that it is a group of consanguinei descended from a common (female) ancestor. The classes, therefore, represent the repugnance entertained by the early Australians against the intermarriage of kinsfolk, and were not due to a reformatory movement intended to prevent the marriage of brother and sister. There would be no occasion for such a movement unless consanguineous marriages were before usual, which is neither certain nor probable. Moreover, if such a reformatory movement took place it had too wide an effect, as it prevented intermarriage between tribal brothers and sisters, whose blood relationship is very slight. The wide extension of the prohibition proves that it arose from some other principle, and this can only have been the powerful objection to the intermarriage of near kinsfolk which is universal among uncultured peoples.

The fact that the class divisions of the Australian

[1] 1883, p. 506.

system comprise a series of totem groups, is confirmatory evidence in support of the opinion that
consanguineous marriages were foreign to it. We have
already seen that the two primary classes among many
of the tribes of South-Eastern Australia were such
groups, their totems being the Eagle hawk and the
Crow. In many cases the distinguishing totems of the
classes have been lost, assuming them to have once
existed, but each class has a group of totem names.
Mr Howitt states [1] that " the totems form two groups,
and are the names of animals, birds, fish, reptiles,
vegetables, or more rarely other natural objects." He
adds, " The fundamental rule appears to be that each
group of totem names is, in fact, a several and collec-
tive representation of its primary ; so that any one of
the totems belonging to a group may, as a rule, marry
with any totem of the complementary group." The
totem groups appear to have been formed before the
sub-division of the primary classes. This is shown by
the fact that in the Kamilaroi system, for example,
the totems belonging to the sub-divisions *Muri* and
Kubi are the same, as are the totems belonging to
Ipai and *Kumbo*.[2] It is proved, moreover, by the
fact that, although where the primary classes have been
sub-divided, children do not take the class name of
their mother, they belong to her totem. The totem
thus answers, so far as descent is concerned, to the
original class, while comprising, however, only a portion of the persons who would have belonged to it
if the original class had retained its character as a
totemic division. Mr Fison remarks,[3] in relation to
the Kamilaroi system, that for all practical purposes

[1] *Ibid.*, p. 498.   [2] *Ibid.*, p. 500.
[3] Fison and Howitt 1880, p. 41.

the totems may be taken as indicating sub-divisions of the classes, and that they affect the marriage regulations only "by narrowing the range of matrimonial selection."

The question arises whether the totemic sub-divisions of the class had originally this object. The probability is that it had not ; for, in the Dieri system, which is less developed than the Kamilaroi, and has no class sub-divisions, a member of any totem belonging to one primary class may marry any member of any totemic division belonging to the other class; so long as they do not stand to one another within certain degrees of relationship.[1] Mr Howitt refers[2] to a system, that of the Wotjoballuk tribe, in which each totem division has associated with it a group of sub-totems. These are probably, as he supposes, totems in a state of development, but he does not explain how they originate. There will be no difficulty in understanding this if it be remembered that the totem is the symbol of a gens, and that a totemic group therefore answers to the gens itself. One of the chief incidents of this association of kinsmen is the obligation not to marry within the gens, and so also in the Australian system "all persons in the community who bear the same totem are looked upon as of common descent, and they are considered to be so closely related that no *connubium* can be permitted between them."[3] It is probable, therefore, that the totemic groups comprised in a class division were developed in the same way as the gentes of the American or Ganowanian system, to which the Kamilaroi system is

[1] Howitt 1885, p. 804.
[2] *Ibid.*, p. 818.
[3] Howitt and Fison 1885, p. 157.

allied. Mr Morgan, when speaking of the Iroquois
phratry, which originated from a pair of gentes, this
being the smallest number ever found in a tribe, states[1]
that "the gens increases in the number of its members
and divides into two; these again sub-divide, and in
time re-unite in two or more phratries," which form a
tribe. In illustration, he refers to the Mohegan tribe,
which had three original gentes—the Wolf, the Turtle,
and the Turkey. Of these, the Wolf gens divided
into four gentes, the Turtle into four, and the Turkey
into three, a new name being taken by each of the
new gentes, while the original retained its own name,
which became that of the phratry. As a rule, however, the name of the original gens out of which other
gentes have been formed is not known. There does
not appear at present to be any evidence that the
phratry is known to the Australian system, unless the
primary classes with their group of totems may, as Mr
Fison thinks, be thus termed.[2] They are, at least,
analogous to the phratry. This is evident from Mr
Morgan's remark that "intermarriage in the phratry is
prohibited, which shows of itself that the gentes of
each phratry were derived from an original gens."[3]
For *phratry* read *class*, and this remark would be
equally applicable to the less advanced Australian
system, which, like that of the Dieri, possesses only
two primary divisions,[4] each composed of several

---

[1] Morgan 1877, p. 99.

[2] Fison and Howitt 1880, p. 24. Mr. Howitt states that the
term "major totems" might be applicable to the primary
classes, as in many cases their designations are "animal
names" (Howitt 1885, p. 800).   [3] Morgan 1877, p. 101.

[4] In some instances the primary classes are lost, or, like
the original gens of the Americans, are themselves totems
(Howitt 1885, p. 801).

totems. That the Australian totems were developed in the same manner as the American gentes is confirmed by the fact mentioned by Mr Morgan in relation to the Delawares,[1] that they have twelve embryo gentes in each tribe, which are lineages within the gentes without having taken gentile names, thus answering to the "pseudo totems" of the Wotjoballuk system referred to by Mr Howitt.[2]

It was stated above that the existence of totem groups in the Australian system is evidence that consanguineous marriages were foreign to it. This statement assumes that such a group is, like the larger class divisions, formed of individuals related to each other by blood. When the origin of the totem system is treated of, it will be shown to be connected with that of female kinship, and that the totem is the sign by which the descendants of a common female[3] ancestor are distinguished. Those who belong to a particular totem are thus of kin to each other, and their relationship is indicated by the totem, which is the recognised name or sign of the kindred. It is argued by Dr M'Lennan[4] that the totem bond could not "unite a kindred scattered throughout different communities, as it now does, unless it had marked it off from other kindreds before systematic interfusion of kindreds had begun;" and therefore that the totem was precedent to the exogamy by which "the interfusion of kindreds is regularly caused." This argument is a fair one, but it will not support the inference made by Dr M'Lennan,

---

[1] Morgan 1877, p. 101. [2] Above, p. 105.
[3] Where descent is traced preferably in the male line, totems may equally be used to identify the descendants of a common male ancestor.
[4] 1885, p. 229.

that when the system of relationship represented by
the totem—that is, kinship traced through a common
female ancestor—was formed, the persons thus united
" had no objection to the intermarriage of related
persons," if by this is meant related by the rules of
female descent.   The argument depends on the meaning attached to " exogamy," which, as used above by
Dr M'Lennan, is equivalent to " capture," whereas it
necessarily implies the existence of an objection to
the intermarriage of kindred, which objection must
have originated almost contemporaneously with the
formation of the totemic groups consisting of the
descendants of a common female ancestor.

With kinship in the female line the offspring of a
marriage will belong to their mother's totem, and under
the operation of the law of exogamy such offspring
will be hindered from intermarrying.   In the absence
of any other regulation, there would be nothing to
prevent a man from marrying his own daughter.   In
connection with this point we will consider the subdivision which the original classes or groups have in
many cases undergone.   The effect of this subdivision
is that " each half of an original class has marital
rights over the women of one particular half of the
other class, whose children do not, however, take the
class name of their mother, but of the sister class,
i.e., of the subdivision which is complementary to
hers."   The rules of marriage and descent which
governed the original classes still continue in operation, their effect, however, being to lessen the groups
which have marital rights over each other, and to
take children out of their mother's sub-class.   Thus,
in the Kamilaroi system, which has been treated so
fully by Mr Fison, the original classes were Dilbi and

Kŭpathin,[1] which intermarried with each other, the children belonging to their mother's class. When these classes were divided they stood as follows :—

$$\text{Dilbi} = \begin{cases} \text{Muri.} \\ \text{Kubi.} \end{cases} \qquad \text{Kŭpathin} = \begin{cases} \text{Ipai.} \\ \text{Kumbo.} \end{cases}$$

The effect over marriage and descent of this subdivision of the original classes is shown as follows :— *

Muri marries Kumbo (f.)	Kubi marries Ipai (f.)
Ipai.	Kumbo.

Ipai marries Kubi (f.)	Kumbo marries Muri (f.)
Muri.	Kubi.

This arrangement has an important effect on the relation between a man and his children. While there were only two intermarrying groups, a man's children, under the influence of the rule as to female descent, belonged to the group which was the wife class of their father, and therefore, in the absence of some special restriction, a man would theoretically be entitled to marry his own daughter. When the classes were subdivided this was no longer the case, as a man's children then belonged to a group with which their father was forbidden to have marital relations. Mr Howitt regards this fact as so important[2] that he thinks subdivision of the classes was intended "to enforce separation between those who had heretofore been mutually eligible under the class rules, but who being of the same blood could not intermarry without committing that which among these aborigines is now universally regarded as a deep pollution." A difficulty in accepting this explanation arises from the fact, re-

---

[1] Howitt 1883, p. 500.

* [See note p. 475.—R.N.]

ferred to by Mr Howitt, that while the prohibition of the intermarriage of parents and children is universal among the Australians, the subdivisions of the classes "have only a local range." If, therefore, the prohibition of marriage between parents and children, or rather of father and daughter,—as under the original class system a mother and son were forbidden to intermarry,—is not dependent on the subdivision of the original groups, and if, as Mr Howitt himself supposes, those unions were "even then forbidden by public opinion," it is probable that the subdivision had some other object in view. Possibly this may be gathered from the further statement,[1] based on the assumption that the division into classes was a reformatory movement, that "the secondary division into sub-classes was intended to prevent the possibility of intermarriage between parents (own and tribal) and children," that is, their (own and tribal) children. This explanation was given by myself[2] before seeing Mr Howitt's remarks, but I suggested that the real origin of that subdivision must be sought "in the division of the original marrying classes into two grades— a parent and a child grade." It was not meant by this that the members of any particular class were regarded as the fathers of any other class, but only that in connection with the question of marital arrangements the members of two classes stand to each other, so far as grades or generations are concerned, in the relation of parents and children. It is evident that no particular class could be identified as the parent or child class in relation to any other, as, to refer

[1] *Ibid.*, p. 504.
[2] Wake 1884, p. 155.

again to the Kamilaroi system, Ipai is both the father
and the child of Muri, and Kubi both the father and
the child of Kumbo. But, taking a class as forming
a child generation or grade, some other class stands
to it, for the time being, in the relation of a parent,
which could not be the case under the original two
class arrangement. For instance, all Dilbi of any
particular grade would be either Muri or Kubi according to their age or generation, and so with Kŭpathin,
who would be divided according to generation into
Ipai or Kumbo. The effect of this would be the
same as the reformatory movement supposed by Mr
Howitt, but as there is no evidence of any custom
which would require such a reform, even so far as
concerns the persons standing to each other in the
relation of *tribal* parents and children, I think we
must regard the division of the primary classes as
intended, not so much to alter or limit the range
within which marital connections were possible, as to
point out more distinctly what persons stood together
in the relation of class parents and children, and,
therefore, could not intermarry. Mr Howitt remarks [1]
with reference to the Dieri, that the contemporary
generation [2] of each class division is comprised of
" brothers and sisters," and that " men of one class,
who are thus 'brothers' to one another, marry the
women of the other class, who are thus 'sisters' to
one another."

Before proceeding further it will be advisable to
examine the explanation given by Dr Morgan, of the
social phenomena exhibited among the Australian
aborigines. The American writer sees in these pheno-

[1] 1885, p. 808.
[2] By which is meant "all those on the same level in a
generation."

mena evidence of the organisation of society simply
on the basis of sex, or rather the organisation into
classes on that basis. The class in its male and female
branches is, says Dr Morgan,[1] the unit of the social
system, " which place rightfully belongs to the gens
when in full development." The gens is formed on the
basis of kin, and therefore we ought to find something
different from this in the Australian social system,
which is of a more archaic formation. We have had
occasion already[2] to criticise Dr Morgan's theory,
which supposes[3] an original condition of promiscuous
intercourse between the sexes, followed by the earliest
or consanguine family. According to that theory, in
the second stage of development the punaluan family
appeared under the influence of organisation upon the
basis of sex, " which broke up the first species of
marriage by substituting groups of brothers who
shared their wives in common, and groups of sisters
who shared their husbands in common,—marriage in
both cases being in the group."[4] The punaluan custom tended to check the intermarriage of brothers and
sisters, and it led to the organisation into gentes on
the basis of kin, which excluded brothers and sisters
from the marriage relation. The latter system is said
by Dr Morgan to exist among the Australians, but
only in an inchoate form, although " advancing to
completeness " through encroachments upon the sexual
organisation.

That Dr Morgan's theory supposes the existence of
marital connections between all persons, however near

[1] 1887, p. 50.   [2] Above, p. 19.
[3] For Dr. Morgan's sequence of institutions connected with
the family, see Morgan 1877, pp. 498 ff.
[4] *Ibid.*, p. 50.

of kin, who were not the children of the same mother, is evident from the remark [1] that the establishment of the classes on the basis of sex, with prohibition of marriage between own brothers and sisters, was treated by the Murdu legend [2] as designed by its authors to avert the evil arising from consanguine marriages. It is true that the consanguine family is said to arise from intermarriage of brothers and sisters *own and collateral*, but if the latter were excluded equally with the former, the Australian system could not be organised on sex. It is clear, indeed, from Dr Morgan's association with it of the punaluan custom, that the Australian system of marriage is not based purely on sex. This would require all the men to be husbands of all the women, excluding own brothers and sisters, whereas in practice collateral brothers and sisters are also excluded. Mr Howitt, therefore, very properly makes his " segmented exogamous commune " answer to the punaluan family.[3] It may be perfectly right, therefore, to say, with Dr Morgan,[4] that the Australian marriage system is only " an extended form of polygamy and polyandry, which, within narrower limits, have prevailed universally among savage tribes," and yet it may be wrong to refer its origin to the exclusion of marriage between brother and sister. The only case in which this also would be true, would be where the intermarrying groups or classes were so small that each consisted only of the children of one woman. Here all the men of one family group would marry all the women except their own sisters, that is, all the

[1] Prefatory note to Fison and Howitt 1880, p. 5.
[2] Above, p. 40.
[3] Fison and Howitt 1880, p. 236.
[4] 1877, p. 54.

women of the other group, and the women in like
manner would marry all the men of the common
group except their own brothers.   We have here on a
small scale a tribe divided into two intermarrying
family groups, or, in Mr Howitt's words, a " segmented exogamous commune," which expression does
not, however, necessarily require a prior undivided endogamous commune, or consanguine family group,   If,
therefore, there is any truth in Dr Morgan's explanation of the nature of Australian native society, it can
be found only in the fact that its laws of marriage
and kinship are based, not on individual marriage, but
on marriage between groups of individuals.   Such a
system as this may be described, in some sense, but
not in the sense stated by Dr Morgan, as based on the
relation between the sexes.   Many men may be
married to many women, but the alliances thus
formed are governed by strict rules which prevent
anything like the approach to promiscuity required
by Dr Morgan's theory.

According to Mr Fison's explanation of the remarkable system in operation among the Australian
aborigines, every member of a particular totem is, in
theory, the born husband or wife of every member
of another totem or group of totems.   We shall see
that there are in practice various restrictions on the
exercise of the group-right, but that it is not purely
theoretical is shown by the facts already referred to [1]
in connection with " expiation for marriage."   Other
examples of the exercise of the group-right are mentioned in " Kamilaroi and Kurnai."   Mr Howitt
says,[2] in relation to Mr Lance's statement that the
women are more or less monopolised by the elder

[1] Above, pp. 34ff.
[2] Fison and Howitt 1880, p. 326.

men, that " the communal rights revive in favour of
the younger men, and are also extended to friendly
strangers visiting the tribe.   These rights arise out of,
and are exercised under, the class rules.   Elsewhere
a man of any one class may claim marital rights over
a woman of the corresponding class wherever he may
meet her, although he never saw her before, and his
right [1] will not be questioned."   Elsewhere,[2] Mr
Howitt mentions that a general licentiousness among
the group of persons allotted to each other as " accessory spouses" by the Great Council of the tribe,
is permitted on the evening of the ceremony of circumcision ; and he states that in its widest sense the
relation of " accessory spouse" is that of the two
primary groups to each other, but that the common
right can be fully exercised only when the whole tribe
occasionally reunite.[3]   If it can be exercised at all it
is sufficient to establish the existence of group
marriage of a very extended character, although in
practice it is limited by various restrictions which
reduce it to " an extremely loose form of polygamy,"
to use the expression of Mr Fison, who remarks[4]
that present usage is everywhere in advance of the

---

[1] Mr. Fison uses the strong expression "thousand miles of
husbands" in relation to this right (Fison and Howitt 1880,
p. 73).   [2] Howitt 1885, p. 805.

[3] *Ibid.*, p. 807. Mr. Howitt affirms that on these occasions
the two groups would "temporarily resemble what one might
suppose an undivided commune to be." This is clearly wrong.
The undivided commune requires communal marriage, that
is, absolute promiscuity, including the consanguineous unions
of Morgan, whereas, except in the doubtful case of the
Kununduburi, "the sexual intercourse of persons who are
considered too nearly related is forbidden under all circumstances by a death penalty" (1885, p. 808).

[4] Fison and Howitt 1880, p. 160.

ancient rules, and that the terms of the Australian system are "survivals of an ancient right, not precise indications of custom as it is."

Let us now see what is the nature of group marriage as now practised by the aborigines of Australia. The Dieri may be referred to as an example of a tribe which approaches the nearest to what is supposed to have been primitive practice. In the first place, men and women are betrothed or otherwise allotted to each other by their parents, forming the individual marriage relation termed *Noa*.[1] The following are the features of Noa marriage as given by Mr Howitt[2] from information supplied to him by Mr Gason.

This relation can only exist between individuals who belong to different classes and totems, and who are not within the prohibited degrees of relationship to each other.

A woman usually becomes the Noa of a man by betrothal to him when she is a mere infant, but sometimes she is given by direction of the Great Council to a man as a reward for his meritorious conduct.

A man may be Noa to two or more women, but a woman cannot be Noa to more than one man, although she may be *Pirauru*, or " accessory wife," to other men.

The right of the Noa is superior to that of the Pirauru, and hence the latter cannot, except by consent, claim a woman when the former is in camp at the same time.

[1] This phrase is also used by the Rev. Richard Taylor in reference to an *unmarried* New Zealand woman, she being then *noa* or common (Taylor 1870, p. 167).

[2] Howitt 1885, p. 807.

A man's Noa never accompanies him when he goes on a mission to another tribe, his female companions being required to grant their favours to all the men of the visited tribe not within the prohibited degrees of relationship, although the women are Noa to other men.

The Noa relation may, subject to the usual prohibitions, exist between individuals of any allied tribes, being usually in this case brought about by the Great Council for tribal purposes.

This system, which is a phase of individual marriage, is supplemented by a form of group marriage, in which a man and a woman, although Noa to others, are allotted to each other as " accessory spouses " by the Great Council of the tribe, in secret session, their names being afterwards formally announced to the people on the evening of the ceremony of circumcision, during which for a time there is " a general license permitted between all those who have been thus allotted to each other." That form of marital relation is called Pirauru, and it is explained by Mr Howitt [1] as follows.

Each Dieri man or woman is the Pirauru of some other Dieri woman or man. [2]

The Pirauru relation may exist between men and women of different local groups or of different tribes, but it may not exist between persons of the same totem, who are regarded as brother and sister, nor between any person and those who stand to him or her in the following relationships :—

Father, father's brother, father's sister ;

[1] *Ibid.*, pp. 805–6.

[2] Apparently only after having passed through the Míndraí (peace) ceremony (*Ibid.*, p. 806).

Mother, mother's sister, mother's brother ;

Brother, brother's child ;

Sister, sister's child ; or

Any person whom we call "cousin," either on the father's or on the mother's side.

Mr Howitt states further that any individual may in course of time have several Pirauru, as a man or woman already standing in this relation to some person may at a subsequent Great Council be given another Pirauru. If a woman has thus two "accessory spouses" who are both in camp with her at the same time, the older man of the two has the temporary right to claim her, thus enjoying the privilege of the Noa. A man will sooner lend his Pirauru than his Noa to a man who is Pirauru to her, but it is not often that the male Noa refuses thus to accommodate the Pirauru, as he is liable to be treated in the same manner under similar circumstances.

Mr Howitt remarks on this curious system that it is clearly a form of group marriage, in which a number of men of one class are married collectively to a number of women of another class, and which, "when the two classes meet at the tribal ceremonies, becomes what may be called regulated communal intercourse between the sexes." He adds that, "at other times when the community is scattered over the tribal country, a man may be found having with him at one time one or more Pirauru, and at another time other women who stand in this relation to him ; or a woman may be found living with several men who are Pirauru to her. To those unacquainted with the custom this presents the aspect of lawless license, or of polygamy, or of polyandry, but it is in fact group marriage." Judging from the application of the term Noa, which is applied not only to a woman's individual husband, but to her husband's brother and her sister's husband, and also to a man's individual wife, his wife's sister, and his brother's wife, that relation was originally the same as the *punalua* of the Hawaiians. The peculiar marriage arrangements of the Australian aborigines are exhibited in the following diagram, where the thick lines represent the Noa marriage and the thin lines the Pirauru relation :—

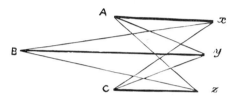

The system of marriage found in practice among the Australian Dieri furnishes a strong example of the rule that the formation of sexual relations is prohibited among uncultured peoples only when natural restraints or social regulations would be interfered with. The latter, which embody the rights of the father or other person and the tribe, are strictly regarded, and the former are no less influential. The restrictions arising from what I have termed "natural restraints on promiscuity" are so numerous, that they materially limit the range within which sexual connections are permitted. Mr Howitt divides[1] those restrictions into three classes, *prohibitions arising out of the class and totem restrictions, prohibitions arising out of blood relationship, and prohibitions arising out of locality.* It is evident, however, that they are all based on the objection which even the lowest savages entertain to marriage between persons near of kin. All the members of a class or

[1] *Ibid.*, pp. 818–20.

totem are supposed to have descended from a common female ancestor, and as her descendants belong to the same family group, they are incapable of intermarrying. Prohibition arising out of blood relationship is of the same nature, but it is based on actual nearness of kin. Not only, however, is kinship through the mother regarded as a ground of prohibition, but also to some extent that through the father. By the former a man is too nearly related to the daughters of his father's brothers, or of his mother's sisters, to allow of marriage between them; and the latter forbids him to enter into this relation with his father's sister or her daughters, or with the daughters of his mother's brothers. Moreover, as Mr Howitt points out,[1] these relatives represent groups, and individuals are included in them who are "very far away" group relations. The prohibition arising out of locality is expressly based on the idea that persons living near to each other are closely related by blood. This prohibition operates the most strongly with the tribes whose class organisation has become weakened or extinct. Thus, among the Kurnai, who have lost the class organisation altogether, all those who are born in the same locality are regarded as necessarily so near akin as to be forbidden to intermarry. A man is compelled, therefore, says Mr Howitt,[2] "to seek a wife in some more distant part of the tribal territory, and from certain local groups to the exclusion of others."

In the Aldolinga tribe of Central Australia all the prohibitions arising out of class, near relationship, and locality found in force in other tribes are combined, and result in "the narrowing down of the matrimonial choice to an incredibly small fraction of the whole

[1] *Ibid.*, p. 819. [2] *Ibid*, p. 809.

number of women." [1] It is often so difficult to determine whether or not a particular man and woman are under marriage disability, that elopement is resorted to as the only means of solving the question, and in Gippsland, where those restrictions are of exceptional extent, elopement is the most prevalent form of marriage. Under these circumstances, it is not surprising that group marriage is in many places being gradually replaced by individual marriage. The beginnings of this are, indeed, to be found in the group system itself. Whether *Noa* relationship or that of *Pirauru* was the first developed, or whether they sprang up together, is doubtful. The former is, however, well named by Mr Howitt, " inchoate individual marriage." The man and woman who are Noa to each other stand in a special relation. They habitually cohabit, and the man is regarded as the father of all the children born to his Noa, whether they are his or not, and he claims the right to dispose of her daughters in marriage. The children call him father, while they call their mother's Pirauru, " little father." The Noa wife, when not given to a man by order of the Great Council of the tribe, is usually betrothed to him when she is a mere infant, and therefore he naturally considers that he has a special interest in her. The custom of betrothal of girls at a very early age is universal with the Australian tribes, even with those whose social system is of the most primitive form. Mr Howitt thinks [2] that it dates back to an early period of the " divided commune," and associates it with the monopoly by one man of one or more women, giving the Australian " pairing family." We shall have occasion

[1] *Ibid.*, pp. 820n.
[2] Fison and Howitt 1880, p. 356.

to refer again to this subject when considering the origin of individual marriage.

The Australian system possesses an individuality of its own which has been developed under special circumstances. It is evidently based on the principle, embodied in the practice of all uncultured peoples in relation to marriage, that sexual conduct is right and proper, so long as the restrictions arising from consanguinity and the social regulations for enforcing the rights of others are observed. The operation of that principle, combined with the recognition of the fact that every male who attains to manhood can claim the right and opportunity of thus acting, would necessarily under the conditions of Australian life result in some such system as that above described. Individual marriage would not under these conditions be sufficient. The men are often away from home for a considerable time, and unless they are then provided with substitutes for their absent wives, they cannot enjoy the sexual hospitality to which they are entitled. Moreover, owing to warfare, infanticide, or other causes, the number of men or women may become unequal, or an individual may be unable for the time to perform his or her part of the marital engagement, in which cases strict compliance with the sexual right would require that some men should have more than one wife or some women have more than one husband. There is, moreover, a special cause in operation among the Australian aborigines which would greatly aid in the development of that system. Reference has already been made to the association of the widespread custom of betrothal with the monopoly of women. Mr Howitt seems to think that this monopoly has largely influenced the development of individual marriage. There can be no doubt, on the other hand, that at first when the sexual rights of every adult member of the tribe were fully recognised, it would have a different effect. Mr Howitt states [1] that monopoly of the women by the older men of the tribe is very common all over Australia, " especially where group marriage is still in the ascendant." He adds, " but this monopoly is not exclusive ; at certain times and on certain occasions the old communal right revives in favour of the younger men, or of friendly strangers visiting the tribe." Those who have sisters or daughters to exchange encourage the perpetuation of the monopoly, which is strengthened also by the custom already referred to of betrothing girls when mere infants. The scarcity of women available to young men for wives thus caused, often leads to the obtaining of women by force, or to elopement where this can be safely accomplished.

If those various causes operated under the restrictions directed against · the intermarriage of persons near of kin, among a race of low culture, who fully recognised the absence of impropriety in sexual conduct so long as the rights of others were not interfered with, and under the semi-nomadic conditions of Australian aboriginal life, a system of group marriage would almost certainly be established. It does not follow, however, that it has always been as fully developed as at present. The fact that originally there were only two class or totemic divisions, all the persons belonging to each of which were supposed to be descended from a common female ancestor, would seem to point to a very simple form of family arrangement. It may have originated in a compound group formed

[1] *Ibid.*, p. 354.

under the conditions of the *punaluan* family, but even this is not necessary. The "divided communes" represented by the class divisions are supposed to require an original "undivided commune," but the greater whole of which they are parts is the tribe. This has, in addition to its social organisation, what has been aptly termed its "local organisation." The Australian tribe is defined[1] as "a larger or smaller aggregate of people, who occupy a certain tract of hunting and food ground in common, who speak the same language with dialectical differences, who acknowledge a common relatedness to one another, and who deny this relatedness to all surrounding tribes." It is, however, divided into smaller groups, each having its own tract of hunting and food grounds, and the tribe is therefore composed of a number of local groups, which "are perpetuated in the same tracts by the sons, who hunt over the hunting grounds of their fathers." We learn from Dr Morgan[2] in relation to the American social system that "to a stranger the tribe is visible, but not the gens," which, as regards the Australian tribe, might be rendered that a stranger sees the local organisation, but not the social organisation of the class divisions. As these divisions represent the two common female ancestors and their descendants, we may suppose the tribe to represent the original male head of the local group of which the classes were the divisions. On this supposition the primitive tribal group would have consisted of a male and two females, each of whom with her children formed a separate family group of persons related by blood. These families formed two exogamous intermarrying groups

[1] Howitt 1885, p. 799.
[2] Morgan 1877, p. 103.

tracing descent through the mother, but recognising descent through the father for certain purposes, and especially for the perpetuation of the local organisation.

We have now to consider the simple phase of group marriage, in which one only of the intermarrying groups consists of persons related by blood, and which, from the name applied by the Hawaiians to such marital associations, is termed *punalua*.[1] We have already[2] had occasion to refer to this curious social feature in connection with the subject of brother and sister marriages, evidence of which is wrongly found in it by Mr Morgan. Whether or not the punaluan family, that is, a group composed of several brothers having their wives in common, or several sisters having their husbands in common, with the offspring of such unions, is known to all the Polynesian peoples or is restricted to the Sandwich Islanders, has not yet been determined. The word *puna-lua* is a compound term, of which the latter part is the Polynesian numeral two. In the New Zealand language a second wife is callèd *pune rua*, the third wife *pune toru*, and so on.[3] The term *punalua* may, therefore, have been at first applied to the case of a man having two wives, or a woman two husbands, and afterwards extended to denote two brothers or sisters having their wives or husbands in common. Mr Morgan states, however, that the word is applied by a man to the husband of his wife's sister, and by a woman to the wife of her husband's brother, meaning "intimate companion." This application of the term might possibly be based on the fraternal relation sub-

---

[1] Above, pp. 99.   [2] Above, pp. 20ff.
[3] The Rev. Richard Taylor (1870, p. 331). The Hawaiian word for ancestor is *ku-puna*.

sisting between those persons, without any reference to a sexual alliance. Judge Andrews however remarks[1] that the punalua relationship arose from the fact that two or more brothers with their wives, or two or more sisters with their husbands, were inclined to possess each other in common ; but the modern use of the word is that of *dear friend* or *intimate companion*. Curiously enough, among the New Zealanders a married woman is termed *he hoa*, a friend, a title which applies also to her husband, who is called *tane*, which, says Mr Taylor, " though literally only a man, has generally the other signification attached to it."

There appears to be a reference to punalua in Mr Ellis's statements,[2] in relation to the natives of the Society Islands, that " those among the middle or higher ranks who practised polygamy, allowed their wives other husbands," and that " brothers or members of the same family sometimes exchanged their wives, while the wife of every individual was also the wife of the *taio* or friend." Similar practices probably prevailed at Tahiti, among the higher classes at least, as Mr Ellis states,[3] that " the marriage tie was dissolved when either of the parties desired it ; and though amongst their powerful chiefs it was allowed nominally to remain, the husband took other wives, and the wife other husbands." Elsewhere,[4] he says, when the rank of the parties was equal, they often separated—the husband took other wives, and the wife other husbands—and if the rank of the wife was in any degree superior to that of her husband, she was at liberty to take as many other husbands as she

---

[1] Quoted in Morgan 1877, p. 427.
[2] Ellis 1832–34, III, 124.
[3] *Ibid.*, I, 256.   [4] *Ibid.*, I, 274.

pleased, although still nominally regarded as the wife of the individual to whom she had been first married." Probably these customs prevailed when the Polynesians were first discovered, but they are not mentioned by Dr Forster, who accompanied Captain Cook in his second voyage round the world. Dr Forster indeed affirms [1] that monogamy was "most universally introduced among the most various nations of the South Sea," and he explains the absence of polygamy to the gentle manners of the females, the equality of the sexes, and the great facility of parting with a wife, and taking another in her stead. He does, however, refer to the supposed polyandry of the natives of Easter Island, which he ascribes to the extraordinary scarcity of females, there being only fifty women on the island out of nine hundred inhabitants, occasioned, it was thought, by many of them having been killed by an earthquake.

The statement of Mr Ellis that in Tahiti, when a woman was of superior rank to her husband and separated from him, she could take as many other husbands as she pleased, although still nominally regarded as the wife of her first husband, has an important bearing on the social phenomena exhibited among the Nairs of Malabar. A consideration of what Dr M'Lennan terms Nair polyandry must be reserved until the next chapter. Reference may be made here, however, to the marriage relations of the Dravidian Todas, which may take a form closely resembling the *punalua* of the Polynesian islanders. The Todas are usually described as polyandrous, and Col. Marshall states [2] that formerly it was their almost universal custom "for a family of

[1] Forster 1778, p. 424, 432.
[2] Marshall 1873, p. 213.

near relations to live together in one mand, having wife, children, and cattle all in common." This writer adds, however, that as each brother may become the husband of a separate wife by virtue of his having paid a dower, and as younger brothers on reaching the age of maturity, and other brothers on becoming widowed, may each " either take separate wives or purchase shares in those already in the family," any degree of complication in married life may be met with, " from the sample of the single man living with a single wife, to that of the group of relatives married to a group of wives." We have here a closer approach to the puna-luan family than to the Australian system of group marriage, although the Toda group of husbands in-cludes relatives more distant than own brothers. With the latter indeed " every man and woman, every lad and every girl, is somebody's husband or wife," but this is because they are betrothed and married at the earliest possible age.[1] The Todas agree with the Aus-tralian aborigines and other peoples among the lower races in regarding with abhorrence marriages between persons near of kin, although Col. Marshall thinks half brothers and sisters are allowed to intermarry.[2]

Group marriage of the Toda type, rather than poly-andry, as Dr M'Lennan supposes,[3] is the real explana-tion of the practice ascribed to the ancient Britons by Cæsar, who says that " by tens and by twelves hus-bands possessed their wives in common, and especially brothers with brothers, and parents with children." The same explanation may be given of the marriage arrangements of the Massagetæ, with whom every man had one wife, yet all the wives were common. Dr

[1] *Ibid.*, p. 220.   [2] *Ibid.*, p. 221.
[3] McLennan 1876, p. 156.

Morgan very justly remarks[1] that "punaluan marriage in the group affords a more rational and satisfactory explanation of these and similar usages in
other tribes mentioned by Herodotus, than polygamy
or general promiscuity." It is not satisfactory, however, if the punaluan marriage referred to supposes anything more than the intermarriage of several brothers,
own and collateral, with each other's wives in a group,
or of several sisters, own or collateral, with each other's
husbands in a group.

The origin of the classificatory system of relationships in use among the Polynesian islanders is traced
by Dr Morgan to the former existence of consanguineous
marriages, which commenced with the intermarriage of
own brothers and sisters, and afterwards embraced
within their range all other persons on the same level
of generation, described as collateral brothers and
sisters. The existence of such marriages is inferred
from facts which show that the marriage of own
brothers and sisters is sometimes permitted, and from
the *punaluan* family, which, says the American writer,[2]
"included the same persons found in the previous consanguine family, with the exception of own brothers
and sisters." This statement is pure hypothesis; for,
although the punaluan group consists of several brothers
having their wives in common, or several sisters having
their husbands in common, there is no evidence that
in either case the husbands are of kin to their wives,
as required by Dr Morgan's theory. After remarking
that the punaluan family was formed out of the consanguine, he says expressly, " Brothers ceased to marry
their own sisters, and after the gentile organisation
had worked society its complete results, their collateral

[1] Morgan 1877, p. 431.   [2] *Ibid.*, p. 502.

sisters as well. But in the interval they shared their remaining wives in common. In like manner sisters ceased marrying their own brothers, and after a long period of time their collateral brothers ; but they shared their remaining husbands in common." Now there is as little evidence of a period when men married their collateral sisters, or women their collateral brothers,[1] as there is of their having married their own sisters or brothers.

The Australian social system is based, as we have seen, on the existence of two primary intermarrying classes, each forming a group of persons related by blood through descent from a common female ancestor, the combination of which groups answers, according to Mr Howitt,[2] to the punaluan family. If by this is meant, however, the hypothetical punaluan family of Morgan, which is supposed to have been formed from the consanguine family[3] by the exclusion of own brothers and sisters from the group of kindred who intermarried, Mr Howitt's view is incorrect. For by the Australian system the marriage between collateral or tribal brothers and sisters is equally forbidden. But if by the punaluan family is intended simply the compound polygynous and polyandrous system in use among the Hawaiians, where two or more brothers with their wives, or two or more sisters with their husbands, lived in common, Mr Howitt's statement is

---

[1] These include the sons of the father's brothers and of the mother's sisters (Fison and Howitt 1880, p. 77).

[2] *Ibid.*, p. 365.

[3] Dr. Morgan deduces the consanguine family from the Malayan system of consanguinity, and he infers promiscuity "as a necessary condition antecedent to" that family, but he thinks the cases of promiscuity usually cited are "better explained as arising under the punaluan family" (1877, p. 502).

correct. In each case the group of men are conjointly married to the group of women, forming with the off-spring of the union a punaluan family.

It was said above[1] that simple punalua has a double phase—(a) where several brothers (own or tribal) have their wives in common, and (b) where several sisters (own or tribal) have their husbands in common. Both forms of punalua are recognised among the Polynesians, but the latter alone is met with among some peoples. When America was first visited by Europeans, the family life of the aborigines was based on the marriage of single pairs, "forming clearly marked, though but partially individualised, families."[2] This Syndymasian or pairing family possessed some of the characteristics of the monogamous family, from which it is said to have differed chiefly in the absence of an exclusive cohabitation. Polygamy was universally recognised as the right of the males, although chastity was required of the wife under severe penalties, but the marriage relation subsisted only during the pleasure of both husband and wife. The pairing family is supposed by Dr Morgan to have been gradually produced within the punaluan family under the influence of the organisation into gentes, that influence being shown first in the exclusion of own brothers and sisters, and the children of own sisters from intermarriage, as they were members of the same gens. According to this view, which must be rejected so far as it requires the consanguine family, own brothers could still share their wives and own sisters their husbands, so that the *range* only of punaluan marriage was affected. There appears to be some evidence of the former existence of punalua on the American

[1] P. 99.   [2] Morgan 1877, pp. 453ff.

continent.   Dr Morgan refers[1] to social phenomena among certain tribes of South America, which he thinks supply traces of the punaluan custom, but they are equally consistent with the optional marriage, which allows either party to divorce himself or herself at pleasure.   As to North America, he remarks that when first discovered the punaluan family seems to have entirely disappeared, and that no tradition remained, so far as he was aware, of its ancient prevalence.   He refers,[2] however, as of punaluan origin, to a custom, which is still recognised in at least forty tribes, according to which, where a man marries the eldest daughter of a family he becomes entitled to all her sisters as wives when they attain the marriageable age.   The right was seldom enforced, owing to the difficulty of one man maintaining several families. Dr Morgan observes on this custom, that " undoubtedly there was a time among them when own sisters went into the marriage relation on the basis of their sisterhood, the husband of one being the husband of all, but not the only husband, for the other males were joint husbands with him in the group.   After the punalua family fell out, the right remained with the husband of the eldest sister to become the husband of all her sisters, if he chose to claim them."   The object of this custom is incidentally pointed out by Lafitau, who states[3] that the Algonkins marry several sisters, and when one is *enciente* they reside with the others in succession.   With other American tribes, who do not practise polygamy, it is usual for a man to marry the sister of his deceased wife, especially if her friends

[1] *Ibid.*, p. 431.
[2] *Ibid.*, p. 432; cf. p. 160.
[3] Lafitau 1724, I, 559.

are satisfied with his conduct. Among some of the
Australian tribes also it is not unusual for a man to
marry his wife's sister either in her lifetime or after her
death. Mr Howitt, who mentions the custom as being
known to the Kurnai, remarks [1] that the alleged reason
for a father giving a second sister to his daughter's
husband, was that the parents would then have a
double supply of food, the son-in-law being under
obligation to supply food to his wife's parents. Mr
Howitt adds that the right of a man to his deceased
wife's unmarried sister would be admitted by the
father in some clans, or " could only have effect in
others if the widower could carry off his wife's sister
from the camp before her relatives could prevent him."
A similar relic of punalua would seem to have been
preserved in Madagascar. Thus, according to Mr
Charnay,[2] among the Betsimisaraka, the younger sisters
of the three wives of a chief belong to him until they
marry. The custom of a man marrying two sisters
was not unknown to the early Hebrews, as shown by
the marriage of Jacob with Leah and Rachel, and it
is evidently referred to in the Mosaic command,
" Thou shalt not marry thy wife's sister to vex her in
her lifetime." It is of course possible that these latter
cases may not be evidences of punalua, as they were
consistent with the practice of simple polygyny.
Punalua is the having by brothers or sisters of wives
or husbands in common, and unless we suppose with
Dr Morgan that other men or women, as the case may
be, formerly joined in these marital arrangements, they
do not come within the punaluan custom.

[1] Fison and Howitt 1880, p. 203.
[2] Cited by the Rev. James Sibree (1880, p. 44) ; Charnay
1870, p. 50.

CHAPTER V.

IN the preceding chapter we treated of group marriage as represented by the complex system of the Australian aborigines, which may be described as hereditary punalua, and the simple punalua of the Polynesian and other peoples. We have now to consider the later developments of the marriage law, where one of the intermarrying groups is reduced to a single individual. Thus, if in the punaluan group the wives on the one hand, or the husbands on the other hand, were replaced by a single individual, we should have *polyandry* in the one case, and in the other *polygyny*. The latter will form the subject of the next chapter, and we will now proceed to a consideration of polyandry.

It has already been stated[1] that there may be two phases of polyandry, one (*a*) where the group of men who have a wife in common are kinsmen, and the other (*b*) where the husbands are strangers in blood. If it be true, as the facts mentioned in the preceding pages would lead us to believe, that polyandry is derived from an earlier system of group-marriage—whether that of the Australian aborigines or preferably that of the Polynesian peoples—we must assume that the earliest phase of polyandry was that in which the husbands are brothers, or at least kinsmen. This is

[1] Above, p. 100.

the usual phase, and it may be doubted whether the existence of systematic polyandry, in which the joint husbands are strangers in blood to each other, can be established.

Dr M'Lennan divides [1] the cases in which polyandry is practised into the ruder form, that in which the husbands are not brothers, and the less rude, that in which the husbands are brothers. The ruder form of polyandry is said to be found among the Kasias, the Nairs, and the Saporogian Cossacks, and the less rude form is represented by the polyandry of the Tibetans, between which extremes, says Dr M'Lennan, all the possible forms must lie. Moreover, the ruder form is said to exist among the lower classes wherever the less rude occurs. Exceptions to this rule are met with (1) in Tibet, where polyandry is universal and the husbands are always brothers ; (2) in Malabar, where polyandry is universally practised by all classes, except the Brahmins only, and the ruder form is used by the high caste Nairs, the less rude being found among the lower castes—the Teers, Maleres, and Poleres. Dr M'Lennan affirms [2] that in the accounts we have we can detect "stages of preparation" for the change from the lower to the higher polyandry. The rudest cases are, he says, "those in which the wife lives not with her husbands, but with her mother or brothers. In these cases a woman's children are born in and belong to *her* mother's house. In the cases next in order of rudeness, the wife passes into cohabitation, according to fixed rules, with the husbands in a house of her own—becoming thus detached from her family, though still connected with it through the right of her children to become

[1] 1876, p. 146. [2] *Ibid.*, p. 152.

heirs to the family estate. Her children would still belong to her mother's family—the want of a community of blood and interests among the husbands preventing the appropriation of the children to them. Such cases, however—detaching the woman from her family—would prepare the way for a species of marriage still less rude, in which the woman passed from her family, not into the house of her own, but into the family of her husbands, in which the children would be born, and to which they would belong. This could only happen when the husbands were all of one blood, and had common rights of property, in short, when they were brothers." This highest form of polyandry is that which is prevalent in Tibet, the rudest form being, as we have seen, that of the Nairs.

Let us examine a little more closely into the nature of what is termed the Nair type of ٭ polyandry, that in which the husbands are not brothers. Dr M'Lennan refers to three separate accounts of this curious social system. According to a writer in the "Asiatic Researches," it is the custom among the Nairs for one woman to have attached to her two males, or four, or perhaps more, and they cohabit according to rules. This account appears to be taken from the Arabic writer Zeen-ud-deen, who says,[1] "Among the Nairs and the castes connected with them, two or four men live with one woman, each of them in turn passing the night with her." It is added that the followers of trades cohabit "two or more together with one woman, but not unless they are brothers or in some way related, lest confusion should ensue in the inheritance of property."

[1] Zeen-ud-Deen 1833, p. 64.

The statement of Hamilton is, that a Nair woman
could have no more than twelve husbands, whom she
had to select " under certain restrictions as to rank
and caste." Buchanan, on the other hand, while
agreeing as to the existence of certain restrictions
as to *tribe* and caste, affirms that *after marriage* the
women are free to cohabit with any number of men.
According to Dr M'Lennan, it is consistent with the
three accounts, and is directly stated by Hamilton,
that a Nair may be one in several combinations of
husbands, that is, he may have a share in any number
of wives. It is remarkable, nevertheless, that the
writer in the " Asiatic Researches " expressly says,
" The Nairs practise not marriage, except so far as
may be implied from their tying a thread round the
neck of the woman on the first occasion." It is
quite consistent with this statement that the "wife"
continues to live with her mother or brothers, although
Hamilton affirms that she has "an house built for her
own conveniency " on being married to the first of
her husbands. Mr Andrew Wilson does not hesitate
to call the Nair polyandry a " mere freak,"[1] and the
system may well be so termed in which a man does
not know his father, and under which a man would
be considered as an unnatural monster "were he
to show such signs of grief at the death of a child,
which, from long cohabitation with, and love for
its mother, he might suppose to be his own, as he did
at the death of a child of his sister." Buchanan states
further, that among the Nairs " a man's mother man-
ages his family ; and after her death his eldest sister
assumes the direction. Brothers almost always live
under the same roof ; but if one of the family separates

[1] Wilson 1875, p. 227.

from the rest, he is always accompanied by his favourite sister."

The explanation of this social system is connected with the fact, only incidentally mentioned by Dr M'Lennan, that a Nair is only nominally married to a girl of his own caste, and never has any intercourse with her; while she may after that marriage have many lovers, provided they are Brahmans, or Nairs other than her nominal husband.[1] No reason is given why the husband and wife are forbidden to have sexual relations with each other, but it may be supplied from an unexpected quarter. When treating of *punalua*, it was stated[2] that in Tahiti a marriage was dissolved when either of the parties wished, and that the husband took as many wives and the wife as many husbands as they pleased. If, however, the husband was a powerful chief, or if the wife was superior in rank to her husband, the original marriage was nominally supposed to continue. We have here a custom answering to that 'of Nair " polyandry," except in the fact that in the latter the marriage, which appears to have been imposed by the Brahmans, is nominal from the first. In the Society Islands, however, there was formerly a practice still more closely resembling the Nair custom. When the islands were first visited by Europeans an institution, known by the name of *Areoi*, had great influence among the people. The Areois are described by Mr Ellis[3] as " a sort of strolling players, and privileged libertines, who spent their days in travelling from island to island, and from one district to another, exhibiting their pantomimes, and spreading a moral contagion throughout society." The Areois

---

[1] *Ibid.*, p. 227.   [2] Above, p. 126.
[3] Ellis 1832–34, I, 234.

comprised individuals from every class, and women as
well as men, the wife of every Areoi being a member
of the "fraternity," which was held in the greatest
repute by the chiefs and higher classes. According to
the legend, which describes its origin, the Areoi
institution was established by the two younger
brothers of the god Oro, who directed them to nomin-
ate certain persons in the several islands to form the
first society, and authority was delegated to them to
admit all who, being wishful to join it, consented to
murder their infant offspring. It might be supposed
from Mr Ellis' account of the institution that its
original motive was licentiousness. Just the opposite
appears, however, to have been the case. Dr Forster,
the companion of Captain Cook, states[1] that the
great chiefs and sages of the islands thought it prudent,
owing to the increase in the number of the "chief"
class, to institute an order of men styled *Arees*,[2] who
should have great prerogatives, and great honours paid
to them, and who were to be the chief warriors,[3] "and
who should be forbidden to marry, in order that they
might not be too much attached to their wives and
children." This was the beginning of the society
called *Areoi*, which so far changed from its original
intention that not only did its members indulge in
sensual conduct at their festivals, but some of them
formed illicit marital connections. It was owing to
this practice, says Dr Forster, that "the sages of the

[1] Forster 1778, p. 411.

[2] In New Zealand the High Chiefs are styled *Arikis* (Taylor 1870, p. 149).

[3] Mr. Ellis states that the chief warriors were called *Aito*,
a title which was highly coveted and was open to men of all
ranks (1832–34, I, 296).

nation made another law, according to which all
infants, the offspring of the connection of the Areeoys
with women should be instantly killed after their birth,
because the increase of the Arees was thought to be
detrimental to the state, and the original engagements
of the Areeoys, never to cohabit with women, would
else have been entirely defeated." The Arees were,
therefore, a military class bound to celibacy, but forming illicit connections, which were allowed so long as
no children sprung from them. The conduct ascribed
to them by Mr Ellis differs somewhat from the account
given by Dr Forster, who says,[1] "At certain stated
times of the year" the Areeoys go from one island to
another, "and there the days are spent in great feasts,
wherein a profusion of the dainties of the country are
consumed, and the nights are spent in music and
dances, which are said to be remarkably lascivious,
and likewise in the embraces of some girls, who officiate on these occasions like the priestesses and nymphs
of the Paphian and Amathusian goddess among the
Greeks."

The Arees, or Areois, evidently in many respects
much resemble the Nairs,[2] who have no children by
their wives, and who are perpetuated as a caste
through their sisters, whose offspring they regard as
their heirs. The Nairs do, however, nominally take
a wife, but this is probably for the benefit of the
woman, who, after marriage, is granted a certain
license as compensation for the loss of her husband.
This custom agrees with the group marriage of the
Australians, except that there is no cohabitation of

---

[1] Forster 1778, p. 412.
[2] Is there not a connection between the names Nair, that is,
Nayar, which means "Master," and Aree or Ari (chief)?

husband and wife as in the Noa relation. The Nair marital arrangement is that of "accessory spouses,"[1] and probably it originated in the necessity of supplying the military caste with the "sexual hospitality" its members required while nominally adhering to their vow of celibacy. If this is so, Nair polyandry cannot be regarded as a ruder system based on promiscuity, or as the source from which the true or Tibetan polyandry has been derived. The right view is expressed by Oscar Peschel, who remarks[2] that polyandry "must not be confounded with the community of wives of the military castes, to whom celibacy was prescribed as a vow of the order, such as the Naiars of Malabar, and formerly certain Cossacks," the Saporogian Cossacks mentioned by Dr M'Lennan.[3]

The Nairs are described by Sir W. W. Hunter as "strictly honest and austerely religious."[4] That they can practise celibacy if necessary is evident from the statement of Zeen-ud-deen[5] that after the death of any near relation the Nair will abstain for a whole

[1] This opinion is held by Mr. Howitt (1885, p. 806n.)

[2] Peschel 1876, p. 222.

[3] Montesquieu almost arrived at the truth when he says,[1] "The Naires are the tribe of nobles, who are the soldiers of all those nations. In Europe soldiers are forbidden to marry :[2] in Malabar, where the climate requires greater indulgence, they are satisfied with rendering marriage as little burdensome as possible ; they have a wife amongst many men, which consequently diminishes the attachment to a family, and the cares of housekeeping, and leaves them in the free possession of a military spirit."

    [1] Book 16, chap. 5, cited by Dr. Charnock in *Anthropologia* (1873), p. 169.

    [2] The Templars and other orders of Christian knights took a vow of chastity.

[4] Hunter 1881, VI, 248.   [5] 1833, p. 62.

year from association with women, during all which time he neither shaves his hair nor cuts his nails.[1]

The position and customs of the Namburis, or Brahmans of Malabar, may have had much to do with the development of the Nair system of marriage. Originally all the country belonged to the Namburis, and was attached to certain pagodas until the era of Cherumah Perumal, under whose rule it was divided between the Rajas and chief Nairs.[2] Hamilton's explanation of the Nair system is that the Brahmans, wanting soldiers and mistresses, instituted the Nair caste with its special features. Sir W. W. Hunter thinks rather that both Nairs and Namburis settled in the country as " part of a general movement southward, which in all but prehistoric times brought the best of its people and its Brahmanism to the rest of Southern India." It is not improbable, however, that the relations between the Brahmans and the Nairs, who are Sudras, were always what they are now, and as custom allows only the eldest son of a Namburi to marry, if he is likely to leave male issue, it is evident that illegitimate unions between the younger sons and the Nair women, who were only nominally married, might easily be established, and in fact the younger Namburis do cohabit with Nair women without marriage, " in the way of the Nairs." There is thus a certain relation between the nominal celibacy of the Nairs and that of the

[1] M. Elie Reclus (1885, p. 193) rejects the view that the social system of the Nairs was invented for the purpose of creating a military aristocracy, but he does not give the point special consideration.

[2] Prichard 1836–47, IV, 160. This epoch was between the fourth and seventh centuries of the Christian era (cf. Hunter 1881, VI, 244).

[3] J. Duncan 1798, p. 13.

Brahmans.[1] The Namburi custom may have been a development from an earlier polyandry of the Tibetan type. According to this all the younger brothers would have been entitled to participate in the marital arrangements of the eldest brother. Supposing the latter to have successfully resisted this right under circumstances which would not allow the younger brothers to marry separately, a means would have to be found for their enjoying the sexual hospitality to which they were entitled by nature. This would be well provided by such a system as that in operation among the Nairs, especially if the celibacy of the latter was originally real. The Nair caste could not be perpetuated unless the women were allowed to form sexual alliances, which would be at first only with the Namburis, but afterwards, when the rule of celibacy was relaxed, with the Nairs themselves. Possibly the development of this system may have been aided by a belief in the sacred character of the sacerdotal class, such as leads the members of the Mahárájas sect of the Bombay Presidency to consider themselves honoured if their wives and daughters receive the attentions of their religious teachers.[2] M. Elie Reclus remarks [3] that all India is imbued with the belief that priestly blood is endowed with regenerative virtues, and he seems to find in this fact some explanation of the connection between the Namburis and the Nairs. Nevertheless, he speaks of the Nair system having been invented for the benefit of the Namburis, who, seeing that the Nairs

[1] Zeen-ud-Deen states that the younger Brahmans abstain from marriage, in order that heirs may not multiply to the confusion of inheritance (1833, p. 64).

[2] Above, p. 92.

[3] 1885, p. 203.

cared only for mothers, determined to present them with fathers.[1] This offers no explanation, however, of the Nair ceremonial marriage, which is attended by the nominal celibacy of the husband and the actual independence of the wife. who gains freedom of conduct by the loss of her husband. The fact that these practices exist among the ruling classes, while the lower classes have the ordinary, or Tibetan, form of polyandry, renders very improbable M. Reclus' notion that the Nairs were without legal marriage until this was required by Brahmanical law.[2] If the opinion expressed above that Nair polyandry was originally connected with the practice of celibacy is correct, the explanation of it given by Dr M'Lennan cannot be accepted, and his " ruder form " of polyandry disappears. Mr Fison argues from Hamilton's remark, " a Nair may be one in several combinations of husbands—that is, he may have any number of wives," that Nair polyandry is really a description of group marriage, and he asserts that, as the Nairs are evidently divided into exogamous classes, their polyandry resolves itself into " cohabitation between permitted groups." Unfortunately for this conclusion, the Nair never cohabits with his legal wife, and it takes no account of the celibacy to which he was originally subject.

It cannot be said that the phenomena presented by the Nair system is evidence of an advanced state of society. A similar condition of society may formerly have been widely prevalent where kinship through the mother was the rule. Professor Smith asserts[3] that the type of marriage found in Arabia along with female kinship, " in which unions are of a very temporary charac-

[1] Reclus 1885, p. 199.   [2] 1885, p. 190.
[3] Robertson Smith 1885, p. 122.

ter, and the wife dismisses her husband at will," is only a development of Dr M'Lennan's ruder form of polyandry. He refers to several facts which he thinks confirm the former existence of this system among the Arabs. He mentions,[1] on the authority of Ibn Batûta, that in Omân, in the fourteenth century, "any woman who pleased could receive from the Sultan licence to entertain lovers at will without her kin daring to interfere." Prof. Smith adds that in Arabia and elsewhere in the Semitic world, "unrestrained prostitution of married and unmarried women was practised at the temples, and defended on the authority of the licence allowed to herself by the unmarried mother-goddess."[2]   Elsewhere[3] he remarks that it is in Yemen that the most persistent traces of polyandry of the Nair type are found down to quite modern times. These facts, however, furnish no evidence of the existence of a primitive condition of society. They prove the prevalence of great licentiousness, based on the notion of sexual hospitality, and if they are evidence of anything further, it is only of the existence of the *beena* form of marriage, in which a woman receives her husband at the house of her father. Prof. Smith further identifies[4] the Tibetan and Nair forms of polyandry with the *ba'al* and *sadîca* marriages of the Arabs, under the latter of which women bore children for their own tribe, and were free to choose their husbands and dismiss them at will. He supposes that such women would not be confined to one husband at a time, although the only ground

---

[1] McLennan 1876, p. 286.

[2] According to this reasoning, the prostitution would not have existed before the worship of the mother-goddess.

[3] Robertson Smith 1885, p. 236.   [4] 1885, p. 139.

for the supposition is that women brought under dominion by conquest or capture had several husbands. Prof. Smith adds, "for such women, in short, the idea of chastity could not exist; their children were all full tribesmen, because the mother was a tribeswoman, and there was no distinction between legitimate and illegitimate offspring in one sense of the word, though, as in cases of Nair polyandry in other parts of the world, there was possibly a law of incest which forbade women to bear children to certain men (men of her own kin)." This may be perfectly true, and yet there does not appear to be any evidence that in *sadíca* marriage a woman could have more than one husband at a time. That term is applied [1] to a marriage which involves no subjection of the woman, and which includes not only cases where, as in *beena* marriages, the husband goes to settle in his wife's village, but also the temporary *mot'a* arrangements [2] "in which a woman only received occasional visits from the man on whom she had fixed her affections." These arrangements did not involve any loss of character on the part of the wife, and so far from this being the case, under *sadíca* marriage generally the position of woman was far higher than it was after the spread of "marriages of dominion." It is an old Arab sentiment, and not a Moslem one, says Prof. Smith,[3] "that the women of the group are its most sacred trust, that an insult to them is the most unpardonable of insults. Under the *sadíca* system every one in the tribe was interested to protect the women, as they were not only their wives, but the mothers of the children of the tribe." [4]

[1] Robertson Smith 1885, pp. 70ff.   [2] See above, pp. 95ff.
[3] 1885, p. 130.
[4] Other evidence of the former prevalence in Arabia of "Nair polyandry" is found by Prof. Robertson Smith (1885,

The former existence in Arabia of a custom of marriage " in which the woman remained with her kin, and chose and dismissed her partner at will, the children belonging to the mother's kin and growing up under their protection," may be considered as established. There are, however, several points of distinction between this custom and the ruder form of polyandry of Dr M'Lennan. This writer states [1] that the first advance from a general promiscuity, would be " to arrangements between small sets of men to attach themselves to a particular woman." He adds that previous to the establishment of a system of kinship, " when men were bound to each other only by the tribal tie," there would be difficulties in the way of forming such combinations. Now, there is no evidence that under the early Arab custom several men were attached to a particular woman. In fact, the *mot'a* marriage is always spoken of as between two individuals, and it was rather a system of temporary monandry than one of polyandry, although, according to Prof. Smith,[2] the real difference between such an arrangement and that which is considered by Mohammedan law regular marriage, " lies not in the temporary character of the union, but in the fact that in the one case both spouses have the right of divorce, while in the latter only the husband has it." Moreover, so far from *mot'a* arrangements having been introduced when, as required by Dr M'Lennan's

p. 170) in the use of the *tent* in the later marriage ceremony. This is traced by him to the custom of *beena* marriage, "in which the tent was the wife's, and after her death passed to her children, so that a husband had no right to bring a new wife into it."

[1] McLennan 1876, p. 136.
[2] Robertson Smith 1885, p. 68.

theory, a system of kinship had not been established,[1]
its existence may be said to have depended on the
operation of such a system.　In this and other *sadíca*
marriages the children of the union belonged to the
woman's kin, who formed a tribe, which, as there are
strong reasons for believing,[2] was originally "constituted or propagated by mother kinship."　Kinship among the Arabs, says Prof. Smith, "means a
share in the common blood which is taken to flow in
the veins of every member of a tribe—in one word,
it is the tribal bond which knits men of the same
group together, and gives them common duties and
responsibilities from which no member of the group
can withdraw."　The bond was strengthened by the
law of blood-feud, and as in the early Arab tribes the
rule of tracing kinship through females was established, they were strictly exogamous.　The Arab
tribe would answer, therefore, to the primitive class
or clan of the Australians, or the gens of the
Americans, and its system of marriage would be
totally different from the ruder polyandry of Dr
M'Lennan, which is but a slight remove from general
promiscuity.

　　It is strange that while the ruling caste of Malabar

---

　[1] It is true that the system of kinship through females only
is said to be always found along with the ruder polyandry
(McLennan 1876, p. 139). Previously, however, Dr. McLennan speaks of the formation of "arrangements between small
sets of men to attach themselves to a particular woman" (p.
136), and the difficulty attending the formation of such
combinations until the systems of female kinship has been
firmly established, "when every group stood resolved into
a number of small brotherhoods, each composed of sons of the
same mother"—that is, Tibetan polyandry.

　[2] Robertson Smith 1885, pp. 24ff.

practise the so-called ruder polyandry, the form in use among the lower classes is of the less rude or Tibetan type. As stated by the Mohammedan writer, Zeen-ud-deen, " the joint concern in a female is among these last, limited to the brethren and male relations by blood." Mr Duncan observes,[1] however, that this polyandry was practised only in a few of the southern districts, and that there was no prohibition against any man keeping for himself either one or as many women as he could maintain. The object of the polyandry of the lower castes of Malabar is said to be to keep property in the family, and the absence of any such motive in Nair marriages is confirmatory evidence that they do not belong to a ruder type. In fact, the so-called Nair polyandry is not polyandry at all, in the proper sense of the term, and it is a mistake therefore to affirm that it represents the earliest stage of development out of a state of promiscuity. In Ceylon there are two sorts of marriage, *deega* or *beena*, according to whether the wife goes to live in the house and village of her husband, or whether the husband or husbands come to live with her in or near the house of her birth. Dr M'Lennan remarks on this,[2] that " sometimes a deega married girl returned to her parents' house and was there provided with a beena husband, who lived with her in family," and he identifies Nair polyandry with the *beena* form of polyandry. This is evidently erroneous, however, as the Nair custom is based on the nominal character of the marriage relation formed by the wife, while the latter is a real marriage between a woman and one or more husbands.

Prof. Smith falls into a similar error when compar-

[1] Duncan 1876–82, II, 14.   [2] McLennan 1876, p. 148.

ing the earliest marriages in use among the Arabs with the Nair practice. He states,[1] that in the latter "the woman remains with her own kin, but entertains at will such suitors as she pleases," and that when a child is born, as " neither its actual father nor the kin to which he belongs can be determined with certainty," [2] it is "reckoned to its mother, and kinship descends in the female line." And he asserts that the type of marriage found in Arabia along with female kinship, "in which unions are of a very temporary character, and the wife dismisses her husband at will," is only a development of Nair polyandry. The remark as to the insecurity of the husband's position is made by Dr M'Lennan in relation to *beena* marriage,[3] which Prof. Smith really means when he speaks of Nair polyandry,[4] although they are quite distinct. The special feature of the latter is, that a husband and wife never cohabit, but each associates with his or her lovers ; whilst in *beena* marriage a woman, while it lasts, lives with her husbands, or perhaps with only one husband ; for more than one is not essential to it.

The distinction between *beena* and *deega* marriages, which depends on whether the wife goes to reside in her husband's village or the husband settles in that of his wife, is not limited to polyandrous unions. The arrangement made between husband and wife, or rather between their friends, has reference to the children of the marriage, and it is a secondary matter

[1] Robertson Smith 1885, p. 122.

[2] This is a very broad statement, and one the truth of which our knowledge of Nair "polyandry" does not allow to be verified.

[3] McLennan 1876, p. 149n.

[4] He refers to "beena marriage or Nair polyandry" (Robertson Smith 1885, p. 146).

whether the children are the offspring of a polyandrous union or not. Prof. Smith distinguishes[1] between polyandry "in which the woman is under dominion, and cannot refuse her favours to the circle that has brought her into their dominion in order to bear children for them and for their tribe," and polyandry "in which the woman lives among her own kin, and, bearing children for them, and not for outsiders, is free to distribute her favours at will." He adds, "What is common to the two systems is, that in each case the children belong by virtue of their birth to a certain group, and are held to pertain to this group in no artificial way, but because the blood of the group flows in their veins." This is simply the rule of the gentile organisation, and it is evident that it is not affected by the question whether the female through whom descent is traced has one husband or a group of husbands. The real point is whether the woman continues to live among her own friends or not. In the one case her children belong to her own[2] family, and in the other case they *may* belong to her husband's family, and will do so if the incidents of wife-purchase have been observed. And, as Prof. Smith remarks when referring to the effect on the law of kinship of the tribal rule that a woman should not leave her own kin but may entertain a stranger as her husband, "the rule of descent is unaffected whether the father comes to settle permanently with his wife's tribe, or

---

[1] This is not so always, however; as with descent in the male line it does not matter whether the married pair reside in the husband's village or in that of the wife. The latter is sometimes the case with the polyandrous Todas, but the children always belong to the husband (Marshall 1873, pp. 212, 218).

whether the woman is only visited from time to time by one or more suitors."[1] Whether actual polyandry ever existed among the Arabs under these circumstances is doubtful. There appears to be no evidence of it having done so, although the learned writer so often referred to infers,[2] that women who were free to choose their own husbands and dismiss them at will could not be confined to one husband at a time, from the fact that " women brought under dominion by conquest or capture had several spouses." The inference is not very clear, and it may be objected that as *beena* marriage does not necessarily imply polyandry, so also it may not be essential to *sadica* marriage. We can thus account for the system in vogue among the Kooch of Northern India, among whom the husband goes to live in the family of his wife and her mother, and who yet practice monogamy ; without supposing, as Dr M'Lennan does,[3] that they have passed through an early stage of " ruder polyandry."

We have now to consider the Tibetan type of polyandry, but we will first refer shortly to the *deega* form of marriage, that in which the wife goes to live in the house and village of her husbands. According to Dr M'Lennan's theory, this would only happen "when the husbands were all of one blood, and had common rights of property—in short, when they were brothers."[4] The order of development required by that theory is strictly logical, but it has no necessary relation to polyandry. In the gentile organisation of the American Indians, which is founded on kinship through females and shows no trace of true polyandry, the husband usually goes to reside near his

[1] 1885, p. 62.
[3] McLennan 1876, p. 151.
[2] *Ibid.*, p. 139.
[4] *Ibid.*, p. 153.

wife's family, although sometimes the wife leaves her home to reside among her husband's kin. In either case, however, the children of the marriage belong to the mother's gens, while in the *deega* marriage of the polyandrous Kandyans the contrary is the case,[1] showing that the mere fact of a woman passing into the family circle of her husband does not give the latter a right to the children of the marriage. Reference has already been made to the curious fact that while the ruling class in Malabar practise the system described by Dr M'Lennan as the ruder species of polyandry, the higher form of polyandry which depends on the husbands being brothers, and which answers to the *deega* marriage of Ceylon, is found among the lower castes. We may be tempted to believe that the latter was at one time universal in South-Western India, and that the former originated among an intruding people for special purposes or under special conditions.

The polyandry of the lower castes of Malabar is of the true or Tibetan type, and it is necessary now to see what light is thrown by its phenomena on the actual origin of polyandry. According to Capt. Samuel Turner,[2] the usual authority quoted as to Tibetan marriage, it is customary for one female to associate with all the brothers of a family, without any restriction of age or of numbers, the choice of a wife being the privilege of the eldest brother. Turner does not offer any explanation of this curious practice, although he hints that it might have originated at

[1] Dr. McLennan says that "the rights of inheritance of a woman and her children are found to depend on whether the woman is a beena or a deega wife" (1876, p. 149).

[2] S. Turner 1800, p. 348.

some remote period of time when females were much fewer in number than males. He suggests that its intention may have been to prevent an undue increase of population in an unfertile country, although he expressly states that the Tibetans can never be charged with infanticide. According to Du Halde,[1] the Lamas apologise for the practice of polyandry on the ground of "the scarcity of women which prevails both in Tibet and Tartary." He asserts, however, that "this excess is trifling, for the Tartars admit of no such irregularity." Du Halde mentions, what does not appear from Turner's work, that the first child of the polyandrous union belongs to the eldest brother, and those born afterwards to the others according to their seniority.[2] A recent writer, Mr Andrew Wilson, who has treated more fully of Tibetan polyandry, confirms the statement that the choice of a wife is the right of the eldest brother, and he adds[3] " that among the Tibetan-speaking people it universally prevails that the contract he makes is understood to involve a marital contract with all the other brothers, if they choose to avail themselves of it." Mr Wilson states [4] that polyandry prevailed among all classes, most instances being of *two* husbands, the usual number of brothers in a family, and that it was superseded by polygyny only where the people were a good deal in contact with Hindus or Mohammedans. The fact that polygyny could be practised shows that scarcity of females was not the cause of polyandry. Mr Wilson affirms [5] in-

---

[1] Du Halde, 1735, IV, 572.

[2] This is said by Dr. Shortt to be the case with the Todas (cited by Dr. R. S. Charnock in *Anthropologia*, 1873, p. 169).

[3] Wilson 1875, p. 233.

[4] *Ibid.*, p. 228.   [5] *Ibid.*, p. 231.

deed that there is in Tibet a large number of surplus women, who are provided for in the Lama nunneries. The origin of the polyandrous system, which is almost general among the thirty millions of Tibetan-speaking people,[1] may be inferred from the great end it serves —that " of checking the increase of population in regions from which emigration is difficult, and where it is also difficult to increase the means of subsistence." [2] Tibetan polyandry thus arises not from a scarcity of women, but from the pressure of population. Few more effectual means to check the tendency to over population could be devised, says Mr Wilson,[3] " than the system of Tibetan polyandry, taken in conjunction with the Lama monasteries and nunneries." A similar opinion as to the effect of polyandry is expressed by Turner, who observes that it has no evil influence on the manners of the people. They are said to be gentle in disposition, obliging and humane. The women occupy a comparatively elevated station in society, and to complete liberty the wife adds " the character of mistress of the family and companion of her husbands." Before marriage perfect chastity is not required in the female sex, but afterwards instances of incontinency are seldom known.[4]

The females of Ladak have a different character, as they are said by Mr Fr. Drew[5] to give themselves

[1] This applies also to the peoples of Assam having Tibetan affinities. M. Reclus says of the Dapla, ''like their neighbours of Tibet they admit all forms of marriage, both polyandry usual among the poor, and polygyny practised ordinarily by the rich'' (1876–94, VIII, 204).

[2] Wilson 1875, p. 234.

[3] *Ibid.*, p. 225.

[4] S. Turner 1800, pp. 350ff.

[5] Drew 1875.

without resistance to the first stranger who solicits
them.   He gives a similar explanation of the object of
Tibetan polyandry to that of other writers—the small
extent of the cultivated land and the absolute isolation
in which the people dwell, by which all emigration is
prevented.   Mr Drew states that generally, when the
eldest brother marries, all his brothers become the
husbands of his wife, in which case the children of the
marriage call them all father.   A woman has a right,
in default of a group of brothers, to choose one or
several husbands.   The result of these polyandrous
unions is that the population remains stationary.   On
the marriage of an eldest son he becomes entitled to
all the property of his parents, although they may be
still living, and he is regarded as the head of the
family.   Probably we have here the explanation of
what is said by Mr Moorcroft as to the position of the
younger brothers.   He states, as quoted by Dr M'Lennan,[1] that they have no authority, " they wait upon
the elder as his servants, and can be turned out of
doors at his pleasure, without it being incumbent upon
him to provide for them."   On the death of the eldest
brother, however, his property, authority, and widow
devolve upon his next brother, whether there has been
a polyandrous arrangement or not.

The phenomena of Tibetan polyandry are somewhat
different from those of the Toda marriage system, which
has already been referred to in connection with group
marriage.   That the Todas are polyandrists is shown
by Col. Marshall's description [2] of the sexual union as
" the lawful marriage of one woman with several men,
either brothers or near relations."   After a young man,

[1] *Ibid.*, p. 159.
[2] Marshall 1873, p. 203.

or his guardian, has made the preliminary arrangements for an exchange of dowers with the father of the girl whom he wishes to marry, he has to obtain her consent. This is given only after a trial for a day and a night, during which period the young man and woman are shut up in a house by themselves. If the girl then tells her mother that she accepts the suitor, they are held to be man and wife, and after receiving a necklace and mantle from her husband, either the wife accompanies him to his own house, or, if it be more convenient to them, they remain together in her father's village. Up to this stage, says Col. Marshall, " the woman is married with her own consent to one man—he who pays the dowry, or gives security to society for his own good behaviour. But now, if the husband has brothers or very near relatives, all living together, they may each, if both she and he consent, participate in the right to be considered her husband also on making up a share of the dowry that has been paid.[1]

Notwithstanding the prevalence of polyandry among the Todas, it would seem that monogamy is growing to be the national form of marriage, and Col. Marshall suggests[2] that possibly they are " merely reverting to an ancient usage—that prior to infanticide." He is not of this opinion, however, and he evidently believes that the polyandry of the Todas is a primitive institution developed out of a system of group marriage, the group of husbands being restricted to a reduced allowance of wives, owing to the scarcity of females arising from the practice of female infanticide. That this custom is not now known to the Todas is admitted

[1] *Ibid.*, p. 213.
[2] *Ibid.*, p. 229.

by Col. Marshall, but he affirms,[1] on the authority
of an aged native, that formerly it was the custom
when they had one girl, or in some families two girls,
to kill the succeeding ones.   As boys were never killed,
there must ultimately, in the absence of other causes to
restore the balance, have been a greater number of
men than women in the tribe, and therefore either
polyandry or the acquisition of wives from other
tribes.   Although the practice of infanticide has
ceased, there is still a preponderance of males over
females, which Col. Marshall regards[2] as an effect
of the former infanticide, the continuance of which
" leads ultimately to the constitutional physical change,
in which a surplus in actual *births* is maintained in
boys over girls."   Hence "the excess of males over
females, bred of infanticide, tends to preserve the
system of polyandry, when infanticide itself has ceased
to be a national practice."

The actual polyandry of the Todas is thus accounted
for as due to the scarcity of females consequent
directly or indirectly on the practice of infanticide,
a conclusion which agrees with that arrived at by Dr
M'Lennan.   It by no means follows, however, that
because polyandry and infanticide are now associated
they always have been so.   The Tibetans do not kill
their female children, and they have no scarcity of
females, and yet they practice polyandry.   The object
of this custom in Tibet is to keep down population,
and, as was shown above, its real reason is " poverty."
And such must have been the origin of polyandry
among the Todas, whose ruling passion is the "necessity for children."[3]   So great is the disgrace attached

_____

[1] *Ibid.*, p. 194.   [2] *Ibid.*, p. 232.
[3] *Ibid.*, p. 208.

to the epithets *baruda* and *barudi*, meaning childless, as applied to young married people, the husband would, says Col. Marshall, connive at any steps his wife might take to obtain children. That such a people would kill their children and thus produce an artificial scarcity of females, unless they had a special reason for it, is extremely improbable. The reason actually assigned by the aged Toda for infanticide was poverty. He said, " We were very poor, and could not support our children." Whether or not the Todas were always so poor as not to be able to provide for a large family, it is now impossible to say ; but as they are known to have resided in their present position only for a few hundred years, we may infer that at one time they possibly did not practise infanticide. The example of the Tibetans proves that poverty alone may lead to polyandry, without resorting to infanticide, and such may have been the case with the Todas also.

Let us see whether any light is thrown on this subject by the practices of other peoples of India. Col. Marshall remarks[1] that the Sikh " bears a considerable though refined likeness to the Toda." The Sikhs belong to the Jat stock, and we learn from Sir William Hunter's work,[2] that in the Punjab, " among Jat families too poor to bear the marriage expenses of all the males, the wife of the eldest son has sometimes to accept her brothers-in-law as joint husbands." The learned writer states, however, that the Hinduized low-castes all over India have domestic customs which are survivals of polyandry, and he thinks that the marriage of Draupadí related in the Maha Bharata with the five Pándavan brethren preserves a trace of

[1] *Ibid.*, p. 4   [2] Hunter 1881, IV, 232.

such a primitive custom.[1]   That the practice of polyandry was widely spread in ancient India is very
probable, and if it be true, as required by Dr
M'Lennan's theory,[2] that descent in the male line
was introduced under the influence of the Tibetan
form of polyandry, that custom must have been
almost universal, as male kinship is now found among
most of the Indian peoples.   The question of the
connection between polyandry and male kinship will
be considered in a subsequent chapter, and we will
here examine into the spread and origin of Indian
polyandry by the light of the marriage of Draupadí
with the Pándavan brothers.

Mr Talboys Wheeler states[3] that the Brahmanical
compilers of the Maha Bharata have endeavoured to
convey the opinion that " such a marriage was so exceptional as to be a shock to the social sentiments of
the period."   This would seem to show that polyandry
had at least ceased to be customary at the date of
the compilation of the poem, but judging from the
incidents attending Draupadí's marriage,[4] we cannot
suppose it to have been an exceptional case.   Arjuna,
one of the Pandavas, won the daughter of Drupada,
the Raja of Panchála, at a Swayamvara or tournament,
the victor at which was to have her as his bride.
The brethern took the princess home, and their mother
Kuntí desired them to take her as their joint wife.
Arjuna was the third son, and according to the rules
of polyandry it is the eldest brother who has the right
of marriage.   Accordingly, we find that it was Yudhishthira, the eldest Pandava, who finally decided that

[1] *Ibid.*, IV, 284.   [2] McLennan 1876, p. 139.
[3] Wheeler 1867, I, 132.   [4] *Ibid.*, pp. 129ff.

the marriage should take effect. Draupadí thereupon became the wife of the five brothers, and she dwelt with them in turn for two days at a time, each of them having his separate house and garden. Now, it was a law among them, says the poem,[1] " that if a brother enter the house of another brother whilst Draupadí was dwelling there, he should depart out of the city and go into exile for twelve years." Arjuna entered the house of Yudhishthira for weapons while Draupadí was there, and although it was urged that his eldest brother stood to him as a father, Arjuna determined to go into exile, and he did so. Mr Wheeler regards this matrimonial law as mythical, and probably the story of the exile is so, but the rule, the breaking of which gave rise to the story, is consistent with recognised custom under similar circumstances. This is shown by the Arab practice, referred to by Strabo,[2] of the man who first visited the common wife, leaving his stick at the door of her house, a practice followed, according to Dr Shortt, by the modern Todas, as well as by the Nairs.[3] Dr M'Lennan refers[4] to the circumstances attending the Pandavan marriage as pointing to a system of polyandry of the Tibetan type, an opinion which appears to be well founded. If it be true, as there are many reasons to believe,[5] that the Pandavas are now represented by the Jats, and that they belonged to the Dravidian stock, we may see in the Maha Bharata story, combined with

[1] *Ibid.*, I, 142.

[2] XVI, 4; Robertson Smith 1885, p. 133.

[3] Reclus 1885, p. 192.   [4]McLennan 1876, p. 174.

[5] This question is considered by the present writer (1886, p. 204).

the existing marriage customs of many of the tribes of the Indian peninsula, evidence that polyandry was at one time a general form of marriage with the Dravidian race. At the same time the Pandavan incident does not supply any confirmation of the theory that polyandry arose from a scarcity of women, whether arising from infanticide or any other cause, unless it be supposed that the Pandavas had a difficulty in obtaining wives owing to their being in exile.

Some light may perhaps be thrown on the subject of infanticide and scarcity of women by a consideration of the customs of the modern Jats and their neighbours the Rajpoots. Female infanticide was at a comparatively recent date very common with both these peoples,[1] and it was sometimes carried so far that the Jat Sikhs belonging to the priestly classes Bedee and Sodhee put all their daughters to death. The nobler Rajpoot tribes appear to have been nearly as much addicted to the practice,[2] and many of them are said to have been " for generations unblessed with the presence of a daughter." What can have been the origin of this crime ?

As to the Jats, the source of their objection to rear female children was their poverty, and consequent desire to lessen the number of mouths to be filled, which will also account for the polyandry so prevalent among them, especially in the lower classes.[3] The female infanticide of the Rajpoots, who appear not to have practised polyandry, cannot be thus explained, although indirectly it may have been connected with poverty. Thus, the Rajpoots, while freely

[1] Browne 1857, pp. 7, 110ff.
[2] *Ibid.*, pp. 31, 58.
[3] *Ibid.*, p. 121.

admitting the crime, affirmed that the chief motive which prompted it was the great cost of a daughter's marriage, the expenditure being so great as to be ruinous in many cases.[1] Mr Browne, after referring to the practice of infanticide by the Mairs, an aboriginal tribe of Rajpootana, remarks[2] that among them, as among the Rajpoots, " the expenditure of enormous sums on the marriage of their daughters may be regarded as the most powerful motive to this inhuman custom. Yet there was a remarkable difference between the two systems. With the Rajpoots the main expenditure lay on the father of the bride, whereas among the Mairs it was on the side of the bridegroom's family," the reason being that the Rajpoot had to pay for a husband for his daughter, while the Mair had to buy a wife for his son. Thus the one, " lest he should be unable to marry and portion his daughter worthily, the other, lest his should be left unmarried, because no one was prepared to pay the high price set on her," murdered them in infancy to avoid the risk of disgrace.[3] Another motive to female infanticide arises from pride of birth. Among the Hindoos it is an established custom that the family into which a female may marry must be of at least equal rank with her own. Therefore, " to marry an inferior is, in their eyes, a degradation, but to remain unmarried is actual dishonour," to escape from which female infanticide was largely resorted to by Raj-

---

[1] *Ibid.*, p. 12.

[2] *Ibid.*, p. 64.

[3] The Khutrees living north of the Myhee River, however, destroy their daughters that their sons may be compelled to seek wives among the Southern Khutrees, who being of an inferior grade, pay a dowry with daughters to secure an alliance with their neighbours (*Ibid.*, p. 55).

poot families of high rank.[1] Mr Browne regarded
"pride of birth" as the primary cause of infanticide
with them, as it became with some of the Jats,[2]
the secondary cause being the ruin which resulted
from the exorbitant expenditure at the marriage of
daughters.

We have already[3] had occasion to consider the
evidence on which Prof. Smith identifies the *sadīca*
marriage of the Arabs with the *beena* form of polyandry, and it was shown to be doubtful whether this
system was ever established among the Arabs.   Let us
now see on what evidence it is asserted that the
Tibetan form of polyandry existed among them side
by side with Nair polyandry or beena marriage.   The
former type of marriage as found by Prof. Smith in
Arabia is termed by him[4] *ba'al* polyandry, " because
in it the polyandrous husbands have jointly the same
sort of control over the woman's person that the individual husband has in *ba'al* marriage," or marriage
of dominion.   Marriages of this kind are " where the
wife who follows her husband, and bears children who
are of his blood, has lost the right freely to dispose of
her person ; her husband has authority over her, and
he alone has the right of divorce."[5]   Prof. Smith
asserts[6] that such marriages were originally formed by
capture, which was afterwards supplemented by purchase or consent, which passed to the husband the right
to live with the woman and to get children by her.   If,
instead of an individual, a group of kinsmen acquired
a woman by either of those methods, all the conditions of Tibetan polyandry would be present, and

[1] *Ibid.*, p. 58.   [2] *Ibid.*, p. 121.
[3] Above, p. 150.   [4] Robertson Smith 1885, p. 126.
[5] *Ibid.*, p. 175.   [6] *Ibid.*, p. 82.

" such polyandry must necessarily arise if it is not possible or not convenient that every member of the group should have a wife to himself." [1] The community of personal estate among the early Arabs is thought to justify the assumption that if women were captured in warfare they would not be assigned to individuals, but would be held by " small sub-groups having property and wives in common, as in Tibetan polyandry." [2] The same thing would occur when a wife was purchased, the prices asked for women in ancient Arabia under the name of *mahr* or dowry being often very high, and then, as now among the Bedouins, many men could not afford to keep a wife. If wives were purchased at all, therefore, they would be procured by a group, and individual men would not have an exclusive right to them.

Prof. Smith goes further than inference, however, and he endeavours to prove that *ba'al* polyandry was at one time no exceptional phenomenon in Arabia, but the rule. He refers [3] to the statement of Strabo (xvi., 4, p. 782), in relation to the people of Arabia Felix or Yemen, that " brothers have precedence over children ; . . . all the kindred have their property in common, the eldest being lord ; all have one wife, and it is first come first served, the man who enters to her leaving at the door the stick which it is usual for everyone to carry ; but the night she spends with the eldest. Hence all are brothers of all [within the stock of συγγενεῖς] ; they have also conjugal intercourse with mothers ; an adulterer is punished with death ; and adulterer means a man of another stock." Strabo illustrates the subject by reference to the case of the daughter of a king married to her fifteen brothers.

[1] *Ibid.*, p. 125.   [2] *Ibid.*, p. 127.   [3] *Ibid.*, p. 133.

We certainly have in this account the special features of Tibetan polyandry, with the addition of the statements that brothers have intercourse with mothers, and that a sister had her brothers for husbands, which, however, refer not to *own* mothers or brothers, but to those who are entitled to these names as belonging to the maternal or fraternal group of kin. Verification of the former existence of polyandry is found in the right of the heirs to take a woman, who was acquired under contract of marriage, if her husband divorced her. This implies, says Prof. Smith,[1] "that the kin had an interest in the woman's marriage even while her husband lived, and that their interest became active as soon as he divested himself of his special claims on his wife." The right of the heir is in fact "a modification of the older right of kinsmen to share each other's marriages," to which is also traced the claim which a man had to the hand of his cousin on the father's side. This is said to depend on the principle that the father's kin are heirs to his daughter's hand as well as to his estate, in illustration of which reference is made to a case where the father's male kinsfolk not only seized his property, but married his daughters without regard to their will. This is evidence, however, only of the existence of a rule such as was in force at Athens [2] to keep property in the family.

That Prof. Smith has established the former existence among the Arabs of polyandry of the Tibetan type must be admitted. But his facts and statements go further than this. As he himself says,[3] the general result of his argument is, "that kinship through the mother alone was originally the universal rule of

[1] *Ibid.*, p. 137.   [2] Above, p. 30n.   [3] *Ibid.*, p. 151.

Arabia, and that kinship through males sprang up in polyandrous groups of kinsmen which brought in wives from outside, but desired to keep the children of these alien women to themselves." Here, however, we have not simply polyandry but group marriage, and not merely such a form of it as is found in the Polynesian *punalua*, where several own brothers have their wives in common, but the wider form in which the group of husbands comprises collateral brothers as well. That *ba'al* polyandry was based on a system of group marriage is required by the origin assigned to the former. It is supposed to have been founded on capture or contract, and it is evident that a group of kinsmen may have captured more than one woman. Prof. Smith states [1] that in old warfare the procuring of captives, both male and female, was a main object of every expedition, and as the local group and the kindred group were identical, " or at least the kernel and permanent element in every local group was a body of kinsfolk," the captured women who were retained by the group as wives would be held in common, unless on the distribution of booty a sub-group of kinsfolk received a particular woman for their share. Even in the latter case the same sub-group would probably acquire other female captives as the result of subsequent expeditions. The same reasoning applies to marriage by contract. This is, however, supposed. by Prof. Smith to have been of later origin than marriage by capture,[2] and it is possible that at the later date group marriage [3] had given place to a system of poly-

[1] *Ibid.*, p. 73.　　　　　　　　[2] *Ibid.*, p. 80.

[3] The "unbridled licence" granted to wives and daughters at the temple of Astarte, at Baalbek, and other sexual irregularities "of a polyandrous kind," associated with the worship of a mother-goddess, referred to by Prof. Robertson

andry approaching that of the Tibetan type, but in which the group of husbands were not necessarily own brothers.

If Arab polyandry was originally a form of group marriage, the question of infanticide is not of much moment in connection with it, but it is important as bearing on the origin assigned by Dr M'Lennan for polyandry.   Whether infanticide ever prevailed to any great extent among the Arabs is somewhat doubtful, although it was practised by some of the tribes, and it is said [1] that " at any rate in some places and at some times, there was a strong pressure of public opinion against sparing any daughter, even though she were the only child of her parents."   If the practice were general, however, it is evident that there would be no women left for wives, and we must suppose that it took place under special influences, as we have seen to be the case with the Rajpoot infanticide, which was primarily due to " pride of birth."   This fact renders it probable that the Arab authors were right in saying that pride was the motive for infanticide, parents being afraid that their daughters might be taken captive, and so bring disgrace on their kin.   Prof. Smith refers to the fact that the earliest Arabs were pure savages, practising cannibalism with other barbarous customs, and he well observes [2] that, like other savages, they would practise infanticide where, as is the case with the present nomad tribes, famine had often to be endured. That female rather than male children were killed

Smith (1885, pp. 136, 180), partake rather of the nature of group marriage, if indeed they were anything more than phases of sexual *hospitality*.

[1] *Ibid.*, p. 129.   [2] *Ibid.*, p. 283.

under these circumstances may perhaps be assumed from the proverb according to which "to bury a daughter was regarded not only as a virtuous but as a generous deed." Prof. Smith is of that opinion, and he is also inclined to see a connection between female infanticide and the custom of classing sons as of the father's kin and daughters as of the mother's, and the proverb just quoted might be applied to such a case on the ground that daughters may become the mothers of warriors for a hostile tribe. There does not appear, however, to be any evidence of a custom of thus tracing descent among the Arabs, and in fact the existence among the early Arabs of female kinship is not consistent with it. The Arabs doubtless practised infanticide when pressed by poverty, and preferred to preserve the future warriors of the tribe rather than those who might not repay the burden of rearing them, even if they did not give birth to warriors for their enemies. That infanticide was much less prevalent at the period when female kinship was universal than it afterwards became is very probable, as the more daughters were destroyed the fewer women would there be to bear children to perpetuate the tribe.

It is advisable now to consider how far the facts above referred to confirm or otherwise Dr M'Lennan's conclusions. He supposes[1] polyandry to be one of the phenomena distinctive of the earlier stages of the social progress of any race of men,[2] and he affirms

[1] McLennan 1876, p. 166.

[2] Dr. Morgan is also of the opinion stated in the text, but he regards polyandry as merely one of the forms of *punalua* (1877, p. 517). Sir John Lubbock agrees that polyandry arises from a scarcity of females, but he regards it as an exceptional phenomenon (1875, p. 133). Mr. Fison, while explaining polyandry as "group marriage in difficulties"

that its origin "can only be ascribed to a scarcity
of women as compared with men," caused by the
balance of the sexes being artificially disturbed, that
is, by female infanticide. Now, we have seen that
Tibetan polyandry exists without either (*a*) female
infanticide or (*b*) scarcity of women, and that it is
actually the result of (*c*) poverty. A reference to
the conditions of Jat polyandry shows that it was
formerly accompanied by both (*a*) and (*b*), and that
it also was due to (*c*); while that of the Arabs, which
was the result of (*c*), when it was not due to pride,
existed with (*a*) or with (*b*), whether the scarcity of
females was owing to infanticide or to the high price
set on females through other circumstances. It is
important to notice that polyandry is the result of
poverty, even in those cases where this is not always
associated with infanticide and scarcity of females.
Moreover, these phenomena existed among the Rajpoots without polyandry, and like this phase of marriage, they were due to "poverty," possible if not
actual, where not owing to pride of birth. Except
in this case, poverty is, indeed, the real parent of
(*a*) female infanticide and (*b*) scarcity of females,
as well as of polyandry, and as (*a*) and (*b*) are not
necessarily associated with polyandry, they cannot
be the original causes of it, as Dr M'Lennan's theory
requires. It is possible, therefore, that the Jats may
at one time have resembled the Tibetans in practising polyandry, while having neither infanticide

(1880, p. 145), declares that the proportion of males to
females among savages would not permit polyandry to be
the system of marriage anywhere at any time (1880, p. 147).
Perhaps here he refers only to savage tribes, and not to such
a people as the Tibetans.

nor scarcity of women, or like the Rajpoots, they may have practised infanticide without being polyandrous. In all these cases, moreover, kinship is traced through males in preference to females, showing that paternity is certain, either actually or constructively.

It may be said that Dr M'Lennan refers to the "ruder form" of polyandry associated with kinship through females, and not to the polyandry of the higher type which has male kinship. The appearance of the latter system is accounted for[1] by assuming that before the establishment of the higher form of polyandry paternity was uncertain, while afterwards there was "certainty as to the father's blood, though not certainty as to fathers." It has been shown,[2] however, to be a mistake to suppose either that paternity is uncertain, or that a child's relationship to his father is not recognised among the lower races of man. It will be hereafter proved, moreover, that female kinship does not depend on uncertainty of paternity, and that although true polyandry is associated with male kinship, these have no necessary connection with each other. Even assuming that this polyandry was developed from a lower form, the latter may have existed without either female infanticide or scarcity of women, as was probably the case with the Arab system of "fornication."[3] According to the hypothesis, in the 'rudest cases of polyandry the wife lives with her mother or brothers, and her children belong to her mother's house. The family is perpetuated through females, and it is extremely improbable, therefore, that female infanticide would be practised, preferably at all events

[1] McLennan 1876, p. 154.   [2] Above, pp. 15, 56.
[3] Above, p. 98.

to male infanticide. From whatever point of view
Dr M'Lennan's argument is considered, therefore, it
fails to account for the origin of polyandry, which can
be explained satisfactorily only as being established,
under the pressure of poverty, either independently
or as an offshoot from the phase of punaluan group
marriage in which several brothers have their wives in
common.

Before leaving the subject of polyandry reference
must be made to the law of the *levirate*, which is the
obligation laid on the younger brother of a man who
has died without leaving a son to take his brother's
widow for the purpose of providing a son for him.
The direction contained in the Institutes of Menu is,
that if a man dies without a son, his brother or other
kinsman appointed for the purpose shall raise up a son
for him, but only one; and it is expressly declared
that an elder brother or a younger brother caressing
the wife of the other are both degraded. An exception
to this is made, however, where the wife has no issue,
in which case it is allowed to the lower classes for the
purpose of providing a son, but it is not permitted to
the "twice-born" classes.[1] Assuming that the law of
the *levirate* originated in the obligation to marry the
widow, which was imposed on a man who succeeded to
his brother's property, what is the object of the rule
laid down by Menu? This question may be answered
by showing what was thought to be attained by having
a son. It is said "by the eldest (brother), at the
moment of his birth, the father, having begotten a son,
discharges his debt to his own progenitors." Again,
"that son alone by whose birth he discharges his debt,
and through whom he attains immortality, was be-

[1] *Menu*, IX. 58 et seq. [Bühler 1886.]

gotten from a sense of duty ; " [1] and thus is the son to be begotten on the widow by the appointed kinsman.[2] The father is regarded as born a second time in the person of his son (ix., v. 8), hence the first-born supports his younger brothers, as the father supports his sons (v. 108). The elder brother is to be regarded as a father and as a mother (v. 110), and his wife is considered as mother-in-law to the younger, and the wife of the younger as daughter-in-law to the elder (v. 57). The performance of the funeral obsequies was one of the chief objects for which a son was desired, and a daughter might be appointed to raise up a son for that purpose (v. 127). The maternal grandfather thus becomes in law the father of a son, who is to " give the funeral cake and possess the inheritance " (v. 136). The right to inherit is thus connected with the performance of the obsequies, but it is very different from the right of succession to his brother's property, which a man takes along with his brother's widow. Here the younger brother succeeds to the children and other property of the deceased, because he marries the widow and becomes the head of the family instead of his elder brother. In the other case, the father is succeeded by a son who stands in his place as head of the family ; but although he may take entire possession of the patrimony for the benefit of the family, if his younger brothers wish to live apart, they are entitled to take their shares (v. 104 *et seq.*). There may certainly be only one son to enjoy the inheritance, and this son may be begotten on the widow by a younger brother or other kinsman, but in this case the son will

[1] *Menu*, IX. 106–7.

[2] Such a son delivers his father from the hell named *put*, and he was therefore called *puttra* (IX. 138).

have to divide the estate equally with his natural father, the representation to the deceased brother not being considered complete for the purpose of inheritance (v. 120-1). Dr M'Lennan remarks on this rule, that in Menu's time the obligation to raise up a son to a deceased brother " had not only been to some extent dissociated from the corresponding right of inheritance, but was falling into disrepute." The aim of the provisions of Menu is, however, so different in every respect, except the mere fact of the taking of the brother's widow to wife, from the system of polyandry that they can hardly have had, as supposed by Dr M'Lennan,[1] any relation to each other. One provision of Menu has certainly at first sight a very polyandrous look. It is said (ix., v. 182), that if among several brothers of the whole blood one has a son born, all of them shall be considered as fathers of a male child by means of that son. This provision appears, however, to be intended to prevent the adoption of a son to the exclusion of a nephew who would be heir. As to inheritance, it is expressly declared (v. 185), "not brothers, nor parents, but sons, if living, or their male issue, are heirs to the deceased, but of him who leaves no son, nor a wife, nor a daughter, the father shall take the inheritance ; and if he have neither father nor mother, the brothers."

Nor is there any stronger reason to believe that the law of the *levirate* as known to the Hebrews had any relation to polyandry. Dr M'Lennan remarks,[2] that in the earliest age the Levir had no alternative but to take the widow; *indeed, she was his wife without any form of marriage.* That the custom had a certain relation to the property of the deceased is

[1] McLennan 1876, p. 160.   [2] *Ibid.*, p. 162.

evident from the statement of Boaz, that he had purchased Ruth, the widow of Mahlon, " to raise up the
name of the dead upon his inheritance." It was not,
however, merely that Mahlon, or rather his father
Elimelech, might have an heir, but that his name
" be not cut off from among his brethren, and from the
gate of his place." [1] The whole story of Ruth and
Boaz is instructive as showing that the Hebrew custom agreed closely with that prescribed by the law of
Menu. Ruth, under the instructions of her mother-
in-law, Naomi, laid herself at the feet of Boaz while
he slept, and when he awoke she revealed herself, and
said, " Spread thy skirt [2] over thine handmaid, for
thou art a near kinsman." Boaz reminded her that
she had a nearer kinsman, but that, if necessary, he
would do the kinsman's part. In the morning Boaz
summoned the nearer kinsman to redeem the inheritance in the hand of Naomi, but the latter excused
himself on the ground that he would mar his own
inheritance, and he asked Boaz to redeem it.   In
confirmation of this arrangement Boaz drew off his
kinsman's shoe. The elders and people were then
called in to witness that Boaz had bought the field
of Naomi, and had purchased Ruth for his wife, " to
raise up the name of the dead upon his inheritance."
The chief difference between the Hebrew and the
Hindoo custom is, that while in the latter case only
one son was to be raised up to the dead man, there
was no such limit in the case of Ruth. It is remarkable that the son she bore to Boaz was credited to

[1] Ruth 4 : 10.

[2] Among the Arabs the casting of a garment over the widow
by the heir was symbolic of his wish to inherit (Robertson
Smith 1885, p. 136).

Naomi,[1] who took the child and became its nurse, and her neighbours gave the child the name Obed, saying, "There is a son born to Naomi." Possibly Naomi merely stood in the place of her husband Elimelech, whose grandson by the appointed kinsman was to prevent his name being "cut off from among his brethren;" as among the Hindoos a man obtained immortality through his son's son.

Whether Ruth bore to Boaz more children than one is not stated, and it was a matter of no importance, as the firstborn son was to perpetuate the name of the dead. This is shown by the old law of the *levirate* as stated in Deuteronomy,[2] where it is said, "If brethren dwell together, and one of them die, and have no child, the wife of the dead shall not marry without into a stranger; her husband's brother shall go in unto her, and take her to him to wife, and perform the duty of an husband's brother unto her. And it shall be, that the firstborn which she beareth shall succeed in the name of his brother which is dead, that his name be not put out of Israel." If a man refused to perform a brother's part, the widow was to remove his shoe and spit in his face, and his name was not to be "called in Israel." Dr M'Lennan remarks[3] on this enactment, that the obligation to marry the widow "is here presented pure—as a *duty* falling on the brother, which it was disgraceful to neglect." The disgrace, however, was not in declining to marry the widow, but in refusing to "build up his brother's house," in other words, to obtain a son for

[1] This answers to the Hindoo rule that a daughter might be deputed to provide a son to perform the funeral obsequies of his maternal grandfather.

[2] 25 : 5–10.   [3] 1876, p. 160.

him, that his name "be not put out of Israel." The
object of the law was the birth of a son, and it was
probably founded on the principle that the dead man
had married for the purpose of perpetuating his name,
and it was the duty of the woman whom he takes for
this purpose to bear him a son, if necessary, by his
brother or other kinsman. That this is the proper
view of the subject is evident from the ideas and
practice which were prevalent among the early
Arabs. Prof. Smith refers[1] to the usage known as
nikáh al-istibdá, that is, when a man "desired
a goodly seed he might call upon his wife to cohabit
with another man till she became pregnant by
him. Here the child was, as according to Hindoo
law, the husband's son." The usage is based on the
fact that the husband on marriage purchased the
right to have children by his wife, who should be
reckoned to his own kin.[2] As the woman did not
change her kin on marriage, the husband's right had
relation rather to the children of the marriage than to
the woman herself,[3] and it found expression in the
rule, which Prof. Smith describes as the fundamental
doctrine of Mohammedan law, "the son is reckoned
to the bed on which it is born." The rule explains
how the Arabs could lend a wife to a guest, or, when
going on a journey, to a friend, and even such a case as
that of a husband entering into "a partnership of
conjugal rights with another man, in return for his
service as a shepherd ";[4] as in these cases the offspring
belong to the woman's husband. The rule had the
curious effect in ancient Arabia that one man might
be the natural father of a child, and another man its

[1] 1885, p. 110; cf. p. 275n.
[2] *Ibid.*, p. 108.   [3] *Ibid.*, p. 101.   [4] *Ibid.*, p. 116.

M

legal father. This would arise where a man died or divorced his wife while she was pregnant, and she married again before the child was born, in which case it belonged to the family of the second husband.[1] It was so even if the first husband arranged with the man who married his divorced wife, that the child to be born should be ultimately returned to its real father, unless the second husband's kin objected.[2] On these facts Prof. Smith very justly observes,[3] "In ancient Arabia, therefore, fatherhood does not necessarily imply procreation, and the family of which the father is the head is held together, not by the principle of physical paternity, but by the rule that the husband is father of all the children born on his bed." This rule has no reference, however, to polyandry, but refers rather to the right which the husband acquires over his wife and her offspring, a right which, so far as the woman is concerned, may belong to the husband's heir on his death.[4] In the custom of the *levirate* there is probably a mixture of motives. The object of its observance is to raise up a son to a deceased brother, and so far Mr Fison is right when he says[5] that "its underlying motive is found in the preferential claim to the birthright vested in the elder branch." The object for which the son has to be obtained has relation directly or indirectly to inheritance, and so far Sir John Lubbock is correct in affirming[6] that the *levirate* is "more intimately connected with the rights of property than with polyandry."

[1] *Ibid.*, p. 110.
[2] *Ibid.*, p. 115.
[3] *Ibid.*, p. 119.
[4] *Ibid.*, p. 114.
[5] Fison and Howitt 1880, p. 146.
[6] Lubbock 1875, p. 135.

CHAPTER VI.

POLYGYNY.

WE have now to consider the phase of the marital relation in which one man has several wives, sisters or otherwise, usually called polygamy, but which is more properly *polygyny*, as opposed to polyandry, in which a woman has more than one husband. The simplest form of polygyny is that in which several sisters become the wives of the same man, answering to the polyandry in which the several husbands are brothers. It appears to have been known to the natives of America,[1] and it is practised among the Australian aborigines;[2] also, as we shall see by the Ostiaks of Siberia and some of the Malagasy tribes. It was not unknown, moreover, to the early Semites, as appears by the marriages of Jacob with Rachel and Leah. This case differs, however, from that in which the husband is entitled to his wife's sisters when they become of marriageable age. The personal service[3] of Jacob was equivalent to a price, and was an actual payment for the woman taken in marriage, in which particular the Semitic practice agreed with that of later polygyny.

It has been shown that polyandry is due chiefly to poverty, which prevents a man obtaining the sole right to the favours of the woman who stands to him

---

[1] Above, p. 132.　　　　　　　[2] Above, p. 133.

[3] In this mode a man acquires a wife among some of the American tribes (Lafitau 1724, I, 561).

in the relation of wife. On the other hand, abundance may be said to be the chief inducement to the practice of polygyny. Even to enable a man to enjoy the privilege of marrying two or more sisters it is necessary that he should be a successful hunter, or otherwise able to maintain more than one family.[1] Among more cultured races similar ideas prevail, and the possession of wealth is generally attended with the practice of polygyny, except where it is forbidden by religious teaching. This accounts for the fact that, while in polyandry the husbands are brothers or other near kinsmen, with a developed system of polygyny, a man's wives, so far from being sisters, are usually not at all related to each other. In the former case poverty limits, while in the latter plenty widens the range of matrimonial choice, it being restricted only by the operation of the law of consanguinity in relation to marriage. Systematic polygyny agrees, however, with polyandry in that both are found chiefly among peoples tracing descent in the male line. This custom is based on the right of the husband or his kindred to the children of the marriage, which usually supposes that the wife leaves her own family to reside among the kindred of her husband. The conditions of polygyny based on wife-purchase would render the adoption of any other course very improbable. The polygynist would live among his own people surrounded by his wives. The exception would be where these are sisters, in which case the man may reside either with his own tribe, or with that of his

---

[1] Mr. Morgan states that polygamy was never prevalent to any considerable extent among the American aborigines, owing to the inability of persons to support more than one family (1877, p. 160).

wives, the latter being probably the most usual practice.

Dr Darwin affirms[1] that most savages are "polygamists," and that polygamy is "almost universally followed by the leading men in every tribe." This statement may be accepted as expressing the general truth, but as developed polygyny takes different forms, I propose to enter into some detail on that point. Moreover, as we have seen, the sexual relations of some of the polygamous races are governed by the rules of group marriage, rather than of systematic polygyny. It is true that in the Australian tribes the monopoly of women by the old men is very common. This polygyny is, however, subject to certain rights of the younger men, which are evidences of the continuance of the operation of group marriage.[2] The *punalua* of the Polynesians is evidence of pure polygamy, for it allowed several brothers to have their wives in common, as well as several sisters to have their husbands in common. Polygyny proper, however, appears to be not uncommon among the islanders of the Pacific, especially with the upper classes. Thus, in New Zealand, although numbers of the lower orders usually had only one wife, chiefs generally had from two to six, of whom the first was the head wife.[3] In the Sandwich Islands polygyny was allowed to all, but it was practised only by the chiefs. It was much more prevalent among the Tahitians. Many of the inferior chiefs had two or three wives, who appeared to receive an equal degree of respect and support.

[1] Darwin 1871, II, 362–63.
[2] Fison and Howitt 1880, p. 354.
[3] Taylor 1870, p. 337.

Although the higher chiefs kept a number of females, it was, says Mr Ellis,[1] "rather a system of concubinage, than a plurality of wives, that prevailed among them." The woman to whom the chief was first married, or whose rank was nearest to his own, was generally considered his head wife, the others being looked upon as her inferiors, so long as she lived with her husband. In Samoa the chiefs, in addition to a legitimate wife, could have numerous inferior wives or concubines, and sometimes these were attached to houses on the public roads where travellers were entertained. Polygyny is said to be universally practised by the Fijians,[2] among whom a man's social position depends on the number of his wives, all of whom, however, except the first would seem to be treated as slaves.

Among the North American tribes polygyny was in theory recognised as the right of the males, although many of them could not afford to practise it. It could only have been general, moreover, if the husband usually lived among his wife's kindred, which, considering the present distribution of the gentes, can hardly have been the case. According to Lafitau,[3] polygyny was much more common in the southern than in the northern part of the American continent. He says that here the practice is restricted to the Algonkin tribes, and he adds that there is always a chief wife, of whom the others are the servants, and whose children are regarded as superior to those of the inferior wives. Mr Catlin affirms,[4] however, that

[1] Ellis 1832–34, I, 273.
[2] Pritchard 1866, p. 372.
[3] 1845, I, 555.
[4] Catlin 1876, I, 118–20.

polygyny was recognised among all the Indian tribes visited by him, and he adds that wives were universally bought and sold, in most cases of the father. The practice of polygyny appears to be known to all the tribes of the Pacific coast, where the husband does not live among his wife's relations, although it is practically restricted to the chiefs. This is the case with the Nootka nations, who have to pay high prices for wives,[1] and the Chinooks, among whom "practically few, and those among the rich and powerful, indulged in the luxury of more than one wife."[2] With the natives of North California, who are so essentially wife purchasers that the children of a wife who has cost her husband nothing are looked upon as bastards and treated with contempt, polygyny is universal, "the number of wives depending only on the limit of a man's wealth."[3] This may be said also of the natives of New Mexico,[4] but in Southern California, although the chiefs had several wives, the common people only had one.[5] Mr Bancroft remarks[6] that a plurality of wives was found among all the wild tribes of Mexico at the time of the Spanish conquest, the first wife taking precedence of the others, while many men had concubines also. Among the Mexican nations polygyny or concubinage was generally allowed. In addition to the principal wife, a man might have less legitimate wives, with whom the "tying of garments" constituted the whole marriage ceremony, the nobles and chief men also

[1] Bancroft 1875, I, 195.
[2] *Ibid.*, I, 241.
[3] *Ibid.*, I, 350.
[4] *Ibid.*, I, 512.
[5] *Ibid.*, I, 410.
[6] *Ibid.*, I, 633.

keeping women who were mere concubines.[1] It is remarkable that with the Maya nations of Central America, although concubinage was indulged in by the wealthy, true polygyny was unknown, and bigamy was severely punished.[2]

Plurality of wives would seem not to have been allowed under the paternal government of the Incas of Peru. The Incas themselves, however, took several wives from among their own relations, and had also concubines. According to Garcillasso de la Vega,[3] the Inca had three kinds of children : those of his wife, who, as legitimate, were destined for the succession to the kingdom ; those of his relations, who were legitimate by blood ; and the bastards born of strangers in blood. The practice of the less civilised peoples of South America appears to be more in unison with that of the North American tribes than with Peruvian custom. Drs Von Spix and Von Martius say of the Brazilian Indian that he takes as many wives as he wishes for, or can afford to keep.[4] The Indians of Paraguay also allowed polygyny, although, according to Dobrizhoffer,[5] it was not much practised, and it was thought to be both wicked and disgraceful for a man to have illicit connection with other women than his wives. Much the same may be said of the natives of Guiana, among whom instances of conjugal attachment are said by the Rev. W. H. Brett[6] to be not uncommon. The Tehuelches of Patagonia, at the southern extremity of

[1] *Ibid.*, II, 265.   [2] *Ibid.*, II, 671.
[3] Lasso de la Vega 1715, I, 354.
[4] Von Spix and von Martius 1824, II, 346.
[5] Dobrizhoffer 1822, II, 138.
[6] Brett 1868, p. 343.

the American continent, may have as many wives as they can support, but, according to Capt. Musters,[1] it is rare to find a man with more than two, and polygyny is not generally practised. This is not surprising when we consider that although wives are purchased, a certain number of horses or silver ornaments being given in exchange, marriages are always governed by inclination. Capt. Musters affirms [2] that the finest trait in the Tehuelches character is "their love for their wives and children; matrimonial disputes are rare, and wife-beating unknown; and the intense grief with which the loss of a wife is mourned is certainly not 'civilised,' for the widower will destroy all his stock and burn all his possessions," and possibly become careless of his life. Great affection between man and wife appears also to be characteristic of the polygamous Esquimaux of North America, who occasionally practise polygyny [3] on a somewhat extensive scale. Capt. Hall met with a man who had thirteen wives, several of whom had, however, deserted him, and one he had left because she "bore no children." [4]

If from the new world we pass to the old, we find that on the Asiatic continent, although the practice of polygyny is widely spread, it is not universal. It appears not to be very prevalent among the Mongolian and other peoples of Central Asia and Siberia. The *Itelmen* of Kamschatka are said by Von Steller[5] to take their female prisoners as concubines, and, accord-

---

[1] Musters 1871, p. 178.   [2] *Ibid.*, p. 187.

[3] Polyandry is sometimes practised by the young men, but probably only under special circumstances.

[4] Hall 1864, II, 100.

[5] Cited in Wake 1878, I, 263.

ing to Castren, the Ostiaks occasionally practise polygyny, but not frequently, as wives are too expensive.
A man may marry several sisters, and a younger brother
is bound to marry the widow of an elder brother.[1]　As
to the Mongols proper, they have only one legitimate
wife, but they can have several concubines.　These
are subject to the wife's authority, and her children
alone inherit, although the children of the concubines
can be legitimatised.[2]　The Tunguses appear to agree
with the Mongols in their marital arrangements.[3]

Among the Chinese, the practice of polygyny is not
general, but it is permitted under certain conditions.
The wife chosen for a man[4] by his father and mother
or near relation is the first or principal wife.　A man
can have other wives, who, although subordinate to
the first wife, are legitimate, and whose children have
a right of succession from their father.　The law
guards the rights of the principal wife, and forbids,
under a severe penalty, a man to reduce her to the
condition of an inferior wife or concubine, or to
elevate another in her place.[5]　The Rev. Julius
Doolittle states that in China rich married men have
often one or more concubines living in their families.
He supposes, however, that a second or inferior wife is
generally married with the consent of the principal
wife, when the latter is childless, the desire to have

[1] *Ibid.*, I, 269.　　　　　　　　[2] Prjévalskii 1880, p. 46.
[3] *Ibid.*, p. 208.

[4] Archdeacon Gray sees in this practice a chief cause of
Chinese polygyny, as the first match being often unsuitable,
the husband chooses himself a second or even a third wife
(1878, I, 184).

[5] Gray 1878, I, 212 ; Renouard de Sainte-Croix 1812, I, 186.

male children " to perpetuate one's name, and to burn incense before one's tablet after death," having great influence over the Chinese mind.[1] Mr Edkins asserts[2] that any number of *tsié*, or handmaids, bought with money, may be taken, although the doing so is not considered altogether reputable. The children of the inferior wives would appear to belong in law to the first wife.[3] The Japanese, like the Chinese, are in theory monogamists, but concubinage is practised among them,[4] and the concubines, although they are subject to the wife's authority are not considered as dishonoured by their position in the family.[5]

A casual survey would lead us to speak in similar terms of the marital arrangements of the Buddhists of the Indo-Chinese Peninsula. Sangermano says,[6] indeed, in relation to the Burmese, that they have only one lawful wife, but that they keep several concubines, of whom each has a separate house. Sir John Bowring also states[7] that, although in Siam a man may have as many wives as he pleases, the head wife is the only legitimate one, the others occupying the position of concubines. Elsewhere,[8] he says, however, that although he only observed two grades of wives, the first wife and the subordinate ones, yet there are said to be four classes of wives. Of these, the first is the wife of royal gift; the second, the legal wife ; the third, the wife of affection ; and the fourth, the slave wife, that is,

[1] Doolittle 1868, p. 76.
[2] Edkins 1859, p. 163.
[3] Douglas 1882, p. 78.
[4] Humbert 1870, I, 104.
[5] Busk 1841, p. 171.
[6] Sangermano 1833, pp. 46, 54.
[7] Bowring 1857, I, 119.
[8] *Ibid.*, I, 184ff.

"the handmaid with whom the owner has cohabited, and who, in consequence, becomes emancipated." In Cambodia,[1] the common people take only one wife, but the law allows a man to have three wives, who answer to the second, third, and fourth wives of the Siamese. Rich men also have a certain number of concubines who are generally purchased, which is the case also with the third wife, who is usually the young slave of a friend or acquaintance.

Polygyny is not unknown to the aboriginal tribes of India, but probably it is not much practised. Thus the Jenadies of Southern India are polygynists, owing to the women being more numerous than the men.[2] The Dravidian Málers of Rajmahal favour a plurality of wives, and if a man leaves several widows they are distributed among his brothers and cousins.[3] Of the Kolarian tribes the Santals of Orissa do not disallow polygyny, but they are usually content with one wife, and where it is otherwise, the first wife is honoured as head of the house.[4] The primitive Juangs of Singbhúm are said to have as many wives as they can support, which is two at the utmost; although Dr Shortt affirms that polygyny is permitted only where a man has not any family by his first wife [5]—a custom not unknown to more advanced races. Many of the Assam tribes appear to have been addicted to both polyandry and polygyny. Among the hill Muris the chiefs practise the latter, and when a man dies his wives descend to his heir, who becomes the husband of them all except his own mother.[6] The Abors permit

---

[1] Moura 1883, I, 335ff.
[2] Wake 1878, I, 111, and authorities there cited.
[3] *Ibid.*, I, 126.   [4] *Ibid.*, I, 134.
[5] *Ibid.*, I, 140.   [6] *Ibid.*, I, 149.

polygyny, although it is not much practised, in which they agree with the Khamtis. The Sissee Abors, however, as well as the Mishmis and the Singphos, take as many wives as they can afford to buy, the last named also having slave concubines, whose children have equal rights with the legitimate offspring.[1] The Kukís of Cáchár, on the other hand, do not permit polygyny, but they do not object to having concubines in addition to a wife.[2] The many points of resemblance between these tribes and the Malays will lead us to expect to find polygyny among the latter. In Sumatra a man may obtain in *jujur*—that is, by purchase—as many wives as he likes, and as such wives are practically slaves, they may be regarded as in the light of concubines.[3] The Battas allow a man to have several wives as well as concubines, and on the husband's death his widows belong to his brother or other nearest male relative, or sometimes even to his son, but a father cannot take his son's widow.[4]

Before referring to the Semitic and Aryan races, it will be well to see what are the ideas prevalent among the African tribes on the subject of polygyny, first of all glancing at the marital notions of the natives of Madagascar. The Rev. Wm. Ellis remarks in relation to this point,[5] that " the only law to regulate polygamy seems to be that no man can take twelve wives excepting the sovereign." The practice of polygyny is not universal, but " most of the nobles or chieftains, who can afford to maintain a plurality of wives, deem it

[1] Rowney 1882, p. 163, 167.
[2] *Ibid.*, p. 186.
[3] Marsden 1783, p. 270.
[4] Baecker 1874, pp. 490, 496.
[5] Ellis 1838, I, 165.

essential to their rank and honour, if not to their happiness, to take more than one wife." It seems to be necessary that a man should obtain the consent of the first wife before marrying again, and Mr Ellis gives an interesting account of the mode in which the husband obtains the sanction, and of the proceedings attending the second marriage. When the ceremony has been completed, the husband either continues to live with both wives in the same house, or the first wife has a separate establishment. Generally, too, says Mr Ellis, "the custom obtains of the husband's soliciting a small portion of his first wife's rice ground, which he presents to his vady-kely (little wife), and in return gives her another piece some time afterwards as a compensation." According to M. Charnay,[1] each Betsimisaraka chief has at least three wives, of whom the first is the legitimate wife, and her children are his heirs; the second is the wife whom the husband repudiates when she is past the prime of her youth and beauty; and the third is a slave, who receives her freedom when she becomes a mother. The French traveller adds that the younger sisters of these wives also belong to the husband until they are married. This system in vogue among the Malagasy has much in common with that of the class wives of the Cambodians and the Siamese as mentioned above, although they do not appear to have the wife of royal gift of the Siamese.

Polygyny may be said to be general among the African races. Mr Brodie Cruickshank mentions the practice in connection with the natives of the Gold Coast, who have both free and slave wives.[2] Du

[1] Charnay 1870, p. 50.
[2] Cruickshank 1835, I, 325.

Chaillu states,[1] that among the Gaboon tribes polygyny is universal, and it is so also among the
natives of Eastern and Northern Africa. In Uganda,
the Wahŭma often obtain wives by exchanging
daughters. The royal harem is supplied by women
received in tribute from neighbouring chiefs, or by
the governors of districts, who present their pretty
daughters to the king in atonement for some offence.
On the other hand, the governors are presented by the
king with women, who are captured abroad, or seized
from offenders at home.[2] A similar practice was
in use among the Ashantees, of whom the higher
classes had many wives and the king 3333, which
number was carefully kept up, in order that the king
might be able to present women to distinguished
subjects.[3] Among the Kafirs and Bechuanas of South
Africa women are valued in cattle, and girls pride
themselves on the high price they fetch. Men buy
as many wives as they can support. The first wife
has, however, a certain pre-eminence, and theoretically
all the cows which a man possesses at the time of his
marriage are the property of his wife, and after the
birth of her first son they are called *his* cattle. If
the first or any subsequent wife furnishes the cattle
to purchase and endow a new wife, she is entitled to
her service, and calls her " *my* wife."[4]

If Africa is not the birthplace of polygyny, it must
be sought in Western Asia. The position of Egypt

[1] Du Chaillu 1861, p. 51.
[2] Speke 1863, p. 250.
[3] Bowdich 1819, p. 289.
[4] Shooter 1857, p. 84.

between the two regions would therefore lead us
to expect to find it a common practice among the
early inhabitants of that country.   M. Ménard affirms [1]
the existence of polygyny on the authority of Diodorus
Siculus, who states that in Egypt the priests married
only one wife, but that other citizens could have
as many wives as they pleased, and that all children
were considered legitimate.   This applied even to the
children of slave mothers.   M. Fontane confirms the
opinion that polygyny was practised by the Egyptians,
at least at the commencement of the Middle Empire.
He says,[2] that "without speaking of the harems, there
were at the side of the legitimate wife, and associated
with her, concubines pleasing to the master by their
talent, their grace, or their beauty."   These females,
who were generally foreigners, seem not to have
caused any disquietude to the Egyptian wife, who
could always retain her influence over her husband if
she became a fitting companion for him.   The Egyptians
appear to have been devoid of the sentiment of love,
and married only for the purpose of forming a family.
Under these conditions, it would not be surprising if,
as M. Fontane suggests,[3] the wandering Egyptians
of the Ancient Empire had a family or a wife in every
city and country where they sojourned.   In modern
Egypt a man may, in accordance with the regulation
of Mohammed, have four wives, and as many concubines as he likes, but if he has only one wife he can
divorce her, and take another whenever he chooses.
He has only to say to her, "Thou art divorced," and
she must return to her friends.[4]

[1] Ménard 1880–83, II, 3.
[2] Fontane 1882, p. 194.
[3] *Ibid.*, p. 365.
[4] Lane 1836, I, 117, 225.

In modern Asia we shall expect to find polygyny more or less prevalent wherever Mohammedanism is established.[1] The condition of society in this respect is, however, far superior to that of the ancient world. As Mr Bosworth Smith remarks,[2] Mohammed "at least put some limitations on the unbounded licence of Eastern polygamy," which among the early Arabs permitted the acquisition of any number of wives. In this respect the Arab prophet compares favourably with the Hebrew lawgiver. The connection of polygyny with wife-purchase is well shown in the regulations of Mohammed. He expressly enjoined the propriety of the latter, and although the price paid is considered the property of the wife, the theory of Moslem law is still, as pointed out by Prof. Robertson Smith,[3] that marriage is purchase, thus settling "a permanent seal of subjection on the female sex" by perpetuating the old marriage of dominion, It has been maintained by a later Jewish writer that, although the Hebrews practised polygyny, monogamy was the rule and polygyny the exception.[4] M. Weill says also that they prohibited marriage with two sisters. This is true, according to Levitical law, but the marriage of Jacob with the two sisters Rachel and Leah proves that if the regulation then existed it was disregarded. The Hebrews, as well as the Arabs, had also concubines, or slave wives, in addition to the legal wife or wives,

[1] Polygyny appears, however, to be now rare among the higher classes in Egypt, and in India among the Mussulmans (R. B. Smith 1876, p. 328).

[2] Ibid., p. 237.

[3] Robertson Smith 1885, p. 100.

[4] Weill 1874, p. 70. The expression "if a man have two wives" (Lev. 21. 15) is consistent with polygyny being exceptional.

as shown in the history of the patriarchs.   Possibly
it may be that, as asserted by the Rabbins,[1] although
the Pentateuch does not forbid polygyny, it was
usually practised only under special circumstances.
Thus, where a women was childless, her husband took
a second wife, a rule, however, which is not consistent
with the existence of the harems of the kings nor with
the polygyny of the patriarchs.   The strongest argument in favour of the belief that polygyny was not
a common practice among the Hebrews, is the fact
that after their return from the captivity it was no
more indulged in, no doubt owing to their improved
moral and religious condition.   In support of the
opinion that the lower classes among the Hebrews and
the Arabs were not generally addicted to that practice,
it may be stated that the Moors of Northern Africa,
and also the Berbers, are usually monogamous.[2]

That polygyny was in use among the Babylonians
and Assyrians is very probable, and it is known to
have been practised in ancient Persia, at least by the
rich and great.   M. Menard remarks[3] that " the
royal harem, raised to the dignity of a state institution, had an immense development and a mag-
nificence without equal.   The historians show us the
king surrounded by his concubines, and living nevertheless with the queen, who took no offence at these
attendants."   The possession of a large harem has
generally been regarded by eastern monarchs as an
essential requirement, but it is only an extension of
the custom which allows a man to have, in addition
to his lawful wife, several inferior wives or con-

[1] Ménard 1880–83, II, 50.
[2] Wake 1878, I, 188, 190, and authorities there cited.
[3] Ménard 1880–83, I, 57.

cubines. Nevertheless, we shall in the next chapter see reason to believe that it was not allowed by the ancient Iranians,[1] and the same must be said of the Aryans of India and of the early Greeks and Romans.

Although concubinage was permitted among the Greeks of the heroic age, as indeed of subsequent times, the practice of polygyny, except under special circumstances, was forbidden.[2] The first person named in Roman history who appears to have adopted that practice was Mark Anthony, but afterwards it became not uncommon, and continued far down into the Christian period. So late as the year 726, a decretal of Pope Gregory II. allowed a man to marry a second wife " if the first is infirm and incapable of conjugal functions." The system of concubinage was doubtless known to other branches of the Aryan stock, and chiefs and great men would always consider themselves privileged in that respect. According to Branicki,[3] the primitive Slavs were polygynists, and their king, Vladimir, before embracing Christianity, had no less than eight hundred concubines in three different localities. That writer states that even to this day there often exists in the Russian *mir* a singular form of incestuous concubinage. The chief of the family voluntarily marries boys of from eight to ten years of age to girls of from twenty-five to thirty, and then he frequently becomes the lover of his daughter-in-law, until the legal husband reaches

[1] It is said that in a province of ancient Media, to make good ravages of war, the citizens were compelled each to take seven wives. In another province women were compelled to take five husbands owing to so many women having been carried away captives of war (*The Popular Encyclopaedia,* art. "Polygamy.")

[2] Duruy 1886–89, I, 164.

[3] Cited by Letourneau 1876, p. 355.

the age of puberty.   A similar custom has been
noted by Dr Shortt as existing among the Reddies
of Southern India ; the children are fathered on the
boy-husband, who in due time "in his turn takes
up with some other 'boy's' wife in a manner precisely
similar to his own, and procreates children for the
boy-husband."[1]   It is difficult to account for such a
custom as this ; but probably it is connected with
the ideas which treat a father as holding his property
for his new-born son, although enjoying its fruits until
the son can enter into possession.[2]

The facts referred to in the preceding pages show
that on the American Continent, in Australia, and
Madagascar, as well as among the Ostiaks of Siberia
and the early Hebrews, polygyny sometimes assumed
the form of marriage with two or more sisters.   With
other peoples, such as the New Zealanders, the Malagasy, the Hill Tribes of India, the early Hebrews, the
Arabs, and many of the North African peoples, as well
as among Mohammedan peoples generally, a man's
wives, although not sisters, are in a position of
equality[3] among themselves.   In the great majority
of cases, however, the first wife occupies a position
of superioriy, whether the other women taken by her
husband are *inferior wives,* as in Tahiti and some
other Polynesian Islands, and in some parts of the
American Continent, and China, and in South Africa ;
or *concubines,* as with the Fijians, the Mayas, the
Malays, the Assamese tribes, the Japanese, the Mon-

---

[1] Shortt 1869, p. 194.

[2] These ideas are entertained by some of the Polynesian
tribes, as well as by the Hindoos to some extent. Does not the
custom of a father taking the name of his new born son
spring from the same source? The son is a reincarnation of
the father.

[3] This does not apply in the case of slave wives or concubines.

gols, the Burmese, the ancient Egyptians, the Persians, and some other peoples belonging to the Aryan stock. In some cases the peoples whose wives were of equal standing were allowed also to have concubines. Such were the early Hebrews and Arabs, and probably the ancient Egyptians. The like privilege as to the enjoyment of concubines was conjoined with the possession of first and inferior wives among many of the Mexican tribes and the Incas of Peru, and still is with some of the tribes of Madagascar. The Siamese occupy the almost unique position of having four classes of wives, of which, however, the slave wife answers to the concubines of other forms of polygyny. The phases of this custom may be practically divided into (a) those in which all a man's wives have equal rights, (b) and those where there is a superior wife (or wives) and inferior ones, the latter being sometimes legal wives, and at others slave wives or concubines.

This classification may be useful, but it does not show that the several phases of polygyny have any relation to race, nor does it throw much light on the causes which give rise to the practice, which causes can be ascertained only from the circumstances of particular cases. From a consideration of these we may infer that, although in many instances man's luxury and sensuality lead to polygyny, yet in other cases it is due to social conditions over which man has no control. The views hitherto held on this subject are far from satisfactory. Lord Kames affirmed [1] that "polygamy" sprang up in countries where women are treated as inferior beings, and that it can never take place where the two sexes are held to be of equal rank. He adds that for this reason polygamy was

[1] Home 1819, I, 256.

never known among the northern nations of Europe. In confirmation of this statement he mentions that Saxo Grammaticus, who wrote the history of Denmark in the twelfth century, " gives no hint of polygamy even among kings and princes," and that Crantz, in his history of the Saxons, affirms that polygamy was never known among the northern nations of Europe.[1] This observation is confirmed by all other writers, and Scheffer in particular states that neither polygamy nor divorce was ever heard of in Lapland, not even during paganism.

As to polygyny itself, Lord Kames declares[2] it to be an infringement of the law of nature, basing his opinion on the false assumption that, " in all countries and at all times," males and females are equal in number, and supporting it by the consideration that " the God of nature has enforced conjugal society, not only making it agreeable, but by the principle of chastity inherent in our nature." Polygynists would probably answer to the first part of this contention, that they find their conjugal society agreeable, and the second part is scarcely supported by the facts referred to in these pages. The practice of polygyny is traced by Lord Kames to two sources—" first, from savage manners, once universal ; and, next, from voluptuousness in warm climates, which instigates men of wealth to transgress every rule of temperance." On the first of these points he says that the low condition of the female sex among savages and barbarians paved the

---

[1] The Scandinavians, or, at least, the Icelanders, had, in addition to a lawful wife, a recognised concubine. According to Tacitus, moreover, the richer German nobles sometimes had several wives for the purpose of adding to their importance (Mallet 1847, p. 202).

[2] Home 1819, I, 277ff.

way to polygamy. Women by marriage became slaves, and it was the universal practice for a man who parted with his daughter to be a slave to require a valuable consideration for her. Moreover, as a man can purchase as many slaves as he likes, so he can take as many wives as he pleases. Thus " the low condition of woman among barbarians introduced the purchasing them for wives, and, consequently, polygamy."

The answer to this reasoning is twofold—first, wives among savages or barbarians practising polygyny are not always treated as slaves ; and, secondly, fathers selling their daughters for wives do not knowingly sell them into slavery. That the condition of women among the lower races is often not much better than slavery may be granted, but in many cases, as we shall see, it is far otherwise. As to wife purchase, it may be doubted whether the ideas which govern such a transaction are very different from those which guide persons under similar circumstances in monogamatic societies. When the savage buys a girl to be his wife, it is for the purpose of having, if not a companion, a helpmate, and a mother of his children, and her father parts with her for those objects. Probably the treatment the woman will receive from her husband is not considered by any one, and it will depend in great measure on her own conduct. The other source of polygyny mentioned by Lord Kames, opulence in a hot climate, is a true one, but it is evidently not the efficient cause of polygyny as a developed system among the lower races.

Very little light has been thrown by more modern writers on the causes which have led to the development of systematic polygyny. Sir John Lubbock has treated the matter incidentally but not exhaustively.

He says[1] that the relations existing between husband
and wife in the lower races of man are sufficient to
remove all surprise at the prevalence of polygyny
(polygamy). He supposes that much influence must
be ascribed to other causes. Thus, "in all tropical
regions girls become marriageable very young; their
beauty is acquired early, and soon fades, while men,
on the contrary, retain their full powers much longer.
Hence, when love depends, not on a similarity of
tastes, pursuits, or sympathies, but entirely on external
attractions,[2] we cannot wonder that every man who is
able to do so provides himself with a succession of
favourites, even when the first wife remains not only
nominally the head, but really his confidant and
adviser." We appear to have here, in other terms, the
two causes of polygyny given by Lord Kames, that is,
the lower condition of women leading through wife-
purchase to polygyny, and the voluptuousness which
induces the wealthy to acquire a plurality of wives.
Sir John Lubbock gives another cause for polygyny
which undoubtedly is often operative, the length of
time which, among some peoples not having domesti-
cated animals, elapses between the birth of a child and
its being weaned. We shall have occasion to refer
again to this point.

Dr Morgan says little directly as to the origin of
polygyny. When criticising Dr M'Lennan's views as
to the prevalence of polyandry, he remarks[3] that the
Malayan, Turanian, and Ganowanian systems of consanguinity and affinity "bring to light forms of polygyny and polyandry which have influenced human

[1] Lubbock 1875, p. 112.

[2] The attractions most valued by a savage are sometimes of
a peculiar character.   [3] Morgan 1877, p. 517.

affairs, because they were as universal in prevalence as these systems were, when they respectively came into existence." In the Malayan system, the marital group was formed of men living in polygyny and of women living in polyandry. In the other systems, punalua was found in either of two forms, in one of which the group was founded on the brotherhood of the husbands, and in the other it was based on the sisterhood of the wives. These systems, says Dr Morgan, exhibit "the forms of polygyny and polyandry with which ethnology is concerned." According to this view, we may regard polygyny as a relic of one phase of the punalua system, and we shall expect to find it most prevalent among the peoples showing traces of that phase, that is, the Turanian and the American (Ganowanian) families. As to the former, it is undoubtedly true that polygyny is very widely spread, but, if what has been said above is correct, chiefly of the kind which allows a man to have several concubines in addition to his legal wife. As to the latter, Dr Morgan affirms[1] that polygyny is allowed by usage among the American aborigines generally. He adds, however, that it was never prevalent to any considerable extent, from the inability of persons to support more than one family. When it was practised the additional wives were usually the sisters of the first wife, to whom a man was entitled on marrying the eldest daughter in a family. Dr Morgan's theory does not, however, offer any explanation of the existence of polygyny among peoples outside of the Malayan, Turanian, and Ganowanian stocks, and probably in all those cases its origin must be traced to special causes independent of any earlier system of marriage. If so, there is no reason why

[1] *Ibid.*, p. 161.

polygyny should in any case be dependent on any such system.

Even if we admit that polygyny may in some cases be a relic of an earlier phase of punalua, other causes may be assigned for its prevalence among many of the peoples who at one time practised it, if they do so no longer. Those causes are, *first*, the sterility of the first wife ; *secondly*, the length of time during which a woman suckles her child ; *thirdly*, the sexual requirements of man while leading a hunting or pastoral mode of life ; *fourthly*, the accidental scarcity of men ; and, *fifthly*, the luxury or sensuality of man, or the desire for influence and power. That in nearly all these cases the polygynous habit is associated with the practice of wife purchase is not improbable. The fact has an important bearing on the effect of that habit on the condition of woman and society. As to the first of these causes of polygyny, the *sterility* of the first wife, we have an illustration of this in the history of Jacob.[1] The Hebrew patriarch had married Leah and Rachel, the two daughters of Laban, his mother's brother. Leah bore children, but Rachel was barren, and being envious of her sister, she gave Jacob her handmaid to wife. This example was followed afterwards by Leah when she ceased to bear children. The polygyny of the Chinese is in most cases connected with the want of children, the second wife usually being taken with the consent of the first wife when she is childless.[2] This circumstance is, as we shall see in the next chapter, a sufficient ground of divorce

[1] Gen. 29, 30.

[2] According to Archdeacon Gray, the strong desire for offspring, and especially for male offspring, is a chief cause of Chinese polygyny (1878, I, 184).

among the Chinese, and with the Japanese it justifies
the repudiation of a wife without the allowance of anything for her support. The Hindoos also are allowed
to marry a second wife if the first one continues childless after long cohabitation. It is strange that the
Juangs, one of the most primitive of the hill tribes of
India, practise polygyny only where a man has no
family by his first wife. Such is the case also among
some of the Esquimaux tribes. Polygyny, on the
ground simply of a wife's childlessness, would probably
be more common if sterility were not so usual a ground
of divorce. That condition may lead to polygyny in
an indirect manner, as where a man dies without
children, and, in accordance with a custom already
sanctioned, his brother or other relation, who has
already a wife, takes his widow to raise up children
to him.

A *second* cause of polygyny is the long period during
which women among the lower races suckle their children, and probably it has been one of the most prolific
sources of polygyny. Dr Livingstone referred to the
prevalence among the African peoples of the habit,
which was known to the ancient Egyptians, as appears
from the discourse of the scribe Ani, who reminds his
son that his mother had suckled him for three years.[1]
Dobritzhoffer remarks, in relation to the Abipones of
Paraguay, that "the mothers suckle their children for
three years, during which time they have no conjugal
intercourse with their husbands, who, tired of this long
delay, often marry another wife." In Fiji the relatives
of a woman would consider it a public insult if, before
her child is weaned, at the end of the customary three
or four years, another child were born.[2] Among the

[1] Lenormant 1868, III, 142.
[2] Seemann 1862, p. 191.

Chinese similar ideas are current, but a man is expected to cease cohabitation with his wife when she has conceived. Any violation of this rule is supposed not only to cause the child to become sickly, but to provoke the displeasure of the ancestors, and bring misfortune on all the members of the family. Archdeacon Gray refers to the case of a young Chinese gentleman being severely chastised by his parents for a violation of the rule of abstinence.[1] It would be surprising if, under such circumstances, polygyny were not indulged in, and probably in the custom of husband and wife remaining apart until a child had been weaned, originated the practice of concubinage. This is distinct from the marriage of secondary or inferior wives, and may have originated in a wife's "handmaid" temporarily taking the place of her mistress, the children of the handmaid being treated as those of the wife if the latter has none of her own, as in the case of Bilhah, the handmaid of Rachel.[2]

A *third* source of polygyny has sometimes been the inequality of the sexes. Where men are more numerous than women, polyandry may result, and if the opposite state of things should occur there may be the practice of polygyny. Mention has already been made of the Median mode of repairing the loss of population by compelling men to take several wives. An analogous case is said to have occurred in Iceland less than two hundred years ago. Lord Kames mentions this fact, as showing

[1] Grey 1878, I, 184.

[2] As to the "law of uncleanness" after child-bearing, etc., see Lev. 12 : 2 *et seq.;* 15 : 19 *et seq.* The law of uncleanness is acted on almost universally. As to the ancient Persians, see Fontane (1881*b*, p. 115).

that if shame, consequent on the loss of chastity, is removed, the natural appetite will prevail. He says, " In the year 1707, a contagious distemper having carried off a large proportion of the inhabitants of Iceland, the King of Denmark fell on a device to repeople the country, which succeeded to his wish. A law was made authorising young women in that island to have bastards, even to the number of six, without wounding their reputation. The young women were so zealous to repeople their country, that after a few years it was found proper to abrogate the law." [1] The greater number of women than of men among the Jenadies of Southern India is the reason assigned for the practice by them of polygyny; and a similar state of things, which might easily be brought about by the ravages of war, would, under the conditions of savage life, nearly always lead to the same practice. Such is, indeed, said by Mr Catlin [2] to have been the case with the natives of North America, among whom, owing to constant warfare, men were much less numerous than women.

A *fourth* source of polygyny may be found in the exigences of a wandering life. Reference has already been made [3] to M. Fontane's suggestion that in ancient Egypt a traveller might have a family or a wife in

[1] Home 1819, I, 281. Lord Kames states also that in Wales and in the Highlands of Scotland, it was scarce a disgrace for a young woman to have a bastard, and he refers to other cases of unchastity before marriage. That lenient feeling appears to have been less shown in Lowland Scotland than in England, if we may accept the statement of Mr. Thos. De Quincey when speaking of the Dalesmen of Westmoreland (1854, p. 112).

[2] Catlin 1876, I, 118.

[3] Above, p. 192.

every city where he sojourned. On the same principle
the pastoral life was, according to Mr Fenton,[1] accompanied by polygyny among the early Hebrews. We
may thus explain much that is strange in the social
relations of the Esquimaux, who exhibit marriage in
most of its phases, and in the marital system of the
Australians, which provides every man with a wife,
as every woman with a husband, wherever they may
be.

The *fifth* and last source of polygyny to be referred to, is the desire for more than one wife which
distinguishes peoples all over the world, arising not
from the causes hitherto mentioned, but from various
motives, such as the love of wealth or influence which
are supposed to attend the possession of several wives
or a numerous progeny, or the cravings of sensual
appetite. The last named motive is dwelt on by
Lord Kames as one of the chief causes of polygyny.
He says, that in hot climates men have " a burning
appetite for animal enjoyment ; and women become
old and lose the prolific quality at an age which
carries them little beyond the prime of life in a
temperate climate." He adds, "These circumstances
dispose men of opulence to purchase their wives, that
they may not be confined to one ; and purchase they
must ; for no man, without a valuable consideration,
will surrender his daughter to be one of many who
are destined to gratify the carnal appetite of a single
man." Unfortunately for this argument, it is by no
means unusual in some countries for the harems of
the great to be recruited by gift rather than by purchase. Thus, in Cambodia,[2] it is not uncommon for

[1] Fenton 1880, p. 13.
[2] Moura 1882–83, I, 344.

the father of a family to offer one of his daughters
to a great personage in acknowledgment of some
favour he has received. The *mi-kha* or concubines
of this sort are better regarded than others, and often
they receive the title of *propon* wives. In Uganda [1]
the governors of districts present their pretty daughters
to the king, who on the other hand rewards them by
presents of a similar description, a custom practised
also in Siam. In Uganda many men obtain wives
by exchanging daughters with each other. This is
not an unusual mode of proceeding in different parts
of the world. The perpetuation of the monopoly of
women enjoyed to a great extent by the older men
of the tribe among the Australians is, according to
Mr Howitt,[2] "encouraged by those interested in it
having sisters or daughters to exchange with each
other for wives." It is aided, moreover, by the
custom of betrothal when girls are very young, and
even mere infants, which "occurs all over Australia
in tribes whose customs prove them to stand low
down as regards other tribes in social development."
That plan, if fully carried out, would result in a
perfect monopoly of wives, but it would also secure
for the females marriage with husbands whom their
father and friends approved of. The custom of betrothal is very widely spread among peoples of all
degrees of culture, polygynous and otherwise, and
although it is often associated with wife purchase,
it generally supposes a certain degree of preference
on the part of one or both of the persons affianced.
The fact is that the connection between wife purchase and polygyny is purely accidental. The former

[1] Above, p. 191.
[2] Fison and Howitt 1880, p. 355.

practice is prevalent also among polyandrous races, and the latter might exist quite as widely if wives were obtained otherwise than by purchase. A woman is sold to her husband by her father or relations in pursuance of the natural right they claim to her and her offspring, and not because she is to become a victim to a man's arbitrary will or passions. The higher the price paid for her the more highly is she considered by herself and her neighbours.

It by no means follows, moreover, that because a rich man in a hot climate has several wives, he acquires them through a burning appetite for animal enjoyment. Where this is the case it will be chiefly among peoples who practise concubinage rather than polygyny proper. The desire for wealth and influence is, however, as strong in the East as in the West, and it has probably more to do with the practice of poly-gyny than the love of pleasure. Thus, in Fiji, a man's social position depends on the number of his wives.[1] Again, among the New Zealanders, the number of a man's wives adds to his importance, "each having her own mara, or farm, and retainers, according to her rank ; and furnishing her share of the supplies for the establishment. When a chief had several wives he could then entertain guests without fear of scarcity, and this was a sign of greatness."[2] A similar testimony is borne by Catlin in relation to the North American Indians, who desire a plurality of wives owing to the advantage to be gained by having a "stock of labourers" by whom a man's wealth may be increased.[3] On the Asiatic continent the same

[1] Pritchard 1866, p. 372.
[2] Taylor 1870, p. 337.
[3] Catlin 1876, I, 118.

ideas prevail. Among some of the Abor tribes the number of a man's wives is held to be a test of his wealth and consequence.[1] Such is also said to be a chief cause of polygyny among the Malagasy. Wealth and influence attends the possession not of wives only, but also of children. The desire for offspring, and indeed for a numerous progeny, has always affected the Eastern mind. The "quiver full of arrows" was a joy to the Hebrew, especially if the arrows were boys, as it enabled him to "meet the enemy in the gate." It was the same also among the early Aryans, and although the desire was not associated with any special phase of marriage, it might in many cases be a strong motive in favour of polygyny. Whatever effect this custom may have on the general population, there is no doubt that under it men often have very large families.[2]

That polygyny is usually attended by a degrading influence on the condition of woman is probably true on the whole. Lord Kames gives,[3] after Gumilla, the pathetic complaint made by an Indian woman when asked why she had destroyed her female infant. After describing the miserable lot of the Indian wife, she said, "A young wife is brought in upon us, who is permitted to abuse us and our children, because we are no longer regarded." It can hardly be denied, moreover, that polygyny is often attended with deleterious social effects through the artificial scarcity of wives, caused by the monopoly of women, or by the high value set upon them. Thus, among the Aus-

[1] Rowney 1882, p. 163.

[2] The Egyptian King, Ramses II, is said to have had 170 children, of whom 69 were sons (Fontane 1882, p. 363).

[3] Home 1819, I, 288.

tralian aborigines, the monopoly of women by the old
men is accountable for some of the objectionable incidents connected with their marriage system.　In
ancient Arabia the prices asked for women under the
name of *mahr*, the dowry paid to the wife's father or
kin, were often so high that many men could not
afford to have a wife, and consequently they resorted
to *zina* "fornication."[1]　According to another writer,
polygyny results "in the subordination, if not degradation, of the female sex, especially with peoples who, like
the Hebrews and Arabs, have a class of secondary or
slave wives."[2]　On the Gold Coast, polygyny appears
to be employed for a peculiar purpose.　It is customary
for the wealthy classes to keep a number of women as
wives, some of whom are "pawns" and slaves, and it
is notorious, says Mr Brodie Cruickshank,[3] that many
of these women are maintained for the express purpose
of "ensnaring the unsuspecting with their blandish-
ments, and carry on their infamous trade with the
connivance of their husbands."　They are thus instru-
mental in consigning "a numerous body of victims to
bondage."　The practice here condemned is not unusual
among peoples of a low degree of culture, but it is
seldom met with under so complicated a form.

That we may be able to judge as to the actual
operation of polygyny, as compared with other primitive systems of marriage, it is advisable to give some
information as to the position assigned to women
among peoples of a low degree of culture.　It has
been shown that the aborigines of Australia present
in their "group marriage" the nearest approach to
the most simple phase of the law of marriage.　Among

[1] Above, p. 98.　　　　　　　　[2] Fenton 1880, p. 13.
[3] Cruickshank 1835, I, 325.

them, also, woman is probably at a point of degradation lower than in any other part of the world. In
South Australia the native woman is said[1] to be
"an absolute slave. She is treated with the greatest
cruelty and indignity, has to do all laborious work,
and to carry all the burthens. For the slightest
offence or dereliction of duty she is beaten with a
waddy or a yam stick, and not unfrequently speared.
The records of the Supreme Court of Adelaide furnish
numberless instances of blacks being tried for murder-
ing their lubras. The woman's life is of no account
if her husband chooses to destroy it, and no one ever
attempts to protect or take her part under any circumstances. . . . The condition of the native woman is
wretched and miserable in the extreme ; in fact, in no
savage nation of which there is any record can it be
worse."

The Polynesian Islanders, who in their *punalua*
had a modified phase of group marriage, differed
somewhat among themselves in their treatment of
the female sex. In New Zealand, when the island
was first discovered, women were "looked upon as
beings calculated for the mere satisfaction of brutal
appetites, nor treated better than beasts of burden,
without being allowed to have the least will of their
own." Boys would even throw stones at their mothers,
or beat them without their fathers' interference.[2] Dr
Forster remarks, that the females at Tanna, Mallicollo,
and New Caledonia were not in a much happier condition than those of New Zealand, "as they were
obliged to carry burdens, and take upon themselves

[1] Woods 1879, p. 17.
[2] Forster 1778, p. 418.

every laborious and toilsome part of domestic business." It would appear to have been the same on the Sandwich Islands. Here women of all ranks were subject to oppressive *tabus,* in accordance with which they could not eat with men; "their houses and their labours were distinct; their aliment was separately prepared. A female child from birth to death was allowed no food that had touched its father's dish." Many kinds of food were forbidden to women, and whatever was savoury or pleasant was reserved for man's own use. Mr Jarves asserts[1] that the Hawaiian woman "was excused from no labours, excepting such as were altogether too arduous for her weaker frame. When young and beautiful a victim of sensuality; when old and useless, of brutality." He might justly say that her lot was worse than that of her sex generally in the Southern islands. In Tahiti and the Society Islands women were never allowed to eat with men, and Dr Forster regarded this custom as a relic of a state of subjection in which women were there formerly held. He states,[2] however, that in those islands women were permitted to mix in all societies, and to converse freely with everybody without distinction, and that their sweetness of temper and winning manner secures them "a just and moderate influence in domestic and even public affairs." The female sex were found to be on an equality with men also in the Friendly Islands and the Marquesas; and such would appear to be the case also in Samoa, where the women are held in much consideration, are treated with great attention, and are supposed not to do anything but what justly

[1] Jarves 1843, p. 84.
[2] Forster 1778, p. 422.

belongs to them.[1] The social position of the female sex in the Polynesian Islands is thus seen to have been on the whole much superior to that of women among the Australians. Dr Forster asserts [2] that monogamy was almost universally practised by the peoples of the South Seas, and it is not surprising, therefore, that when such was the case, women were more highly esteemed.

Among the allied race of Madagascar, although women " are not reduced to the humiliating state of degradation in which they are found among some uncivilised portions of the human race," yet they are far from being treated as the equal of man. Woman is there, says the Rev. Wm. Ellis,[3] " held in esteem chiefly as the creature of his caprice and ungoverned passions, or of his sordid and heartless avarice." The Malagasy husband had almost absolute power of divorce, and where this followed on a dispute which led to the wife running away to her parents or relations, he often treated her personally with extreme cruelty, and exercised his power in such a manner as to prevent her ever marrying again. Mr Ellis ascribed [4] the frequency of divorce among the Malagasy to the domestic disputes and jealousies arising from the practice of polygyny,[5] of which it is one of the great evils, and he states that it is attended by envy, hatred, and interminable family resentments, waste of property and frequent litigation, making polygyny a

[1] Wilkes 1849, II, 148.
[2] Forster 1778, p. 424.
[3] Ellis 1838, I, 174.   [4] *Ibid.*, p. 171.
[5] This is the chief objection to polygyny named by Peschel, who says, "Even in ordinary families envy and jealousy estrange the children of different mothers" (1876, p. 222).

curse to the land. A similar result attends this practice among the East Africans, particularly the chiefs, to which, says Capt. Speke,[1] is to be traced the wars which disorganise the country, as half-brothers quarrel among themselves and fight for the right of succession to their father. Here, as in Western Africa, women are considered property. Wife purchase is, indeed, the rule with all the dark races of Africa, and in too many cases women are, as stated by Du Chaillu,[2] treated more harshly than slaves. What their condition must have been in Northern Africa before the spread of Mohammedanism may be judged of by the benefits conferred on women by that religion. Mr Winwood Reade[3] says : "Women can no longer be married by a great chief in herds, and treated like beasts of burden and like slaves. Each wife has an equal part of her husband's love by law, it is not permitted to forsake and degrade the old wife for the sake of the young. Each wife has her own house, and the husband may not enter into it until he has knocked at the door and received the answer, *Bismallah,* in the name of God." Among the Ba-ntu tribes of South Africa the first wife appears to have certain pre-eminence.[4] The superiority of the first wife furnishes some amelioration of the evils attendant on the practice of polygyny, but the condition of women generally among the South African tribes is

[1] Speke 1863, p. 18.   [2] Du Chaillu 1861, p. 333.

[3] Reade 1874, p. 282. Mr. Bosworth Smith affirms, however, that polygyny "tends to depress love into an animal passion, and so to unspiritualise all the relations between the sexes" (R. B. Smith 1876, p. 234).

[4] See above, p. 191. This is shown also in the fact that only the chiefs and their principal wives are buried (Thompson 1827, I, 337).

not much better than slavery. The life of a female is but little regarded, and the killing of a wife was formerly too common an occurrence to attract much notice.[1] Among the Zulus young boys were allowed to kill their mothers if they attempted to chastise them.[2] The Kaffirs appear to care less for their women than for their cattle, and by Hottentots and Bosjesmans women are treated as little better than animals. With the Berber tribes of Northern Africa, who are usually monogamous, woman holds a much higher position. According to General Faidherbe,[3] a Berber woman is really a wife, the mother of a family, and not an article of property or a beast of burden, as with the Arabs. The Moors more nearly approach the latter than the former in their treatment of women, whom they look upon as created for their pleasure and caprice, and value in proportion to their stoutness,[4] in pursuance of a notion very common among African peoples.

The position of woman among the polygynous Mongols is much the same as with the generality of African peoples. Wife purchase is fully established among them, and a wife becomes in some sense the slave of her husband. All the hard work of the household, including the tanning of skins and the fulling of cloth, devolves entirely upon her.[5] According to the Rev. James Gilmour, the Mongolian woman works hard and is badly treated. He says,[6]

[1] Moffat 1842, p. 464.
[2] Thompson 1827, II, 418.
[3] Faidherbe 1874.
[4] Durand 1806, IV, 130.
[5] Huc 1851, I, 52, 185.
[6] Gilmour 1883, p. 178.

" Her place in the tent is next the door, the felt she sleeps on is the thinnest and the poorest. . . . She takes little care of herself, and has little care bestowed upon her. An old woman spoke some truth, at least, when she said to me, ' The women are treated like the dogs, which are fed outside the tent.' " It must be added, however, that, according to M. Prjévalskii,[1] wives are the equals of their husbands in private life, although they are seldom consulted in relation to anything which does not concern the household. The Russian traveller says also [2] that the Tangoutes, who present in every respect a strong contrast to the Mongols, allow women equal rights with themselves. It is very different with the Ostiaks, who also allow polygyny. This Turkic people sell their girls to the highest bidder, and treat their women as slaves. Castren relates [3] that when among them he was frequently roused from sleep by the cries of ill-used women, and sometimes a man would literally beat his wife to death.

The Asiatic peoples referred to trace descent preferably in the male line, but if we consider the condition of women among the American tribes, who usually have female kinship, we do not find it much improved. Throughout both North and South America wives are purchased by the giving of presents,[4] and generally they occupy a position of great hardship, and their lives are spent in the most laborious drudgery.[5] Moreover, they have no power of divorce,

[1] Prjévalskii 1880, p. 47.
[2] *Ibid.*, p. 207.
[3] Castren 1856, p. 56.
[4] Catlin 1876, II, 233 ; Lafitau 1724, I, 565.
[5] Catlin 1876, II, 229.

which is the privilege of the husband, who also can take a second wife if he wishes. A man dare not, however, ill-treat his wife, and, apart from actual divorce, she appears to have nearly as much freedom of conduct as the husband himself.[1] The condition of women among the American tribes is thus more favourable than among some tribes of a similar degree of culture; but, on the whole, the hardships complained of by the Indian wife on the banks of the Orinoco are common to her native sisters of both North and South America. Cranz says of the Greenland women,[2] that after all they "have a hard and almost slavish life of it. While they are little, or as long as they tarry with their parents, they are in an agreeable condition enough. But from their twentieth year to their death, their life is a concatenation of fear, indigence, and lamentation."

Nevertheless, it must not be thought that where polygyny is practised the condition of woman is always one of hardship and degradation. The predatory races of Central and Western Asia are chiefly Mohammedans, and therefore polygynists, at least in theory, and whether their religion or their general culture is the source of the improvement, there is no doubt that with them woman occupies a higher social position than with the Mongolian peoples. Elsewhere[3] I have written concerning these races:—"That wives should continue to be acquired by purchase in accordance with the practice of most primitive peoples is not to be wondered at, seeing that the marriage price

[1] Lafitau 1724, I, 584ff.
[2] Cranz 1767, I, 165.
[3] Wake 1878, I, 375. See authorities there cited.

is too valuable a property to be hastily abandoned by a parent. Marriage has ceased, however, to be a mere bargain and sale, and the wife, instead of being little better than a slave, has become the companion of her husband. Among the Afghans a man may, by cutting off a lock of his sweetheart's hair, snatching away her veil, or throwing a sheet over her, declaring at the same time that she is his affianced wife, secure her as his wife, although he must pay the usual price for a bride. Marriages of affection are by no means rare, and the sentiment of love appears to be strongly developed among them, most of their songs and tales speaking of it in the most glowing and romantic language. Elopements and secret engagements, where a man has not sufficient property to purchase the object of his affections, are not uncommon. The tender passion having so much to do with the union of the sexes, it is hardly surprising that wives often exercise great influence in the household, the husband, indeed, sometimes sinking into a secondary place. Marriages founded on the affections are no less common with the predatory Toorkmans, owing no doubt to the freedom of intercourse allowed between the sexes, and the necessity of paying a high price for a bride leads also among them to frequent elopements. . . . As with the Afghans and Toorkmans, women among the Bedouins enjoy a considerable degree of liberty, and hence, although wealth frequently overbalances in the eyes of parents the claims of affection, their marriages are often governed by choice. Burckhardt goes so far as to say that the Bedouins are perhaps the only Eastern people who can be entitled lovers. This we have seen to be incorrect, but that marriages of affection are not rare, among the Syrian Bedouins at least, may be inferred from the fact that they think it scandalous to demand the 'daughter's price.' Moreover, woman is highly respected, and is treated after marriage as a companion rather than as a slave. The respect is exemplified by the fact that, if a homicide can succeed in concealing his head under the sleeve of a woman and cry *fy ardhék* ('under thy protection'), his safety is insured."

Although the practice of polyandry is more repugnant to the feelings of an European than that of polygyny, the former system is less degrading than the latter to women. This is necessarily so under the conditions of the so-called "ruder polyandry" of the Nairs, in which a woman after marriage continues to live with her mother, brothers, and sisters, and the household, owing to the operation of the rule of female kinship, is controlled by females.[1] Here, says M. Elie Reclus, "the mother reigns and governs. She has for first minister in the house her eldest daughter, who transmits her orders to all her little world. Formerly, on state occasions, the reigning prince himself gave place to his eldest daughter. With much more reason he recognised the supremacy of his mother, in whose presence he never dared to seat himself until she had given him permission. Such was the rule in the palace and in the most humble dwelling. Brothers obey their eldest sister, respect their younger ones, with whom during their early youth they avoid being alone, through fear of forgetting themselves."[2]

With the Todas, whose sexual relations partake of

[1] We shall see, when treating of female kinship, that among the non-polyandrous Basques the wife is the head of the household.

[2] Reclus 1885, p. 195.

the group marriage of the Australians and the polyandry of the Tibetans, the condition of woman is
hardly less favourable than with the Nairs. Col.
Marshall states [1] that they hold a position in the family
" quite unlike what is ordinarily witnessed amongst
Oriental nations. They are treated with respect, and
are permitted a remarkable amount of freedom. They
perform the legitimate offices of women in Europe ;
tending children, cooking the family meals, bringing
water from the spring, and cleaning the house and
premises." Men and women do not eat together at
home ; the adult males usually eating first, and then
the adult females, the children of both sexes having
their meals either with the men or with the women.[2]
This may be, however, only a matter of convenience,
and not a sign of inferiority on the part of the woman,
as a wife never bows down before her husband to do
the *Adabuddiken* greeting,[3] although she performs the
ceremony before her father-in-law, mother-in-law, and
her husband's elder brother. The ceremony is never
performed by one man to another, but women do it to
men and to other women older or superior to themselves.

The polyandry of Tibet has no more degrading effect
on the condition of the female sex than that of the
Todas. The influence of that custom on the manners
of the Tibetans cannot be injurious, if it be true, as
stated by Capt. Turner,[4] that they are distinguished
for humanity and gentleness of disposition. This
writer says of them, " Without being servilely officious,

---

[1] Marshall 1873, p. 43. [2] *Ibid.*, p. 82.

[3] The woman crouches down before the person she is saluting, who places first the right foot and then the left foot on
her head.

[4] G. Turner 1861, p. 350.

they are always obliging; the higher ranks are unassuming; the inferior, respectful in their behaviour.
Nor are they at all deficient in attention to the female
sex; but, as we find them moderate in all their passions,
in this respect also their conduct is equally remote from
rudeness and adulation. Comparatively with their
southern neighbours, the women of Tibet enjoy an
elevated station in society. To the privileges of unbounded liberty, the wife here adds the character of
mistress of the family and companion of her husbands."
It is possible that the position of woman in Tibet has
been beneficially affected by the teachings of Buddhism. Such has undoubtedly been the case in some
other countries; but the mild disposition of the peoples
among whom that religion has been established is
probably chiefly accountable for the social elevation
of woman, so far as this is not directly referable to the
system of polyandry itself.

It would be surprising if under the social conditions
found to exist among polygynous peoples, especially
where wife purchase is established, a man did not
exercise considerable authority over his wife and her
offspring. This would be justified on the ground that
a man's wife is his "property," and the property right
acquired by purchase would extend to the women's
children. If a man has several wives under these
conditions, his authority is enlarged, and he may
become the head of a numerous household or of a
series of households. We have an example of this
in the *patriarchal family*, which, in the system of
Dr Morgan,[1] is founded upon the marriage of one man
with several wives, followed, in general, by the seclusion of the wives. Morgan remarks,[2] however, that,

[1] Morgan 1877, p. 384.   [2] *Ibid.*, p. 465.

although the chiefs lived in polygyny, this was not
the material principle of the patriarchal institution.
" The organization of a number of persons, bond and
free, into a family, under patriarchal power, for the
purpose of holding lands, and for the care of flocks
and herds, was the essential characteristic of this
family. Those held in servitude, and those employed
as servants, lived in the marriage relation, and, with
the patriarch as their chief, formed a patriarchal family.
Authority over its members and over its property was
the material fact. It was the incorporation of members in servile and dependent relations, before that
time unknown, rather than polygyny, that stamped the
patriarchal family with the attributes of an original
institution." This is true, and it is true also that
the institution became fully established only under a
monandrous system of marriage, but the patriarchal
family had its greatest development under the fostering
influence of polygyny, and the wife purchase with
which the latter is usually connected. This view may
be supported by reference to the patriarchal family as
established among certain African peoples. Mr Cruickshank gives a graphic description of the formation of
patriarchal authority among the negroes of Western
Africa."[1] The acknowledged head of a family possesses the right to dispose of his descendants and
collateral relations as he may think fit; "they are,
in fact, so much property, which he can sell, pawn, or
give away at his pleasure." The foundation of this
right is very properly found in the nature of African
marriage as wife purchase. The father purchased a
wife for his son, and thus acquired the right of a
master over their offspring; "while he united his

[1] Cruickshank 1835, I, 311ff.

daughter, failing any suitable collateral relation, to a favourite slave, perhaps, or allowed her to cohabit with an adopted son or friend, upon conditions which secured to him an addition to the consequence of his house in their children." In the absence of an actual sale of the female, the children of the marriage are subject to the authority and disposal of the head of the mother's relations. But even in this case the mother and her offspring may become the "pawns" of the husband, as security for advances made by him to his wife's family, and the pawn bond may be converted by proper formalities into a distinct sale. On the Gold Coast wealth in slaves and dependents is considered the most desirable species of riches, and means of all kinds are adopted for increasing their number. This is true generally all the world over wherever the conditions of the patriarchal family are developed, although probably the means employed for strengthening the family group are seldom so objectionable as those ascribed to the natives of West Africa.

Further consideration of the patriarchal family will be reserved until the next chapter, and this may be fitly brought to a close by reference to the question which has been raised, as to whether the practice of polygyny or polyandry has any effects on the relative number of male and female births. It has been asserted that more male children are born where polyandry is established, and more females where polygyny is the rule. If there were such a law on this, we should expect to find that with monogamy there would be an equality of male and female births. As a fact, however, there is a preponderance of male births among European peoples, although owing to an excessive death rate among male children, combined with other causes affecting the adults, it is found that there are considerably more females than males in all old settled countries where statistical records have been kept.[1] The preponderance of male births among the monogamous peoples of Europe could be connected with polyandry only on the assumption that the ancestors of these peoples were polyandrous. This inference might perhaps be allowable, if it could be shown that a preponderance of male births always accompanies polyandry. Col. Marshall, indeed, affirms[2] that among the polyandrous Todas males of all ages bear to the females the proportion of 100 to 75, and that the paucity of females can be accounted for only by acknowledging " either that infanticide is, or has recently been practised to a very sensible extent, or that more boys are *born* than girls." Until a comparatively recent date, female infanticide was largely resorted to by the Todas, but Col. Marshall does not see in this fact the explanation of the smaller number of females. He prefers to believe that owing to the practice of female infanticide, there is formed a bias in favour of males which strengthens with each generation until families " grow to have habitually more sons than daughters. This habitude outlasting the depraved practice which caused it, indurates, more or less, into a fixed characteristic of the people, and a male-producing variety of man is formed."[3] This is ascribed rather to infanticide than to polyandry, but it would not be safe to make any general inference from the social phenomena of Toda life. A similar paucity of female births is met with among the Jews of some parts of Europe. Moreover, there is reason to believe that

[1] Darwin 1871, I, 301. [2] Marshall 1873, p. 110.
[3] *Ibid.*, p. 111.

a larger proportion of male births take place whatever the form of marriage.

Statistics have been furnished by Mr John Sanderson, of the number of children born in the polygynous marriages of the Kafirs of Natal.[1] Of fifteen households, two, which embraced nineteen marriages, had an equal proportion of children of each sex; while in twenty-five marriages the boys were in excess, and in ten only were there more girls than boys. Here female infanticide appears not to have been practised, the weak and ailing, and perhaps twins, alone being destroyed. Statistics collected by Mr James Campbell in Siam,[2] where polygyny is the rule, show that instead of female births preponderating, as we should expect if polyandry is accompanied by an excess of male births, the proportion of the sexes is nearly the same as at Berlin. The male birth rate in Siam is, therefore, higher than it is in Great Britain. Dr Darwin mentions[3] in connection with this subject, that hardly any animal has been rendered so highly polygamous as the English race-horses, and that their male and female offspring are almost exactly equal in number, although some mares, as some women, produce more of one sex than of the other. Why this should be we do not know, and possibly the causes, whatever they are, or other causes equally unknown, which produce a disproportion of the sexes with some women, may operate more generally, so as to give a similar disproportion in some races.

[1] Sanderson 1879, p. 254.
[2] James Campbell 1870, p. 192.
[3] Darwin 1871, I, 303.

CHAPTER VII.

In tracing the developments of the law of marriage, we found that its earliest systematic expression was the *group marriage*, which is still in active operation among the aborigines of Australia. Each of the Australian tribes was originally divided into two exogamous intermarrying classes, or groups ·of persons related, actually or theoretically, among themselves through descent from a common female ancestor. Marriage within the group was not allowed, but, *in theory,* all the male members of one class were collectively married to all the female members of the other class. In practice, the marital relations between the two classes, or the sub-groups into which they are now usually divided, are very complex. A simpler form of group marriage is the *punalua* of the Polynesians, which has two phases, in one of which several brothers have their wives in common, and in the other several sisters have their husbands in common. It is not necessary that all the members of the intermarrying groups should reside together, and, in fact, among the Australian aborigines, while every individual belonging to the intermarrying groups is recognised as the husband or wife of some other members, each man or woman may cohabit temporarily with other members of the group to which they do not belong. Moreover, if either group is reduced to a single individual, a corresponding change will take place in the form of the marriage itself. Thus, where one female is married to a group of men, we have *polyandry* of the true or Tibetan type, in which all the husbands are brothers, and of the so-called Nair type, in which the members of the male group are usually strangers in blood. Where one man is married to a group of women, we have, if the wives are sisters, the simple *polygyny* formerly largely practised by the American peoples; while, if the members of the female group are strangers in blood, we have the advanced polygyny of the Asiatic and African peoples. If each of the intermarrying groups is replaced by a single individual, *monandry*,[1] or individual marriage, takes the place of primitive group marriage.

A little consideration will show that monandry may arise among peoples addicted to any of the earlier systems of marriage. Thus, the rights associated with group marriage or punalua may be denied by an individual to the other members of the marital group, or may be tacitly abandoned by them in his favour. We have here the origin of the individual marriage practised by the more advanced Australian tribes, and perhaps also by some of the islanders of the Pacific. In polyandry among kinsmen, the first or principal husband may decline to let his kinsmen share in the wife he has obtained, or they may consent not to press their right to join in the marital bond; in which case we should have the individual marriage of the Kandyans of Ceylon, and of some other previously polyandrous peoples of Asia. In the so-called polyandry

[1] This term is used by Dr. McLennan, but "monogamy" would be preferable if this term were not required for a still more developed phase of marriage.

of the Nair type, the same result would follow if the woman restricted herself to the companionship of one man. This would give the individual marriage of the early Arabs, when they were not compelled by poverty to practise " fornication," or to be satisfied with a share in a wife. Again, among a people allowing the polygyny in which the wives form a related group, a man may decline, or not be able through poverty, to take his wife's sisters, or they may be refused to him, which is often the case among the American aborigines, who have the pairing family. Finally, where the later form of polygyny is practised, a man may determine not to take more than one wife, or to have slave wives or concubines, which would give rise to individual marriage, as often met with among Asiatic and other peoples who are not usually regarded as monandrous.

Notwithstanding the fact that individual marriage may exist alongside of group marriage, polyandry, or polygyny, its existence under such conditions must be regarded as exceptional, and in some sense accidental. The poverty which furnishes the true explanation of polyandry may cease, and this practice may give place to monandry, or even polygyny ; while, on the other hand, the pressure of poverty may cause monandry to take the place of polygyny, or rather prevent a plurality of wives being indulged in, if, indeed, it does not lead to the practice of polyandry. Such changes in the economic conditions of society cannot be regarded as furnishing a sufficient explanation of the origin of systematic monandry, which could be produced by *both* wealth and poverty, only under totally different social conditions in each case. Possibly, however, that origin must be sought, not in the material surroundings of the persons preferring individual marriage, but in ideas formed consequent on the development of mental culture.

It has been suggested by Sir Henry Maine that liberty of divorce may have been one of the causes of the transition in some societies from polygamy to individual marriage, where it was not effected under the influence of religion ; and he affirms[1] that " the monogamy of the modern and western world is, in fact, the monogamy of the Romans, from which the license of divorce has been expelled by Christian morality." The existence of individual marriage has, however, first to be accounted for, and the infrequency of divorce among the Romans in the early·period of their history, at least where marriage had been contracted in its most solemn form,[2] proves that some powerful influence must have been at work long before the introduction of Christianity. That influence, which operated with all the civilised nations of antiquity, must have been strong indeed, considering the inducements to the practice of polygyny afforded by the social conditions of Eastern life. These were referred to when treating of the probable causes which led to that practice. Much light ought to be thrown on the question by a consideration of the ideas entertained on the subject of marriage by the Asiatic race who have perpetuated a state of society which doubtless was at one time common to a large part of the civilised world. Archdeacon Gray affirms[3] that the Chinese have always regarded the marriage relation as a personal one,[4] and therefore,

[1] Maine 1875, p. 60.

[2] Dionysius affirms that marriage by *confarrentio* could not be dissolved, but divorce was afterwards allowed (Smith, W. 1842, art. "Divortium").

[3] Gray 1878, I, 184.

[4] The death of a grown-up son or daughter unmarried is

in theory at least, they are monandrists. The rule
thus enforced by morality is strictly enforced in some
of the northern provinces of China, especially in that
of Shantung, but in other parts polygyny is not uncommon. It is not considered respectable, however,
to take a *tsiĕ*, or handmaid bought with money, if a
man has sons by his wife, and every additional *tsiĕ*
he takes sinks him in the estimation of his friends.[1] If
we may believe the Abbe Huc,[2] concubines were formerly allowed only to mandarins and to men of forty
years of age who had no children. Mr Doolittle suggests[3] that many a man whose life is childless marries
a second or inferior wife, with the consent and appro-
bation of the first one, and while she is living, who
would not have taken such a step in other circumstances. To die without leaving a son to perform the
burial rites,[4] and to offer up the usual sacrifices at the
tomb, " is one of the most direful fates that can over-
take a Chinaman." To prevent this catastrophe he
marries young, and if his wife is childless he either
marries a second wife, or he adopts a child for the
purpose of performing the necessary rites and sacri-

regarded as a deplorable evil, and parents call on their children to marry as soon as they reach the age of puberty. It is
considered a crime not to give female slaves in marriage.
Moreover, marriages are performed between the spirits of
males who die in infancy or boyhood, and those of females
who have also died young. (*Ibid.*, I, 186, 226.)

[1] Edkins 1859, p. 163. Prof. Douglas seems to be in error
in saying that a man must divorce his first wife before taking another (1882, p. 71).
[2] Huc 1855, II, 226.
[3] Doolittle 1868, p. 76.
[4] Douglas 1882, p. 70. If the rites were omitted or improperly performed, the spirit of the dead might lose his
way to the infernal regions (Doolittle 1868, pp. 134ff.).

fices. Mr Doolittle, in referring to the adoption of an
heir to an eldest son, remarks[1] that " it is regarded as
indispensable that there should be some one to burn
incense to the manes of the dead from the eldest son
down to posterity in the direct line of the eldest son,
either by an own child or an adopted child." The
utmost importance is attached by the Chinese to the
worship of the ancestral tablet, which is supposed to
be the *bonâ fide* residence of one of the three spirits of
the departed,[2] and which passes from eldest son to
eldest son, or the son by adoption.

Notwithstanding the advance made by the Chinese
towards monandry, they are more backward in some
other matters connected with social life. Thus, they
still practise the ancient custom of wife-purchase, not
in name, but in the form of marriage presents, including money, which is expended in providing the bride's
outfit.[3] The wife may be said, therefore, to come
under the power of her husband, who has a kind of
property in her. In fact, a wife may be sold, although
probably only with her own consent, and as a wife and
not as a slave. Huc declares,[4] however, that a man
may strike his wife " with impunity, starve her, sell
her, or, what is worse, let her out for a longer or
shorter period, as is a common practice in the province
of Tche-kiang." Her position of inferiority is such
that she has no right to take meals with her husband,
or even with his male children. She " must eat
alone, after they have done, and in a corner; her
food is scanty and coarse, and she would not be
allowed to touch even what is left by her own sons."
Huc declares that the judicial annals are full of

[1] Doolittle 1868, p. 508. [3] *Ibid.*, pp. 49, 51.
[2] *Ibid.*, p. 158.
[4] Huc 1855, I, 248ff.

the most tragical events arising from the perpetual humiliation and wretchedness to which the women of China are reduced, and that the number of female suicides is very considerable.[1] The position formerly assigned to Chinese women may be seen from the " Family Sayings " of Confucius.[2] This sage taught that man is the representative of heaven, and that woman is to obey his instructions—" When young she must obey her father and elder brother; when married she must obey her husband; when her husband is dead she must obey her son. She may not think of marrying a second time. . . . Beyond the threshold of her apartments she should not be known for evil or for good." It is not surprising that the Chinaman has very wide powers of divorce. Confucius gives seven grounds of divorce, of which the first is disobedience to a husband's parents. The other grounds on which a woman may be divorced are, not giving birth to a son, dissolute conduct, jealousy of her husband's attentions to other members of his harem, talkativeness, thieving, to which is added, virulent disease or leprosy. According to Mr Doolittle,[3] however, the last two reasons are not now regarded among educated men as sufficient, and he affirms that very few divorces occur in China.[4] This refers only to the case of a man putting away his wife. The idea of a woman separating from her husband of her own accord would be thought

[1] See Gray 1878, I, 185.
[2] Legge 1869, p. 106.
[3] Doolittle 1868, p. 75.
[4] This hardly agrees with the statement of Archdeacon Gray as to Canton (Gray 1878, I, 220ff.).

ridiculous. There are certain exceptions to the husband's power of divorce, which show considerable
thoughtfulness on the part of Chinese legislators for
the condition of woman. As given by Confucius,[1]
they are : if a wife has no home to return to ; if she
passed with her husband through three years' mourn-
ing for his parents ; and if the husband has during
the marriage become rich from being poor. Probably
on the whole the female married life is usually more
bearable than might be supposed from what has been
said above. Wives " possess equal rank with their
husbands, and are joined with them in the worship
of ancestors. Mothers are allowed a certain degree
of influence over their sons, who are obliged at particular seasons to pay homage to them,[2] and the
emperor himself is not exempt from performing the
ceremonies of the *kotow*. Honorary tablets or portals
are sometimes erected to the memory of virtuous
widows who have obeyed with filial devotion " the
parents of their husbands. Moreover, widows who have
committed suicide on the deaths of their husbands, and
betrothed girls whose husbands have died before the
marriage day, are entitled to have their names recorded on the large general tablets erected in the
temple, which they visit before they commit suicide."[3]

[1] Legge 1869, p. 106. Japanese women are subject to the
same dependence on the male members of the family as
Chinese women, and to unlimited liability of divorce. They
are, however, well educated, and are not required to remain
in seclusion. They join in the "innocent recreations" of their
fathers and husbands, and "the fidelity of the wife and the
purity of the maiden are committed wholly to their own
sense of honour" (Busk 1841, p. 170).
[2] Huc 1855, I, 21 ; Gray 1878, I, 234.
[3] Doolittle 1868, p. 78.

We have seen that "impropriety" is the ground on which the having a plurality of wives is condemned by the Chinese. The idea of "propriety" has great influence over their conduct, it being one of the five active qualities or virtues of Chinese philosophy.[1] It forms the basis of the feeling of self-respect and sense of honour which delight the good man, and in its application to the subject of marriage we have a proper starting-point for the development of systematic monandry out of a preceding condition of polygyny. Whether the idea of propriety would alone have been sufficient to ensure this result, is doubtful. It was aided, however, by certain other notions which had much influence over the philosophic teaching of the ancient world. The Chinese firmly believe in the doctrine of the transmigration of souls, and, in their opinion, at the end of five generations the spirits of the dead may be born again into the world as men, or, according to their deserts, become birds, beasts, or reptiles.[2] This belief shows its practical influence over the Chinese mind, in that after the descendants of an individual have reached the fifth generation, his ancestral tablet is no longer worshipped. In that teaching we have the addition to the old doctrine that certain animals, and possibly all animals, are the re-embodiment of human souls, of the belief that such incarnation is consequent on the performance, in the earlier human life, of actions which are morally wrong, or, at least, which are disapproved of by some super-human being, who has power to condemn the soul to existence under an animal form. The doctrine

[1] Wake 1878, II, 40, 53; Meadows 1856, pp. 342ff.
[2] Doolittle 1868, pp. 143, 595.

of re-incarnation is intimately connected with that
of the emanation of souls from the Universal Soul, on
which is based the ancient idea of the evil influence
of matter. There is nothing, however, in Chinese
philosophic teaching to condemn marriage as perpetuating a condition of impurity, a notion which is almost
precluded · by the belief that a man's happiness in the
spirit world may depend on his having a son to perform the necessary funeral rites, and to make the
usual offerings to the ancestral tablets. It might
be justly inferred, however, that a man who indulged
in a plurality of wives was unduly influenced by the
objective world, and therefore such conduct, as contrary to the sense of self-respect, would be condemned
as improper.

The characteristics of the family among the early
Semites was much the same as with the Chinese.
The system of wife-purchase was prevalent among the
former, although the price was usually in the form
of presents to the relations of the bride. There
appears to have been nothing like the extension of
that custom which obtained among the early Babylonians, of whom Herodotus says,[1] " Once in every
year the following course is pursued in every village.
Whatever maidens were of a marriageable age, they
used to collect together and bring them in a body to
one place ; around them stood a crowd of men. Then
a crier having made them stand up one by one, offered
them for sale, beginning with the most beautiful ; and
when she had been sold for a large sum, he put up
another who was next in beauty. They were sold on

[1] *Clio*, 196 (Bohn's edition, p. 85). Herodotus approves of
the custom mentioned in the text, and states that it was practised also by the Venetians of Illyria.

condition that they should be married.   Such men
among the Babylonians as were rich and desirous of
marrying, used to bid against one another and purchase the handsomest.   But such of the lower classes
as were desirous of marrying did not require a beautiful form, but were willing to take the plainer damsels
with a sum of money.   For when the crier had
finished selling the handsomest of the maidens, he
made the ugliest stand up, or one that was a cripple,
and put her up to auction, for the person who would
marry her with the least sum, until she was adjudged
to the man who offered to take the smallest sum.
This money was obtained from (the sale of) the handsome maidens ; and thus the beautiful ones portioned
out the ugly and the crippled."   We have here the
explanation of the custom referred to, which was
evidently intended to provide a marriage portion for
those girls who, owing to some personal defect, would
otherwise remain unmarried.   It was, moreover, a
public regulation, as Herodotus states, that a father
was not allowed to give his daughter in marriage to
whom he pleased, and subsequently another regulation
was adopted to prevent men from ill-treating their
women, or carrying them away to other cities.   The
public sale of girls came to an end at Babylon on its
capture by Cyrus, and the "meaner sort," from want
of a livelihood, prostituted their daughters.   This
practice would be, however, merely a continuance of
ancient usage, if the true interpretation is given by
Bachofen and others of the statement made by Herodotus,[1] that "every native woman was obliged, once

[1] *Clio*, 199. Herodotus states that the same custom was
practised in Cyprus.

in her life, to sit in the temple of Venus, and have intercourse with some stranger."

The early Hebrews probably had the practice of wife-purchase, whether by personal labour, as in the case of Jacob, or by actual payment of a price. At a later date, a girl was, until puberty, at the disposal of her father, who could either sell her or marry her to whom he pleased, being a Hebrew. There were, however, certain conditions, one of which was that the purchaser could not sell the girl to another person, and if he did not espouse her, or marry her to his son, he was bound, when she reached the age of puberty, or at the end of six years, to aid her in obtaining freedom by reclaiming from her father the price paid for her services. If married, however, she was only a concubine, a position which, although conferring full conjugal rights, was one of inferiority. These conditions were probably introduced in restriction of the privileges claimed at an earlier date, when children were absolutely in the power of the head of the family.[1] At the later period neither daughter nor wife was capable of inheriting except under certain special circumstances, and a woman was not allowed to give testimony in a court of justice. Women were not reckoned among the members of the religious assembly, and they had no part in the performance of any fixed religious observance, their place being to attend to the interests of their home and family.[2] A man could repudiate his wife for the most trivial reason, but the free use of the power was probably not approved of by the more cultured Hebrews, and a wife herself could, on certain grounds, demand a dis-

[1] Weill 1874, pp. 11, 12.
[2] *Ibid.*, pp. 117ff.

solution of marriage.   These grounds were : if her
husband was affected with some contagious disease,
such as leprosy; if he adopted certain occupations of
a repulsive character ; if he deceived his wife; if he
habitually ill-treated her ; if he refused to contribute
towards her maintenance ; finally, if after ten years
of marriage his impotence was established, particularly
if his wife asked for a divorce because she desired a
son to support her in her old age.   By a fiction, however, it was always the husband who was reputed to
put away his wife, showing that in early times Hebrew
women had no power to obtain a divorce.[1]   It is probable that, notwithstanding her legal incapacity, the
Hebrew woman was practically on a social equality
with her husband.   M. Weill well says,[2] " According
to circumstances, she could be poetess, prophetess,
judge and warrior, without her sex being the least
obstacle to her legitimate influence ; nor was she
thought unworthy of taking part in the most important public affairs.   But the respect which she at
all times inspired, perhaps manifested itself still better
in the bosom of the family, of which she was not only
one of the constituent elements, but she is proclaimed
by the Bible as the firmest support."

   Semitic society is supposed by Dr Morgan [3] to have
produced the *patriarchal family*, which was in the
early period common with the chiefs, but soon sub-
sided into the " monogamous " family, which was
common among the people.   The American writer
regards [4] the Hebrew and the Roman forms of the
former institution as exceptional in human experi-

[1] *Ibid.*, pp. 76ff.   [2] *Ibid.*, p. 123.
[3] 1877, p. 480.
[4] Morgan 1877, p. 466.

ence. This depends, however, on what is meant by the patriarchal family. According to Sir Henry Maine,[1] it "consists of animate and inanimate property, of wife, children, slaves, land, and goods, all held together by subjection to the despotic authority of the eldest male of the eldest ascending line, the father, grandfather, or even more remote ancestor. The force which binds the group together is power." In this form the patriarchal family was established among the Romans, with whom the *patria potestas* was fully developed, the father having life and death over all the members of his *familia*, or "body of servants," with full control over its property.[2] Was such a system in existence among the Semitic peoples and the Aryan peoples generally, or was it restricted to the Romans? Dr M'Lennan answers the former question in the negative, and he asserts[3] that in the early Hebrew family instead of *patria potestas* and agnation we find *beena* marriage, and the relationships consistent therewith; while "from not the Hebrews only, but from the Germans and from the early Greeks, we appear to get unquestionable indications of a system of kinship only through women having preceded the acknowledgment of kinship through the father."

That the patriarchal family as defined by Sir Henry Maine did not exist among the Hebrews[4] may be admitted, but has it been established that they practised *beena* marriage? The argument in favour of this opinion is based on the Scriptural command (Gen. ii. 24), that "a man shall leave his father and his

[1] Maine 1875, p. 310.
[2] Morgan 1877, p. 469.
[3] McLennan 1885, p. 352.
[4] On this point, see *Ibid.*, pp. 35ff.

mother, and shall cleave unto his wife." This implies
that on marriage a man quitted his father's household,
but it does not necessarily follow that, as in *beena*
marriage, he was to pass into the family of his wife,
and that his children were to belong to it. The only
Hebrew marriage referred to by Dr M'Lennan in
support of his contention is that of Jacob and the
daughters of Laban. So far, however, from this being
a *beena* marriage, it is evidently a case of marriage by
purchase. It is true Dr M'Lennan asserts[1] that
"marriage by purchase of the bride and her issue
can hardly be thought to have been primeval practice." The question is not, however, one of primeval
practice, which the passage in Genesis can hardly be
said to attest, but whether wife-purchase was practised
by the Hebrew patriarchs. As to Jacob's marriage,
Dr M'Lennan remarks that "Jacob had to buy his
place in Laban's family as husband of Laban's
daughters, by service;" and that the children born
to him belonged to Laban's family. The latter point
is supposed to be proved by the fact that Jacob
stole away with the children from his father-in-law,
and that Laban on overtaking the fugitives claimed
Jacob's wives and their children as his own, calling
them his "sons and daughters," in which he was right,
argues Dr M'Lennan, as Jacob had not purchased
them. But what does Jacob say on the subject?
When he had served Laban twenty years he wished to
return to his own country, and he said to Laban (Gen.
xxx. 26), "Give me my wives and my children, for
whom I have served thee, and let me go, for thou
knowest my service wherewith I have served thee."
Here Jacob claims to have bought, not "his place in

---

[1] *Ibid.*, p. 45.

Laban's family as husband of Laban's daughters," but the daughters and their children. If he was wrong, Laban would have denied the claim, but instead of doing so he asks Jacob to stay, because "the Lord hath blessed me for thy sake." Moreover, Jacob's claim is supported by the testimony of his wives.[1] When Jacob told them he was directed by God to return to his native land, they said (ch. xxxi. 14), " Is there yet any portion or inheritance for us in our father's house ? Are we not counted of him strangers ? for he hath sold us, and hath also quite devoured the price paid for us," adding, " For all the riches which God hath taken away from our father, that is ours, and our children's," which could be the case only if the wives and children belonged to Jacob and not to Laban. Moreover, Laban did not follow Jacob in his flight because the latter had *stole away*, that is, " gone away secretly," with Laban's daughters and their children, but because he had lost his household gods or *teraphim* (Gen. xxxi. 30, 34). Laban certainly complained of the secret flight, and that he had not been suffered to give a parting salutation to his sons and his daughters, meaning his daughters' children, to which Jacob replied that he feared Laban would have taken his daughters away by force. The only ground for contending that Jacob had not purchased his wives and their children is that Laban calls the latter his sons and daughters and claims them for his own. Possibly he may have considered that, as Jacob had not actually paid a bride-price, he was not entitled to the children, but it is evident that Jacob did not

---

[1] Dr. McLennan says that they only wished to justify to themselves what they proposed to do (1885, p. 46n.) ; but such an explanation is not sufficient.

admit the claim, the nature of which shows, indeed, that it was not well founded. Laban said (v. 43), "The daughters are my daughters, and the children are my children, and the flocks are my flocks, and all that thou seest is mine." The fairness of the claim may be judged of by the reference to Jacob's flocks, and it fully justified Jacob's suspicion that Laban had intended to send him empty away, notwithstanding his twenty years' service, an action which would have been consistent with Laban's conduct throughout.[1] The expression, "sons and daughters," given by Laban to his daughters' children may be compared with the statement of Jacob to Rachel (Gen. xxix. 12) that he was her father's " brother," although in reality he was the son of her father's sister. Rebekah, the sister of Laban, had married his father's cousin, Isaac, the father of Jacob, who was therefore of the same generation as her brother Laban. Jacob and Laban were also descended from the same ancestor, Terah, the paternal grandfather of both Isaac and Bethuel, the father of Rebekah, and they were, therefore, "tribal" brothers.[2] With descent in the female line, which seems to have been the custom so far as the regulation of marriage was concerned, the children of Jacob were the "sons and daughters" of his "brother" Laban, and they would be so in a double sense, seeing that Jacob's wives were Laban's own children.

The marriage of Jacob with the daughters of Laban was as much an example of wife-purchase as was that

---

[1] It is possible that Laban feared Jacob would marry a Canaanite if he returned to his native land (31 : 50), a fear which Rebekah had before entertained (27 : 46).

[2] Bethuel, the father of Rebekah, is called by Abraham's servant his master's "brother" (Gen. 24 :48).

of Isaac and Rebekah, which Dr M'Lennan cites[1] as proving that *beena* marriage was not exclusively practised in the land of Haran. We may infer, therefore, that *beena* marriage is not indicated in Genesis ii. 24, which requires a man on marriage to leave his father and his mother. The command means merely that on marriage a man shall live with his wife instead of with his father and mother. This view is confirmed by the addition that man and wife shall be one flesh, a notion which is not consistent with the uncertain duration of *beena* marriage. There is another incident in the narration of Jacob's sojourn at Padan-aram which renders it improbable that his marriages there were of the *beena* type. It is said (Gen. xxxi. 1) that Jacob heard Laban's sons complaining that he had taken away all their father's wealth. This shows that Laban's sons were living with their father, and we may assume that they and their wives and children formed part of their father's *familia*, but without the *patria potestas* of the strict patriarchal family. This appears to have been the case with Jacob and his sons, whose family life was probably much the same as that described by M. Weill. Every man would be the head of his own family group, with power over his own wife and children,[2] the wife as mother having almost equal authority in the household with her husband. As to the question of descent, there is no doubt that kinship through females was considered by the early Hebrews a bar to marriage,

[1] McLennan 1885, p. 44.

[2] This seems to be implied in the words of Reuben to Jacob, "Slay my two sons, if I bring him [Benjamin] not to thee" (Gen. 42 : 37), as well as in the proposed sacrifice of Isaac by Abraham.

while it was not so with kinship through males.   In
fact, Abram married his paternal half-sister.   So,
also, Nahor married his niece, the daughter of his
brother Haran, and Isaac the daughter of Abram's
"brother," his nephew Bethuel.   The early Hebrew
patriarchs, while tracing kinship through females in
relation to marriage, evidently, nevertheless, recognised
descent in the male line for other purposes.[1]   Terah
is the common male ancestor from whom they all
traced their descent, and this fact accounts for Abram
being called the brother of his nephew, the son of his
brother Bethuel, and Jacob the brother of his uncle
Laban, the son of Bethuel.   The mother of Jacob was
also descended from Terah, and it is remarkable that
none of the wives of the patriarchs are mentioned
except those who had that descent.   While, therefore,
the early Hebrews had not agnation, they traced
descent from the father for the purposes of what
we may call rank, or a feeling of *caste*, and this was
the source of their patriarchal authority.

That we have in ideas similar to those of the
Chinese an explanation of the origin of individual
marriage among the Hebrews and early Aryans, can
hardly be doubted.   The feeling of self-respect would,
under favourable influences, be developed among
them all alike, and, while enforcing marriage for the
purpose of perpetuating the family and continuing the
rites of ancestral worship, it would forbid marriage
with more than one wife unless the taking of a second

[1] We have an analogous case in the Polynesian custom of
tracing descent in the male line, while rank descends in the
female line. In the time of the Judges of Israel, Abimelech
claims the assistance of his mother's brethren in obtaining
the succession to the rule of his father Jerubbaal (Judges
9 :1, 2).

wife was necessary to provide a son. Dr M'Lennan incidentally mentions the existence among a polyandrous race of a feeling of propriety in connection with marriage. Thus, he says,[1] that with the Kandyans of Ceylon polyandry is universal among the lower and middle classes, " but the chiefs are strictly monogamists, apparently regarding polyandry as a low practice, unworthy of men in their position." The cause of this improvement, assuming that the Kandyan chiefs formerly practised polyandry, is not given, but perhaps it may be inferred from the statement, that "as settled habits arose, as property accumulated, and the sexes became more evenly balanced, the example of the chiefs would find more and more imitators, and their cases would furnish a model for an improved system of succession." Thus would arise, says Dr M'Lennan, a practice of monogamy *or* of polygyny ; an alternative which may perhaps lead us to think that the monogamy of the Kandyan chiefs was originally due, not to any of the changes referred to, but rather to the force of example. In Tibet polyandry prevails among all classes, and was superseded by *polygyny* " only where the people were a good deal in contact with either Hindoos or Mohammedans."[2] Dr M'Lennan's supposition that when Tibetan polyandry was once reached an improving race would slowly advance from it to monandry, may be true, but in the absence of a keen sense of propriety it might advance equally to a condition of polygyny.

With Sir John Lubbock "individual marriage " is an infringement of communal rights, and originated

[1] McLennan 1876, p. 195.
[2] Wilson 1875, p. 228.

in the appropriation by a man of his female captive, in derogation of the rights of the whole tribe. He says[1] that women taken in war were not the common property of the tribe, as other women were, and that their captors reserved them to themselves as wives. In this practice he sees the origin of individual marriage, which was thus founded on capture, leading to exogamy,[2] the existence of which thus becomes evidence of a prior condition of promiscuity. Mr Fison remarks on this point,[3] that Sir John Lubbock's "whole theory rests upon the assumption that a warrior has a sole right, as against his tribe, to a captive taken by him in war." He adds that " in support of this right Sir John advances nothing whatever beyond the assertion that it would be likely to accrue." On this fallacy is founded his whole theory of the origin of individual marriage. Sir John Lubbock naturally takes exception to this statement, but nevertheless it is perfectly true. He cites many facts in support of his theory, but they are really beside the question, as, instead of being examples of marriage by capture, or rather by force, they are merely phases of exogamous marriage. Not having had a clear notion of the distinction between the tribe and the gens or clan, he refers to the former what has to do with the latter. There is " capture " in both cases, but in the one case it is the forcible abduction of a woman from another tribe, presumably against her and its will; while in the other it is the marriage of the woman, possibly sometimes against her will, but with the real, although veiled, consent of her relations, that is the members of the family group to which she belongs, the tribe having nothing at

[1] Lubbock 1875, p. 125.   [2] *Ibid.*, p. 95.
[3] Fison and Howitt 1880, p. 151.

all to do with the matter. This view derives support
from Dr M'Lennan's statement,[1] that "in almost all
cases the form of capture is the symbol of the group
act—of a siege, or a pitched battle, or an invasion of
a house by an armed band, while in a few cases only,
and these much disintegrated, it represents a capture
by an individual. On the one side are the kindred of
the husband, on the other the kindred of the wife."
In its bearing on the general argument, he adds[2] that
the correct view is that, assuming communism and a
practice of capture, the individual captor would have
no exclusive right to a war captive.

Mr Howitt considers the same question, and he
states[3] it is quite certain that marriage is brought
about throughout Australia by capture, but after considering various examples of the practice, he affirms
that among the Australian aborigines "marriage by
capture was only permitted when the captor and the
captive were of some classes which might legally intermarry," and that "its practice amounts merely to a
violent extension of the marital rights over a class in
one tribe to captured members of the corresponding
class in another tribe." Sir John Lubbock, in reply-
ing to the criticism of Messrs Fison and Howitt,
admits that the right of a man to his female captive
is limited by the tribal laws, that is, the man may not
marry her if she belongs to an excluded gens, but he
contends[4] that if the man might marry her at all, she
would become exclusively his ; in which case, in
accordance with his general theory, "no expiation for
marriage" would be required. This conclusion, how-

[1] McLennan 1876, p. 444.   [2] 1877, p. 447.
[3] Fison and Howitt 1880, p. 343.
[4] Lubbock 1885, p. 297.

ever, does not agree with fact; as, in nearly all the cases referred to by Messrs Fison and Howitt, a man has the exclusive right to his female captive, *only after* the rights of the other members of the group have been satisfied.   In some cases the "expiation" is not actually mentioned, but the accounts are not complete, and by analogy it may be inferred.   The fact of its being required is evidence that a female captive is regarded as in theory the property of all the men of the family group to which the captor belongs, and therefore it shows conclusively that individual marriage cannot have arisen in the way supposed by Sir John Lubbock, that is, by a man having the sole right to his female captive.   Individual marriage in one sense of the term, or "true marriage," is of much later origin, and if it has any connection at all with capture, it is so only after the group right has been compounded for.

Sir John Lubbock refers to Mr Howitt's statement,[1] that marriage by elopement was very common among the Australian aborigines, and that it differs from marriage by capture only in the presence or absence of the woman's consent, as though this fact is in favour of his own views.   It is just the opposite, however, as Mr Howitt adds that "both these forms occur not only as producing *individual* marriage, *where the class rules have become weakened*,[2] but also *group* marriages, *where the class rules are still full of vitality*." The case of the Kurnai, which is thought to be opposed to Mr Fison's views, belongs to the former category. The fact that they exact the strictest fidelity from their wives, shows that the old class rules have be-

---

[1] Lubbock 1875, p. 354.   [2] These italics are mine.

come weakened, and the most usual mode of acquiring a wife in use among them is by elopement.[1]

Mr Howitt gives an explanation of the origin of individual marriage which differs entirely from that of Sir John Lubbock. He says[2] that, in Australia at least, individual marriage did not arise "by the monopoly of female captives in disregard of the common tribal right." His own opinion[3] is, that individual marriage arose from the monopoly of women by the older men of the tribe, combined with the custom of betrothal, "especially when aided by elopement and by capture, which, being at first completely under the control of the class laws, afterwards received greater prominence as these class laws became weakened." Elsewhere,[4] Mr Howitt says that he sees at the root of betrothal the belief that a child is derived from the male parent only, the mother being no more than its nurse, and he thinks this belief, together with betrothal, "which produces the sense of separate ownership," has tended to bring about ultimately individual marriage. This may be a proper explanation of the origin of the monandry of the Australian aborigines, but it is not sufficient to account for the development of the *monogamy* of the higher races, any more than for the prevalence of individual marriage among many peoples who are usually regarded as polygynists.

According to the theory of Dr Morgan, the development of individual marriage among the American aborigines, who when first discovered had attained to the "pairing family," was connected with that of

---

[1] Fison and Howitt 1880, pp. 200, 205.

[2] *Ibid.*, p. 343. [3] *Ibid.*, pp. 354ff.

[4] Howitt 1885, p. 821.

paternal authority, the growth of which " steadily advanced as the family became more and more individualised, and became fully established under monogamy, which assured the paternity of children."[1] The
object of individual marriage, the essential feature of
which is an exclusive cohabitation, was, according to
this view, to ensure legitimate heirs, and to limit their
number to the actual progeny of the married pair,
and it was really due to the " growth of property, and
the desire for its transmission to children."[2]   Dr
Morgan adds,[3] that the portraiture by early writers of
society, in what he calls the upper status of the barbarian, " implies the general practice of monogamy,
but with attendant circumstances, indicating that it
was the monogamian family of the future struggling
into existence under adverse influences, feeble in
vitality, rights, and immunities, and still environed
with the remains of an ancient conjugal system."
The pairing or syndyasmian family of the American
peoples was, in fact, developed out of the *punaluan*,
which from the first had a tendency towards the
syndyasmian, seeing that in the former " there was
more or less of pairing from the necessities of the
social state, each man having a principal wife among
a number of wives, and each woman a principal husband among a number of husbands."[4]   This is equally
true, however, of group marriage, and this also may,
therefore, be said to have a tendency towards the
pairing family, and thence to the monogamian.
Moreover, notwithstanding the approach towards
monandry observed among the American aborigines,
polygyny, which is universally recognised as a man's

[1] Morgan 1877, p. 466.   [2] *Ibid.*, p. 477.
[3] *Ibid.*, p. 480.   [4] *Ibid.*, p. 457.

right, would be largely practised if it was not that the people are too poor to indulge in it. Dr Morgan's supposition that monogamy arose from the desire to transmit property to children is not correct. This desire is also said by him[1] to have changed descent from the female to the male line, thus furnishing a foundation for the paternal authority which he regards as intimately connected with the development of monogamy. On this it may be observed that so far from descent in the male line being limited to monogamous peoples, it is almost universal among the races of Asia and Africa, whether practising polygyny or polyandry. Moreover, the desire to transmit property to children would be gratified as well under polygyny as under monogamy, there being certainty of paternity in both cases. Property was so transmitted among the ancient Hebrew patriarchs, notwithstanding that kinship was traced in the female line preferably to the male line where marriage was in question. This is no less true in relation to polyandry where several brothers have a wife in common ; a system of marriage the origin of which Dr M'Lennan connects with the alteration in the right of succession to property from the children of the eldest sister to her brother's own children, who "would be born in the house and would become its heirs."[2]

There are so many difficulties in the way of accepting any of these social explanations of the origin of systematic monandry among peoples long accustomed to the practice of the earlier phases of marriage, that we cannot doubt the true cause must be sought in the development of a sense of self-respect such as the Chinese exhibit in relation to marriage. The

[1] *Ibid.*, p. 470.   [2] McLennan 1876, p. 192.

monandry of the Kandyan chiefs may perhaps be accounted for by such a feeling, although it may be due really to the force of example. This no doubt has had much to do with the fact that polygyny is gradually losing its hold among the higher classes in Egypt, and in Asiatic countries where the people are brought much into close contact with European civilisation. The introduction of Western ideas has largely affected social life in those countries, and a prejudice in favour of monandry thus established may give rise to the feeling that it is required by a sense of self-respect. Something more than this, however, is found in the monogamous unions of certain races, further reference to which must be reserved for a later chapter.

CHAPTER VIII.

WE have in the preceding chapters considered the subjective phase of the sexual instinct, that which has to do with the active agents, and the outward expression of which is the marital union of the persons concerned. We have now to treat of the objective phase of the social instinct, that which has relation to the offspring of such a union. It was remarked above [1] that " the birth of offspring gives rise to feelings in the minds of its parents so active and so general as to be regarded as constituting a secondary instinct. This is usually referred to as the maternal instinct, but it would be more properly termed the *parental instinct*, as it is common to both parents, although it is generally more strongly developed with the mother, owing to her closer connection with the child as its nourisher or nurse, both before and after its birth." This greater intimacy has an important bearing on the subject about to be discussed, as the idea of kinship was probably in the first instance based on the special association between mother and child. It was not necessarily so ; but on whichever side, maternal or paternal, the parental instinct became the more influential, the *objective* phase of the sexual instinct may be said to underlie the idea of *kinship*, as its *subjective* phase is at the base of the law of *marriage*.

[1] Above, pp. 2, 56.

The origin of the idea of kinship has already been referred to in connection with the development of the law of marriage. These subjects are, indeed, closely related ; for, as we have seen, one of the most important checks on sexual promiscuity arises from the influence of the natural restraints based on the feeling, which has been referred to as the fraternal instinct, that persons closely related by blood ought not to intermarry. The authority of this instinct is so generally recognised, that marriages between persons near of kin are not only forbidden, but are looked upon with horror even by peoples of the lowest degree of culture.[1] We may suppose that the parental instinct would show its action in the recognition of a relationship between a child and *both* its parents. This question will have to be considered fully hereafter, but it is necessary to point out here the distinction between *relationship* and *kinship*, a distinction which is usually lost sight of.[2] The former of these terms is wider than the latter, as two persons may be related to each other, and yet not be of the same kin. Systems of kinship have reference to the particular, and not to the general, relationship of persons to each other, and they are based on the existence of special ties between certain individuals, who by virtue thereof are subject or liable to certain claims and disabilities as between each other. The subject may be illustrated by what Dr Morgan says [3] as to the origin of the gens. This " came into being upon three principal concep-

---

[1] Above, pp. 58ff., 72ff.

[2] It is noted, however, by the Rev. Lorimer Fison, who expresses the distinction in saying that "the line of descent does not at all affect the personal relationships" (Fison and Howitt 1880, p. 119).

[3] 1877, p. 69.

tions, namely, the bond of kin, a pure lineage through
descent in the female line, and non-intermarriage in
the gens." The bond of kin implies the personal
protection of each individual member of the gens. It
is evident that kinship, which here is limited to persons in the female line of descent, does not preclude
the more general relationship due to descent from a
common *male* ancestor, which relationship may be
accompanied by its own rights and liabilities. It
would hardly be possible in small communities to
enforce the same rules in connection with general
relationship, as with special relationship or kinship.
If the prohibition of marriage between persons near of
kin were extended so as to apply to all persons nearly
related, marriage would become almost impossible;
although, as a fact, most peoples in a primitive condition include among the persons forbidden to intermarry those most nearly related through both father
and mother. This implies that relationship to both
parents is fully recognised, and such we shall show is
actually the case, notwithstanding what has been said
by many writers as to uncertainty of paternity.

As the *parental* instinct has to do with relationship
in general, so the *fraternal* instinct has to do more
especially with kinship. The law of kinship is based
on that phase of the sexual instinct, the objective,
which has relation to the offspring of marriage. The
children of a common parent stand in a special relation to each other, which shows itself in the development of the feeling referred to as the fraternal instinct.
The position of each mother as the *nurse*, using this
term as meaning, not only the suckler, but also the
rearer of her own children, makes the tie which binds
them together much stronger than that between the

children of different mothers, except occasionally,
where the milk-tie has been added, as in the case of
fosterage. This remark is particularly applicable to
uncultured peoples, although there are certain ideas
connected with paternity which may cause kinship in
relation to the children of a common parent to be
traced through the father and not through the mother,
thus largely increasing its range.

It is not surprising, however, that kinship based on
the idea of a special relationship subsisting between
the children of the same mother, should be usually
regarded as the earliest phase to be developed. This
is the view entertained by Dr M'Lennan, who endeavoured to establish[1] that " the most ancient system in
which the idea of blood relationship was embodied,
was a system of kinship through females only." This
conclusion has been almost generally adopted by succeeding writers, and the system has been found to
prevail so widely, while so many traces of it have
been discovered where kinship through males is now
established, that its universality in primitive times is
possible. We shall see hereafter, however, that it is
not necessary, or even probable. Dr M'Lennan finds
the origin of the custom of tracing kinship through
females only in the uncertainty of paternity, arising
from the supposed fact that in primitive times a
woman was not appropriated to a particular man for
his wife, or to men of one blood as wife. The children,
although belonging to the horde, would remain attached
to their mothers, and, according to his views, the blood
tie observed between them would, as promiscuity gave
place to polyandry of the ruder kind, in which the
husbands are strangers in blood to each other, become

[1] 1876, p. 124.

developed into the system of kinship through females.[1]
Dr M'Lennan affirms that this conclusion was reached
by a process of reflection, beginning in the perception of the fact that a man has his mother's blood in
his veins, after which it would be quickly seen that
" he is of the same blood with her. other children."
A little more reflection would enable him to see that
" he is of one blood with the brothers and sisters of
his mother." The man then perceives that " he is of
the same blood with the children of his mother's
sister;" and " in process of time, following the ties of
blood through his mother, and females of the same
blood, he must arrive at a system of kinship through
females."[2] It is evident, nevertheless, that this reasoning does not exclude the recognition also of kinship
through males, and Dr M'Lennan himself states that
if paternity were usually as indisputable as maternity,
" we might expect to find kinship through males acknowledged soon after kinship through females," showing that the real origin of the latter system, according
to Dr M'Lennan's theory, is uncertainty of paternity.

A very different explanation is given by an earlier
writer, who also assumes that originally mankind
consorted without any of the restrictions of marriage.
Bachofen believed, as we have already had occasion
to show,[3] that women were at an early period supreme,
not only in the family, but in the State. He supposed
that they had revolted against the condition of promiscuity which originally subsisted in the intercourse
between the sexes, and established a system of marriage
in which the female occupied the first place as the
head of the family, and as the person through whom

[1] McLennan 1876, p. 139.   [2] *Ibid.*, p. 124.
[3] Above, pp. 14, 16.

kinship was to be traced. This movement, which had a religious origin, was followed by another resulting from the development of the idea that the mother occupied a subordinate position in relation to her children, of whom the father was the true parent, and therefore the person through whom kinship should be traced. Dr M'Lennan, who objects to this theory that if marriage was from the beginning monogamous, kinship would have been traced through fathers from the first, affirms[1] that " those signs of superiority on the woman's part were the direct consequences (1) of marriage *not* being monogamous, or such as to permit of certainty of fatherhood ; and (2) of wives not as yet living in their husband's houses, but apart from them in the homes of their own mothers." The meaning of this is, that the phenomena referred to by Bachofen were due to the prevalence of a system of polyandry such as that ascribed to the Nairs.[2] It is very improbable, however, that we have here a sufficient explanation of those phenomena. According to Dr M'Lennan's opinion, one cause of the superiority of woman was the fact of wives living apart from their husbands in the homes of their mothers. This custom must, therefore, have preceded woman's superiority, assuming this to have existed, and the tracing of kinship through females which gave rise to it. This would require us to believe that, as soon as promiscuity in the sexual relations ceased, women lived alone with their children, the only male members of their families being their sons, who would be subordinate to them ; unless, indeed, a son were to set up a separate establishment for himself, under the control of his favourite

[1] McLennan 1876, p. 418.   [2] Above, pp. 135ff.

sister, as is sometimes the case with the modern Nairs.[1]
If we consider, however, the customs of uncultured
peoples of the present day, we shall see that such
a domestic condition as that of the Nairs can hardly
represent that of mankind in the early ages. Among
savages there is seldom that subordination of the man
to the woman which we should have to assume, and
where it does exist it has been developed under special
social conditions.[2]

Sir John Lubbock's views on the subject of kinship
are expressed as follows : [3] " Children were not in the
earliest times regarded as related equally to their
father and their mother, but that the natural progress
of ideas is, first, that a child is related to his tribe
generally ; secondly, to his mother, and not to his
father ; thirdly, to his father, and not to his mother ;
lastly, and lastly only, that he is related to both." It
has already been shown [4] that there is little, if any,
evidence of the existence of the " communal marriage "
on which Sir John Lubbock founds his opinion as to
the relationship of children to the tribe. The evidence
in support of his view that tribal relationship was
replaced by exclusive relationship between mother and
child is as unsatisfactory. He asserts [5] that under
communal marriage, and even where polygamy prevails, the tie between father and son would be very
slight, and that "the tie between a mother and child
is much stronger than that which binds a child to its

[1] McLennan 1876, p. 150.

[2] In the gentile institution of the American tribes, even
with descent in the female line, the chiefs and sachems are
men, notwithstanding the power of the women in their elec-
tion and deposition (Morgan 1877, p. 71).

[3] Lubbock 1875, p. 149.   [4] Above, pp. 31ff.

[5] Lubbock 1875, p. 139.

father." In this Sir John Lubbock sees the explana-
of the fact that "among many of the lower races
relationship through females is the prevalent custom,"
a custom which he regards[1] as "the relic of an ancient
barbarism."

Mr Herbert Spencer shows how the idea of a
special relationship between mother and child may
have arisen. Unlike the writers hitherto referred
to, he does not think that promiscuity in the relations between the sexes ever existed in an unqualified form.[2] Mr Spencer is of opinion, indeed, that
monogamy must have preceded polygamy, although,
owing to the extension of promiscuity and the birth
of a larger number of children to unknown fathers
than to known fathers, a habit arose of thinking of
maternal kinship rather than of paternal kinship.
Where paternity was manifest, children would come
to be spoken of in the same way.[3] He adds that the
habit having arisen, the resulting system of kinship
in the female line will be strengthened by the practice
of exogamy. The defect of this explanation lies in its
requiring uncertainty of paternity, and it appears,
moreover, to be inconsistent with the fact, mentioned
by Mr Spencer himself, that where the system of
female kinship now subsists, "male parentage is habitually known." It is true that he supposes male kinship to be disregarded, but this conclusion will be
found to be inconsistent with fact.

What, then, are the notions of savages as to the
relation between a child and its parents? When
De Hontan enquired of the American natives why
they always bore their mother's name, they replied

[1] *Ibid.*, p. 148.　　　　　　[2] Spencer 1876–96, I, 662.
[3] *Ibid.*, I, 665.

that as children received their souls from their
father and their bodies from their mother, it was
reasonable that the maternal name should be perpetuated.[1] Bachofen might have had this reasoning
in mind when he wrote,[2] in referring to the importance of the paternal conception of man, "Maternity
belongs to the corporeal side of man ; the paternal
psychical principle belongs to him alone." The
remarks of M. Giraud-Teulon[3] (made in connection with Bachofen's theory), that the search for paternity is the first sign of moral progress among all
peoples, and that "the first who consented to acknowledge himself 'father' was a man of genius and of
courage, one of the great benefactors of mankind,"
must be regarded as having no justification in fact.
Among the Greeks, the father, as endowed with crea-
tive power, was clothed with the divine character, but
not the mother, who was only the bearer and nourisher
of the child.[4] This idea, which was common to all the
ancients, was fully recognised by the Egyptians,
among whom, says Strabo, no child was reputed illegitimate, even though he was born of a slave mother,
as they looked upon the father as the sole author of
the being of the child, to whom the mother supplied
little more than nourishment.[5] This opinion agrees
closely with that held by the natives of Australia,
among whom the belief is generally entertained that

[1] Lahontan 1728, II, 154 ; see also Carver 1778, p. 378.
[2] Bachofen 1861, p. 27.
[3] Giraud-Teulon 1867, p. 32.
[4] This was the defence of Orestes, who avenged his father's
death by slaying his mother.
[5] Wilkinson 1837–41, II, 64.

the child is derived from the male parent only, and
that the mother is only the nurse. Mr Howitt, who
mentions this fact,[1] states that a black fellow once
remarked to him, "The man gives the child to a
woman to take care of for him, and he can do whatever he likes with his own child." In some tribes,
indeed, the son is recognised as the re-incarnation of
his father, notwithstanding that the son is of his
mother's class division.[2]

These ideas throw light on the curious and widespread custom of *la couvade*, or "hatching," which
requires that immediately after childbirth the mother
shall rise and attend to the duties of the household,
while the father goes to bed with the new-born infant.
This custom, which is known to us by the name given
to it in France, where traces of it are still to be met
with among the Basques, was also anciently observed
in Corsica, among the Iberians of Spain, and by the
Tibareni of the country south of the Black Sea. It is
still practised in Southern India, in Yunnan by the
Miau-tze, in Borneo, Kamschatka, and Greenland, and
as mentioned by Lafitau,[3] by many of the tribes of
South America. Dr E. B. Tylor, who has brought
together all these cases, remarks[4] that the *couvade*
"implicitly denies that physical separation of 'individuals' which a civilised man would probably set
down as a first principle, common by nature to all
mankind. . . . It shows us a number of distinct and

[1] Howitt 1885, pp. 813, 821.
[2] Howitt and Fison 1884, p. 145.
[3] Lafitau 1724, I, 257.
[4] Tylor 1865, p. 292.

distant tribes deliberately holding the opinion that the connection between father and child is not only, as we think, a mere relation of parentage, affection, duty, but that their very bodies are joined by a physical bond, so that what is done to the one acts directly upon the other." Professor Max Müller [1] offers the curious suggestion that the *couvade* custom arises from some "secret spring in human nature," which led the husband at first to be "tyrannised over by his female relations, and afterwards frightened into superstition. He then began to make a martyr of himself till he made himself really ill, or took to his bed in self-defence." Sir John Lubbock sees in that custom a connection with the change which he supposes to have taken place from female to male kinship. He says,[2] "As soon as the change was made, the father would take the place held previously by the mother, and he instead of she would be regarded as the parent. Hence, on the birth of a child, the father would naturally be very careful what he did, and what he ate, for fear the child be injured." The suggestion made in this passage is carried further by M. Giraud-Teulon,[3] who regards the *couvade* as an imitation of nature, intended to give a colour to the fiction that the father had brought forth the child, and was for it a second *mother*, such a pretence being the only way in which a bond between the father and his child could be established. The French writer shows that "adoption by the imitation of nature" was practised among the Romans down to the first century of the empire. This was with a people who recognised relationship through both father and mother, and it was

[1] Müller 1868, II, 284.   [2] Lubbock 1875, p. 148.
[3] Giraud-Teulon 1867, p. 33.

not a true instance of the *couvade.* So far, moreover, from this custom having any relation to a change from female to male kinship, it is most strongly pronounced among peoples having preferably a system of kinship through females. This is the case with the Arawaks and Caribs of British Guiana, and probably with the Abipones of Paraguay.[1] M. Giraud-Teulon[2] dwells on the domestic superiority of women among the Basques, with whom a husband "n' entre dans le maison que pour *reproduire* et travailler pour la bien de sa femme."

This "reproduction" furnishes the explanation of the custom in question. With some of the Brazilian tribes, when a man becomes a father he goes to bed instead of his wife, and all the women of the village come to console him for "la peine et douleur qu'il a eu de faire cet enfant."[3] This agrees with the idea entertained by so many peoples that the child is derived from the father only, the mother being merely its nourisher. When such an idea is held, it is not surprising if, as among the Abipones, the belief is formed that "the father's carelessness influences the new-born offspring, from a natural bond and sympathy of both,"[4] or if the father abstains, either before or after the child's birth, from eating any food or performing any actions which are thought capable of doing it harm.[5] Still more so, if the child is regarded, as is sometimes the case, as the reincarnation of the

[1] See Morgan 1877, p. 183.
[2] Giraud-Teulon 1867, p. 38.
[3] Gravier 1881, p. 45.
[4] Dobrizhoffer 1882.
[5] The Motumotu of New Guinea say that after conception the *mother* must not eat sweet potato or taro, lest the head of the child grow out of proportion, and the *father* must not eat crocodile or several kinds of fish, lest the child's legs grow out

father, a notion which is supported by the fact, pointed out by Mr Gerald Massey,[1] that in the *couvade* the parent identifies himself with the infant child, into which he has been typically transformed. The explanation given by Prof. Douglas of the *couvade* as practised by the aborigines in the Chinese province of Kwei-chow agrees with that view. He states that the father goes to bed with the infant for a month, " the idea being that the life of the father and child is one, and that any harm happening to the father will affect injuriously the well-being of the infant." [2]

Dr Tylor, while explaining the practice of the *couvade* as chiefly due to the confusion of imaginary and real relations, remarks that these nearly always " involve giving over the parentage to the father, and leaving the mother out of the question." This is an important statement, as it is confirmatory of the opinion that male parentage is fully recognised by peoples of a low degree of culture ; in fact, so fully that the parentage of the mother is almost lost sight of. We have evidence that among a race which, according to Dr Morgan, ranks below the Polynesians and African negroes, and far below the American abori-

of proportion. At Suau, a husband shuts himself up for some days after the birth of his *first* child, and will eat nothing. (Chalmers 1887, p. 165.) The severe fasting of the Caribs was only on the birth of the first child. The Mongols are said to nurse the first child to prevent the mother dying at the next birth. The birth of the first son is an important incident with the Hindoos, the Polynesians, the Kafirs, and other peoples.

[1] Massey 1883, I, 117ff. Mr. Massey explains the *couvade* by reference to Khefr, the Egyptian scarab god, who was the *creator by transformation*.

[2] Douglas 1882, p. 90.

gines, there is no such uncertainty of paternity as is required by Dr M'Lennan's theory of the origin of female kinship. In treating of Australian group marriage, we have seen[1] that in the groups which have a marked social organisation with uterine descent, there are two kinds of marital connections—one where two individuals are given to each other in permanent marriage by their parents; the other, where a man and woman are allotted to each other as *accessory spouses*, each of whom may stand in this relation to other individuals. In the marital group thus formed the permanent husband is the "father" of all his wife's children, and he claims the right to dispose of her daughter in marriage, although she may be actually the child of the woman's accessory husband, who is known as "little father."[2] This agrees with the fact that in the Tibetan polyandrous system the eldest brother is regarded as the father of all the children of the marriage; and as under the conditions of the Australian class system the father's blood, though not the father, is certain, kinship through males should have been established, if Dr M'Lennan's theory were correct.

It is surprising that Dr Morgan says little as to the origin of the system of kinship through females. He agrees with Dr M'Lennan so far as to say that "prior to the gentile organisation, kinship through females was undoubtedly superior to kinship through males, and was doubtless the principal basis upon which the lower tribal groups were organised." He affirms, however, that "descent in the female line, which is all that 'kinship through females only' can possibly indicate," is the only rule of a gens, and that relationship through the father is recognised as fully

[1] Above, pp. 115ff. [2] Howitt 1885, 813.

as that through the mother.[1] He says, further,[2] that the " gens, though a very ancient social organisation founded upon kin, does not include all the descendants of a common ancestor. It was for the reason that when the gens came in, marriage between single pairs was unknown, and descent through males could not be traced with certainty. Kindred were linked together chiefly through the bond of their maternity." We have here apparently two reasons stated for the establishment of kinship through females : the absence of marriages between single pairs, and the uncertainty of paternity. Both of these conditions are found by Dr Morgan in the *consanguine* family groups which he supposes to have been formed when promiscuity ceased. The classificatory system of relationships, the origin of which he traces to the consanguine family, can, however, receive a totally different interpretation, and the existence of that family itself is, as I have already shown,[3] very doubtful.

There is reason to believe that, notwithstanding the antiquity of the system of female kinship, relationship through the father, if not a developed system of male kinship, was fully recognised at an equally early period. To show the grounds for this opinion it is necessary to refer again to what was said above as to the distinction between *relationship* and *kinship*. Systems of kinship are based on the existence of a *special* relationship of persons to each other, as distinguished from the general relationship subsisting between such persons and other individuals. For instance, while a man may be related generally through his father to one class of individuals, and through his mother to another class, he may be of kin only to one

[1] Morgan 1877, p. 516. [2] *Ibid.*, p. 67.
[3] Above, pp. 23, 129.

class or the other. This special relationship or kinship is accompanied by certain disabilities, particularly in connection with marriage, which it would not be possible in small communities to extend to all persons related to each other through both parents. Kinship, as distinguished from mere relationship, must be restricted, therefore, to one line of descent. If the theory of Dr M'Lennan, or that of any of his successors, is correct, kinship must almost necessarily have been established through descent in the female line, as they all suppose the uncertainty of paternity in the early ages of mankind. Reasons have been given, however, for doubting the existence of such uncertainty, and it can be shown, moreover, that paternity is of secondary importance in relation to the question of kinship. This follows from the principle already laid down[1] that the objective phase of the sexual instinct, that which is at the base of the idea of kinship, has relation to the offspring of marriage. The primitive test of kinship was the right to the children born of the sexual union, and this right depended on the social customs of early races. In its absence there would be no *special* relationship, although there would be the general relationship based on the recognition of the ties between an individual and the persons connected with him through his two parents. We may have in this fact an explanation of the system of relationships which exists among the islanders of the Pacific and of the Indian Archipelago. This is said by Dr Morgan, to whose labours we are indebted for a knowledge of the subject,[2] to be the most primitive

---

[1] Above, p. 253.

[2] Lafitau, however, long since pointed out the existence of the classificatory system among the aborigines of North America (1724, I, 552).

form of the system under which all persons nearly related by blood to an individual are placed together in certain categories or classes, according to the generation to which they belong, instead of being distinguished by names denoting their special relationship to the individual or to each other.

Before treating of the Malayan system of relationships, we will endeavour to ascertain the principles which govern the right to the offspring of marriage, and in so doing we shall be able to show the origin of the different phases of kinship indicated by the custom of tracing descent preferably in the male or in the female line. It is evident that a child may be treated as specially related to either parent, and be reckoned of his or her kin to the exclusion of the kin of the other parent. There must be some reason for the preference in any particular case other than that based on paternity or maternity, seeing that uncultured peoples as a rule fully recognise the relationship of a child to both parents. As a fact, the kinship of the child depends on the conditions of the marital arrangement between its parents. Among the social restraints on promiscuity one of the most powerful is that which arises from the rights of a woman's father or kindred. These rights extend not only to her conduct before marriage, although they are often not strictly enforced, but also to the marriage itself and its consequences. Thus, the woman's father or her kin, *in the absence of any agreement to the contrary,* claim her children as belonging to them, whether she remains with them after her marriage, or goes to reside among her husband's kin. A woman may never leave her place of birth, where she may form a temporary or permanent marital alliance with one or more men, and then all her children will usually belong to her own kin. Such may be the case also whether she remain at home for a time, and afterwards goes to the place of abode of her husband's family, or becomes at once a permanent resident among them. In all cases the relationship of both parents to their offspring is fully recognised, but whether descent shall be traced in the female or the male line, depends on whether or not the woman's kin have given up their natural right to the children of the marriage. Ratification by the woman of the contract of marriage may be necessary, but the contract is generally entered into without her consent, and often without her cognizance, although on the terms of it depends the kinship of her offspring. If the husband does not give anything in return for his wife she continues a member of her own family group, and her children belong to their mother's kin. If, however, the husband pays a bride-price, she may have to give up her own family for that of her husband, and her offspring will belong to the latter.

The principles here laid down will be applied when we come to treat of what may be termed male kinship and female kinship. It should be noted here that either of these systems of kinship may exist in connection with any phase of marriage. This must be so, if the right to the offspring depends on whether or not the bride-price has been paid by the father. In fact, among the Australian aborigines, who have group marriage, not only do we find that in some tribes descent in the female line is preferred, and in other tribes descent in the male line, but that the so-called polyandry of the Nairs is associated with kinship through females, while the Todas, with their modified form of group marriage, have only kinship through males.

Again, some of the Islanders of the Pacific prefer one line of descent and some the other, those who practise *punalua* usually having male kinship ; while on the American continent, where traces of punalua have been found, and the pairing family was established among the natives, the gentile institution with descent in the female line appears to have been formerly nearly universal, although some of the tribes have, now at least, descent in the male line. Among polyandrous peoples the Tibetans have the system of male kinship, while in India and Ceylon female kinship is associated with polyandry of the *beena* type, and male kinship with that of the *deega* type, as was the case also among the polyandrous Arabs. Descent in the male line appears to be almost universally associated with systematic polygyny and monandry. Female kinship was, however, established among the monandrous Basques, and it exists also with some of the polygynous peoples of Africa. Sometimes, no doubt, there has been a change,[1] under the influence of new social conditions, from one system of kinship to another, and owing to the numerous traces of female kinship met with among peoples now preferring male kinship, it has been supposed that descent was at one time traced by such peoples in the female line. Reasons will be given hereafter for doubting whether this practice was ever universal, a view which loses sight of the fact that relationship in both lines of descent may have preceded the special relationship through one line only, which is expressed as kinship.

We will now proceed to consider the classificatory system of relationships as exhibited in its simplest form among the Polynesian islanders, whose system

---

[1] This point will be considered when treating of male kinship.

of consanguinity is pronounced by Dr Morgan[1] to be the oldest known among mankind. Under the Malayan system all persons nearly related by blood to an individual are placed together in certain categories or classes, according to the generation to which they belong, instead of being distinguished by names denoting their special relationship to the individual or to each other. The following table shows what persons in each generation are classed together by that system.

Grandparent Grade.

Grand-father's sister.	Grand-father's brother	Grand-father.	—	Grand-mother.	Grand-mother's brother.	Grand-mother's sister.

Parent Grade.

Father's sister.	Father's brother.	Father.	—	Mother.	Mother's brother.	Mother's sister.

Fraternal Grade.

Father's sister's child.	Father's brother's child.	Brother.	*Ego.*	Sister.	Mother's brother's child.	Mother's sister's child.

Child Grade.

Father's sister's grandchild.	Father's brother's grandchild.	Brother's child.	Child.	Sister's child.	Mother's brother's grandchild.	Mother's sister's grandchild.

Grandchild Grade.

Father's sister's child's grandchild.	Father's brother's child's grandchild.	Brother's grandchild.	Grandchild.	Sister's grandchild.	Mother's brother's child's grandchild.	Mother's sister's child's grandchild.

Dr Morgan, when referring to the agreement between this curious system and the Chinese " Grades of Relatives," remarks[2] that " if we make the application, commencing with grandfather, it will be seen that my grandparents, and such kinsmen of theirs as stand to me in the relation of grandparents, form one grade or class ; that my parents, and such relatives of theirs as stand to me in the relationship of parents, form a second grade or class ; that my-

[1] 1877, p. 403.
[2] Morgan 1871, p. 455.

self, with my brothers and sisters, and my collateral brothers and sisters, form a third grade or class ; that my children and the children of collateral [1] brothers and sisters form a fourth grade or class ; and that my grandchildren and my collateral grandchildren form a fifth grade or class: Those of each grade stand to ego in the same identical relationships, and the individuals of the same grade or class stand to each other in the relationship of brothers and sisters."

According to Dr Morgan's views the Malayan system here described represents all the blood relationships of a consanguine family as follows :—As all the brothers cohabit with their sisters, each child of the complex union must be equally related to every brother, and so must every child of such children. Moreover, each sister is in some sense mother to·all the children, since she is the wife of all her brothers. It is clear that the principle thus involved is applicable to all the members of the grade above that of the brothers and sisters who are thus supposed to cohabit, on both the father's and the mother's side ; seeing that, according to the assumption, the children of the father are those of all his brothers and sisters, and the children of the mother those of all her brothers and sisters. A more simple explanation, however, would be that all members of each grade intermarry in a group, and the offspring also intermarry in a group, giving the most perfect lineal and collateral blood relationship possible. The requirement that each sister should be mother to all the children furnishes a strong objection to Dr Morgan's theory. Although, under the conditions supposed, all the children of several brothers would be brothers and sisters to each

[1] This should be "own and collateral."

other, each father being equally the husband of all the mothers, yet these mothers can distinguish each her own children, who have clearly but one mother, although having apparently several fathers. Dr Morgan sees this difficulty, but he endeavours to put it on one side by the statement that the children of each wife would, as all the wives have the same husband, be step-children of the others, which relationship being unrecognised, they really fall into the category of sons and daughters. This explanation is not satisfactory, however, and as it has already been shown that there is no evidence of the former existence of the practice of own brothers and sisters intermarrying in a group, some explanation of the Malayan system must be found without having recourse to such a consanguine family.

In the first place, we may refer to the fact that in the classificatory system of the natives of America, although the children of brothers are described as brothers and sisters to each other, and the children of sisters are brothers and sisters to each other, yet the children of a brother and a sister stand to each other in a different relation.[1] The explanation of two of these cases is not difficult, as by the rules of the gentile institution, children take the family name of their mother, and a man must marry a woman of a different family group from that of his sister, so that their children must belong to different families. According to the same rule, the children of two sisters must bear the same name, and hence they will be more nearly related than the children of a brother and a sister. The nearness of relation between the children of two brothers cannot, however, be thus explained, unless it be assumed, as must have been the case if ever there were

[1] Morgan 1871, p. 144.

only two intermarrying groups, that the wives of all the brothers belonged to the same group. We should have an example of such a case in the *punaluan* custom, if the wives which several brothers had in common were own or collateral sisters belonging to another family. Here all the children of the complete union would take the name of their mothers, and would therefore be classed as brothers and sisters, and would stand in the relation of children to all the parents. The same result would follow if several sisters married several brothers, own or collateral, of another family group, and possessed their husbands in common.

If relationship is determined by reference to a common ancestor, through both the male and female lines, not only will the offspring of such an union as that first supposed be classed as brothers and sisters, but the children of a brother and those of a sister must also be brothers and sisters, although belonging to different families—in the one case that of the brother's father, and in the other that of the sister's father-in-law— seeing that they have on one side the same grandparents. The same is true of the children of several sisters, and in either case, therefore, the grandparents occupy the position of common ancestors. It is clear that all the descendants from the common ancestor in the same grade will stand in the same relation to him, and therefore in a special relation to each other. All his children are brothers and sisters, and so are all their children. Moreover, the latter are equally children to each of the persons in the grade above them, who are parents equally to all the children. Not so actually but relatively ; as in the earliest form taken by the classificatory system all the members of each

grade are classed together as standing in a special relation to the persons in the grade above them.   Hence
they are all equally related as " brothers" and "sisters,"
or " parents " and " children."   This class relationship
does not, however, exclude relationship by blood.   The
latter is indeed implied by the former, as all the persons belonging to the family group formed by its
living members are descended from a common ancestor.

The Malayan system of relationship can thus be
satisfactorily accounted for on the basis of the punaluan family, combined with reference to a common
ancestor, without resorting to the consanguine family,
which is essential to Dr Morgan's theory.   Punalua
belongs, as we have seen, to the earliest type of group
marriage, which is accompanied by the full recognition of relationship on both the paternal and the
maternal sides.   That there was such a perfect recognition of relationship is confirmed by the marriage
regulations in force among the peoples who possess
the Malayan system.   Such regulations may, indeed,
be used as a test of kinship.   Judging from Dr
Morgan's statement, that it was only necessary to
exclude own brothers and sisters from the intermarrying groups, " to change the consanguine into the
punaluan family," the Malayan system would allow
any persons to intermarry so long as they were not
own brothers and sisters.   In comparing this system
with that of the Australian aborigines, he says,[1] " The
number of persons in the Australian punaluan group
is greater than in the Hawaiian, and its composition
is slightly different ; but the remarkable fact remains
in both cases, that the brotherhood of the husbands
formed the basis of the marriage relation in one group,

[1] Morgan 1877, p. 425.

and the sisterhood of the wives the basis in the other. This difference, however, existed with respect to the Hawaiians, but it does not appear as yet that there were any classes among them between whom marriage must occur." The question is really, however, whether among the Polynesians there were any restrictions on marriage such as those provided by the Australian system, the "must" of which arises from the limitation placed on marriage by natural and social restraints.

Unfortunately little has been written with reference to the rules of marriage among the Polynesians, but there can be no doubt that, notwithstanding the brother and sister unions of the Hawaiians, stringent regulations existed for the prevention of the intermarriage of persons near of kin. An important remark bearing on this subject is made by the Rev. George Turner, who says,[1] after referring to the great prevalence of immorality among the Samoans, "considerable care is taken to prevent any union between near relatives; so much so, that a list of what they deem improper marriages would almost compare with the 'Table of Kindred and Affinity.' They say that of old custom and gods frowned upon the union of those in whom consanguinity could be closely traced. Few had the hardihood to run in the face of superstition; but if they did, and their children died at a premature age, it was sure to be traced to the anger of the household god on account of the forbidden marriage." It is a pity Mr Turner has not supplied a list of the forbidden marriages among the Samoans, who are probably the parent stock from which spring the Hawaiians, the New Zealanders, and the islanders

[1] Turner, G. 1861, p. 185.

of the East Pacific. From what we know, however, of the customs of peoples allied to the Polynesians, we are able to establish that descent in the male line and descent in the female line are both fully recognised by all the Oceanic races, and that whenever kinship is traced in one line, the other line of descent is regarded for certain purposes.

Let us first consider the question of descent in the male line. This is the established custom among the Malays of Sumatra, as might be inferred from the statement of Marsden [1] that marriages are forbidden between the children of two brothers, while allowing marriages between a brother's daughter and a sister's son. Probably we may accept the regulations in force among the Battas, as representing pretty nearly the primitive custom of the natives of the Indian Archipelago on the subject of marriage and relationship. As a rule, says Willer,[2] the Battaks forbid marriage between persons of the same *marga*, or family, and also between persons of different *margas* when they are already allied by blood. As, however, relationship through the mother is not here considered, children of a brother and those of a sister can be united, but not those of two brothers, unless they belong to a *marga*, the members of which cannot intermarry. Marriage connects the husband, but not his family, to his wife, while it unites the wife not only to her husband but to his family. Therefore, on his death he transmits his right to her and his duties to his nearest male relations, even to his son by a former wife if he has had no children by the widow. It

[1] Marsden 1811, p. 228.
[2] Cited in De Baecker·1874, pp. 489ff.

would be incest, however, for a father to take the widow of his son.[1] The children are of the *marga* of their father, and they, with marriageable girls and widows, belong to the father, the nearest male relation or the chief of the community.[2] Even if the male relation renounces his right to the widow, she cannot claim possession of her children, the right to whom depends on the payment of a bride-price, which is regulated by that paid for the mother and the grandmother of the intended bride.[3] Wife-purchase is practised by all the peoples of the Indian Archipelago, and when a man has received payment for his daughter, she and all the children born of the marriage belong to her husband. If he cannot pay the bride-price, he must live with his wife among her family to whom her children will belong.[4] Agreeably with the fact that descent is traced in the male line, and that females on the maternal side cannot inherit,[5] public offices are hereditary in the sense that they pass from father to son or to the nearest male relatives, although selective in the sense that the community can choose between sons or between brothers and other near relations.[6] Nevertheless, that descent in the female line is for certain purposes regarded, is evident from the fact that the nobility is divided into two classes, one of which includes persons whose father and mother both belong to the nobility, and the other persons whose fathers only are noble.[7] Moreover, where colonies are established under the leadership of men who are the sons of the same father, but not of the same mother, they are distinguished after the *sepantur*,

[1] De Baecker 1874, p. 496.
[2] *Ibid.*, p. 470.   [3] *Ibid.*, pp. 494, 497.   [4] *Ibid.*, p. 498.
[5] *Ibid.*, p. 507.   [6] *Ibid.*, p. 483.   [7] *Ibid.*, p. 471.

that is, the marriage from which they have originated.[1]

If now we examine the phenomena of social life
among the Polynesian islanders, we shall find them
to agree with the Malay institutions just referred to.
That descent is traced in the male line is shown by
the fact that in the Society Islands, when discovered
by Cook,[2] the possessions of families descended to the
eldest son, who was obliged to support his brothers
and sisters, and allow them houses on his estates.
Among the Maories of New Zealand, when a man
died his eldest son had all the rights of primogeniture,
and took the family name which his father had before
him, the second son assuming his father's second
name.[3] According to the Rev. Lorimer Fison, in
the Friendly Islands a man's children belong to his
tribe, and on his death his property descends to
them, while on their mother's death her property
remains with her husband and children.[4] Capt.
Cook remarks that on the death of a man of
wealth his property went to the king, who usually
gave it to the eldest son, conditional on his making a provision for the other children.[5] In the
Hervey Islands, the eldest son "as the future head
of the family, is called 'the chief,' special honour
being paid to him at his birth and death."[6] Among
the Samoans, the brother of a deceased husband

[1] Cited in De Baecker 1874, p. 478.
[2] Cook 1784, II, 113.
[3] Taylor 1870, pp. 326, 355.
[4] Morgan 1871, p. 579.
[5] Cook 1784, I, 304.
[6] Gill 1876, p. 30.

considered himself entitled to his brother's wife, and to be regarded by the orphan children as their father. The principal reason for the custom was "a desire to prevent the woman and her children returning to her friends, and thereby diminishing the number and influence of their own family. And hence, failing a brother, some other relative would offer himself, and be received by the widow."[1] That descent is traced by the Polynesians in the male line, either alone or jointly with descent in the female line, is confirmed by the remark of the Rev. R. H. Codrington, quoted by Mr Fison,[2] that the natives of Banks Islands and of the neighbouring groups reckon descent in the female line, "excepting where the Polynesian element is strong."

The Polynesian custom agrees with that of the Malays, in that the son of a chief succeeds to his father's title and office. This is so in the Friendly Islands, where the *Natché* ceremony was performed to initiate the king's son into the privilege of eating with his father, which was equivalent to a recognition of the son's right of succession to the sovereignty.[3] It was, indeed, an admission of his equality with his father, and afterwards the same obeisance was paid by the people to the heir apparent as to the king himself.[4] In the Society Islands, although the king had absolute power, his authority lasted only so long as he had no son to occupy the throne. On the birth of a son the sovereign invariably abdicated, the royal name was conferred on the infant, and his father was the first

[1] Turner, G. 1861, p. 190.
[2] Fison 1881, p. 314.
[3] Cook 1784, I, 241, 253, 350.
[4] *Ibid.*, I, 198.

to do him homage, by saluting his feet and declaring
him king. This practice was not confined to the royal
family, but was customary also among the nobility and
the *raatiras,* or proprietors of the soil, in both which
classes, says the Rev. Wm. Ellis,[1] "the eldest son
immediately at his birth received the honours and
titles which his father had hitherto borne." This
writer supposes that the practice was adopted to
secure a son the undisputed succession to his father's
dignity and power, and such might well be the case
where rank usually descends in the female line.
I would suggest, however, that it was rather in accordance with the notion, prevalent among peoples of all
degrees of culture, that a man is re-incarnated in
his son.[2] The Laws of Menu declare that a man
is born again in his son, and that by his eldest son
the father at the moment of birth discharges his
obligations to his own progenitors, and the eldest son
ought, therefore, to manage the whole patrimony.[3]

Notwithstanding what has been said above, the
Polynesians fully recognise descent in the female line.
This is proved by the fact that where rank is hereditary it is traced chiefly through females. In the
Sandwich Islands, females frequently reigned in their
own right.[4] It is possible, however, that this was
an innovation on ancient custom, according to which
offices would descend in the male line. We see
the influence of the Malayan idea that the highest
rank is that where both parents are noble, in the

---

[1] Ellis 1832–34, III, 99ff.

[2] Above, p. 262. Is the not unusual custom of a father taking the name of his eldest son connected with the same idea?

[3] Chap. 9. 8, 106.

[4] Jarves 1843, p. 33.

Hawaiian law, which requires that in order to prevent competition for the throne, the wife of the king should be as high born as any other female in the nation. This accounts for the marriage by the king of his own sister, the offspring of such an union being regarded as of the highest possible rank.[1] In the Friendly Islands great respect was shown for the aunt of the king, who·was considered as of divine origin.[2] Capt. Cook remarked that the king was not of the highest rank. He was inferior to four persons having the title of Tammaha, who were his father's sister, of equal rank and older than himself, and her three children.[3] As the woman in question was the king's paternal aunt, the reverence shown for her could not have been connected with female kinship. Its explanation is probably to be found in the custom of tracing nobility through both lines of descent. Among the Tongans rank descended through females, except with the Mataboole and Mooa classes, and if a woman was of superior rank to her husband he was obliged to pay her respect,[4] although a man has absolute authority in his own household. The recognition of relationship in the female line is shown also in the fact that the children of a free woman and a slave man take the social condition of their mother,[5] although possibly the absence of a bride-price in this case may have something to do with the result.

If we now turn to another branch of the widespread Oceanic race, we shall find that while descent is usually traced in the female line, relationship in the male line

[1] Wilkes 1849, IV, 31.   [2] *Ibid.*, III, 27.
[3] Cook 1784, I, 306.
[4] Mariner 1817, II, 86, 94ff.
[5] Spencer 1874, p. 10.

is also acknowledged. The Rev. Lorimer Fison, when speaking of a certain Fijian burial custom, states[1] that "the relationship between the paternal grandfather and his grandchild is closer than that which exists between the child and its father," and traceable to the "former prevalence of descent through females, which is indeed the rule among some of the Fijian tribes." In treating of land tenure in Fiji, Mr Fison remarks[2] that among the tribes who have uterine descent, "and who have not been brought into contact with tribes having agnatic descent, so as to be influenced by them," hereditary chieftainship does not exist. Mr Fison affirms that hereditary ruling chiefs are at first nothing more than heads of families who, under the influence of descent through males, have taken precedence of other heads of families by birthright. Thus, among the original *Mataveitathini*, or "Band of Brothers," from whom the various sections (yavusa), of which a *matagali* or division of a village (koro) belonging to a land-owning tribe are descended, "the elder brother takes precedence of the younger, and the yavusa, of which he is the ancestor, takes precedence of the other yavusa," the descendants of the elder brother being elder brothers for ever. There is something of the same kind in Samoa, where a village may contain ten or twenty titled heads of families, and one of the higher rank called chiefs. The titles of the heads of families are not hereditary, but the pedigree of the chiefs is carefully traced to the ancient head of some particular clan.[3] With the birthright is com-

[1] Fison 1881, p. 145.

[2] *Journal of the Anthropological Institute* 10 (1881), p. 346.

[3] Turner, G. 1861, p. 280. The system described in the text answers to that in use among the Chinese, whose laws recognise heads of families under a chief, who is the head of the clan (Doolittle 1868, p. 508).

bined the influence of polygamy. The operation of this practice in connection with the distinctions of rank is explained by Mr Fison as follows :—" Every chief of high rank has a certain wife, or certain wives, who are marama (high-born women—of ' good families'). These are called Watina Mbau, and his children by them are chiefs in their own right. But though all these wives are marama, one of them may be of a ' better family' than the others, and her child is consequently of higher rank than are their children, for rank is derived from the mother as well as from the father ! Hence a man may be of higher rank than his own father, if his mother be of a better family than that of his paternal grandmother." This agrees exactly with the Polynesian custom already referred to. As a further case in point, it may be mentioned that in the Sandwich Islands daughters by a wife of more elevated rank were preferred to sons by a wife of lower rank.[1]

Before leaving the Pacific Islanders, reference should be made to the curious custom found among the Fijians, according to which one man becomes *vasu* to another. This title is borne by the son of a man who has married into a strange tribe, and it expresses the connection in which he stands to his mother's brother, and the privileges he possesses over his uncle's moveable property. This the *vasu* is said to have at his absolute disposal, and he can at any time take whatever he chooses. Mr Fison regards this right as a survival of inheritance through the mother, under which the sister's son becomes the heir, to the exclusion

[1] Wilkes 1849, IV, 31.

of the son.[1] It may be doubted, however, whether this is a sufficient explanation of the custom. Mr Fison speaks of the great vasu (vasu levu), who is vasu to the whole community, and according to Dr Seemann,[2] there are vasus not only to families, but to towns and states, and it is considered shabby to resist their exactions. When the vasu right is exercised, however, a return is expected to be made, and most probably the custom in question is equivalent to that of adoption as practised in the neighbouring Polynesian Islands. In Samoa it was formerly the general rule for a man to give away his child to his sister. In return, she and her husband gave to the father some foreign property (tonga). The child was viewed as *tonga*, and was a channel through which foreign property would flow from its parents to the family by which it was adopted. On the other hand, the child was to its parents " a source of obtaining foreign property (oloa)[3] from the parties who adopt it, not only at the time of its adoption, but so long as the child lives." The Rev. George Turner regarded the custom of adoption as "not so much the want of natural affection, as the sacrifice of it to this systematic facility of traffic in native and foreign property."[4] The Fijian custom of vasu appears to have a similar effect, and probably it is intended as an acknowledgment of the actual existence of a certain relationship, rather than a relic of an earlier system of kinship.

[1] *J.A.I.* 10 (1881), p. 339.

[2] Seemann 1862, p. 216.

[3] *Oloa* denotes foreign property as distinguished from *toga*, native property. See Pratt 1878.

[4] Turner, G. 1861, p. 179.

The Malagasy, like the Islanders of the Pacific, have a system of relationship resembling that termed Malayan. The Rev. James Sibree says, with reference to the former,[1] " It is often difficult to ascertain exactly the relationship of members of a family, for first cousins are usually termed brother and sister, and uncles and aunts—father and mother respectively ; and it is only by asking distinctly of persons whether they are ' of one father,' or are ' uterine brother and sister,' that we learn the exact degree of relationship. These secondary fathers and mothers seem often to be regarded with little less affection than the actual parents." The nature of the marriage restrictions associated with the Malagasy system of relationships shows that, for certain purposes at least, descent in the female line is preferred. Thus marriage is forbidden between the children and descendants of two sisters by the same mother to the fifth generation, that is, says Mr Sibree, to the great-great-great-grandchild of such two sisters. Such marriages are " regarded with horror as incest, being emphatically *fady*, or tabooed . . . so that when a man divorces his wife, he calls her *anabàvy*, sister, implying that any intercourse between them is henceforth impossible." Marriage between brothers' and sisters' children are permissible on the performance of a slight prescribed ceremony, which is supposed to remove any impediment arising from consanguinity.[2] Marriage between the children of two brothers is not only allowed but is very common, being regarded as " the most proper kind of

[1] Sibree 1870, p. 192 ; cf. Sibree 1880.

[2] This expiation is practised also by the Malays (Marsden 1811, p. 225).

connection, as keeping property together in the same family." It is called *lova-tsi-mifindra*, "inheritance, not removing." Marriage restrictions among the Malagasy are thus evidently based on the idea of kinship through the mother, and Mr Sibree refers to their having the practice of inheriting rather through the female than the male line. In accordance with this principle,[1] the genealogy of the sovereign and the nobles is traced by the female and not by the male line.

And yet relationship through the father is fully recognised by the Malagasy. Mr Sibree states that, owing to the former prevalence of polygamy and divorce, half-brothers and sisters are much more numerous among the Malagasy than in European nations, and that there is no distinctive word for that half-relationship; but he adds, "They say that such an one is *miray ray*, ' of one common father ' with another, or *miray tam-po*, ' of one common mother,' or literally ' joined from the heart.' "[2] By Malagasy custom, if an elder brother dies childless his next brother must marry the widow to keep up his brother's remembrance, the children of such marriages being considered as the heirs and descendants of the elder brother.[3] The existence of the law of the Levir among the Malagasy is conclusive evidence that relationship in the male line is fully recognised by them, although for certain purposes, and particularly in connection with marriage, that in the female line may be preferred. We have an analogous case among the

[1] Reference to it is probably to be seen in the Council of Twelve Old Women, whom it was customary for the Hova sovereign to consult.

[2] Sibree 1870, p. 39.   [3] *Ibid.*, p. 37.

negroes of the African Gold Coast, with whom children
do not inherit their parent's effects, brothers' and
sisters' children being a man's heirs, and yet the eldest
son of a· king, or of a governor of a town, succeeds
to his father's office.[1]

Reference has already been made [2] to the agreement
which exists between the classification adopted in the
Malayan system of relationship and the five grades of
relations of the Chinese, and it is advisable to consider whether the latter system throws any light on
the former. Dr Morgan remarks [3] that " the Hawaiian
system of consanguinity realises the nine grades of
relations (conceiving them reduced to five by striking
off the two upper and the two lower members) more
perfectly than that of the Chinese at the present time.
While the latter has changed through the introduction
of Turanian elements, and still more through special
additions to distinguish the several collateral lines, the
former has held, pure and simple, to the primary
grades which presumptively were all the Chinese
possessed originally." He continues, " It is evident
that consanguinei, in the Chinese as in the Hawaiian,
are generalised into categories of generations ; all
collaterals of the same grade being brothers and sisters
to each other. Moreover, marriage and the family are
conceived as forming within the grade, and confined,
so far as husbands and wives are concerned, within its
limits. As explained by the Hawaiian categories it is
perfectly intelligible. At the same time it indicates
an anterior condition among the remote ancestors of
the Chinese, of which this fragment preserves a knowledge, precisely analogous to that reflected by the

[1] Bosman 1721, p. 172.
[2] Above, p. 272.
[3] Morgan 1877, p. 416.

Hawaiian. In other words, it indicated the presence of the punaluan family when these grades were formed, of which the consanguine was a necessary predecessor." The consanguine family was not, however, the necessary predecessor of the punaluan,[1] and there is no warrant for the statement that marriage is conceived by the Chinese system as being formed within the grade. Although the Chinese do not consider it worth while to observe the tie of consanguinity after the fifth generation, yet all the descendants of a single pair are related, as is shown by the fact that persons having the same family name, which is that of the paternal ancestor, cannot intermarry ; a restriction which is inconsistent with the assertion that marriage is formed within the grade. The Chinese system recognises more remote grades of ancestors and descendants than the Malayan, but the name given to the grandfather, *tsŭ*, shows that originally it was not so, the word *tsŭ* meaning "one who begins or founds a family."[2] Moreover, the remote progenitors and descendants are expressed by similar terms. Thus, according to Mr Hart, in the Chinese system "my great-great-grandfather is the more remote of my practically recognised forefathers ; while, in the same way, my most remote practically recognised descendant is my great-great-grandson." Beyond these limits individuals are classed generally as "ancestors" and "descendants," as in the Malayan system, a practical application of the general rule being found in the Malagasy custom which disallows marriages between the descendants of two sisters down to the fifth generation.

Although the Chinese usually prefer descent in the

---

[1] On this subject, see above, p. 21.
[2] Hart 1871, p. 432.

male line, yet relationship in the female line is fully
recognised by them. An example of this is seen
in the mode of address, in use by the natives of
Keang-se, known as *Laon-peaon*, which, as translated by Mr Hart, is, " O you old fellow! brother
mine by some of the ramifications of female relationship." That this is not a mere local idea is
evident from the actual expressions to denote such
relationship given in Mr Hart's Table of Consanguinity.[1] Thus, not only are the names given to
the mother, "mother-relation" and "house-mother,"
similar to those given to the father, "father-relation"
and "house-father," but the word *tsŭ*, ancestral, is
applied to the grandmother as well as to the grandfather on the father's side. The *maternal* grandmother is not designated, but the great-grandmother
on the mother's side is termed ancestral (*tsŭ*), although with the addition of the word *wae* (outer),
denoting that she is out of the (father's) family.

In one case a son takes the family name of his
mother. This is where a man having only a female
child, instead of marrying her out brings to his own
house a husband for her, and then, says Mr Hart,[2] " if
more sons than one are the fruit of the marriage, the
second one generally takes the mother's family name,
and is considered literally her father's race." [3] The
Japanese have analogous customs. Among them the
eldest son, who inherits the property, is not allowed
to leave the paternal home, and when he marries he
takes his wife to his father's house, and she assumes

[1] *Ibid.*, p. 432.   [2] *Ibid.*, p. 435.

[3] This is equivalent to the rule laid down by the laws of
Menu (9. 127), that a man having no son may appoint his
daughter to raise up a son to him.

his family name.   Nor can the eldest daughter leave
her father's house when she marries.   Her husband
must go to reside with her and take her family
name.   Moreover, if a man "buys a house for his
second or younger son, and he marries, his wife
takes the family name ; but if the wife's father
provides the house, then he loses his family name
and takes that of his wife."[1]   The Malay marriage
customs show the influence of the same ideas.   They
have a mode of marriage called *ambel ana*, in which
the father of a maiden acquires a husband for her
and takes him into his own house, the husband's
family renouncing all further right to him.[2]

The influence of the idea of kinship is shown among
the Chinese in the rule that cousins who have not
the same ancestral names may intermarry, that is,
children of sisters, or of a brother and of a sister,
but not children of brothers.[3]   This rule is founded
on the custom of tracing descent through males, and
agrees with the Malay rule rather than that of the
Malagasy, who in relation to marriage prefer descent
in the female line.   Mr Douglas states[4] that the
only ancient bar to marriage was consanguinity, as
evidenced by the possession of the same surname,
and he ascribes the illegality of marriage with a
cousin on the mother's side, and with a step-
daughter or a mother's sister, to later legislation.   If
this is true, the primitive system would answer to
the class system of the Australians, but the date of
the Chinese penal code, which also forbids marriage

[1] Morgan 1871, p. 428.
[2] Marsden 1811, p. 262.
[3] Doolittle 1868, p. 69.
[4] Douglas 1882, p. 84.

with a relation within four degrees and between persons nearly connected by marriage, is uncertain.[1]

Mr Hart supposes the Chinese system of relationships to have had its origin in the cradle land of humanity, when " each successive birth was considered as increasing the *one* family, and as being in relationship with every individual composing that family, and when from the original pair of parents down to their coeval great-great-grandchildren, the relationship of each to the other through every successive grade, and upwards and downwards, could be distinctly traced, accurately expressed, and was in actual being, having a personal interest for, and being patent to the observation of all." [2] This is equally true of the Malayan system, the analogy between which and the Chinese system of relationships is so close, we cannot doubt that a similar explanation will apply to them both, especially as in most cases each of them is associated with descent in the male line. Relationship in the female line is, however, fully recognised by the Chinese, and it would be surprising if it were not so also among the Polynesians. This is, indeed, admitted by Dr Morgan, who says,[3] that the Malayan system of consanguinity shows " plainly and conclusively that kinship through males was recognised as constantly as kinship through females. A man had brothers and sisters, grandfathers and grandmothers, grandsons and granddaughters, traced through males as well as through females." He qualifies the admission, however, by the statement that " the maternity of children was

---

[1] *Ta-Tsing-Leu-Lee*, div. III. 108, 109; div. VI. 368; see also Staunton 1810, introduction.

[2] Morgan 1871, p. 425. [3] Morgan 1877, p. 515.

ascertainable with certainty, while their paternity was not ; but they did not reject kinship through males because of uncertainty, but gave the benefit of the doubt to a number of persons—probable fathers being placed in the category of real fathers, probable brothers in that of real brothers, and probable sons in that of real sons." This is very ingenious, but the uncertainty of paternity assumed by Dr Morgan did not exist ; or at least there was a certainty of the paternal blood in the punaluan family, which in combination with descent from a common ancestor would give all the relationship of the Malayan system. The very nature of punaluan marriage as defined by Dr Morgan [1] would suppose the recognition of relationship through both parents. There " the brotherhood of the husbands formed the basis of the marriage relation in the one group, and the sisterhood of the wives the basis in the other." Now, the latter is the phase of punalua of which traces have been met with among the natives of North America, who show so perfect a development of the gentile organisation, the original rule of descent in which appears to have been in the female line. On the other hand, as we shall see in a subsequent chapter, the phase of punalua which is based on the brotherhood of the husbands is associated with descent in the male line. We should expect, therefore, to find that where, as with the Hawaiians, both those forms of punalua were in use, *relationship* would be traced through both males and females.

It does not follow, however, that descent in both lines is equally regarded for all purposes. In fact, descent in either the male or the female line is usually

---

[1] *Ibid.*, p. 426.

preferred for the purpose of tracing kinship as distinguished from mere relationship, a distinction which
Dr Morgan loses sight of. There must be such a
preference where, as is always the case among primitive peoples, consanguinity is looked upon as a bar
to marriage, as otherwise in small communities there
would be often great difficulty in marrying at all. It
is so occasionally under ordinary conditions, as mentioned by Mr Howitt in connection with some of the
Australian tribes. He says:[1] "I have endeavoured
to show in the Dieri the prohibition arising out of
class and close relationship, and in the Kurnai those
arising out of close relationship and locality. In the
Aldolinga all these restricting forces combine, and
result in the narrowing down of the matrimonial
choice to an incredibly small fraction of the whole
number of women."[2] With kinship in the male line
all persons who bear the name of the father's family
will be debarred from intermarriage, and where the
female line is chosen the persons forbidden to intermarry will be those who belong to the mother's family.
As, however, relationship by both lines of descent is
regarded for certain purposes, marital unions between
any persons closely related on either side are often
forbidden. We have already seen that marriage
regulations in force among some of the lowest Australian tribes, who have also uterine descent, do not
permit marital unions between persons standing towards each other in any of the following relations :—
Father or mother, father's or mother's brother or sister,
brother's or sister's child, brother, sister, or any of our

---

[1] Howitt 1885, p. 821n.

[2] We have here a chief cause of elopement, and the stealing
of women from other tribes. [For an argument against the

"cousins" on either the father or the mother's side. If relationship through females was the only bar to the formation of sexual unions, a man might marry his aunt or his niece if her mother belonged to a different totem or family group from his own. Moreover, in such a case a woman might marry not only her half brother,[1] but even her own father, as he would not belong to her totem. The fact that such alliances are not permitted shows that the recognition of blood relationship is not restricted to the female side. What is true of the Australian aborigines is probably true also of the Polynesian Islanders, who have the Malayan system of relationships. Here all the members of a common grade are brothers and sisters, and if we apply the remarks made by Mr Howitt, that in the Australian system "the filial relations were inherited, carrying with them fraternal relations in ever-widening lines," combined with an equally extended prohibition of intermarriage,[2] it may be safely inferred that the Malayan system instead of giving evidence of the intermarriage of brothers and sisters, own or collateral, proves on the contrary, that the restrictions on marriage arising from consanguinity were even more wide-reaching than those in force among the Australian aborigines, and therefore that such marriages must have been at one time absolutely prohibited.

common misconception that the choice of spouse in an Australian section-system is particularly restricted, see Claude Lévi-Strauss, "Diogène couché," *Les Temps Modernes*, X, 1955, 1187–1220 (pp. 1209–10).—R.N.]

[1] Marriage with a half sister is allowed by some Australian tribes, but it appears to be exceptional.

[2] Howitt 1885, pp. 816, 820.

CHAPTER IX.

KINSHIP THROUGH FEMALES.

IN the preceding chapter it was shown that the peoples who possess the earliest types of marriage fully recognise the relationship of an individual to the persons composing each of the family groups to which his father and his mother belong, although they may prefer one line of descent to the other for the purposes of kinship. That conclusion is contrary to the views of Dr M'Lennan, Dr Morgan, and other writers, who regard the system of female kinship as the most ancient, and an examination has been made, therefore, of their arguments, with the result of showing that they have entirely failed to establish the uncertainty of paternity to which they ascribe the origin of that system. Dr Morgan, indeed, when criticising Dr M'Lennan's phase, *the system of kinship through females only*, affirms[1] that "the Turanian, Ganowanian, and Malayan systems of consanguinity show plainly and conclusively that kinship through males was recognised as constantly as kinship through females." This admission is spoilt, however, by the remark that the former is consistent with uncertainty of paternity, the benefit of the doubt being given to a number of persons. Mr Fison more truly asserts[2]

[1] Morgan 1877, p. 515.
[2] Fison and Howitt 1880, pp. 119, 126.

that "the line of descent does not at all affect the personal relationship," and that "father and son are none the less related as father and son because they are of different gentes, when descent is reckoned through females," although under the group system a father may have many "sons," and a son many "fathers," that are not actually his own. The same may be said with reference to a mother and her children, whose descent is traced preferably through males.

We have now to show how the custom of tracing kinship or descent through females rather than through males originated. There is no doubt that the former has been preferred by many peoples from a very early period, and there is evidence, moreover, that it has in some cases been replaced by the tracing of descent through males, while it does not appear that the converse process ever takes place. Whether the special relationship expressed in the phrase "kinship through females," was actually developed before the system of male kinship, depends on the conditions of the earliest marital arrangements. It has already been stated that the right to the offspring of the marriage will decide whether descent is to be traced in the female line or in the male line. If the woman's father or her family group have given up their natural right to her children, the offspring of the marriage will be classed as of the kin of their father, but if not, they will be considered as belonging to their mother's kin. This will always be the case in the absence of an agreement to the contrary, whether the woman remains after her marriage among her own family, or goes to reside with that of her husband.

We may refer, in illustration of these remarks, to the social arrangements of the ancient Arabs, who, according to Prof. Robertson Smith,[1] possessed a form of polyandry in which " the woman lives among her own kin, and, bearing children for them and not for outsiders, is free to distribute her favours at will." Under these circumstances, the children belong to the mother's family group, not on account of any uncertainty of paternity, as Prof. Smith supposes, but because the right to them has not been transferred to their father or his kin. In later Arab marriages, under the system of male kinship, the wife follows the husband and bears children who are of his blood. This is so whether constituted by capture or by contract.[2] In the latter case, the husband by his contract with the wife's kin, purchases " the right to have children by her, and to have these children belong to his own kin." [3] This assumes that in the absence of such a contract the children would belong to their mother's kin, which would be the case almost universally where the wife did not leave her own family, the husband residing either permanently or temporarily with them.[4] The property acquired by a husband under a contract of marriage was not so much in the woman herself, who did not change her kin or marriage, as in the right to live with her and get children by her. [5] The woman is thus regarded as a child-bearer, and it is evident that she is valued by her kin chiefly in that character. Formerly, whether a wife remained with her own family, or went with her husband to live among his tribe, she and her children formed a separate group, having their own hut or tent. In Arabia

[1] Robertson Smith 1885, p. 146.　　[2] *Ibid.*, p. 75.
[3] *Ibid.*, p. 108.　　[4] *Ibid.*, p. 62.　　[5] *Ibid.*, p. 101.

even now, where a man has more wives than one, they usually live apart each with her own children, and in the early times when, according to Prof. Smith,[1] *beena* marriage prevailed, the tent was the wife's, and after her death passed to her children. In the *beena* marriage of Ceylon, the husband or husbands of a woman live with her in or near the house of her birth, and here also the children belong to the family group of their mother.

Where a woman remains with her own kin, and her children are retained by them, it may be a matter of indifference by whom the children are begotten and under what circumstances, so long as the woman does not act contrary to the natural or social regulations of marriage. The early Arabs allowed a woman not only to form a *mot'a* marriage, in which she could choose and dismiss her husband at will, but also to receive occasional visits from a lover, although he might be of a hostile tribe. They appear indeed to have recognised any marital connection formed by a woman while she remained with her own tribe, so long as it did not involve loss of character or prevent the tribe from recognising her children.[2] Such connections, which involve no subjection to a husband, are termed by Prof. Smith, *sadíca* marriages, as " a woman who was visited by a man from time to time was called his *sadíca*, or female friend." [3] These arrangements were regarded as marriages, a woman having only one husband at a time, but a condition of sexual morality, in which every woman freely received any suitor she pleased, appears to have been common down to the time of Mohammed.[4] So long as such a system did not

[1] *Ibid.*, p. 169.   [2] *Ibid.*, p. 72.   [3] *Ibid.*, p. 75.
[4] *Ibid.*, p. 174.

infringe the recognised rules of social propriety, and
was not objected to by the woman's kinsfolk, there was
nothing wrong in it from the natural standpoint, and
it would be accepted without difficulty if, as was the
case under such conditions among the Arabs, the offspring belonged to the woman's kin and became members of her tribe.

It would seem to have been a general custom in
ancient Arabia for the husband to live among his
wife's kinsfolk. Professor Smith remarks[1] that
"when something like regular marriage began, and a
free tribeswoman had one husband or one definite
group of husbands at a time, the husbands at first
came to her and she did not go to them." Under
these circumstances, the woman bore children for her
own kin, to whose group they belonged by virtue of
their birth, "because the blood of the group flows
in their veins."[2] Among the American tribes, the
husband and wife always belonged to the cabin of
their mothers,[3] and the wife usually remained in her
mother's cabin, where her relations exercised a strict
surveillance over her conduct, in order that the marriage should not be consummated for the first year.[4]
The Australian aborigines differ from the Americans
in that, even among the tribes who have uterine
descent, a wife usually goes to reside with her husband's family, a son always remaining in his father's
horde.[5] The son is under the dominion of the father,
of whom in some tribes he is regarded as the actual
re-incarnation, and who represents the original male

[1] *Ibid.*, p. 301.   [2] *Ibid.*, p. 146.
[3] Lafitau 1724, I, 577.
[4] *Ibid.*, I, 569, 574.
[5] Howitt and Fison 1885, p. 145.

ancestor of the horde. Mr Fison remarks that the
succession of the son to the father's horde can scarcely
be called inheritance from the father, as among nomad
hunters like the Australians, "there is little or nothing
to inherit, except a hunting right which is common to
all the members of the horde, of whatsoever social
division they may be."[1] The inheritance has relation
to the local organisation of the clans or local groups
of which the tribe is now made up. Each clan has,
says Mr Fison,[2] perpetual succession through males,
who hunt over the same tracts of country as their
father hunted over before them, while its females
have to become the wives of men belonging to other
groups, whose sisters come to it as wives. Thus,
"while the clan has perpetual succession through
males, and its local name remains constantly the same,
the class and totem names of its members, being transmitted through females, change with each generation."
If the custom of sons remaining with the horde has
been the rule from the earliest period, the two original
exogamous intermarrying classes may have had separate territories and local organisations. To perpetuate
this organisation in the same clan, it would be necessary for sons to remain in the clan territory, and this
necessity would account for the fact of women leaving
their parental home on marriage, although their
children were reckoned among their own and not
their husband's kindred. It is not improbable that
the Australian system supplies an explanation of the
fact that, with the natives of North America, a wife
often accompanied her husband to reside among his

[1] Mr. Fison adds that among agricultural tribes, who have
descent through the mother, the land goes with the "name."

[2] Howitt and Fison 1883, p. 34.

family; in which case, although the children of the marriage would belong to their mother's gens, the daughters, like their mother, going elsewhere on marriage, the sons would remain near their father and represent his tribe. Under these conditions, the American tribe would closely resemble the clan or local organisation of the Australian aborigines, with its perpetual succession through males, combined with descent through females in the family groups or totems of which it is composed.

The same thing takes place among some of the African tribes. On the Gold Coast,[1] when a man marries he takes his bride home to reside with him, although she is not acquired by purchase. The man makes certain presents to his wife's relations, which he can again claim if she afterwards leaves him. From the fact that a man's property descends not to his children but to his eldest nephew on the mother's side, a woman's property going to the eldest daughter of her mother's sister, we may judge that kinship is traced through the female line. Relationship in the male line, however, is recognised, as appears from the fact that the son is not allowed to eat what his father is restrained from, and that a man is responsible for the actions of his sons, as well as of his nephews.[2] The second, or *bossum*, wife is not a free woman like the first, but a slave bought by a man for the purpose of being consecrated to his god. As she has been purchased and thus consecrated, she is the favourite wife, and her husband is very jealous of her,[3] and Dr M'Lennan is right in supposing that her children

[1] Bosman 1721, pp. 168 ff.
[2] *Ibid.*, pp. 130, 174.
[3] *Ibid.*, p. 169.

would be of the kindred of their father, differing in this respect from the children of other wives. He is in error, however, when he treats the giving of nuptial presents by the West African as constituting wife-purchase, and therefore, in inferring that wife-purchase is not in this instance sufficient to carry the children to the father from the kindred of their mother.[1] Where the offspring of the marriage are not classed among the father's kin,[2] there is no true wife-purchase. The difference is shown in the practice of the American tribes, with whom a man may make presents to his wife's relations, but the gift only secures him the personal service of his wife, and does not give him any ownership over her offspring.[3]

Wife-purchase is usual with most of the peoples of the Indian Archipelago, and when the agreed price has been received by the father, his daughter and her children belong to the husband. If he cannot pay the price, however, he must reside with his wife's family, and will have no right over the children of the marriage.[4] This appears to be the case also in some instances where a price is paid to the wife's relations, but the husband after marriage lives among them. Thus, with the Sengirese,[5] a man pays to his wife's parents a dowry (*harta*) which varies with the rank of the woman. The husband always goes to the

[1] McLennan 1885, p. 235. In this work, Dr. McLennan finds in wife-purchase a cause of change in kinship, but nothing more.

[2] Sometimes, however, a child may, when grown up, choose whether he will belong to his father's or his mother's kin.

[3] Lafitau 1724, I, 565ff.

[4] Above, p. 279.

[5] Hickson 1887, p. 138.

house of his wife, whether she lives in the same village or not, and becomes a member of her family, the only exceptions being the sons of the rajahs, who may follow their wives or not as they like.   The children belong to the *kampong* of the wife, but it is said elsewhere that "the children of the marriage when they are old enough may choose the family to which they will belong, that is, whether they will belong to the family of their father or mother."   The *harta* of the Sengirese is much the same as the *touhor* of the Battaks,[1] although the payment of the former does not, like the latter, operate as a bride-price.   The reason for the difference is probably that in the one case and not in the other the husband resides among his wife's family, who therefore claim her children.   Kinship is thus usually traced by the Sengirese through the mother, but there is no evidence of the existence among them of the matriarchal system, such as is established among the Garos of Eastern Bengal. The Garo villages, or clans, are divided into *Maharis*, or motherhoods, some of which are especially connected with others and intermarry with them.[2]   They are like the primary exogamous intermarrying classes of the Australians, as "a man's sister marries in the family from which he derives his wife ; his son may marry a daughter of that sister, and, as male heirs do not inherit, the son-in-law, succeeding his father-in-law in right of his wife, gets his father's sister, who is his wife's mother, as an additional wife to live with."[3]   The Garos practise ceremonial marriage by

[1] De Baecker 1874, p. 494.

[2] These Maharis answer to the *Margas* of the Battaks, who have *male* kinship.

[3] Rowney 1882, p. 194.

capture, but it is the female and her friends who catch the bridegroom, and not the reverse. The Khasiahs, who are probably related to the Garos, also marry away from home. A man when he marries goes to live with his wife at her father's house, and his sister's children and not his own are his recognised heirs.[1] Polyandry is said to have been prevalent at one time among the Khasiahs, and their marriage system probably answers to the *beena* marriage of Ceylon, in which the husband, or husbands where there are more than one, live with a woman in or near the house of her birth. Among the Kocch tribe, also, a man goes on marriage to live with his wife and her mother, of whose family he is a subordinate member.[2] In all these cases the children of the marriage belong to the wife's family, and descent is traced, therefore, in the female line, but no special social organisation springs from that custom.

It is different where a woman abandons her father's house to live among her husband's kin, and yet the offspring of the marriage are classed with the kin of the wife. The woman and her children form a group distinct from that among which they reside, and as the sub-group increases from generation to generation, it is necessary to have some means of identifying its individual members to prevent the intermarriage of kinsmen, and to ascertain the persons who are bound together by obligations of mutual assistance. The use of totems, as badges of fraternity, had probably those ends in view, although they may be used also where all the members of a group are kinsmen. When we come to treat of totemism we shall

---

[1] *Ibid.*, p. 189.
[2] McLennan 1876, pp. 149, 151.

see that with the American tribes the word *totem* signifies the symbol or device of a gens, and that the expression "totemic institution" is employed by Schoolcraft
as synonymous with the gentile organisation. A consideration of the nature of the primitive gens will show
that it is a development of the group composed of the
descendants of a woman who had on marriage left
her father's house to reside among her husband's kin,
under conditions which retained her offspring as members of her own family group. The gens is, according
to Dr Morgan,[1] "a body of consanguinei descended
from the same common ancestor, distinguished by a
gentile name, and bound together by affinities of
blood." It includes, however, only a moiety of such
descendants, and where descent is in the female line,
"the gens is composed of a supposed female ancestor
and her children, together with the children of the
female descendants through females in perpetuity."
That definition would apply equally well to the *hayy*
or kindred group of the Arabs. The whole group
conceives itself, says Professor Smith,[2] "as having a
single life, just as in the formula, 'our blood has been
spilt,' it speaks of itself as having but one blood in its
veins." This conception shows its influence in three
things in which the whole *hayy*, or its active members,
have a common interest—the rights and duties of
blood-feud, the distribution of inheritance, and the
distribution of booty.[3] This implies that the kinsfolk
lived together, and the *hayy* was in fact a group which
not only fought together, but usually migrated together within the limits of its own pastures, forming
a single settlement, and guided by one chief.[4] This

[1] Morgan 1877, p. 63.   [2] Robertson Smith 1885, pp. 23, 40.
[3] *Ibid.*, p. 54.   [4] *Ibid.*, pp. 36ff.

was the ancient Arab tribe, composed of the descendants of a common female ancestor, having descent in the female line, and requiring its women to remain with the tribe when they marry, that their children may not be lost to it. The use by the early Arabs of totems to distinguish groups of kinsfolk appears now to be well established by Professor Smith's careful investigations.[1]

The American gens differs from the Arabian *hayy* in the fact that, while the latter generally includes the whole body of kinsfolk, the former usually exists by the side of other gentes within the tribe, and is spread throughout several tribes. Dr Morgan remarks[2] that the gens came into being upon three principal conceptions—" the bond of kin, a pure lineage through descent in the female line, and non-intermarriage in the gens." These conceptions embody merely the fact that the descendants of a common female ancestor are regarded as kinsfolk, and as such not able to marry among themselves. Among other privileges and obligations associated with the membership of a gens is the obligation not to marry in the gens ; mutual rights of inheritance of the property of deceased members ; and reciprocal obligations of help, defence, and redress. The functions and attributes of the gens, says Dr Morgan,[3] " gave vitality as well as individuality to the organisation, and protected the personal rights of its members," who, as being specially connected by the ties of blood relationship, may be regarded as forming an enlarged family group, or rather a fraternal association based on kinship. The gens would, however, form too large a group for all social purposes, and a

[1] *Ibid.*, Chap. 7   [2] Morgan 1877, p. 69.
[3] *Ibid.*, p. 71.

smaller group would be composed of those more immediately allied by blood. Thus, although theoretically the effects of a deceased person were distributed among his gentile relations, yet Dr Morgan admits[1] that " practically they were appropriated by the nearest of kin." It could not have been otherwise where the members of the gens are numerous or widely distributed. The same principle would apply in relation to rights over children, who are " the wealth of savages." Among the natives of North America each gens had personal names used by it alone, and a gentile name conferred gentile rights. Now, although a child was not fully " christened" until its birth and name had been announced to the council of the tribe, its name was selected by its mother with the concurrence of her nearest relatives. Nothing is said by Dr Morgan of any right of the gens over the marriage of its members, and it would seem not to have had any voice in the matter. The formation of the alliance was usually left to the two individuals more immediately concerned, or to their near relations.[2] With descent in the female line, the children belong to the gens of their mother, and, as being of the same family group, they are considered as more nearly related to their mother's brother than to their father. This maternal uncle is in some respects the head of his sister's family, and Mr Morgan states[3] that, among the Choctas, if a boy is to be placed at school, his uncle, and not his father, makes the arrangement. The uncle's authority over his nieces is still more significant, as he is a party to their marriage contracts,

[1] *Ibid.*, pp. 75, 528.
[2] Lafitau 1724, I, 564ff.
[3] Morgan 1871, p. 158.

which in many tribes are founded " upon a consideration in the nature of presents."   Lafitau affirms [1] that
the nuptial presents is a true coemption, but it is so
only in the sense that it purchases a marital alliance
between the man's cabin and that of his intended wife,
which gives the husband certain rights over the
personal service of his wife during the continuance of
the marriage.

The gens has not undergone so full a development
among the Australian aborigines, or apparently among
any other existing uncultured race, as it exhibits with
the natives of America.   The totemic subdivisions of
the Australian class divisions answer, however, to the
gentes of the American system, each of which has a
badge of fraternity, or totemic device, to distinguish it
from others.   Moreover, the Australian totem, as a
fraternal group, has the same ultimate aim as the
American gens, the benefit of its members.   Mr
Howitt says [2] that each man is the " totemic brother "
of every other man and woman of his totem of his
generation, and that each totem is under the direction
of a head man, who is the oldest of the name.   When
a stranger arrives at an encampment from another
tribe, " the first question put to him is, ' What is your
totem ?'   This being ascertained, his totemic brethren
tàke charge of him, protect him, and treat him with
hospitality, even to the extent of providing him with
a temporary wife of that totem with which his own
intermarries."   Here there is the activity of a reciprocal obligation which is essential to the existence
of the group of kinsfolk under any phase of development.   That obligation is not limited to help or

[1] Lafitau 1724, I, 568ff.
[2] Howitt 1885, pp. 803–4.

hospitality, but it extends also to the redress of injuries. The blood-feud is a matter of the group and not of the individual or his immediate kinsmen. As Mr Fison says,[1] "to revenge an injury done to it is the duty of its every member; and in revenging that injury it is not absolutely necessary to strike at the injurious person himself. Any one of his group will do; for not he alone is responsible for his act—the whole body to which he belongs is involved in it." Among the Australians, also, marriage and inheritance have reference to the group and not to the individual.[2] The Australian gens or totem group must have a certain organisation to bind its members closely together, and to enforce their rights as against others. The nature of that organisation is shown by Messrs Fison and Howitt, who state[3] that the tribe possesses a social organisation based on the totems into which the tribe is divided, as well as a local organisation represented by the clans or local groups of which the tribe is made up. The former organisation permeates the latter; "it rules in many cases the assemblies and ceremonial of the tribe; it regulates marriage, descent and relationship; it orders blood-feud, it prescribes the rites of hospitality, and it even determines the sides to be taken at the ball-play." How the authority of the social organisation is exercised is not very certain, but it appears to be under the direction of the head man of the totem group, and possibly it possesses, as suggested by Messrs Howitt and Fison,[4] a "council of elders" answering to the ruling council of the gens of

[1] Fison and Howitt 1880, p. 157.
[2] *Ibid.*, p. 156; cf. Howitt and Fison 1885, p. 145.
[3] Howitt and Fison 1883, p. 33.
[4] Howitt and Fison 1885, p. 159.

ancient Greece. The great council of the tribe deals, however, with offences against both the local and the social organisations, and it answers to the Council of chiefs in which the government of the American tribe is vested, and which can even depose the chiefs and sachems elected by the Gentes.[1]

The rights, privileges, and obligations conferred and imposed upon the members of the American gens,[2] like those of the analogous organisation among the Australians and the Arabs, are only an extension of what must have attached to the members of the primitive group to which the gens can be traced. Such would be the case with the obligation not to marry in the gens, mutual rights of inheritance of the property of deceased members, reciprocal obligations of help, defence and redress of injuries, together with the right of bestowing names upon its members. The right of electing or deposing the person or persons chosen to act as the official head of the group or as its chiefs would not be required at the early period when the group first took its rise, as it would be under the authority of its natural head. The council of the gens, which in its simplest and lowest form consisted of every adult male and female member of the gens, is merely, however, a more extended form of the "family council" by which the affairs of the primitive group of kinsfolk would be considered. How far the possession of a common burial place and of common religious rites can be ascribed to this group is doubtful. Mr Fison, who states[3] that he knows of no case in which the worship of female ancestors is

[1] Morgan 1877, pp. 74, 116ff.
[2] *Ibid.*, pp. 71ff.
[3] Fison and Howitt 1880, p. 110.

practised among savage tribes, endeavours to prove
that ancestor worship, or the worship of the household gods, is the outcome of descent through males.
Nevertheless, the Fijians, who at one time traced
descent through females, have a phase of ancestor
worship.[1] The aborigines of Hainan, who call their
legendary female ancestor *Les*, or the Le mother, who
was produced from an egg, their patron saint,[2] may be
supposed to worship a female ancestor. It must be
remembered, however, that the totem was in some
sense identified with the ancestor where descent was
traced in the female line, and when it came to be
traced in the male line, the eponymous male ancestor
may, as suggested by Mr Fison, have taken the place
of the totem, or at least the worship accorded to him
may have been added to the superstitious practices of
totemism, if he did not himself become identified with
the totem.

We may now fitly give some consideration to the
important question of the nature and origin of
totemism,[3] which attained its most characteristic
development among peoples whose system of kinship
is based on descent through females. The word *totem*
or *dodaim* signifies in the Ojibwa dialect of North
America, from which it is derived, the symbol or
device of a gens, all the members of a particular gens
having the same totem. Hence Mr Schoolcraft used
the expression "totemic system" as synonymous with
gentile organisation.[4] The Australian totem is of the

[1] *Ibid.*, p. 114.

[2] Henry 1886, p. 397.

[3] This subject is more fully discussed by the author in
Wake 1887.

[4] Morgan 1877, p. 165.

same character, and it is described by Mr Fison as the badge of a group rather than of an individual, the individual taking it only as a member of the group.[1] The Rev. George Taplin remarks that each Narrinyeri "tribe" is regarded as a family, all the members of which are blood relations; and the totem borne by the Australian tribe, or rather tribal division, is thus the symbol of a family group, in like manner as the American totem is the device of a gens. The first question asked of a strange native by the Dieyeri or Dieri tribe of Cooper's Creek, in Central Australia, is, "Of what family (*murdoo*) are you?" Each *murdoo* is distinguished by a special name, being that of some object which, according to a tribal legend, may. be animate or inanimate, such as a dog, mouse, emu, iguana, rain, &c.[2] It is evident that the Australian totem is a "badge of fraternity," and equivalent to a family name, a name which belongs to all the members of a particular group, who are regarded as of kin, and which cannot be held by any person not belonging by birth or adoption to that group. The possession of a particular totem by any person is proof, therefore, that he is entitled or subject to all the rights, privileges, and obligations of the kindred group with which the totem identifies him, and which answers to the gens.

Reference has already[3] been made to the obligations of the "totemic system" among both the American and the Australian natives. We have seen also that the gens originated in the idea of kinship, with descent in the female line, and prohibition of marriage in the

[1] Fison and Howitt 1880, p. 165.
[2] Gason 1879, p. 260.
[3] Above, pp. 308ff.

gens. The bond of kin has associated with it the obligation of mutual aid and defence among the members of the group, which implies the duty of doing nothing to injure a fellow-member. All individuals having the same totem must, therefore, treat each other as brethren, and this rule applies not only to human beings, but also to the totem objects. Sir George Grey, in referring to the *kobongs* or totems of the natives of Western Australia, says,[1] "A certain mysterious connection exists between the family and its kobong, so that a member of the family will never kill an animal of the species to which his kobong belongs should he find it asleep; indeed, he always kills it reluctantly, and never without affording it a chance of escape." He adds, "This arises from the family belief that some one individual of the species is their nearest friend, to kill whom would be a great crime, and to be carefully avoided. Similarly, a native who has a vegetable for his kobong, may not gather it under certain circumstances, and at a particular period of the year." So also the natives of North America will not hunt, kill, or eat any animal of the form of their own totem. When, therefore, we find particular animals forbidden for food to a class of individuals, we may assume that such animals have a totemic character. Some light may thus be thrown on the origin of totemism. The Samoans supposed certain animals to be incarnations of household deities, and no man dare injure or eat the animal which was the incarnation of his own god, although he would eat freely of the animal incarnation of another man's god.[2] Notions of

[1] Grey 1841, II, 229.

[2] Turner, G. 1861, p. 238. The sacred animals of the different nomes of ancient Egypt were dealt with in much the same way (Maspero 1886, p. 29).

the same kind were prevalent throughout the islands of the Pacific.[1] Thus, the Fijians supposed every man to be under the protection of a special god, who resided in or was symbolised by some animal or other natural object, such as a rat, a shark, a hawk, a tree, &c. No one would eat the particular animal associated with his own god.[2] It is probable that the Fijian family gods, who answer to the household deities of the Samoans, are regarded as incarnate in the sacred animals, &c., of the tribe, towards whom, as being re-embodiments of deceased ancestors,[3] they necessarily stand in a fraternal relation.

These ideas show a close connection between animal-worship and ancestor-worship, and they have an important bearing on the origin of totemism. We have seen that the obligations of the totemic system or gentile organisation are based on the conception of kinship. This is also essential to ancestor-worship, which, like totemism, rests on the duty of giving mutual aid and protection. The worshippers make the offerings and perform the rites required by their deceased ancestors, who in return give their protection and assistance to their descendants. This mutual obligation is associated with the superstitious regard for certain animals and other objects. The venerated animals are not killed or eaten by those who are connected with them by superstitious ties, and they are supposed, on their part, to act as protectors to their

[1] Tylor 1871, II, 213.

[2] Wood 1868–70, II, 271, 290.

[3] On the temple at Dorey in New Guinea are sculptured the representations of the crocodile and serpent ancestors of some of the Dorians (Meyners d'Estrey 1881, p. 132).

human allies, by whom they are viewed as guardian spirits.

Dr M'Lennan saw a necessary connection between totemism and ancestor-worship, and he affirms[1] that the ancient nations passed in prehistoric times " through the totem stage, having animals and plants, and the heavenly bodies conceived as animals, for gods before the anthropomorphic gods appeared." By " totem," Dr M'Lennan evidently understood merely the animal or plant friend or protector of the family or tribe, and if this has any reference to *spirit*, it is the spirit of the animal or plant. He speaks[2] of men believing themselves to be " of the serpent breed derived from a serpent ancestor," and so of other animals. He does not see in the totem any reference to the actual human progenitor of the family, and he could hardly do so in accordance with his view of the mental condition of man in the totem stage, where " natural phenomena are ascribable to the presence in animals, plants, and things, and in the forces of nature, of such spirits prompting to action as men are conscious they themselves possess." Prof. Robertson Smith accepts, in his admirable work on the social condition of the early Arabs,[3] Dr M'Lennan's views in relation to totemism and animal worship, and gives as one of the three points which supply "complete proof" of early totemism in any race, " the prevalence of the conception that the members of the stock are of the blood of the eponym animal, or are sprung from a plant of the species chosen as totem." When Prof. Smith comes to consider this point, however, it appears that among the Arabs cer-

[1] McLennan 1869, p. 408.
[2] *Ibid.*, p. 569 ; 1870, p. 214.
[3] Robertson Smith 1885, pp. 186ff.

tain animals were not eaten because " they were thought to be men in another guise "—that is, they were not merely animals, but were men in disguise.[1] This is very different from the theory which makes men trace their descent from animals or plants, although these may be supposed to have the same kind of spirits as men.

According to Sir John Lubbock,[2] *totemism* is the stage of human progress in which natural objects, trees, lakes, stones, animals, &c., are worshipped, and it is regarded by him as equivalent to *nature-worship*. Totemism is said,[3] further, to be the deification of classes, so that " the Redskin who regards the bear or the wolf as his totem feels that he is in intimate, though mysterious association with the whole species." The explanation given [4] of the phase of totemism which relates to the worship of animals is that it originated " from the practice of naming, first individuals, and then their families, after particular animals. A family, for instance, which was called after the bear would come to look on that animal first with interest, then with respect, and at length with a sort of awe." This does not go far enough, however, as it is not shown why the totem objects are not only viewed with veneration, but are regarded as friends and protectors. Dr E. R. Tylor well objects,[5] moreover, " as to animal worship, when we find men paying distinct and direct reverence to the lion, the bear, or the crocodile as mighty superhuman beings, or adoring other beasts, birds, or reptiles as incarnations of spiritual deities,

[1] *Ibid.*, p. 204.
[2] Lubbock 1875, p. 199.
[3] *Ibid.*, p. 227.   [4] *Ibid.*, p. 253.
[5] Tylor 1871, II, 215.

we can hardly supersede such well-defined developments of animistic religion, by seeking their origin in
personal names of deceased ancestors, who chanced to
be called Lion, Bear, or Crocodile."

It may now be affirmed that the description of the
totem as a "badge of fraternity" or the "symbol of a
gens" is not sufficient. It is more than a symbol or
a badge. That description might answer for the
pictorial representation of the totem, but not for the
totem itself, which has actual vitality, and which can
only be regarded as the embodiment or re-incarnation
of a human ancestral spirit. Any object is fitted for
this spirit embodiment, and therefore totemism may be
conceived, not as a phase of nature-worship, but as a
combination of this cult with ancestor worship. The
ancestral character of the totem accounts for the association with it of the idea of protection, which is based
on the existence of a fraternal relationship between the
totem and all the individuals belonging to a particular
group of kin. The totem as a badge or symbol, therefore, represents the group of individuals, dead or alive,
towards whom a man stands in a fraternal relation,
and the protection of whom he is, therefore, entitled
to, so long as he performs all the obligations òn his
part which flow from the existence of such a relationship between them.[1] The belief that the spirits of the
dead do take on themselves animal forms is widely
spread.[2] At the same time, it is very probable that

[1] Mr. J. G. Frazer, in his excellent little work on "Totemism," which I met with only after the text was written, describes the system as both religious and social. "In its religious aspect it consists of the relations of mutual respect
and protection between a man and his totem; in its social
aspect it consists of the relations of the clansmen to each other
and to men of other clans" (Frazer 1887, p. 3).

[2] Tylor 1871, II, 6.

some savages do not distinguish between the man and
the animal incarnation, and that if they think at all
of the ancestor of the race, it is under the animal form.
For instance, as Dr Morgan remarks,[1] among the
Moqui Village Indians of New Mexico, " the members
of the gens claimed their descent from the animal
whose name they bore—their remote ancestors having
been transformed by the Great Spirit from the animal
into the human form." The Crane gens of the Ojib-
was appear to have a similar legend.[2] This must be
considered, however, as of later origin than the more
general opinion that certain animals are the embodi-
ments of the spirits of deceased men, in accordance
with which view the totem in its original idea may be
explained as *the re-incarnated form under which the
legendary ancestor of the gens or kindred group allied
to the totem is venerated.*

The existence among the natives of Australia and
America of systematic totemism may have been due
to the establishment of the gentile institution on the
basis of female kinship, and the intermingling of the
gentes or groups of kin owing to wives on marriage
leaving their own families to live among the husband's kindred, as the result of the practice of
exogamy. Some of the Australian tribes have a
legend according to which the use of totems was
introduced, by command of the Supreme Being, to
put a stop to consanguineous marriages.[3] This shows
that the totem is connected with marriage and kin-

---

[1] 1877, p. 86.

[2] Mr. Frazer refers to numerous cases in which the members of a totem believe themselves to be descended from their
totem. In other cases a human ancestress is said to have given
birth to an animal of the totem species.

[3] Above, p. 47.

ship, but considering how universal, not only with the Australian aborigines, but also among savages in general, is the objection to marriage between near blood relations, it is more than probable that the legend in question, like that of the Moqui Village Indians, arose to explain an already existing phenomenon, that of totemism.[1]

There is another feature of totemism which should not be lost sight of when viewing its origin. The Rev. Lorimer Fison remarks,[2] "The Australian totems have a special value of their own. Some of them divide not mankind only, but the whole universe, into what may almost be called gentile divisions." The natives of Port Mackay, in Queensland, allot everything in nature into one or other of two classes, Wateroo and Yungaroo, into which their tribe is divided. The wind belongs to one, and the rain to the other. The sun is Wateroo, and the moon is Yungaroo. The stars are divided between them, and the division to which any star belongs can be pointed out. The Mount Gambier tribe of South Australia have a similar arrangement, but natural objects are allied with the totemic subdivisions. Mr Fison gives examples of this, as supplied to him by Mr D. S. Stewart, from which he concludes that the native of South Australia "looks upon the universe as a great tribe, to one of whose divisions he himself belongs; and all things, animate and inanimate, which belong to his class are parts of the body corporate whereof he himself is part."

There is a curious parallelism between this system and the ancient doctrine of the separation of the

[1] Mr. Frazer makes the general observation that "persons of the same totem may not marry or have sexual intercourse with each other" (1887, p. 58).

[2] Fison and Howitt 1880, pp. 167ff.

intelligent universe into two great divisions, the celestial and terrestrial, or that of light and that of darkness. In the totemic system one great division includes the sun and summer, answering to the realm of light, and the other division comprises moon, stars, winter, thunder, clouds, rain, hail, answering to the realm of darkness. The American natives also show traces of this notion of the dual division of nature in their hero-myths, which, according to Dr Brinton,[1] are intended to express "the daily struggle which is ever going on between Day and Night, between Light and Darkness, between Storm and Sunshine." It is not improbable that the American totem system is based on the idea of duality. Although the totem divisions or gentes are now so numerous, there is reason to believe that, as long since mentioned by Lafitau[2] in relation to the Iroquois and Hurons, they had at one time not more than two gentes. That the Iroquois commenced with two gentes may indeed be inferred from the fact that the gentes in each of their tribes are divided between two phratries or brotherhoods,[3] and it is probable, therefore, that the original totems of all the North American tribes were only two in number. The Wolf and the Bear, which would seem to answer to Light and Darkness,[4] are the only totems common to all the great families of tribes of that area.

The Australian totem system, notwithstanding its

[1] Brinton 1882, p. 65.

[2] Lafitau 1724, I, 465.

[3] Morgan 1877, pp. 90ff.

[4] Gubernatis 1872, *passim*. Dr. Brinton shows that the Great Rabbit of Algonkin mythology is the Light God (1882, p. 47).

dualism, appears to lose sight of the opposition between light and darkness, and to look upon the two great divisions of nature represented by those phenomena as forming parts of a great whole. This idea answers to the fundamental connection which the Magism of the ancients found between the opposing principles in nature, as emanating equally from one and the same pre-existent principle.[1] We may not yet be in a position absolutely to affirm that toetmism is derived from the ancient doctrine of emanations, but they are certainly allied.[2] The early Scandinavians supposed that "from the supreme God were sprung (as it were emanations of his divinity) an infinite number of subaltern [subordinate] deities and genii [spirits], of which every part of the visible world was the seat and temple. These intelligences did not merely reside in each part of nature; they directed its operations. It was the organ or instrument of their love or hatred of mankind. Each element was under the guidance of some being peculiar to it. The earth, the water, the fire, the air, the sun, moon, and stars, had each their own divinity. The trees, forests, rivers, mountains, rocks, winds, thunder, and tempest, had the same, and merited for that reason religious worship, which at first could not be directed to the visible object, but to the intelligence with which it was directed."[3] These subordinate intelligences are none other than the celestial beings of the Zoroastrian

[1] Lenormant 1878, pp. 228, 231.

[2] Mr. Frazer takes a different view, and states that social changes have favoured "the passage of totemism into a higher form of faith" (1887, p. 89).

[3] Mallet 1847, I, 79.

cosmogony, prototypes of things on earth, which emanated from the Deity. As Lenormant remarks,[1] "Stars, animals, men, angels themselves, in one word, every created being had his Fravishi, who was invoked in prayers and sacrifices, and was the invisible protector who watched untiringly over the being to whom he was attached." We have here the idea of guardianship by a mysterious being, which is so important in connection with the totem, and when we consider that, according to the doctrine of transmigration of souls, which is subsidiary to that of emanations, the forms through which the human soul is supposed to pass on its progress towards perfection include not only beasts, birds, and fishes, but also trees, stones, and other inanimate objects, there is no difficulty in believing that any of these objects might become the totem of a particular individual or of a group of persons descended from him. Dr M'Lennan saw a connection between totemism and the doctrine of transmigration, which teaches that "everything has a soul or spirit, and that the spirits are mostly human, in the sense of having once been in human bodies."[2]

Whatever the origin of totemism, the practical value of the totem under the conditions of early society cannot be doubted. Dr M'Lennan, who supposes that the totem was originally taken from the mother, remarks,[3] "A stranger is at once recognised by those who bear the same totem mark[4] and totem name

---

[1] Lenormant 1878, p. 199.

[2] McLennan 1869, p. 423.

[3] McLennan 1885, p. 227.

[4] This must not be confounded with the tribal mark. Tattooing has to do with this, rather than, as Dr. McLennan supposes, with the totem or family mark. I think this view is supported by the facts as to tattooing referred to by Mr. Frazer (1887, pp. 28ff.).

with him as their relation connected with them (though in an unknown way) by feminine[1] descents. The totem or kindred name is the more prominent, because personal names are usually carefully concealed. It more than serves the uses of a family name. It is the totem mark alone that is placed upon a grave. It is with it alone that in intercourse with Europeans, the representative of a kindred signs a treaty." So long as the members of a family group reside together, there is little reason for the establishment of any special sign of "fraternity" by which persons near of kin may be recognised. In a small community all persons thus related would be known, so as to prevent the intermarriage of such persons, which is one of the most important functions of the totem, even if all the members of the community, except perhaps the strangers who had settled there on marriage, were not of the same kindred. It might be different, however, where a woman left her own family to reside with her husband among the members of another group. In this case, unless the wife had been acquired by purchase, she would retain her tribal connection, and her children would bear a special relationship to her family. The same result would follow where a tribe is composed of two or more intermarrying groups, if the females on marriage leave their homes to live among their husbands' kin. In like manner, if a man left his own tribe or family to reside with that of a woman whom he marries, and by arrangement acquires the right to her offspring, the children of the marriage would have a special relationship to their father's family. The connection created

[1] The totem is evidence of kinship in the *male* line, where this line is preferred for tracing such relationship.

between a tribal or family group and an individual living at a distance from it, is accompanied by certain rights, obligations, and disabilities, and it is necessary to have some means by which that connection can be easily and certainly ascertained. The chief disability has relation to marriage, which is not allowed between persons of the same kindred, and as such marriages are regarded with great dislike by primitive peoples, it is on this ground especially necessary that persons related by blood can be known with absolute certainty.

Dr M'Lennan, in pointing out that the totem bond unites a kindred scattered throughout different communities, affirms[1] that it must have marked the kindred off from other kindreds before the existence of exogamy, by which the systematic interfusion of kindreds is regularly caused. He adds, " We are thus carried back to a time when there were bodies of kindred having each a common totem, which were usually bound together for common defence—that is, essentially by the blood-feud—which were connected by that system of relationship which first was formed, and which had no objection to the intermarriage of related persons." It has been shown in the preceding pages, however, that Dr M'Lennan's views as to the earliest social condition of mankind are untenable, and that the practice of exogamy is really due to the restraint on promiscuity arising from the dislike of intermarriage between persons near of kin, which is a fundamental fact of savage life. Instead of the use of the totem preceding exogamy, they may be said to depend on each other. The totem shows what persons are kinsmen, and therefore not only bound together for self-

[1] McLennan 1885, p. 229.

defence, but not able to intermarry, while exogamy is
the intermarriage of persons who are not akin in the restricted sense of this term, this being evidenced among
primitive peoples by their possession of different totems.

When the conditions of social life were changed,
consequent on the establishment of descent in the
male line as the test of kinship,[1] totemism as a system
would gradually become effete. That change, combined with the practice of wives leaving their own
family to live among their husband's kin, would take
from the totem one of its most important uses, as all
the members of a kindred group would dwell together,
instead of being, like the individuals belonging to
different totems under the American or Australian
systems, intermingled in one tribal group. Totems
would then come to be useful chiefly as ensigns, or as
furnishing surnames to establish community of descent,
and therefore the existence of marriage disability ; as
with the Chinese, among whom no persons of the same
family name can intermarry, however distant may be
the actual relationship.

There is another point bearing on what has gone
before which may be considered here. Although the
gens or totemic group is theoretically a body of kinsfolk, some of its members may in reality be wholly
wanting in the blood which binds the group together.
This result arises from the exercise of the right allowed
by the totemic system or gentile institution of adopt-
ing strangers into the gens or totem. Among the
American tribes,[2] captives taken in war, when not put

---

[1] Where male kinship was always preferred, the "totemic
system" was never developed.

[2] Morgan 1877, p. 80; cf. Lafitau 1724, II, 308.

to death, were adopted into some gens, and when adopted they often occupied in the family the places of persons slain in battle. Captive women and children were usually thus incorporated with the tribe. Sometimes, by arrangement, individuals were transferred from one gens to another, which had become a small number of persons, and thus liable to extinction. Whether or not such a systematic adoption is practised among the Australians is doubtful. An example of adoption among the natives of Victoria is referred to by Mr James Dawson, who states[1] that should a child of another family be born on an estate, it is looked upon as one of the family to which the estate belongs, and has an equal right to a share of the land if it is six months old at the death of the head of the family. He adds that this adopted child " is called by a special name, *woork*, by which also it addresses the owner of the land." Mr Fison refers to adoption as an Australian practice, and he remarks[2] that the adopted person not only enters into all the relationships of his fresh gens, but abandons all those of his own gens. This undoubtedly is the effect of adoption as practised by the American tribes, and it was the same among the early Arabs. With this race, young children whom a woman took with her to the house of her husband, and whom he brought up, were, says Professor Robertson Smith,[3] often adopted into his stock. Moreover, freedmen living with a tribe of alien blood were adopted into it, and so also refugees were often admitted by adoption into the tribe of their protector. This was based on a fiction of kinship, as " to preserve the doctrine of tribal homogeneity, it was feigned that

---

[1] Dawson 1881, p. 7.   [2] Fison and Howitt 1880, pp. 104, 112.
[3] Robertson Smith 1885, p. 112.

the adopted son was veritably and for all effects of the blood of his new father."[1] From this fact we may judge how erroneous is the reason assigned by Sir John Lubbock[2] for " the frequency of adoption among the lower races of men, and the fact that it is often considered to be as close a connection as real parentage." Instead of being evidence of such a social condition as communal marriage or promiscuity, it is evidence of the importance attached to relationship by community of blood. This opinion is confirmed by the view of adoption entertained by the Greeks and Romans, who did not consider it complete unless it was accompanied by the ceremony of the mock-birth.[3] The Roman law required that adoption should in its consequences agree with that which it imitated, but this principle was not fully regarded by the Greeks, who permitted an adopted son to marry the daughter of his adopted father.[4] This was not allowed by Hindoo law, which probably expresses the general practice where adoption is recognised. The effect of the Hindoo law is stated by Mr Sutherland as follows :— " The adopted son cannot marry any kinswoman related to his father and mother within the prohibited degrees, as his consanguineal relation endures ; nor can the son of two fathers marry in the general family of either."[5]

[1] *Ibid.*, p. 44.

[2] Lubbock 1875, p. 88. Dr. Letourneau falls into a similar error when, in referring to the frequency of adoption among the Polynesians, he says that "elle montre combien on attachait peu d'importance à la filiation" (1876, p. 370).

[3] M. Giraud-Teulon connects the "mock-birth" with the *couvade* custom (1867, pp. 34ff.).

[4] Daremberg and Daglio 1877–1919, p. 76, art. "Adoptio."

[5] See the *Dattaka-Mímánsá*, translated by Sutherland (1865, pp. 113, 219).

Before leaving this part of our subject, mention may be made of the curious custom which requires a man and his wife's mother to avoid each other. This custom is found among primitive peoples in all parts of the world,[1] particularly among those who trace kinship through females. Sir John Lubbock regards the avoidance of a mother-in-law as a natural consequence of marriage by capture. He says,[2] " When the capture was a reality, the indignation of the parents would also be real; when it became a mere symbol, the parental anger would be symbolised also, and would be continued even after its origin was forgotten." It is not very apparent, however, why the pretended anger, if even there had ever been a reality answering to it, of a woman against her son-in-law should be " symbolised " by her avoiding him. Mr Fison points out[3] that in some Australian tribes the feeling which gives rise to the custom referred to exhibits itself in the form of respectful formality. The man and his mother-in-law " are ceremoniously polite to one another, always using the respectful forms of address— *e.g.*, the pronouns in the dual or the plural instead of the singular—and in all things treating one another with a certain formal courtesy, as if they were strangers of rank, to whom such respect is due." The simple explanation of the custom is that a man's mother-in-law belongs to the same class or totem as his wife, and therefore to a group of possible wives.* She is forbidden to him, however, and such being the case they must keep out of each other's way. Mr Fison adds[4]

---

[1] Lubbock 1875, pp. 11ff.   [2] *Ibid.*, p. 114.

[3] Fison and Howitt 1880, p. 103.

* [She is not a possible wife, however, in a four-section system. — R.N.]

[4] *Ibid.*, p. 104. Mr. Fison states that among the Fijians a brother and sister avoid each other for the reason mentioned

that "the slightest familiarity between them would be indecent—nay more, it would be pollution, bringing down who knows what terrible punishment from the Unseen Powers." This explanation is confirmed by the fact that among peoples tracing kinship through the male line, a woman must shun the presence of her father-in-law.[1] It is a curious fact that in many of the Australian tribes who have uterine descent, the son-in-law has to fight on the side of his father-in-law in time of war, and to provide food for him, and not for his mother-in-law's cabin as with the Americans. This difference is probably owing to women among the Australians leaving their own families to reside with their husbands, and occupying a position of subordination which they do not exhibit on the American continent ; to which must be added the fact mentioned by Mr Fison,[2] that an Australian is of his father-in-law's class division by birth. Among the New Zealanders, who trace kinship through males, a man often joins his father-in-law's clan, in which case he may have to fight against his own kinsmen, but this occurs only when he goes to reside with his wife's family.[3]

Reference must now be made to the system of relationship associated with the custom of tracing kinship through females. It was from a consideration of the phase of the classificatory system in use among the Polynesian islanders, Mr Morgan came to the conclusion that marriages between brothers and sisters were at one time universally prevalent, giving rise to what he terms the consanguine family. Reasons have

in the text. Probably the same thing occurs between father and daughter where there is uterine descent.

[1] Lubbock 1875, p. 12.   [2] Fison and Howitt 1880, p. 106.
[3] Taylor 1870, p. 337.

already been given for believing that this family never existed in the sense supposed by Mr Morgan, and this becomes the more probable when the system of relationships in use among the Australian aborigines is considered. It may be remarked first, however, that, as descent in the female line is regarded by Mr Morgan as the rule of a gens, if we find among a people who have formed the idea of a gens a system of kinship differing from the Malayan system merely so far as it would be affected by the tracing of descent in the female line only instead of in both lines, we may be sure that the explanation before given of the last named system must be correct. We have such a people in the Australian aborigines, whose totemic groups answer to the gentes of the American tribes, and whose system of relationships is regarded by Mr Morgan as exhibiting the most archaic form of organisation, that on the basis of sex, a view which, however, requires serious modification.

In the chapter on group-marriage, it was mentioned that the Australian tribes are divided into classes, which are again divided into family groups or totems. With many of the tribes of New South Wales and Queensland the classes are four in number, each with a masculine and a feminine name, which among the Kamilaroi natives are Muri and Matha,[1] Kubi and Kubbitha, these forming one pair, and Ipai and Ippatha, Kumbu and Butha, which form another pair. The primary classes were *Dilbi*, the subdivisions of which are Muri-Kubi and *Kupathin*, whose subdivisions are Ipai-Kumbu, and they each comprise a number of totemic sub-groups, distinguished by the

---

[1] *Tha* is the feminine termination.

names of animals.[1]   The rules of marriage do not
allow Muri to intermarry with Kubi, nor Ipai with
Kumbu, but the Muri-Kubi group intermarries with
the Ipai-Kumbu group according to certain rules,[2] the
effect of which will be given at a later page.   These
rules apply also to the totemic sub-divisions of the
classes, which consist of two triplets of totems, each
group intermarrying with the other, but not among
themselves.   The general rule which forbids marriage
within the class has an exception,[3] found, however,
only with certain tribes, by virtue of which a man is
permitted to marry his half-sister on the father's side,
but this privilege does not interfere with the operation
of the law of exogamy, or affect the rule of descent.
By this rule, children never take the class name of
either parent, although they have their mother's
totem, and every family passes, therefore, through
each of the classes in the course of four generations.
The operation of those rules is shown by the following
diagrams, which are framed on the basis of the marriage of Muri (*Ego*) with Butha, and which give the
collateral relationships on the mother's side (A.) and
on the father's side (B.).

An examination of the diagram A shows, on
comparing the names which denote to what class the
several individuals belong, that, with a single exception, all those bearing a common class name in the
same grade stand in the same degree of relationship

[1] Fison and Howitt 1880, p. 42; Howitt 1883, p. 500; cf.
Howitt 1884.

[2] As to the rules of marriage, see further Fison and Howitt
1880, pp. 43ff.; Howitt 1884, pp. 341ff.

[3] Fison and Howitt 1880, pp. 45ff.

AUSTRALIAN SYSTEM.

Female Stem.

Matha duli, *marries* Kumbu dinoun, *grandmother.* *grandfather.*

Kubbitha duli, *marries* Ipai dinoun, *mother.* *father.*

Kubi duli, *marries* Ippatha dinoun. *uncle.*

Ipai dinoun *marries* Kubbitha duli, *mother.*

Butha din. *m.* Muri d., *brother.* Matha d., *m.* Kumbu din *m.* Matha duli, *sister.*

Muri duli, *m.* Butha din. Muri d., *m.* Butha din. *Ego.* *brother.*

m. Butha din., Kumba din, *m.* Matha duli. *cousin.*

Ippatha din., *daughter.* Ipai din., *son.* Kubi duli, *nephew.* Kubbitha duli, *niece.* Kubi duli, *nephew.* Kubbitha duli, *niece.*

Ipai din., *son.* Ippatha din., *daughter.* Ipai din., *son.* Ippatha din., *daughter.* Ipai din., *son.* Ippatha din., *daughter.* Kubi din., *nephew.* Kubbitha duli, *niece.*

Ippatha din., *daughter.* Ipai din., *son.* Kubbitha duli, *niece.* Kubi duli, *nephew.*

AUSTRALIAN SYSTEM.

Male Stem.

Muri duli, *marries* Butha dinoun, *grandfather.* *grandmother.*

Ipai dinoun, *marries* Kubbitha duli. *father.*

Ipai dinoun, *marries* Kubbitha duli, *father.* *mother.*

Kubi duli *marries* Ippatha dinoun, *aunt.*

Kumbu din. *m.* Matha duli, *sister.* Muri duli, *m.* Butha din. *Ego.*

Muri duli, *m.* Butha din. Kumbu din *m.* Butha din. Muri duli, *m.* Butha din. *brother.*

Muri duli, *m.* Butha din. *brother.*

Butha din., *m.* Muri duli, *cousin.* Kumbu din., *cousin.*

Matha d. *m.*

Kubi duli, *nephew.* Kubbitha duli, *niece.* Ipai din., *son.* Ippatha din., *daughter.* Ipai din., *son.* Ippatha din., *daughter.* Kubi duli, *nephew.* Kubbitha duli, *niece.* Ipai din., *son.* Ippatha din., *daughter.*

Ipai din., *son.* Ippatha din., *'daughter.*

Kubi duli, *nephew.* Kubbitha duli, *niece.*

to *ego*. Thus, Muri and Matha are brothers and sisters; Kumbu and Butha, cousins; Ipai and Ippatha, sons and daughters; Kubi and Kubbitha, nephews and nieces. The exception is in the parental grade, but it is explicable according to the principle that women belonging to different classes must stand in a different relationship to *ego* among themselves, this being true of men also in the same grade. The consequence of this rule is that the mother's brother being of a different class from her husband, the former must be "uncle" to *ego*, while the father's sister belonging to a different class from that of his wife must be "aunt" to *ego*. The latter result appears on diagram B, which gives the relationships through the father according to the Australian system, the class names being here reversed. Exactly the same result follows, whichever member of the several subdivisions is taken as *ego*, except that the relationships are expressed by other terms. Difference of class names denotes difference of relationship when in the same grade, in the parental grade the comparison being between mother and father's sister, and father and mother's brother.

It is necessary to remark on some of the terms of relationship used above, that they must not be taken absolutely. Dr Morgan uses the words uncle, aunt, nephew, niece, and cousin in connection with the Turanian system of consanguinity in an accommodated sense. Mr Fison remarks on this,[1] that the relatives indicated "are fathers-in-law and mothers-in-law, rather than uncles and aunts, sons-in-law and daughters-in-law rather than nephews and nieces; while the meaning of the term cousin varies with

[1] *Ibid.*, pp. 76ff.

the sex of the speaker, and with that of the person spoken to." Elsewhere he says that the mother's brothers, own and collateral, are uncles to *ego*, or rather his fathers-in-law, because they are the fathers of those over whom *ego* has matrimonial rights.   This is a better explanation than that given in accordance with his peculiar views by Dr Morgan, who states[1] that the brothers, own and collateral, of *ego's* mother are uncles because they are no longer husbands of the mother of *ego*, and must stand to him in a more remote relationship than that of father.   The mother's brother stands in a special relation to the sister's children where descent is traced through females, and often he exercises more authority over them than their own fathers.   This is because they belong to the same gens or totem group as himself, for which reason they and not his own children are his heirs. For the same reason a man and his paternal grandfather are supposed to stand together in a special relation,[2] which accounts for children being called after their grandfather instead of their father.

The term " cousin " is deserving of further notice, as it practically points out the group of individuals to which a man stands in the marital relation, or from which he must obtain a wife.   That group comprises the children of his mother's brother and of his father's sister, as they do not belong to his class.   Thus, Muri and Kumbu are cousins, and therefore intermarrying classes, and so also are Ipai and Kubi, because they are respectively the children of a brother and of a sister, and not of two brothers or of two sisters, who, as belonging to the same class, are distinguished as " brothers " and " sisters."   This is shown

[1] Morgan 1877, p. 444.   [2] Fison and Howitt 1880, p. 167.

by the following table, formed on the assumption that Muri-Kubi represents one of the original intermarrying classes, and Ipai-Kumbu the other.

Ego.	Marries.	Children.	Nephews and Nieces.	Cousins.	Brothers and Sisters.
Muri.	Butha.	Ipai. Ipatha.	Kubi. Kubitha.	Kumbu. Butha.	Muri. Matha.
Kubi.	Ipatha.	Kumbu. Butha.	Muri. Matha.	Ipai. Ipatha.	Kubi. Kubitha.
Ipai.	Kubitha.	Muri. Matha.	Kumbu. Butha.	Kubi. Kubitha.	Ipai. Ipatha.
Kumbu.	Matha.	Kubi. Kubitha.	Ipai. Ipatha.	Muri. Matha.	Kumbu. Butha.

This table shows at a glance the operation of the Kamilaroi rules of marriage and descent, and proves that all the members of the four classes of which the tribe is composed are related to each other, while marriage is restricted to one-fourth only of the females of the tribe. Moreover, by the rule which prohibits marriage between persons nearly related, a man is not allowed to form a marital connection with the daughter of his own mother's brother, or the daughter of his own father's sister. This is proof that relationship by the father's side is fully recognised; as those females, unlike the daughter of a father's brother or of a mother's sister, belong to the "cousin" group with which the man marries.[1] Reference has already been made to the exception in the Kamilaroi system to the

[1] Howitt 1885, pp. 805–6. The Rev. William Ridley states that a man cannot marry "a first cousin related both by the father and the mother's side" (Ridley 1875, p. 161).

rule that a man can only marry with his "cousin" group, arising from the fact that marriage is permitted with a half-sister where the relationship is on the father's side and the female belongs to a particular gens. This innovation, which appears to be purely local and peculiar to a portion only of the Kamilaroi tribes, is explained by Mr Fison [1] as "a partially successful assertion of the independent right of a gens to chose its wives where it will, provided always that it goes beyond its own boundaries in choosing them." The children of such a marriage take the class name which they would have had if their father had belonged to the class with which their mother could intermarry under the general rule. Possibly the innovation was introduced under special circumstances, which limited the number of females available for wives at a particular time. We have seen,[2] however, that marriage with a half-sister has been not uncommon among peoples of more advanced culture than the Australian aborigines, and that with kinship in one line only it is not contrary to the natural restraint on promiscuity arising from consanguinity.

It was remarked above that if the rule of female kinship is combined with a system of classification differing from the Malayan system only so far as this would be affected by the tracing of descent in the female line, we may be sure that the explanation already given of the Malayan system is correct. Now the effect of that rule is that all the persons in each generation who belong to different groups have a different classificatory title. For example, in the diagram A. of the Australian system, Ipai and Ipatha are sons and daughters, and all Kubi and Kubitha are

---

[1] Fison and Howitt 1880, p. 115.   [2] Above, pp. 24, 31.

nephews and nieces. That is because, in the grade above, Butha is mother of Ipai and Ipatha, whereas Kubi and Kubitha are the children of Matha. Again, all Muri and Matha are brothers and sisters, while Kumbu and Butha are cousins to *ego*, because the former are the children of Kubitha, the mother of Kumbu and Butha being Ipatha. In the absence of the rule of descent in the female line only, there could be no nephews and nieces, because Muri-Matha and Kumbu-Butha are intermarrying classes—that is, the Muri group marries the Butha group, and the Kumbu group marries the Matha group, and with kinship reckoned through both father and mother all the children of such a group marriage must be sons and daughters. On the same principle all the members of the grade above would be brothers and sisters, and those of the parental grade fathers and mothers. Thus, let Muri and Matha be Aa and Kumbu and Butha Bb, and we have—

$$\frac{A+b}{Aa,\ Bb} \qquad\qquad \frac{B+a}{Bb,\ Aa}$$

Whereas with descent in the female line we have—

$$\frac{A+b}{Bb} \qquad\qquad \frac{B+a}{Aa}$$

Descent in the male line would give—

$$\frac{A+b}{Aa} \qquad\qquad \frac{B+a}{Bb}$$

With only two intermarrying classes, that would result in alternate generations. If, however, there are the four Kamilaroi classes, let Kubi and Kubitha be Cc, and Ipai and Ipatha Ee, then with paternal and maternal kinship we have, in addition to the above—

$$\frac{C+e}{Cc,\ Ee} \qquad\qquad \frac{E+c}{Ee,\ Cc}$$

Whereas with descent in the female line we have—

$$\frac{C+e}{Ee} \qquad\qquad \frac{E+c}{Cc}$$

Descent in the male line would give—

$$\frac{C+e}{Cc} \qquad\qquad \frac{E+c}{Ee}$$

These examples would seem to show that the two systems of descent in the male and female lines respectively result from the disintegration of the system which recognises kinship on both sides ; while with female kinship only we have such a series of changes in the relationships of the Malayan system as are exhibited in that of the Australian Kamilaroi.

The classification of relationships exhibited by the Kamilaroi system is, as stated by Mr Fison,[1] the same as the Ganowanian system of the American Indians, who usually trace descent in the female line. Dr Morgan classes together the Ganowanian and the Turanian as one system, and he states,[2] that although this and the gentile organisation in its archaic form are usually found together, they are not essentially dependent. According to this view the formation of the Turanian system, which is associated with descent in the male line, was a consequence of the prior existence of punaluan marriage and the punaluan family, "the change of relationships which resulted from substituting punalua in the place of consanguine marriages" turning the Malayan into the Turanian system. As an example of the change, Dr Morgan mentions the fact, that in the latter the son of a man's sister is his nephew, while in the former he is "son." I have shown, however, this change to be due to the

[1] Fison and Howitt 1880, p. 26n.
[2] Morgan 1877, p. 435.

operation of the rule of female kinship on the earlier system, according to which all the members of the child grade are sons and daughters of all the persons in the grade above. Dr Morgan has throughout fallen into the error of making the classificatory systems in use among different peoples depend on the form of marriage and of the family prevalent among them. He says,[1] " The form of the family keeps in advance of the system (of consanguinity). In Polynesia it was punaluan, while the system remained Malayan; in America it was syndyasmian, while the system remained Turanian; and in Europe and Western Asia it became monogamian, while the system seems to have remained Turanian for a time, but it then fell into decadence, and was succeeded by the Aryan." The simple explanation is, that the classificatory system of the Polynesians is based on the recognition of relationship through both parents, combined with the practice of both phases of punaluan group marriage; while the Ganowanian system is associated with the preference for female kinship over male kinship connected with the use of the form of punalua based on the sisterhood of the wives. The preference for male kinship associated with the prevalence of the other form of punalua based on the brotherhood of the husbands, has given rise, as will be seen in the next chapter, to the Turanian system of classification. At the same time, it cannot be said that the use of a particular line of descent for tracing kinship depends on the system of marriage in vogue. Kinship has relation primarily to the offspring of marriage, and hence the practice of group marriage or polyandry may be associated among one people with male kin-

[1] *Ibid.*, p. 442.

ship, and among another people with female kinship; and the same may be said also of polygyny and monandry, although they are chiefly combined with male kinship, except where relationship is traced equally through both parents, as is the case with the peoples among whom the highest phase of marriage has become established.

Note.—I have not thought it necessary to consider Dr M‘Lennan's explanation of the classificatory system of relationships as "a system of mutual salutations merely." Dr M‘Lennan asks,[1] "What duties or rights are affected by the relationships comprised in the classificatory system?" He answers the question by saying, "Absolutely none. They are barren of consequences, except, indeed, as comprising a code of courtesies and ceremonial addresses in social intercourse." From what has been said above, however, we cannot doubt that the relationships of the classificatory system are real, and that it has a very intimate connection with the rules of marriage and descent. A criticism of Dr M‘Lennan's views will be found in Dr Lewis H. Morgan's work, "Ancient Society," page 517 *et seq.*

[1] McLennan 1876, p. 366.

CHAPTER X.

KINSHIP THROUGH MALES.

In a former chapter it was shown that among the lower races the practice of tracing kinship through females was at one time very widely established, and that such practice arose, not from any uncertainty of paternity or from the special connection which subsisted between a woman and her offspring, but from the fact that such offspring belonged to the mother's family group, whether she went after marriage to reside among her husband's kindred, or, as probably in the earliest ages was usually the case, her husband lived with her among her own relations. It is evident that this explanation of the rule of descent in the female line is quite consistent with the full recognition of paternity. Among the aborigines of Australia, indeed, a son is regarded as the re-incarnation of his father, although by the rule of descent the son belongs to his mother's totemic group. The same idea probably underlies the Arab belief that a child can be recognised as a particular man's son by certain bodily marks, to the discovery of which a class of wise men devoted themselves.[1] In like manner with the full recognition of maternity, descent through males may be preferred for the purpose of tracing kinship. This rule must, indeed, have been established wherever the father's kindred had a right to the offspring of a

[1] Robertson Smith 1885, pp. 143, 287.

marriage, whether it was preceded by an earlier system of female kinship or was itself the original practice.

Before proceeding to consider more fully the origin of tracing descent in the male line, it is advisable to ascertain the opinions entertained on this subject by other writers. Usually it is assumed that there has been a change of descent from the female to the male line. Thus Dr M'Lennan says:[1] "As civilisation advanced, the system of kinship through females only was succeeded by a system which acknowledged kinship through males also, and which in most cases passed into a system which acknowledged kinship through males only." The first step in the progress from the earliest to the latest of these systems was the affiliation of children to mothers instead of to groups, the members of the same stock associating as a gens or house, and the mother and their children occupying separate homes. The formation of the gens, and afterwards of the family, would be accompanied by rude proprietary rights in the common home, weapons, and garnered food. This stage of progress is supposed to be represented by the Nair type of polyandry, in which kinship would be of importance chiefly in relation to the right of intermarriage and as determining the right of succession. Kinship through females would first lose its importance in regard to successions, which would be restricted to the children of the eldest sister of the Nair family group, instead of there being a general succession of all the sister's children. Fathers would, moreover, come to make gifts *inter vivos* to children whom they had reason to think their own, and as this practice grew, there would be further practical restriction of the right of

[1] McLennan 1876, p. 187.

succession through females. With the practice of gifts *inter vivos* to putative children, "would grow a feeling against allowing estates to pass from the house of the brothers to that of—or to the putative children of—the polyandrous husbands of the sister, and a corresponding disposition towards a system of marriage which would allow of property passing to the brother's own children." This would lead to the Tibetan system of polyandry, which "would produce certainty of the children being of their own blood; they would be born in the house, and would become its heirs."[1] In this system the eldest brother was a sort of paterfamilias, the right to succeed him being in his younger brothers in their order; after them in their eldest son. The idea of fatherhood thus attained something like maturity, and "paternity having become certain, a system of kinship through males would arise with the growth of property, and a practice of sons succeeding as heirs direct to the estates of fathers; and as the system of kinship through males arose, that through females would—and chiefly under the influence of property—die away." We thus see that, according to Dr M'Lennan's theory, which will be again referred to in connection with Tibetan polyandry, kinship through males accompanied certainty of paternity, but that "the right of inheritance, as property became abundant, tended to become, and did become, the test of kinship."[2] This view practically agrees with that expressed by Sir John Lubbock, who states that a child was at one time thought to be related to his mother and not to his father, although now it is almost universal among civilised races to trace relationship through the father. The change which has

[1] *Ibid.*, p. 192.   [2] *Ibid.*, p. 197.

thus taken place he supposes[1] " to have been effected
by the natural wish, which every one would feel, that
his property should go to his own children," a view
which, however, requires an antecedent recognition of
the paternal relationship.

Like the other writers referred to, Dr Morgan
regards descent in the female line to have preceded
descent in the male line, and where the latter now
prevails, he supposes it to have taken the place of the
former.[2] Such a change is said to have happened
among many of the American tribes, and also in the
Grecian and Latin gentes. The change in the last
named cases Dr Morgan ascribes to the influence of
property, the accumulation of which " in masses, and
assuming permanent forms, and with an increased
proportion of it held by individual owners," would
give rise to an antagonism " against the prevailing
form of gentile inheritance, because it excluded the
owner's children, whose paternity was becoming more
assured." This would cause the overthrow of descent
in the female line, and substitution of descent in the
male line. Such a change, says Dr Morgan, " would
leave the inheritance in the gens as before, but it
would place children in the gens of their father, and at
the head of the agnatic kindred," ultimately resulting
in their having exclusive inheritance ; the son, moreover, being brought in the line of succession to the
office of his father. The change from the female to
the male line among the American tribes is, however,
thought by Dr Morgan[3] to be due to some other cause
than the influence of property and inheritance, seeing
that among them, when first known, " the idea of

[1] Lubbock 1875, p. 147.   [2] Morgan 1877, pp. 343ff.
[1] *Ibid.*, p. 157.

property was substantially undeveloped, or but slightly beyond the germinating stage," and he suggests that it has occurred at a recent period under American and missionary influences.

The change of descent from the female to the male line, as seen among the Australian aborigines, has been explained in another way by Messrs Howitt and Fison. These writers point out[1] that in the localised "clans" we have the germ of descent through the father, which was fostered under the influence of the custom of betrothal. The husband by betrothal is the real husband, and claims as his own the children of the woman with whom he habitually cohabits. Eventually he would come to insist on the strict fidelity of his wife, and this would be accompanied by a change in the conception of descent. In a more recent memoir[2] Mr Howitt takes a somewhat different view. He sees at the root of betrothal the belief "that the child is derived from the male parent only, and that the mother is no more than its nurse. This belief has, moreover, aided the local organisation, whose perpetuation from father to son is its direct expression, to over-ride the social organisation; and, together with betrothal, which produces the sense of separate ownership, it has tended to bring about ultimately individual marriage, with a change of descent from the 'group of female Pirauru,' to the individual male 'Noa.'" Here the change from female to male descent is connected with individual marriage, and is traced ultimately to the belief that the child belongs to the father, expressed in the custom of betrothal, producing a sense of "separate ownership."

[1] Howitt and Fison 1883, p. 37.
[2] Howitt 1885, p. 821.

Neither of the above explanations of the substitution of descent in the male line for female descent is correct. According to Dr M'Lennan, as already mentioned, the right of inheritance became the test of kinship. That writer, however, states [1] that when wives were captured they would be regarded as property, and they would be still so regarded when, by purchase, they passed from the houses of their birth into alien houses. A sense of property in children would then arise, these being "additional features of the patria potestas." What Dr M'Lennan here regards as secondary in relation to the origin of male kinship is primary. In the case of the Greeks and Romans "property" in the sense used by Mr Morgan may have been at the root of the change, but as a rule the property considered was that represented by children, as Dr M'Lennan would seem ultimately to have recognised.[2] The change from the female line to the male line for tracing descent, where it took place, had in fact relation to the children rather than to any other kind of property, and descent in either line, therefore, originated no doubt in the same cause. The rule of female kinship was the expression of the fact that a woman's children were regarded as belonging to her group of kin, and therefore male kinship

[1] 1876, p. 197.

[2] In *The Patriarchal Theory*, Dr. McLennan says that in many cases it was secured by means of contract alone that "a woman's relatives should cease to have rights over her children" (1885, p. 223), which rights were given up to the husband and his relatives. He speaks, however, of the contract as merely a "device," although this is hardly a proper phrase to apply to wife-purchase, which Dr. McLennan states is of itself in a certain class of cases "sufficient to carry children to their father from the kindred of their mother" (pp. 234, 315ff.).

must be supposed to have been originally associated with ownership of children by their father's kin. Where there has been actual change from one line of descent to the other, there must have been some cause for the change in the group with which a woman's children were classed. The latter alteration could only have relation to the woman herself, as it is owing to the special connection between her and her kin that the latter claim a right to her offspring. We have seen reason to believe that primitively it was a general custom for a woman to receive her husband or husbands among her own kin. At a later date when she went to reside among her husband's relations, the children of the marital association were still considered as belonging to her family group in pursuance of the rule of female kinship. The principles which govern the change to male kinship were referred to at a preceding page,[1] and their application may be seen in the development of the law of marriage among the early Arabs.

It is stated by Prof. Smith[2] that three types of marriage can be shown to have existed in Arabia : one in which a woman did not leave her own kin, but might entertain a stranger as her husband, the children remaining with their mother's tribe ; another in which the woman followed her husband to his tribe, but where, owing to a want of fixity in the marriage tie, the rule of female kinship prevailed ; and the third where the woman leaves her tribe and dwells permanently among her husband's kin, in which case the children of the marriage will follow their father and belong to his tribe. The third type of marriage ultimately prevailed, and it is supposed to have

[1] Above, p. 269.   [2] Robertson Smith 1885, p. 61.

necessarily given rise to the rule of male kinship. The mere fact of the wife's residence with her husband's kin did not, however, give them the right to her children, and Prof. Smith connects this right with the nature of the marriage with which it was associated. He says[1] that the marriage, which in homogeneous tribes is associated with the rule of male descent, might be constituted either by *capture* or by arrangement with the woman's kin. The so-called "marriage by capture" of the Arabs was rather forcible marriage consequent on capture, and it originated in the old style of Arab warfare, which had for its object the procuring of captives. Marriage by arrangement with the woman's kin, who received from the husband a dowry or *mahr* as compensation for the loss of the woman, is supposed to be of later origin than the other type of marriage, as the subjection of women to their husbands which distinguishes both types "is regarded by the Arabs themselves as a virtual captivity."[2]

Prof. Smith appears to have established, that among the Arabs these "marriages of dominion" were originally formed by capture, and that this was afterwards supplemented by purchase, both of them being in use down to the time of Mohammed, and that wherever they existed the children of the marriage were of the husband's blood.[3] That which a man acquired at first by force was afterwards obtained by purchase —the right to have children by the woman whom he had married, and "to have these children belong to his own kin,"[4] the woman herself, however, not changing her kin. We see from this the truth of the

[1] *Ibid.*, p. 72.   [2] *Ibid.*, p. 80.
[3] *Ibid.*, pp. 75ff.   [4] *Ibid.*, pp. 101, 108.

observation above made, that the change from female descent to male descent for purposes of kinship had relation to children, and a confirmation of it is found in the remark of Prof. Smith,[1] in referring to the disabilities laid on women by the law of property and inheritance, that "where a woman leaves her own kin and goes abroad to bear children for an alien husband, there will always be a tendency to reduce her rights of property and inheritance as far as possible, because everything she gets is carried out of the tribe or out of the family." This assumes, not that, as Dr M'Lennan says, the right of inheritance is the test of kinship, but rather that the right of inheritance is dependent on kinship. It is not improbable that in some cases the question of property has largely aided in bringing about the change from female to male kinship, especially where neither forcible marriage nor wife-purchase is practised, but, as a rule, the originating cause must have relation to the children of the marriage, the element which gives strength to the tribe, gens, or family.[2]

The question arises, whether kinship through males has ever been established as an original institution, and not as a change from an earlier rule of descent in the female line. We have seen that the classificatory system of the Polynesian islanders recognised relationship in both the male and female lines, while usually tracing kinship in the former and rank in the latter. The Polynesians have the punaluan form of marriage,

[1] *Ibid.*, p. 94.

[2] Prof. Smith says: "When Mohammed asked the Hawâzin whether they would rather get back their goods or their women and children captured in war, they unhesitatingly chose the latter" (1885, p. 79).

and as among the peoples who have the Ganowanian
system of relationships, kinship through females is
associated with the phase of punalua, which is based
on the sisterhood of the wives, we may expect to find
that with the other phase of punalua, that based on
the brotherhood of the husbands, kinship is traced
through males. Now, as a fact, the latter phase of
punalua is associated with male kinship among the
Turanian peoples, who possess a system of relationship
similar to the Ganowanian system in use with the
American tribes who have the gentile institution with
female kinship. Indeed, the Turanian and the Ganowanian classifications differ only in the line of descent
through which kinship, as distinguished from simple
relationship, is traced. There is no reason, therefore,
in the nature of things why the male kinship represented in the former should be less original than the
female kinship of the latter, and priority cannot be
granted to either of them if, as their common connection with punalua would lead us to suppose, they have
diverged from a common source.

In a preceding chapter[1] reasons were given for
believing that Tibetan polyandry was a phase of
punalua, which was treated as a form of group marriage, and as male kinship is said by Dr M'Lennan to
have replaced female kinship under the influence of
the Tibetan system, it is necessary to consider his
reasoning on this question. In Dr M'Lennan's theory
of progress, Nair polyandry answers to female kinship
and Tibetan polyandry to male kinship. It has already[2]
been shown, however, that these two forms of polyandry do not stand to each other in the relation of
lower and higher, and it is possible, therefore, that the

[1] Above, pp. 91, 138.   [2] Above, p. 149.

male kinship associated with Tibetan polyandry may not have been preceded by female kinship among the peoples practising that form of group marriage. Elsewhere,[1] however, Dr M'Lennan lays stress on two other factors as affecting the question of kinship. He states that where a woman lives with her mother or brothers, her children are born in and belong to *her* mother's house. Afterwards the wife cohabits with her husbands in a house of her own, becoming thus detached from her family, but her children would still belong to this family, " the want of a community of blood and interests among the husbands preventing the appropriation of the children to them." This would prepare the way for the Tibetan system, " in which the woman passed from her family, not into a house of her own, but into the family of her husbands, in which her children would be born, and to which they would belong." This would happen only when the husbands were brothers, own or collateral, and " when this form of marriage became general, and when conjugal fidelity was secured by penalties, we should expect to find that the system of kinship through males would appear, this species of marriage allowing of certainty as to the father's blood, though not of certainty as to fathers."

The reasoning here appears to be that male kinship depends on certainty of paternity, or rather of paternal blood, and that this depends on the fact of the wife residing with her husband's family and the enforcement of conjugal fidelity. It may be asked, however, whether there is any trace among polyandrous peoples of a previous system of female kinship, or whether with them the wife ever remains among her own

[1] 1876, pp. 152ff.; cf. note above, p. 348.

family, and if so, whether this fact is attended by any
change in the mode of tracing descent. The Todas,
among whom formerly it was customary for "a family
of near relations to live together in one mand, having
wife, children, and cattle all in common," have descent
through males. All the children of both sexes belong
to the father's family,[1] and even where, after a child
has been born of the marriage, this is cancelled, owing
to the husband not having fulfilled his contract for
payment of the dowry, the child, whether son or
daughter, remains with the father.[2] This is supposed
by Colonel Marshall to arise from the influence of the
property law. Inheritance runs through the male line
only. No females, whether married or single, can
possess property, and they are supported by their
male relations.[3] The practice of a brother, or other
near relation of a deceased husband, taking his widow
to wife, is supposed also to have arisen from the law
of property, and to have originated in the desire " to
avoid the complications that would arise in the matter
of food and the guardianship of property, from the
marriage of widows, if they entered other families,
taking their children with them." The Todas do not
mind the marriage of a widow out of the family
if she has no child. They have, moreover, a strong
desire for children, so strong, indeed, that Colonel
Marshall thinks[4] it may be termed their ruling
passion, and he refers it rather to a plain instinct
than to "an intelligent human feeling." Agreeably
with this view, sons are not required by them for
religious objects, as among the Hindoos.[5]

The right of the father to his children does not

[1] Marshall 1873, p. 206.   [2] Ibid., p. 218.
[3] Ibid., p. 206.   [4] Ibid., p. 208.   [5] Ibid., p. 171.

depend with the Todas on their mother residing with his family. Usually on marriage the wife accompanies her husband to his own house, but if more convenient to them they remain in her father's village. In either case the marriage, both in name and in fact, is the same. That right is more likely to have arisen from wife-purchase, although the evidence of this is not quite satisfactory. The man certainly gives a *keikuli*, or dowry of cattle, to the girl's father, but he receives in exchange from the latter a present of cattle, less or more in number than those he gives. The bargain thus made requires confirmation by the girl, and to enable her to decide whether she will marry or not, she and her suitor are left in a house together for a day and night. By the expiration of this period the girl has to make up her mind, and if she tells her mother that she will have the man, they are held to be man and wife without further ceremony.[1]

We find no trace of female kinship among the Todas, nor is there any evidence of its former existence among the Tibetans. Mr Andrew Wilson states,[2] on the authority of Herr Jaeschke, that the polyandrous system of this people must be indefinitely old, as they have no tradition as to its origin. Herr Koeppen asserts[3] that it existed in the country before the introduction of Buddhism. There is no evidence, moreover, that Tibetan polyandry was developed through a ruder form, as supposed by Dr M'Lennan. According to Mr Wilson[4] there is no other kind of polyandry in Tibet than fraternal, and he states that it prevails among all classes, although where the people are a good deal in contact with Hindoos or Mohammedans, it is super-

[1] *Ibid.*, pp. 210ff.   [2] Wilson 1875, p. 233.
[3] *Ibid.*, p. 225.   [4] *Ibid.*, p. 227.

seded by polygyny.   Nor is there any probability that
female kinship ever prevailed among the Tibetans.
Their polyandry has the effect of checking, if it was
not at first intended to check, the increase of population in the country, where it is difficult, says Mr
Wilson,[1] to increase the means of subsistence, and from
whence it is difficult to emigrate.   A large number of
surplus women [2] even now exist in Tibet, and they are
maintained in the Lama nunneries, but if group marriage, or the sisterhood phase of punalua, with which
female kinship is usually associated among primitive
peoples, had prevailed, the number of both males and
females would have very largely increased, thus occa-
sioning the very evils which polyandry is found to
prevent.   The population might of course have been
kept down by infanticide, but there is no evidence of
this having been practised by the Tibetans, and that
it did not prevail may be inferred from the existence
of polyandry before the introduction of Buddhism.
Even if it could be shown that infanticide was practised, the custom need not necessarily have anything
to do with any particular phase of marriage or kinship.
The polyandrous Todas, who have male kinship, were
at one time compelled by poverty to practise infanticide, and Col. Marshall thinks[3] that the killing of
female children was so long continued as to have
formed a male-producing variety of the human race.
If a Toda is asked how many children he has, he will
reply that he has so many sons.   This ignoring of

[1] *Ibid.*, p. 234.

[2] Mr. Wilson says that childless women are not regarded in
any particular manner. This is contrary to the Toda views,
but it is not surprising, considering the aim of the polyandrous system.

[3] Marshall 1873, pp. 111, 194ff.

daughters, which is not unusual among Eastern races, shows that they are not so highly thought of as sons, and it is not surprising therefore, that where infanticide is practised, especially where the system of male kinship is established, the victims are usually females. The Chinese have been accused of the systematic practice of female infanticide. There has probably been much exaggeration in relation to this subject, but Prof. Douglas affirms[1] that, although a law exists in the statute-book making infanticide a crime, it is never acted on. He states that in some parts of the country, more especially in the provinces of Keang-se and Fuh-Keen, female infanticide prevails among the poorer classes to an alarming extent, and it is justified on the ground that it is useless rearing daughters,[2] as " when they are young they are only an expense, and when they reach an age when they might be able to earn a living, they marry." Prof. Douglas adds, that it is only abject poverty which drives parents to the commission of infanticide, and that in the more prosperous and wealthy districts the crime is almost unknown.

It is equally questionable whether female kinship has prevailed among many of the non-polyandrous races who now have the system of kinship through males. Let us first take the case of the Chinese. It has been shown in a preceding chapter[3] that this people, like the Polynesians, recognise relationship through both parents. The Chinese system of kinship proves this conclusively, as it differs from other

[1] Douglas 1882, p. 91.

[2] This reasoning would not apply where wife-purchase was practised, a custom which is a safeguard against female infanticide (cf. Wake 1878, I, 421).

[3] Above, p. 291.

forms " in possessing a double set of terms for ancestors, one for those on the father's side and another for
those on the mother's." This, says Mr Morgan,[1] was
rendered necessary by the descent of the family name
in the male line, and unless evidence can be furnished
that descent was ever traced in the female line only,
we must assume that the Chinese always preferred
male kinship for that purpose. There appears, indeed, to be a tradition that "marriage was unknown"
in China till the reign of Fouhi, but this does not
imply that such a condition of promiscuity prevailed
as that from which Dr M'Lennan infers the existence of
kinship through females only.[2] The marriage referred
to by the tradition would be that with which the
Chinese system of relationships is associated, a system
which, as Mr Hart states,[3] has existed for thousands
of years, and which is based on the marriage of two
individuals. Before the development of this phase
of marriage it is possible, or perhaps probable, that
the Chinese possessed a form of group-marriage, such
as the brotherhood phase of punalua still existing in
Tibet. Prof. Douglas quotes[4] from a Chinese book
a passage descriptive of the Tibetan system, which,
after referring to the practice of polyandry, says,
" Adultery is not considered shameful; and when a
married woman forms a *liaison*, she frankly informs
her husband or husbands that such and such a one
has become her '*ying-tuh*,' or 'gallant bachelor.'
The husband or husbands make no objection; and
husbands and wife 'averting their eyes' from the
doings of each other, contentedly follow their own

[1] 1871, p. 416.
[2] McLennan 1876, p. 139.   [3] Above, p. 293.
[4] Cited in Wilson 1875, p. 229.

devices." There is no wonder that the Chinese should consider such a system as this, viewed in the light of tradition, as not marriage. Nevertheless the Tibetans, like the Chinese, prefer male descent, and we may say of the latter as of the former, that there is no evidence of their ever having done otherwise.

The Hindoos also trace descent in the male line, and as they show traces of what may be supposed to have been polyandrous marriage similar to that of the Tibetans, they have probably never had a system of kinship through females only. This question is important, and it is advisable to consider it in the light of recent enquiries. Prof. Hearn, after remarking[1] that there are three possible ways in which consanguinity may be traced, that is, in the male line, or the female line, or both the male and the female, states that the last form, under the name of *cognation*, is used in modern times among races of European descent, but that formerly *agnation*, or relationship through the male line only, was universal among the Aryan nations. This system traces through the father, and through his sons, and not through the daughters, the descendants of a sister, therefore, not being related to her brother or his descendants. According to Prof. Hearn,[2] the archaic household " formed an organized permanent body distinct from its individual members, owning property, and having other rights and duties of its own. In it, all its members, whatever might be their position, had interests according to their rank. Over it the housefather presided with absolute power, not as owner in

[1] Hearn 1879, p. 147.
[2] *Ibid.*, pp. 64ff.

his own right, but as the officer and representative
of the corporation . . . . . The tie between the
members was neither blood nor contract, but community of domestic worship . . . . . Its one great
aim was the perpetuation of the *sacra.* The *sacra*
were essential both to the unity and the continuity
of the houshold. If they ceased, the household was
gone. The *sacra* could be performed only in a particular way. It was a worship of males by males, of
past fathers by present fathers. . . . . Thus the
house-father for the time being was the visible representative and head of the household ; and was
bound not only to administer its temporal affairs,
but to perform the ceremonies of its religion, and to
maintain the purity of its ritual." The household,
moreover, had perpetual succession, and included in
its members both the living and the dead. When
the house-father died his place was at once filled
by his heir, who retained all the household's property
" which it was his special function to administer."
The property of the household and the performance
of its *sacra* were indissolubly connected. The person
charged with that performance was the heir, or in
other words, the heir was the person bound to perform
the *sacra.*[1]

Prof. Hearn finds in the theory of house worship an
answer to the questions why kinship through the
father was limited to males, and " why this limited
form preceded instead of following the more general
form under which daughters were first admitted in the
absence of sons, and ultimately admitted upon an
equal footing." The Hindu, he says,[2] " makes his

[1] *Ibid.,* p. 79.
[2] *Ibid.,* p. 162.

offerings to his father, his father's father, and his
father's grandfather ; but he has no offering for his
mother, or his mother's father, or for any person
in the maternal line. It was the house father, too,
that made these offerings, and not his wife or his
daughters. None but males could present the funeral
repast to the Manes. None but males, therefore,
could, as regards each other, be fellow-partakers of
the cake (Sapindas), or fellow-givers of the water "
(Samanodoeas). Agnation was a consequence of this
system of house worship. Prof. Hearn explains the
fact that the house spirit was always a male and
never a female, by reference to the belief, common
to many of the lower races,[1] that there is an intimate
physical connection between father and child, and that
the mother supplies nutriment to the child and gives
it birth, but nothing more. The Aryans may never
have entertained any notion of a direct physical connection between father and child, but, for some purposes, they " held the theory of paternal generation
in its full extent." Assuming this to have been so,
Prof. Hearn gives the following as the line of thought :
—" A male was the first founder of the house. His
descendants have ' the nature of the same blood ' as
he. They, in common, possess the same mysterious
principle of life. The life spark, so to speak, has been
once kindled, and its identity, in all its transmissions,
must be preserved. But the father is the lifegiver.
He alone transmits the life spark, which from his
father he received. The daughter receives, indeed,
the principle of life, but she cannot transmit it.[2] She

[1] See above, p. 261, and Tylor 1865, p. 29.

[2] Nevertheless, under certain circumstances a son could
be raised to a man through his daughter.

can, at most, be the medium for transmitting another, and quite different life spark. None but males possessed this capacity of transmission. None but males, therefore, could maintain the identity of the original life principle, or could perform the worship if that principle was the centre. Thus males were exclusively the lineal representatives of the founder of the kin ; and as collateral kinship means only the fact that certain persons are alike lineal representatives of a common ancestor, it follows that all relationship, whether lineal or collateral, so far at least as it implied the possibility of celebrating the house worship, and the consequences of that worship, was confined exclusively to males."

That Prof. Hearn's theory of male kinship is correct, may be granted, so far as it applies to "the possibility of celebrating the house worship, and the consequences of that worship." It does not go further, however, and it is open to the objection that male kinship is put after that which depends upon it. This is well shown by Mr Fison, who says,[1] "Ancestral worship seems clearly to have been an outcome of the descent through males. At all events, there must have been this descent before there would be that worship. For, since the household gods were the male ancestors, the forefathers must have come into the direct line of descent before they could be household gods. And when ancestral worship had become established, men worshipped the same gods because they were related—because they were descended from the same forefathers who had grown into gods. A common worship, therefore, was only a mark of common descent." By similar reason-

[1] Fison and Howitt 1880, p. 111.

ing it can be shown that, so far from it being remarkable that the Aryan house spirit is always masculine, it must be so where the rule of kinship through males is established. With descent in the male line, the family group or gens virtually consists of males alone. Hence, says Mr Fison,[1] as the ancestors are the household gods, " the house spirit can be none other than a male, for all the female members are of another gens. For the same reason the celebration of his worship is necessarily limited to males. The only females who could join in that worship by right of birth forfeited their birthright by marrying into another gens ; and none but males are left to make the offering. ' No female, says Prof. Hearn, ' is counted in the line of descent, because no offering is made to a female ancestor.' But the fact is that no female is counted in the line of descent for the sufficient reason that no female can possibly be in that line when descent is through males. Every female ancestor was a woman of another line, and therefore no offering could be made to her."

Prof. Hearn is no less in error when he supposes that under the rule of agnation the descendants of a sister would not be related to her brother or his descendants, or, in other words, that all relationship would be confined exclusively to males. It has been shown in a preceding chapter,[2] that where uterine descent is preferred, relationship through the father is fully recognised, and the same is true as to maternal relationship where male descent is established. Prof. Hearn makes the mistake of using indifferently the words " relationship" and " kinship," a mistake made also by Dr M'Lennan, when he says,[3] that under

[1] *Ibid.*, p. 113.　　　　　　　　　　[2] Above, p. 267.
[3] 1885, p. 211.

agnation "a person could belong to one gens or family only, and could not have relationship with persons in any other," and elsewhere,[1] that with kindred depending upon female descent, children "would not be the relatives of their own fathers." This idea has already been disproved, and the testimony may be added of Mr Fison, who says,[2] "Relationship is wider than kinship; for, in addition to the relationship between the members of the same gens, there are also relationships between them and the members of the gens or gentes with which their gens intermarries.[3] None of all these relationships are in anywise dependent on the line of descent."

The question whether the early Hindoos had a system of female kinship is incidentally considered by Dr M'Lennan when criticising the Patriarchal Theory. He says,[4] "Reason has been shown for concluding that marriage was commonly among early Hindoos (as among other peoples in a rude state) an affair of sale and purchase; and that the peculiarities of Hindoo family law sprung out of an early system of contracts for marriage made on that footing." He adds that "the facts are exactly what we might expect to find were such a system of contract superinduced upon the system of counting kinship through females only." This conclusion is a just one, but how far it is actually supported by the facts is very doubtful. At a preceding page reasons were given for thinking the early

---

[1] 1885, p. 222.   [2] Fison and Howitt 1880, p. 121

[3] That this is so even with the Polynesians is proved by the fact that by the sprinkling of the blood of the mothers of the married pair, the two families to which they belong are ever afterwards regarded as one (Ellis 1832–34, I, 272).

[4] McLennan 1885, p. 315.

Hindoos practised wife-purchase, but the evidence of it, arising from the giving of marriage presents, is not conclusive. It by no means follows, moreover, that the system of contract was preceded by the custom of tracing kinship through females only. Dr M'Lennan's argument[1] is that among the early Hindoos "a man had no right to a child merely as being its father. There was no affiliation of children to the mother ; and children following the mother were also affiliated to the man, who was 'lord' of the mother. . . . The 'lord' of an unmarried woman was her father ; and was affiliated to her father, and of his stock and family. Her issue also were affiliated to her father, and of his stock and family." Marriage, however, passed a woman and her issue, although born before marriage, into the stock and family of her husband, who was now her 'lord,' and such a transfer was the result of a contract of sale and purchase, which gave to the husband the whole right to the woman's family. It should be noted, however, that the Toda system of exchange of dowries was attended with the same result. All children of both sexes belong to the father's family, and inheritance runs through the male line only.[2] This rule applies even where a marriage is cancelled on the ground of the husband not having, by the time a child is born of the marriage, carried out his contract as to payment of dowry. In this case the child, whether son or daughter, belongs to the father, although the mother nurses it during infancy.[3] The birth of a child before marriage would seem to be unknown to the Todas, as everybody is somebody's husband or wife. We can

[1] *Ibid.*, pp. 313ff.   [2] Marshall 1873, p. 206.
[3] *Ibid.*, p. 218.

hardly doubt, however, that an illegitimate child would follow its mother, and be maintained by her father before her marriage, and by her husband afterwards, as with the early Hindoos. The right to the child would depend on the duty of maintaining it, and a woman's offspring while she was unmarried would, therefore, belong to the same stock as herself, whether kinship was traced through females or through males only. Dr M'Lennan says, however, we know that the children of a woman born before marriage belonged to her father, and if this was so, instead of kinship being counted through females only, it must have been reckoned through males, as otherwise the children would have belonged to the woman's maternal stock.[1] As a fact, the contract of wife-purchase will transfer to the husband and his family the right to the offspring of the marriage, whether, in the absence of such a contract, the right to the woman's children would be governed by the rules of kinship in the female line or the male line, and there is, therefore, no occasion to call in the aid of the former system to account for the peculiarities of Hindoo family law.

Let us see what was the custom of other Aryan peoples in relation to kinship. Dr M'Lennan endeavoured to prove that, according to both tradition and fact, the custom of tracing kinship through females only preceded kinship through males among the early Greeks.[2] He says that, although Homer prefers the father in tracing genealogies, yet the blood ties through

---

[1] Dr. McLennan remarks that kinship through females only, "makes children of their mother's stock, and affiliates them to their mother's family" (1876, p. 316). The unmarried woman and her issue of the text, answer to the children in this quotation.

[2] 1876, pp. 241ff.

both father and mother are acknowledged, and few
of the genealogies ascend many steps before terminat-
ing in an unknown or divine father, showing that
pedigrees through fathers were not old inheritances.[1]
Dr M'Lennan refers[2] to various cases to show " that
Homer had no idea of there being no affinity between
mother and child ; that, on the contrary, he regarded
uterine connection generally as especially close and
tender." Moreover, that " there are traditions in the
poems which prove that among some Hellenes affinity
through the mother founded the blood-feud, and gave
rights of succession ; and that among the ' Pelasgi,'
and possibly Hellenes in Troy and Lycia, the tie
through the mother was superior to that through the
father, and that the latter was not regarded as a perfect kinship." So far as the examples referred to are
Trojan or Pelasgic, they do not support Dr M'Lennan's contention that female kinship was preferred by
the Greeks. The only case which would be of much
value if it were applicable is that of Tlepolemus, who
inadvertently slew his grand-uncle, Licymnius, the
brother of Alcmene, mother of Hercules. Tlepolemus
was the son of Hercules and Astyoche, and he had to
flee to escape the vengeance of the other sons and the
grandsons of Hercules. This, Dr M'Lennan says,[3]
shows the recognition of the blood-tie through the
mother as creating the right and obligation of the
blood-feud. But surely this is a mistake. According
to that view the right of blood-feud should be in the
descendants of Alcmene in the female line, but the
sons of Hercules would belong to their own mother's

---

[1] The fact mentioned may prove only that Homer knew
little of the pedigrees of his heroes.

[2] McLennan 1876, p. 253.   [3] Ibid., p. 249.

kin, and not to that of their father, and they would therefore not be of the kindred of the slain Licymnius if descent were traced through females only. This is shown by the following diagram, in which the kindred of Licymnius by female kinship are given in italics.

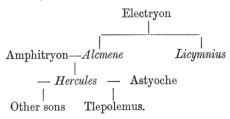

Here, with descent traced in the female line only, although Hercules is through his mother akin to Licymnius, his sons are strangers in blood. On the other hand, with male kinship only, so far from the law of blood-feud requiring the "other sons" of Hercules to slay Tlepolemus, they would have to protect him. As Mr Fison points out,[1] when considering the case of Orestes, where the criminal is of the same gens[2] as the avenger of blood, he is out of reach of the latter, " who could not kill him without bringing upon himself the guilt of shedding the blood of his own gens." Man was powerless in such a case, and the gods had to step in to punish the crime. Mr Fison agrees with Dr M'Lennan in explaining the suit against Orestes as being based on " the claim of the Erinnyes to the right of punishing matricides," but they differ in that while the latter supposes this function to have belonged to them by " special ordination," the former thinks it arose " directly out of the constitution of the gens."

[1] Fison and Howitt 1880, p. 124.

[2] With male kinship they would belong to their father's gens, and they would be of a common gens with female kinship, if their mothers belong to the same gens.

It appears to me, however, that there is not any real evidence in this case of male kinship having supplanted an earlier system of female kinship. When the Erinnyes speak of the "ancient views," they certainly refer to the belief that a mother is related by blood to her child, but this belief does not preclude that of a similar relationship between a child and his father, any more than the latter precludes the former relationship. The Erinnyes are enraged that Orestes should escape them, but the ties of blood between him and his father are closer than those which connect him with his mother, and so he escapes their fury. It does not matter, therefore, so far as its bearing on the argument is concerned, whether Orestes is pre-Homeric or not. This really appears from Dr M'Lennan's own words, when he says[1] at first, that "in Homer we have acknowledgment of the blood ties through both the father and the mother," and afterwards, that "kinship through the mother had been in Homer's time undisputed among the Greeks, and had come by the time of Æschylus to be a subject of controversy, and to a great extent, if not wholly, to be ignored."

Dr M'Lennan has still another argument in favour of the existence of the system of kinship through females in the indications met with in the Greek legends of the "ancient supremacy of women." He refers to the Homeric legend of Meleager, as evidencing "a time when inheritances descended from a man to his sister's children, and when *e converso* a man's maternal uncles were among his nearest heirs." This is an inference from the fact that the two brothers of Althæa, the mother of Meleager, took from Atalanta the spoils of the boar of Calydon which Meleager had

[1] McLennan 1876, pp. 242, 266.

given to her, and which the brothers claimed the right to have rather than Atalanta. According to the legend as related by Ovid,[1] all the companions of Meleager were jealous of his attentions to Atalanta and the honour he paid her, and it was evidently that jealousy, and not any right as next of kin, that made Meleager's maternal uncles claim the head and skin of the boar. The conduct of Althæa, moreover, so far from being governed by the idea of kinship through females, is, on the contrary, consistent only with male kinship. She bewails the death of her brother because her father has lost his two sons, while Meleager, covered with glory, survives to his father. The tie is between father and child in accordance with the notion of kinship through males, and the conduct of Althæa, in avenging her brothers, can only be accounted for on the supposition that a mother was not regarded as so nearly allied to her child as its father, an opinion which is quite opposed to that on which descent in the female line is founded. If this had governed Althæa's conduct she would have been more likely to take the part of Meleager, who was her son, than that of her brothers. The former, equally with the latter, would belong to her own gens, which would preclude her from acting as the avenger of blood.

Evidence of "the ancient predominance of women" among the Greeks is further proved, according to Dr M'Lennan,[2] by the number of their female divinities, and especially by the number of their Eponymæ. The facts that "there were so many goddesses in the early time," and that "so many cities and tribes were named after women," may possibly show that women were anciently of high social importance, but it does

---

[1] *Metamorphoses*, bk. VIII, fab. 4.   [2] McLennan 1876, p. 283.

not necessarily furnish evidence that they were " the chiefs of the groups of kindred." Dr M'Lennan says, further,[1] however, that not only were the tribes named after women, but " they explained their affinities to one another by pointing to the relationship of their primitive mothers." He refers in proof of this assertion to the case of the Thebans and Æginetans, who were said to be the next-of-kin of each other, because Thebe and Ægina had been sisters. This is not, however, the exact statement of Herodotus. He says, " Thebe and Ægina are said to be daughters of Asopus. Now, because these were sisters, " the Æginetæ were entreated to assist the Thebans as being their " nearest friends." Here the common ancestry is traced to Asopus, and hence there is as much evidence of male kinship as of kinship through females. If the facts prove anything as to descent, it is that relationship could be traced through either parent.

Dr M'Lennan finds a confirmation of his views in the custom of naming children after their mother, which he thinks " has never been found in a case where relationship to the father was fully acknowledged." This opinion is not correct, as that custom was observed by the Egyptians,[2] and is not unknown to the Turks, who do not trace kinship through females only, and it has been ascribed to the practice of polygamy, " which makes it easier among a number of children of the same family to distinguish them by their mother's names, than if each had his father's prefixed."[3] Dr M'Lennan mentions, however, certain

[1] *Ibid.*, p. 285. [2] Below, p. 383.
[3] Winterbottom 1803, I, 151.

cases in which it was the custom for children to take
their mother's family name. The most important is
that of the Lycians, of whom Herodotus says,[1] "They
take their name from their mothers, and not from their
fathers; so that if any one ask another who he is, he
will describe himself by his mother's side, and reckon
up his maternal ancestry in the female line. And if
a free-born woman marry a slave, the children are
accounted of a pure birth; but if a man who is a
citizen, even though of high rank, marry a foreigner
or cohabit with a concubine, the children are infamous." Dr M'Lennan cites Nicolaus Damascenus
as stating, moreover, that the Lycians leave their
inheritances to their daughters and not to their sons.
That these facts support the inference drawn from
them as to the existence of kinship through females
cannot be denied. It may even be granted, as affirmed
by Dr Morgan,[2] that the Lycians were "organised in
gentes, with a prohibition against intermarriage in the
gens, and that the children belonged to the gens of
their mother." It is not justifiable, however, to assume
that, therefore, the Grecians also had descent in the
female line only. Dr M'Lennan omits to refer to the
statement of Herodotus, that, although the customs of
the Lycians were partly Cretan and partly Carian, the
custom of taking their mothers' names was peculiar to
themselves, and one "in which they differ from all
other nations." This fact is consistent with the origin
ascribed by Herodotus to the Lycians, whose affinity
to the Greeks is by no means so certain as Dr M'Lennan
supposes. The "modern Lycians"—all of whom,
except eighty families whose ancestors were from home
when their city was captured by Harpagus the Mede,

[1] Bk. I. 173. [2] Morgan 1877, p. 347.

are said by the Greek historian to be strangers—may have been Greeks.

The Lycians were originally, however, if we are to believe Herodotus, sprung from Crete, and the custom of female kinship was no doubt carried by them from this island. The Cretans are stated by Dr M'Lennan to have had that system in ancient times. He refers[1] to Plutarch's remark that they spoke of "motherland" instead of "fatherland," and he adds that there are numerous hints of the system of female kinship in the Cretan legends. But who were the Cretans? That the primitive Cretans were not of Grecian origin is evident from Herodotus' statement that "in ancient time Crete was entirely in the possession of barbarians."[2] According to tradition, when the Lycians first left Crete, under the leadership of Sarpedon, they were called Termilæ. Sarpedon had been driven from the island by his brother Minos, with whom he disputed the sovereignty on the death of Europa. In accordance with the tradition[3] which said that Europa was the daughter of the king of Tyre, the primitive Cretans were Phenicians, and therefore, as not being Greeks, "barbarians." The existence of female kinship among the Cretans, and their offshoot the Termilæ or Lycians, proves only, therefore, that the custom was derived from the Phenicians, who anciently dwelt on the Red Sea, and who were primarily related to the Egyptians and

---

[1] McLennan 1876, p. 295.

[2] This is consistent with the fact that the early inhabitants of Crete were supplanted by invaders of the same stock as the Dorians of Sparta (Daremberg and Saglio 1877–1919, p. 1563). The Dorians are expressly said by Herodotus to be Hellenes (bk. I. 56).   [3] Herodotus, bk. I. 2.

secondarily to the Semitic race.[1] It is true that Dr
Morgan speaks[2] of the Lycians as being Pelasgian in
lineage, and says that Minos, the brother of Sarpedon,
is usually regarded as the head of the Pelasgians in
Crete. But to what race did the Pelasgians belong ?
If we may judge from their Cyclopian architecture
they must have sprung from the same stock as the
Phenicians, and this idea is supported by certain statements of Herodotus. When referring to the use by
the Athenians of certain images of Mercury, he says[3]
it was derived from the Pelasgians, and that it could
be explained in the mysteries of the Cabiri, which the
Samothracians had adopted from the Pelasgians. The
Cabiri were, however, Phenician deities. The common
origin of the Pelasgians and Phenicians here supposed,
is supported by the account given by Herodotus of the
ancient oracle of Dodona.[4] This was in some manner
derived from Egypt, apparently through the agency
of the Phenicians, and the country in which it was
established was formerly called Pelasgia, although
afterwards Hellas.

By reference to the Pelasgians we may account for
certain facts connected with the Greeks which Dr
M'Lennan cites[5] as proof that "at one time in Athens
marriage was unknown in the modern forms, and that
children were named after their mothers." Under the
government of Cecrops "a double wonder sprang out
of the earth at the same time ; in one place the olive
tree, and in another water." The oracle at Delphi
said that the olive tree signified Minerva (Athene),
and the water Neptune (Poseidon) ; and that the

[1] Lenormant 1881–88, I, 275.
[2] Morgan 1877, p. 347.   [3] Bk. II. 51.
[4] Bk. II. 54–57.   [5] McLennan 1876, pp. 292ff.

burgesses should choose after which of the two they would name their town.   Cecrops summoned an assembly, at which the men voted for Poseidon and the women for Athene.   The latter was chosen by one vote, and Poseidon, enraged, caused the sea to flow over all the lands of Athens.   To appease the god, the burgesses punished their wives, by declaring that they should lose their votes, that children should no more receive their mother's name, and they themselves should no longer be called Athenian after the goddess.   Dr M'Lennan is perfectly justified in affirming that this is a tradition of a genuinely archaic state, but it does not prove that children at Athens were anciently named after their mother.   What the tradition really proves is that a contest took place between two peoples, one of whom had the system of kinship through females, and the other that of male kinship.   The parties to the dispute are shown by their respective deities, Athene being the deity of the Greeks, while Neptune (Poseidon) was a Phenician, if not Pelasgian deity.   Herodotus affirms[1] that the Greeks learned the god Neptune from the Libyans, but the Libyans were Phenician, as we have seen reason to suppose the Pelasgians also were.   The tradition, as preserved by Varro, had probably undergone change.   Athene is said to be the champion of "mother-right," but in the Eumenides it is she who by her vote decides that a child is more closely related to its father than to its mother.   There is no inconsistency in her conduct, if, as the result of the contest between the goddess and Poseidon, children ceased, as stated in the tradition, to be called after their mothers.

The real struggle was between the early inhabitants

[1] Bk. II. 50.

of the country represented by Poseidon, who had the
system of female kinship, and the later comers, represented by Athene, who had male kinship. The former
were undoubtedly Pelasgians, and there is reason to
believe, not as Mr Morgan says, that the Grecian and
Pelasgian tribes were derived from a common stock,
but that the former were in great measure derived
from the latter. Herodotus says,[1] "The Athenians,
when the Pelasgians possessed that which is now
called Greece, were Pelasgians, and went by the name
of Cranai; under the reign of Cecrops, they were sur-
named Cecropidæ; when Erectheus succeeded to the
government they changed their names for that of
Athenians; and when Ion, son of Xanthus, became
their leader, from him they were called Ionians."
Elsewhere Herodotus affirms that all the Ionians were
anciently Pelasgians. Possibly another explanation
of the facts may be given. The Greek historian states[2]
that all the Pelasgian tribes of his day spoke the same
language, and that this language was different from
that of any of their neighbours. The Hellenic race
have always used the same language since they became
a people, "though, when separated from the Pelasgians,
they were at first insignificant, yet from a small
beginning they have increased to a multitude of
nations." From all which it may be inferred that the
Greeks were a small tribe, having male kinship, who
settled among and intermarried with Pelasgians having
female kinship, and that the latter custom was perpetuated among some of the tribes down to a comparatively late period, but that it had to contend with,
and was ultimately entirely supplanted by, the former

[1] Bk. VIII. 49; cf. bk. I. 56, 57.
[2] Bk. I. 57, 58.

system. Possibly political considerations had something to do with the final extinction of the Pelasgian custom, as it appears from the tradition preserved by Herodotus[1] that the Pelasgians were driven out of Attica by the Athenians.[2]

Finally, Dr M'Lennan thinks that the indications of the existence in Greece of the Nair family system are irresistible. In support of this conclusion, he refers[3] to Greek tradition as representing the early inhabitants of the country as "emerging from the depths of the savage state. . . . Everywhere the Greeks believed in a past of savage rudeness, and cherished the memories of those who helped them to take the first steps of progress. Their ancestors, according to their legends, were cannibals, and offered human sacrifices to their gods; were ignorant of agriculture, and lived on roots and shell-fish; had no marriage and no laws. Then came one who taught them to prune the vine and to plough the soil; and another who gave them marriage, laws, and social order." According to this view, the association of the sexes among the earliest Greeks was subject to no regulation, and the first approach to permanent cohabitation must have been a system like the polyandry of the Nairs, or one still ruder, " under which it would be possible for children of the same mother to acquire the feelings of relationship, and become bound to one another by a sense of common interests." At the Nair stage women would be the heads of families,

[1] Bk. VI. 137.

[2] The existence among the ancient Etruscans of the custom of describing relationship with reference to the mother and not to the father referred to by Mr. Morgan (1877, p. 348) is evidence of the non-Aryan origin of that people.

[3] McLennan 1876, pp. 299ff.

daughters the heirs and continuers ; and the position of women would probably become one of high consideration. There would be "kinship only through the mother, because paternity would be uncertain ; and men would, for distinction, be named after the mother as naturally as at a subsequent stage they were named after the father." Such a series of phenomena Dr M'Lennan thinks he finds to have existed in ancient Greece, whose family system he supposes, therefore, to be really " that of Nair polyandry, and the close relationship to the mother, which forms an incident of it, the system of kinship through females only."

The answer to this general argument is that the existence of a restricted promiscuity, such as Dr M'Lennan intends by " Nair polyandry," cannot be inferred from the facts supposed by him to evidence a system of female kinship, or from the high position accorded to women. At the worst, it can be said only that among some of the early Greek tribes women received their husbands among their own kin, and that in such cases female kinship was preferred to male kinship for the purpose of tracing descent. There is great probability, however, that those tribes were of Pelasgic and not Hellenic descent. Herodotus states[1] that Cresus, King of the Lydians, found on inquiry that, among the Greeks, the Lacedemonians and Athenians excelled all the rest, the former being of Dorian and the latter of Ionic descent, " for these were in ancient times the most distinguished, the latter being a Pelasgian, and the other a Hellenic nation." The opinion expressed by the Greek historian that when the Hellenic race first separated from the Pelasgians

[1] Bk. I. 56.

they were insignificant, but that they "have increased to a multitude of nations, chiefly by a union with other barbarous nations," is consistent with the conclusion that the peculiar social phenomena mentioned by Dr M'Lennan were not truly Greek, or rather Hellenic, and that they must be referred to the earlier and less warlike race whom they dispossessed. Nor is this conclusion inconsistent with the traditions supposed to prove the absence of marriage among the early ancestors of the Greeks. Such traditions were probably those of their Pelasgian forerunners, and if they prove anything, it would be merely that these "ancestors" had peculiar ideas on the subject of marriage, and not that they lived in a condition of promiscuity.

There appears to be good reason to believe that among the early Greeks and the allied Asiatic peoples kinship through females only was never generally established. Dr Morgan, however, remarks[1] that "it is impossible to conceive of the gens as appearing, for the first time, in any other than its archaic form." He infers, therefore, that the Grecian gens must have been originally in this form, notwithstanding the fact that descent is always limited in the male line.[2] Sufficient causes for the change from the male to the female line of descent have then to be found, and these Mr Morgan finds in the growth of the idea of property and the rise of monogamy. By this was "assured the paternity of children, which was unknown when the gens was instituted, and the exclusion of children from the inheritance was no longer possible." A sufficient answer to this reasoning is found in the fact that paternity was not necessarily uncertain when the gens was established, and that if paternity was not certain,

[1] Morgan 1877, p. 231.   [2] *Ibid.*, p. 223.

yet there was certainty of paternal blood before monogamy was established.   Dr Morgan assumes that
descent in the female line was universal in the archaic
period,[1] from which he infers that it was so in the
earliest Greek period.   This inference is not justifiable,
however, as when the Greeks were first separated from
the parent stock they may already have had descent
in the male line.   He states also [2] that the gens existed
among the Aryans when the Latin, Greek, and Sanskrit
speaking tribes were one people, and he supposes
that they had it in the archaic form, and that the
change in descent from the female to the male line
took place "during the long periods of time which
elapsed between the separation of these tribes from
each other, and the commencement of civilization."
Evidence of this in relation to the Aryans of India
or Irania there is none.   Against that statement may
be set the opinion of another writer, who strongly
favours the view that mother right was a primitive
institution with many ancient peoples.   M. Giraud-
Teulon affirms [3] that the Aryas before quitting the
cradle of their race possessed in germ the spirit of the
same institutions which they afterwards developed.
Elsewhere,[4] he says, "Dans Bactriana, déja la 'gens'
s'annonce sous le principe du père de famille, et les
plus anciennes légends des Aryas reflètent elles-mêmes
le souvenir d'un progrès accompli.   Elles représentent
l'enfant comme 'tombe' du sein maternel et 'relevé'
par le père qui court avec lui autour de la flamme du
foyer, ce premier autel domestique, le purifiant ainsi
du péché de sa naissance. . . . Partout où les Aryas
se sont établis, ils ont introduit avec eux la famille

---

[1] *Ibid.*, p. 63.   [2] *Ibid.*, p. 231.
[3] Giraud-Teulon 1867, p. 7.   [4] *Ibid.*, p. 62.

gouvernie par le père : famille chaste, dans laquelle la femme, ni esclave, ni souveraine, mais campagne respéctée du maitre, relevait, comme les enfants, du chef commun. Quand sur quelques points, et exceptionnellement, comme en Lycie, ils ont transigé avec les peuples vaincus, ils ont transformé la société ancienne : continuant les honneurs à la mère, ils ont detroné, humilié, la déesse Hétaïre."

On the other hand it is affirmed by Dr M'Lennan,[1] as confirming his opinion that kinship through the mother existed among the Homeric Greeks, that "where the ruder forms of the family system prevail, the position of woman is necessarily very high," and he declares[2] that after the time of Homer the degradation of women was "consentaneously with the appearance and growth of the principle of agnation." This opinion certainly does not agree with what took place among the Iranians. The primitive Zoroaster, "organisateur du peuple Iranien, moralisateur excellent, réformateur pratique, sachant son but et le voulant," declared that woman was entitled to be on an equality with man when she was worthy of such a position.[3] The presumption is that previously, although the wife may have been the head of the household, she did not occupy so high a social position as she afterwards attained to. The change is just the opposite to that supposed by Dr M'Lennan to have taken place among the Greeks, and at the same time it was associated with a system of *male* kinship. This may be positively inferred from the curious graduated scale invented by Zoroaster to express the ratio of obligation subsisting

[1] McLennan 1876, p. 265.   [2] *Ibid.*, p. 268.
[3] Fontane 1881*b*, p. 229.

between certain classes of individuals.[1] In this scale woman is only once mentioned, and that as the wife, in which character she owes only sixty degrees of duty to her husband, while brothers owe one hundred degrees, and a father and son one thousand degrees to each other. M. Fontane well says that in relation to the family this gradation is remarkable. The "assistance and friendship" required to be shown between father and son is consistent only with the principle of male kinship occupying a fundamental position such as it occupies in the code of Menu, and this conclusion is confirmed by the entire absence of any reference to the relation between mother and child, although the family is said to comprise father, mother, and children. As M. Fontane remarks elsewhere,[2] "it is through the male the Aryan tradition is transmitted and perpetuated."

It must be concluded, from what has been said above, that primitively among the peoples belonging to the widespread Aryan or Indo-European stock, while relationship was acknowledged through both parents, descent was traced preferably in the male line. This conclusion may be tested by reference to the custom of a people supposed by Dr M'Lennan[3] to have an affinity with the Greeks. He sees a relic of the Lycian custom of female kinship in the fact mentioned by Herodotus[4] in relation to the Egyptians, that "no necessity binds sons to help their parents when they do not choose; whereas daughters are obliged to do so, even if against their choice." There is good ground for believing that there was an Egyp-

[1] *Ibid.*, p. 290.   [2] Fontane, 1881*a*, p. 58.
[3] McLennan 1876, p. 291n.
[4] Bk. II. 35.

tian element among the Greeks, and it would not be surprising, therefore, if some of the Grecian customs resemble those of the Egyptians. In reality, however, Herodotus mentions the fact as to the support of parents, among other peculiarities, as evidence that the Egyptians "have adopted customs and usages in almost every respect different from the rest of mankind." Moreover, that fact cannot bear the interpretation put upon it by Dr M'Lennan, or, at all events, it does not prove that the system of female kinship was established among them. This is evident from what is known of marriage and family life among that people. It is true that Egyptian women occupied a high position, as not only could they occupy the throne or belong to the priesthood, but they were on an equality with their husbands in the household, of which they were mistresses. Moreover, children took their names from their mothers rather than from their fathers. Nevertheless, the father was considered as the real parent of his child, the mother being regarded merely as furnishing it with nourishment and a dwelling-place. For this reason all children were treated as legitimate, even though born of a slave mother. M. Ménard, who mentions these facts, says,[1] moreover, "The Egyptians, as the Chinese, with whom they have so many points of agreement, regard filial love as the first of all the virtues, and, by a singular association of ideas, they consider it as an essential part of the worship which they rendered to the king," as shown by reference to a book on morality written as early as the fifth dynasty.

[1] Ménard 1880–83, I, 4. M. Ménard says the idea that the father is the creator of the child, the mother being merely its nourisher, was common to all antiquity (p. 63).

In Egypt, as in Greece, ideas in relation to the family were considerably modified, but man was always regarded as its head, and the son succeeded to the authority and property of his father by the rule of descent in the male line. M. Ménard remarks[1] that " the two formative principles of the ancient family, including that of the Greeks, are, 1st, the worship of ancestors, a worship which addresses itself to the ancestors of the masculine sex, but not to those of the female sex, who are not considered as clothed with the divine character ; and, 2ndly, the absolute subordination of the woman to the man, a subordination which is the more and more pronounced the farther back we go into antiquity." He says further,[2] that the wife " has no personal right ; she is honoured if fruitful, but if she is sterile she is repudiated or driven away." If she has children, they belong to the father, and " increase his wealth, in the same way as the lambs which his sheep give birth to." That is consistent with the recognition of woman's position as mistress of the household ; but where she is the head of the family, and kinship is traced through her, we must look for traces of a foreign element, such as appears to have been influential in various countries of Western Asia, and not for a primitive institution native to the race. This view is opposed to that which ascribes the subordinate position or the degradation of woman, among the Greeks at least, to the appearance and growth of the principle of agnation.

In criticising Sir Henry Maine's theory of the Patriarchal Family as based on the *patria potestas* and agnation, Dr M'Lennan says,[3] " Given a body

---

[1] *Ibid.*, I, 63.
[2] *Ibid.*, I, 49.
[3] McLennan 1885, p. 199.

of people acknowledging kinship through males, and acknowledging relationship to one another, among whom no relationship was acknowledged outside the body (clan or gens), and who did not marry within it —whose marriage custom, that is, was exogamy—then there appears to be the strongest likelihood that their system of relationship would in time exhibit every feature of agnation." He asserts, however, that agnation has always been uncommon, and that Sir Henry Maine has never been able to find it anywhere except in Rome,[1] and he suggests that, when it did exist, it arose among a people having inheritance to children in the families of their mothers, giving a rule the counterpart of agnation, by virtue of a change " sufficient to make children of the gentile connection of their father."[2] Such a change, however, would not be necessary if agnation was produced among peoples having a system of kinship through males, and this Dr M'Lennan admits may have been the case under proper influences, although he believes that male kinship in general has originated in " relationships through female descents."[3]

This question has already been considered, and we have reason to believe that, although there has been a change from female kinship to male kinship among some peoples, there is no trace of the former having ever existed among the polyandrous and monandrous or monogamous races of Asia and Europe, who have the system of male kinship fully developed. The fact that traces of polyandry, combined with descent in the male line, have been found among peoples belonging to the Aryan stock, such as the ancient Britons and

[1] *Ibid.*, p. 214.   [2] *Ibid.*, p. 210.
[3] *Ibid.*, p. 216.

the Spartans, render it possible that the system of male kinship has been derived not only by the Mongolians, but by the Aryans also, from a polyandrous source, although there is no reason why relationship through both father and mother should not have been fully recognised by them.   The question of kinship depends, not on the phase of marriage, but on the family group who are regarded as having a claim to the children of the marriage.   This again does not depend merely on the fact of a woman continuing to reside after marriage with her own kin, under which condition female kinship probably originated, or going to reside among her husband's kin, as is generally the case with male kinship.   The latter practice would not alone, however, give a right to the woman's offspring.   In connection with the forms of marriage among the early Arabs, we have seen that the capture of a woman from a hostile tribe, or the purchase of a woman from her friends, vested a right in the kindred of the captor or husband to the children born of the woman.   Probably the same effect was due to like causes among other races, and we shall be prepared to find, therefore, that the right of the father's kin to the children of his marriage, which gave rise to male kinship, is usually associated either with " capture " or with wife-purchase, which we shall see exists among most peoples having ceremonial capture in marriage.

It by no means follows that with kinship through the male line, there is no relationship through females. This opinion would be as incorrect as that expressed by Dr M‘Lennan when he states[1] that, among the American aborigines, " relationship being counted only through women, a son was not even a relative of his

[1] *Ibid.*, p. 101.

father." As a fact, where *kinship* is established in either the male or the female line, *relationship* is fully recognised in both lines. Hence a system of kinship through males may have been established without reference to a preceding system of kinship through females, and either system may come to be established, under differing social conditions, among peoples recognising relationship through both parents. It has been shown in the preceding pages that the islanders of the Pacific fully recognise the double relationship, and Dr M'Lennan indirectly confirms this view. He refers,[1] when speaking of the transition from one system of kinship to the other, to cases "in which, for a time, the gentile connection of children was not taken regularly from either father or mother, but sometimes from one and sometimes from the other—it being settled in some cases by the relatives before marriage, in others by the parents when the birth of the child was at hand, which clan a child belonged to." Dr M'Lennan traces these as cases of transition from kinship through the mother only towards kinship and gentile connection being taken from the father. But it is much more probable that the "sense of relationship on the side of both father and mother," which he supposes to "subsist and develope" (though carrying no gentile effects) with the father's kinship, was the beginning of the development. Whether in the final result kinship would be traced preferably in the male or the female lines would depend on circumstances. Curiously enough the peoples of the widespread Oceanic stock show both these systems in operation, the Polynesians generally having kinship in the male line,

[1] *Ibid.*, p. 239.

and the Melanesians generally preferring the female line, while all fully recognise the fact of relationship through both parents.

The existence of a connection between wife-purchase and male kinship has already been incidentally referred to, and a few facts bearing on this point may now be mentioned. For example, the Turanian peoples, including the polyandrous Tibetans, have a developed system of male kinship, and with them marriage is in pursuance of a contract of sale. Thus, in Mongolia the marriage presents given by a man's parents to the family of his bride are really a price, as is shown by the language used in relation to the marriage. They say, "I have bought for my son the daughter of so-and-so," or "We have sold our daughter to such-and-such a family." M. Huc adds,[1] "When it is settled how many horses, oxen, sheep, pieces of linen, pounds of butter, what quantity of brandy and wheat flour shall be given to the family of the bride, the contract is at length drawn up before witnesses, and the daughter becomes the property of the purchaser." The Chinese practice is much the same, although more ceremonious. Valuable presents of money besides other things are always made to the family of the bride by the bridegroom's parents.[2] That this is in effect wife-purchase, appears in the statement of Mr Doolittle[3] that very poor families are sometimes unable to be at the expense of buying a wife for a son, and of marrying her according to the established customs. Occasionally they purchase the wife of a *living* man who wishes for some reason

[1] Huc 1851, I, 185.
[2] Doolittle 1868, p. 51.
[3] *Ibid.*, p. 76.

to part with her. The price paid for such a wife is much less than for a girl or a female slave.

Wife-purchase is the general rule with the hill tribes of India,[1] and with very few exceptions they trace descent through males. Many of the Assam tribes practise polyandry, and of the Meeris it is said[2] all the girls have their price, " the largest price for the best looking girl varying from twenty to thirty pigs, and, if one man cannot give so many, he has no objection to take partners to make up the number." Of the Kookies we learn[3] that they obtain a wife either by purchase or " in the old Jewish fashion, by serving for her in bondage for a term of years." Wife-purchase is customary also among the polygynous tribes of the African continent, who have in most cases the practice of male kinship. Thus, a Kafir, who usually has as many wives as he can maintain, always buys them, and the girls pride themselves on the high price they fetch. They are valued in cattle ; and as each wife costs so many head of cattle, so daughters " will sell for so many—ten, twenty, or fifty—according to their rank, ability, or beauty."[4]

Mr Morgan has the remark[5] that after the Syndyasmian or pairing family began to appear, and punaluan groups to disappear, " wives came to be sought by purchase and by capture." He states elsewhere,[6] with reference to the Indian tribes, that " prior to the marriage, presents to the gentile relatives of the bride,

[1] Lewin 1870, *passim.*

[2] *Ibid.,* p. 154.

[3] *Ibid.,* p. 186.

[4] Grout 1864, I, 5, 116 ; cf. Shooter 1857, p. 50.

[5] Morgan 1877, p. 435.

[6] *Ibid.,* p. 454.

nearest in degree, became a feature in these matrimonial transactions." They did not constitute, however, a true wife-purchase. They are rather, as appears from Lafitau's work,[1] a sort of purchase of the alliance of the wife's cabin. After marriage a man usually went to reside among his wife's relations, and presents were exchanged between the two cabins of the intended spouses, their acceptance being equivalent to the formation of a marriage contract between the parties.[2] Mr Morgan's opinion as to the late appearance of wife-purchase is not consistent with the fact that it is found among peoples having the practice of polyandry, nor, it may be, with the fact that among the Polynesians the suitor made presents to the parents of the woman whom he wished to marry, in order to gain their consent.[3] Where, however, the rank of the wife's family was inferior to that of the husband's, the latter received a dowry with his wife, and probably the present to the family of the latter was not intended so much for purchase as for obtaining the goodwill of the wife's parents. The Rev. Richard Taylor states[4] that it is a common custom for a bridegroom to live with his wife's family. More usually, however, the wife resided among her husband's relations, in which case her children were lost to her father's family. Where, in accordance with custom, a man took away his bride by force, and her relatives came down upon him for the abduction, "after much speaking and apparent anger it ended with his making a handsome present of fine mats, &c., and giving an abundant feast."

This is important in relation to the question of the

[1] Lafitau 1724, I, 568.   [2] *Ibid.*, I, 565.
[3] Ellis 1832–34, I, 269.
[4] Taylor 1870, p. 337.

intention of "marriage by capture," as we shall see in the next chapter. The presents in that case evidently represent the price given for the offspring which the woman may have, an opinion which is confirmed by reference to the marriage customs of an African people. Mr John Kizell, in his correspondence with Gov. Columbine, respecting his negotiations with the chiefs in the River Sherbro, says,[1] "The young women are not allowed to have whom they like for a husband, the choice rests with the parents ; if a man wishes to marry the daughter, he must bring to the value of twenty or thirty bars to the father and mother ; if they like the man, and the brothers like him, then they will call all their family together, and tell them ' we have a man in the house who wishes to have our daughter, it is that which makes us call the family together, that they may know it.' Then the friends enquire what he has brought with him ; the man tells them ; they then tell him to go and bring a quantity of palm wine ; and then give him his wife. In this case all the children he has by her are his, but if he gives nothing for his wife, then the children will all be taken from him, and will belong to the mother's family, he not having anything to do with them."

This case, which is illustrative of the marriage customs in the greater part of the African continent, is very important, as it shows conclusively that the payment of a price for the wife has relation to the ownership of her children, or in other words, that there is an intimate connection between wife-purchase and kinship in the male line. It proves, moreover, that in the absence of such purchase, children may be regarded

[1] Sixth Report, Directors of the African Institution, 1812, p. 128.

generally as belonging to the wife's family, and such is the usual custom among all peoples but those belonging to the Aryan stock, who appear to have recognised kinship through the father from the earliest date. That agrees with the practice of the Arabs, with whom, as already mentioned,[1] the contract of marriage was a purchase by the husband of a right to have children by his wife, and "to have these children belonging to his own kin." So long as this right is recognised, the question of paternity may possibly be considered a secondary matter, especially if the right to the child belonged not so much to the husband of the woman as to his kindred as a whole.[2] This applies particularly to the early Arabs, among whom "fatherhood does not necessarily imply procreation, and the family of which the father is the head is held together, not by the principle of physical paternity, but by the rule that the husband is father of all the children born on his bed."[3] The rule is equally operative among all peoples at an early stage of culture who have the system of male kinship, and it partly accounts for the readiness with which such peoples make a temporary exchange of wives, or offer their wives for the use of guests or strangers. The idea of sexual hospitality is, however, an important element, and one which naturally presents itself to the savage mind. We can well understand, therefore, that although fatherhood does not necessarily imply procreation, yet that it may be fully recognised while very loose ideas are entertained on the subject of sexual propriety.

Prof. Smith affirms,[4] indeed, that the rule which "makes a son of the blood of his father cannot be

---

[1] Above, p. 350.   [2] Robertson Smith 1885, p. 116.
[3] *Ibid.*, p. 119.   [4] *Ibid.*, p. 147.

primitive," because individual fatherhood is a comparatively modern notion, and because " men were reckoned to the stock of their mother's lords before they were one man's children," a conclusion which cannot be arrived at until it is settled that the mother's husbands are themselves of one blood. The " conception of a group of men conveying their common blood to a child," can, however, have been led to only by " the desire to take the child away from the mother's stock." This reasoning, which leads Prof. Smith to the conclusion that " we need an older system of kinship through the mother alone to supply the conditions for the rise of male kinship through *ba'al* polyandry," may be perfectly just when applied to social phenomena, such as are observable among the early Arabs, without being universally true. By *ba'al* polyandry is meant polyandry in which all the husbands are of one *blood*, as distinguished from Tibetan polyandry, in which they are all brothers.[1] The only difference is, that in the one case the husbands are own, and in the other, collateral or tribal brothers ; and it has already been shown that there is no trace of female kinship having ever existed among the peoples having Tibetan polyandry ; and there is no absolute reason therefore why it should have existed among peoples having the analogous system to which Prof. Smith gives the name of *ba'al* polyandry. The utmost that can be said is that *where female kinship prevailed*, the idea of a group of men conveying their common blood to a child can have originated only in the desire to take the child away from the mother's stock. Even this must not be taken too absolutely ; as in marriage by capture, which is associated with the rule of male

[1] *Ibid.*, p. 125.

descent, and which is supposed by Prof. Smith to have preceded marriage by contract among the Arabs,[1] the object would be to take the woman herself, and therefore her offspring from her kindred. In the marriage contract a man acquired the right to have children by his wife, which children should belong to his kin, but he did not purchase any property in the woman herself. It was different with women captured in warfare, who were often sold in the slave market, or were ransomed by their people for money, though when a woman became pregnant by her captor, it was not thought proper in the time of the prophet that she should be either sold in the market or ransomed.[2]

It is pointed out by Prof. Smith, that people reckon themselves of one blood for some other reason than that of parentage, from which he infers that, so far as Arabia was concerned, kinship through the mother was the universal rule. He instances[3] the suckling of "fosterage," which was regarded as constituting a real unity of flesh and blood between the foster-mother and foster-child, or between foster-brothers. This milk-kinship, which, however, Prof. Smith supposes to be evidence in favour of all kinship having been originally through women, was equally with blood relationship a bar to marriage, according to Mohammed's laws of forbidden degrees. Again, the Arabs attached the greatest importance to the bond created between men by eating together, as though a connection was thought to exist "between common nourishment and common life." The Arabs had a maxim, "thy true son is he who drinks thy morning draught," which, says Prof. Smith, "acquires the same significance in constituting kinship as mother's milk had formerly done, after the

[1] *Ibid.*, pp. 72, 80.   [2] *Ibid.*, p. 73.   [3] *Ibid.*, p. 149.

weight formerly given to the bond of motherhood is transferred to fatherhood." This reasoning may be accepted so far as concerns the Arabs, as the fact of kinship through the mother alone having been originally the rule among them can apparently be established from other data. It would be difficult, however, to establish the universal truth of the statement[1] that " procreation and nurture together make fatherhood, but the first is too weak without the second," in the face of the belief entertained by so many peoples that the mother is only the nourisher of the child which has been confided to her by the father. It is true that some races who hold this opinion have the system of female kinship, while others prefer male kinship, but the real question is not whether the father or the mother is the most intimately connected with the child, but whether, according to established rule, the child belongs to the kin of the father or to that of the mother.

Much the same must be said in relation to a rite or ceremony which is supposed by Prof. Smith[2] to have been used by the heathen Arabs to denote that children renounce their original mother-kinship and are received into their father's family group. In that rite, which was practised on infants in connection with a sacrifice called 'acîca, the child's head was shaved and daubed with the blood of the sacrificial sheep. When no 'acîca was offered, the child was named and its gums rubbed with masticated dates on the morning after birth. Prof. Smith thinks that " in general the sacrifice, the naming, and the symbolical application of the most important article of food to the child's mouth, all fell together, and marked his reception into

[1] *Ibid.*, p. 151.   [2] *Ibid.*, pp. 152ff.

partnership in the *sacra* and means of life of his
father's group." The rite of ʿacîca was not performed
on girls, as though to prove that daughters were not
made of their father's kin, an inference which is thought
to be supported by the exclusion of women from
inheritance and the connection made between this and
the practice of female infanticide. There is nothing,
however, in the offering of the hair of the child to the
deity, or in the shedding of the blood to ensure his
protection for the child whose head was daubed with
it, to show that the sacrifice had any relation to the
mother's kin. This presumption is founded entirely on
the fact that the verb ʿacca, "to sever," "is not the one
that would naturally be used either of shaving hair or
cutting the throat of a victim, while it is the verb
which is used of dissolving the bond of kindred,"
either with or without the addition of *ul-rahim*, the
"womb," which is the most general Arabic word for
kinship.[1] This may prove that so far as the Arabs are
concerned the sacrificial rite was intended to represent
the severing of any tie which might be thought to
subsist between the child and its mother's kin, although
the intention may not have gone so far as this. The
idea may have been that until the protection of the
father's god was secured, the mother as its nourisher,
and through her her kin, may have some claim on it,
seeing that on marriage a woman was not adopted into
her husband's stock.[2] This is very different from a
change in the line of descent, which must be proved
from other data before the ʿacîca sacrifice can be referred to in support of it.

This view is confirmed by reference to the use by
other people of the ceremony of head shaving. The

[1] *Ibid.*, pp. 150, 154.   [2] *Ibid.*, p. 101.

Santals of Orissa have a strong feeling of kinship, and, like nearly all other Indian tribes, they trace descent in the male line. Dr Hunter states [1] that the chief ceremonies in a Santal's life, six in number, all bear upon that feeling. The first, which is the admission of the newly-born child into the family, is a secret rite, "one act of which consists in the father placing his hand on the infant's head and repeating the name of the ancestral deity." The second, the admission of the child into the tribe is a more public ceremony, at which the child's head is shaved, and the clansmen drink together to show that they are of one flesh. According to Mr Gerald Massey,[2] the former custom, as practised by various peoples, is symbolical of the birth and adoption of the child into the community ; but it is more. The hair was, as pointed out by Professor Smith,[3] an offering to the Deity, and this view is confirmed by the cases referred to by Mr Herbert Spencer [4] of sacrifice of the hair as an act of worship. The head shaving was therefore not merely a sign of the admission of the child into the group or tribe of the father, but it was a placing of the child under the protection of the family deity, without which the former would be useless. Where a woman is on marriage adopted into the family of the husband, she has to give up the father's clan and gods, and the acquisition of her husband's gods is an essential feature of the marriage. Professor Hearn remarks [5] that the marriage ceremony among the Aryans consisted of three essential parts—first, "the abandonment of, or

[1] Hunter 1881, IV, 177.   [2] Massey 1883, I, 111.
[3] Robertson Smith 1885, p. 153.
[4] Spencer 1876–96, II, 64.
[5] Hearn 1879, p. 87.

at least the agreement to abandon, his authority by the House Father of the bride. The second was the formal delivery of the bride to the bridegroom. The third was the presentation of the bride to the House Spirits in her new home, for which purpose, on her entrance into the house, " she was presented with the holy fire and the lustral water, and she partook, along with the husband, in the presence of the Lord, of the symbolic meal." By this ceremony the wife gave up her father's house and ceased to worship his gods, and she was admitted to a new household and to the worship of its gods.

Before bringing this chapter to a close, it is desirable to refer to the classificatory system of relationships associated with kinship through males. It will not be necessary to say much on this subject, as it has already been pointed out that the Turanian system differs from the American or Ganowanian system only so far as is required by the change of the line of descent, a change which, as Mr Fison observes,[1] does not affect personal relationship. To show this more closely, I here supply two Tables, C and D, giving the male and the female stems under the Turanian system, for comparison with the Australian form of the Ganowanian system shown in Tables A and B, given in the preceding chapter.[2] *

A comparison of these Tables with Tables A and B, giving the relationships according to the classificatory system where the rule of female kinship prevails, shows that the personal relationships are really the same whether descent be traced in the male or in the female line. It will be seen that the *cousin* relation, which

---

[1] Fison and Howitt 1880, p. 26n.   [2] Above, p. 334.

* [For Tables C and D, see pp. 476 ff.—R.N.]

points out the persons with whom *ego* can intermarry,[1] is in different places under one system than it is in the other, due to the fact that kinship is traced through the male stem in the Turanian system, whereas it is traced through the female stem in the Australian system.[*] The former, with slight variations, is in operation throughout nearly the whole of the Asiatic continent, and its distribution would almost seem to constitute it a race character. The relation of the two systems to each other, and the fact that they are equally explainable as the result of the disintegration of the Malayan system,[2] which recognises kinship on both sides, under the influence in the one case of the rule of female kinship, and in the other case of the rule of male kinship, is consistent moreover with their having had independent origins under special social conditions. These special conditions were the prevalence of the form of punalua based on the sisterhood of the wives among the peoples having the Ganowanian system; while among those having the Turanian system, the other form of punalua, that which was based on the brotherhood of the husbands, was the more prevalent.

Dr Morgan remarks[3] that when descent was in the female line the gens possessed two chief characteristics: marriage in the gens was prohibited, children being thus placed in a different gens from their father; and property and the office of chief were hereditary in the gens, children being thus excluded from inheriting the property or succeeding to the office of their father. With descent in the male line the same characteristics belong to the gens, but with very different results.

[1] Above, p. 336.   [2] Above, p. 376.   [3] Morgan 1877, p. 345.

[*] [It is not evident what Wake could have had in mind in making this statement. Structurally, cousins are in "the same place" in both types of system.—R.N.]

Children in the latter case belong to the gens of their father, and they inherit his property and are capable of succeeding to his office. This is the case whether there has been a change from female kinship to male kinship, or whether the latter was independently developed. The political effect attending the operation of those systems was important. Where a woman continued to reside after marriage among her own kin, her children would, with female kinship, increase and continue the kindred group or gens ; but where she went to reside with the family of her husband, her children would continue among their father's gens, but they would form a branch of that to which their mother belonged. Members of two or more gentes might thus exist side by side within a common tribal group, which might come to be endogamous in the sense that its members could marry within the group, although not within the gens to which they belonged. With descent in the male line the opposite result would take place. If a man remained with his wife's family, a branch of the gens to which he belonged would be formed alongside the gens of the wife. That seldom occurs, however. The wife usually goes to the husband's family, and as the children of the marriage belong to them, there is the introduction of another element. The husband's gens is increased, and it is evident that under such conditions the gens must form a homogeneous whole, and that in the absence of the earlier operation of the law of female kinship a gens might be co-extensive with the tribe. Professor Smith points out[1] that "the Arabian *hayy* with male kinship was a perfectly stable unity, and could go on multiplying from generation to generation without loss

[1] Robertson Smith 1885, p. 233.

of homogeneity and local continuity, so long as it had
room to expand." Such was probably the case with
the original thirty confederated tribes of the Romans,
among whom, according to Dr Morgan,[1] " descent was
in the male line from Augustus back to Romulus, and
for an unknown period back of the latter." The fact
that the Ramnes tribe, which settled on the Palatine
Hill, comprised one hundred gentes would seem to
show that the Latin gentes were simple family groups,
or parts of families as supposed by Dr Morgan. This
writer assumes[2] that descent in the female line
anciently prevailed in the Grecian and Latin gentes,
because such descent " is archaic, and more in accordance with the early condition of ancient society than
descent in the male line." When we are told, however, that among all the Italian tribes, with the exception of the Etruscans, descent "had become changed "
to the male line, if at all, before their occupation of
Italy,[3] we may doubt whether any such change really
took place.

[1] Morgan 1877, p. 284.   [2] *Ibid.*, p. 344.
[3] *Ibid.*, pp. 68, 286.

CHAPTER XI.

MARRIAGE BY CAPTURE.

It was stated in the last chapter that the right of the father's kin to the children of his marriage, which gave rise to the system of male kinship, or descent in the male line, is usually associated either with " capture " or with " wife-purchase." The existence of varying phases of the curious custom of what is usually termed " marriage by capture," but which is rather the use of the form of capture as part of its ceremonies of marriage, among peoples in different parts of the world has been fully established, but neither its origin nor its significance has been satisfactorily explained.

Dr M'Lennan, who may almost be called the discoverer of this curious custom, has framed an ingenious theory to account for it, but this theory is not sufficient to explain the importance attached to its existence in connection with marriage. He affirms that " capture in marriage ceremonies " cannot be explained by the fact that women of foreign tribes could be got for wives only by theft or by force, and that therefore it implies something more than the " mere lawlessness of savages." He believes that the " symbol " of capture at weddings became a recognised ceremony " among exogamous tribes, out of respect for immemorial usage when friendly relations came to be established between tribes and families, and their members intermarried by purchase instead of capture." [1] Elsewhere [2] Dr M'Lennan

[1] McLennan 1876, pp. 33ff. [2] *Ibid.*, p. 17.

says, "The symbol of capture occurs whenever, after a contract of marriage, it is necessary for the constitution of the relation of husband and wife, that the bridegroom or his friend should go through the form of feigning to steal the bride, or carry her off from her relations by superior force. The marriage is agreed upon by bargain, and the theft or abduction follows as a concerted matter of form, to make valid the marriage. The test, then, of the presence of the symbol in any case is, that the capture is concerted, and is preceded by a contract of marriage. If there is no preceding contract, the case is one of actual abduction."

Although Sir John Lubbock, in opposition to Dr M'Lennan's theory, regards capture as having preceded the establishment of the rule of exogamy, yet he endorses the opinion expressed by the latter as to the origin of the form of marriage by capture. He says, " So deeply rooted is the feeling of a connection between force and marriage, that we find the former used as a form long after all necessity for it had ceased; and it is very interesting to trace, as Dr M'Lennan has done, the gradual stages through which a stern reality softens down into a mere symbol." [1] Sir John Lubbock adds, that gradually capture " came to be more and more a mock ceremony, forming however a necessary part of the marriage ceremony." This agrees with Dr M'Lennan's statement [2] that " when friendly relations came to be established between tribes and families, and their members intermarried by purchase instead of capture," the form of invasion and capture became an " essential ceremony at weddings;" which means in effect that when neighbouring tribes, who as enemies

[1] Lubbock 1875, p. 100.   [2] McLennan 1876, p. 44.

stole their wives, became friends, they continued to steal their wives to retain a remembrance of their enmity. This is, however, a wholly inadequate explanation of the phenomena, and it does not account for the fact that the ceremonial capture is essential to the validity of the marriage in question. A consideration of the examples of such marriages which have been brought together will enable us to supply a better reason for the importance attached to the form of capture.

In a very interesting article on bride-catching, which appeared in *The Argosy Magazine* more than twenty years ago,[1] Dr M'Lennan gives a number of examples of the form of capture, "which," he says, "occurs whenever after a contract of marriage, it is considered essential to the constitution of the marriage that the bridegroom and his friends should carry off the bride as the prize of victory in a simulated conflict with her relations, should feign to catch or steal her, or to make her a captive after pursuit." Dr M'Lennan moreover classifies his examples of the form of capture, and he places them in the following categories :—*First*, "cases in which the leading idea symbolized is the capture of the bride after a conflict with her kinsmen," the most prominent of which are those in which there is " the idea of a siege of the bride's house ;" *secondly*, " cases in which the simple 'catching' of the bride, or her capture after a race, is feigned ;" *lastly*, " instances of the form in states of disintegration." Such a classification is valuable, as it brings clearly into view a distinction between the several series of examples which might otherwise be lost sight of. In nearly all cases of a siege or invasion of the bride's house, and of a simulated conflict, the consent of the bride and also

[1] McLennan 1866.

of her relatives has previously been obtained. The only apparent exceptions are the customs found down to the sixteenth century in Muscovy, Lithuania, and Livonia, of women being carried off for wives before negotiations were opened with their relations, and the similar practice which seems to have been prevalent until recently among the Irish peasantry of Derry, and also with the Kalmucks, Kirghiz, Nogais, and Circassians. Among these peoples, says Dr M'Lennan,[1] if the parties cannot agree about the price of the bride, she is carried off by force of arms, and the wooer "having once got the lady into his yourt, she is his wife by law, and peace is established by her relatives coming to terms as to the price, after the thing has gone so far that they cannot help themselves." The Scandinavians also appear to have often acquired their wives by force, without making subsequent compensation to the relations of the woman carried away, and there is no trace of symbolised capture in their case.

Before considering the examples of bride-racing and bride-catching, reference may be made to two other series of cases given by Dr M'Lennan, in one of which clandestine intercourse is the chief feature, and in the other the form of capture is said to be in a "state of disintegration." What the former cases have to do with "capture" is not very evident. Among the early Arabs it was not unusual, says Prof. Smith,[2] for a woman to receive stealthy visits at her father's dwelling from her lover, and such temporary connection came under the category of *mot'a* marriage. Probably we have in this custom the explanation of the clandestine intercourse after marriage of the Nogais, Circas-

[1] McLennan 1876, p. 57.
[2] Robertson Smith 1885, p. 71.

sians, and Spartans ; unless, indeed, it is in pursuance
of the ancient. usage referred to by Lafitau,[1] which forbade consummation of the marriage until the expiration
of a year from its being contracted.   It also explains
the " bundling " custom of Celtic and other peoples.
The other examples of such intercourse between husband
and wife related by Dr M'Lennan, may be explained
as due to a certain delicacy of feeling which is occasionally met with among savages, and which may
be illustrated by the conduct of the Fijians.   Dr
Seemann says : [2] " It is quite against Fijian ideas of
delicacy that a man ever remains under the same roof
with his wife or wives at night. . . . Rendezvous
between husband and wife, of which no further explanation can be given, are arranged in the depths of
the forest, unknown to any but the two."   Such
cases have nothing to do with "capture."   It is different
with the examples given by Dr M'Lennan of the form
of capture in disintegration.   Thus, among the Pat-
ricians at Rome,[3] according to Plutarch, the bridegroom
carried the bride over the threshold of his house,
" because the Sabine women did not go in voluntarily,
but were carried in by violence," and parted her hair
with a spear, " in memory of the first marriages being
brought about in a warlike manner."   Again, the
game of Kökburi, " green-wolf," is in imitation of the
bride-racing which is or was in use, says Mr Vambery,[4]

[1] Lafitau 1724, I, 574.

[2] Seemann 1862, p. 191.

[3] This case is not really in point, however, as M. de Coulanges has shown that the "rape" had for its object to obtain
the right of marriage with the Sabine populations, which end
it attained only because it was followed by celebration of
marriage by the recognised religious rites (Fustel de Coulanges 1876, p. 441).

[4] Vambery 1864, p. 323.

among all the nomads of Central Asia. Dr M'Lennan's suggestion, that the throwing of the old shoe at English weddings is a sham assault on the person carrying off the lady, cannot be accepted. Brand, who refers to the custom of throwing the old shoe,[1] does not mention it in connection with weddings, and it is intended merely to indicate the wish that success may attend the mission on which the person favoured with the shoe is setting out.

In the second series of examples referred to by Dr M'Lennan, the consent of the bride has not been obtained to the marriage, and probably is never actually asked before the catching or racing ; but the ceremony usually has the effect of giving her the opportunity of escaping from a distasteful alliance. In some cases, indeed, there is no ceremony at all ; as with the Australians, who not uncommonly carry off women for wives by force, and with the Coinmen and the Caribs, who systematically capture women "with a view to the raising of children."[2] In these and other examples of capture *de facto*, referred to by Dr M'Lennan in chapter iv. of his work on " Primitive Marriage," the absence of the contract shows them to be merely cases of abduction. The contract is the essential feature of the transaction, where there is a formal capture, and it must therefore be considered a little more particularly. It is in the nature of an arrangement, made between a man or his relations and the relations of a woman, that the man and woman shall become husband and wife, and it is usually perhaps in effect a bargain for the sale of the hand of the latter, constituting a case of wife-purchase. The contract is not, however, merely a bargain for the sale of so much property. The pro-

---

[1] Brand 1877, p. 672.   [2] McLennan 1876, p. 49.

posed marriage requires the consent of the two persons more immediately concerned. That of the man may be implied from the nature of the case, but not that of the woman, who is often assumed to be ignorant of the negotiations taking place, and it therefore has to be expressly obtained.

According to Dr M'Lennan, however, the woman is not considered in the transaction. He affirms[1] that "no case can be cited of a primitive people among whom the seizure of brides is rendered necessary by maidenly coyness." Elsewhere[2] he declares that the chance of escape which the wife-chasing "offers to a reluctant bride, is an accident of a ceremony, the origin of which cannot possibly be referred to the desire to consult the bride's inclinations." But Dr M'Lennan's statement is certainly incorrect. In many of the instances where the suitor forcibly removes the bride after the completion of the bargain with her friends, she strongly resists. This often occurs among the Tunguses, the New Zealanders, and the Mandingos. With the New Zealanders, if the girl who is being carried off can break away from her captor and regain her father's house, the suitor loses all chance of ever obtaining her in marriage. So also among the Fijians, if a woman does not approve of the man who has taken her by force to his house, she leaves him for some one who can protect her. With the Greenlanders, if after the bride has been captured by the old women who negotiate the marriage, she cannot be persuaded by kind treatment, she is "compelled by force, nay, sometimes by blows, to change her state." But even in Greenland, if a girl had great repugnance to her suitor, she could escape marriage by betaking herself to the

[1] *Ibid.*, p. 15.   [2] McLennan 1866, p. 38.

mountains. A still more efficacious plan was the cutting off of her hair, which freed her from all importunity, as it was accepted as a sure sign that she had determined never to marry.[1] At the other extremity of the American continent the Fuegians have, according to Captain Fitzroy, an analogous custom. As soon as a youth is able to maintain a wife, he obtains the consent of the relatives of the girl he has made choice of, and does some work for her parents. He then builds or steals a canoe, and when he has an opportunity, carries off his bride. It happens occasionally that the girl is unwilling, in which case "she hides herself in the woods until her admirer is heartily tired of looking for her, and gives up the pursuit."[2] Sir John Lubbock refers[3] to a similar practice among the Ahitas of the Philippine Islands, but here the lover has to find the girl and bring her back before sunset, otherwise he must give up all claim to her. According to Mongol custom the bride hides herself with some of her relatives, and the bridegroom has to search for and find her. This he would seem always to do. The Dravidian Gonds have a similar custom, and so have the Kolarian Hos, with whom, however, the flight and concealment do not take place until three days after marriage.[4]

Marriage by capture, in the sense in which the term is used by Sir John Lubbock, presupposes the absence, not only of the consent of the female, but of that of her relations; but in the instances of such capture usually referred to the marriage is, as Dr M'Lennan's

[1] Cranz 1767, I, 138.
[2] Fitzroy 1839, II, 182; McLennan 1876, p. 30.
[3] Lubbock 1875, p. 109.   [4] Dalton 1872, pp. 192, 280.

theory requires, nearly always made by arrangement with them. The only apparent exception to this rule mentioned by Sir John Lubbock is met with among the inhabitants of Bali. Here the man is said to forcibly carry off his bride to the woods, and to afterwards effect reconciliation with her "enraged" friends. It is not improbable, however, that the rage is simulated, or there may be a recognised understanding that the abduction be atoned for.[1] In some parts of Russia and Prussia it was not unusual, down to the sixteenth century, for women to be carried off by their admirers before any negotiations for marriage with their relations, and Dr M'Lennan refers to a similar practice as being prevalent among the Irish peasantry of the present century.[2] Sir John Lubbock himself explains an apparent act of lawless violence among the Mandingos, as an incident of "marriage by capture," on the ground that the bride's relatives "only laughed at the farce, and consoled her by saying that she would soon be reconciled to her situation," and it appears that her mother had previously given her consent to the proceedings.[3] A mere general understanding, if universally recognised, would, indeed, be as efficacious as a special consent, and whether the consent of the parent has to to be obtained previously to overcoming the opposition of the bride, or whether this has to be overcome as a condition precedent to the consent being given, is

[1] Among the Mechs and Kachars of the Assam Valley the bridegroom gives his father-in-law a money present *after* the sham fight (Dalton 1872, p. 16).

[2] Above, p. 405.

[3] So also among the Finnish Vêpses, the Tchoudes of the North, a suitor sometimes carries off the girl whom he wishes to marry, but always with the consent of her father (Ujfalvy 1880, p. 79).

practically of no importance. We seem to have an example of the latter in the marriage customs of the Afghans as described by Elphinstone.[1] Among this people wives are purchased, and the necessity for paying the usual price is not done away with, although a man is allowed to make sure of his bride by cutting off a lock of her hair, snatching away her veil, or throwing a sheet over her, if he declares at the same time that she is his affianced wife.

It is evident that in these cases the will of the bride elect is a very important consideration, and it is no less so in the examples of bride-racing and bride-catching referred to by Dr M'Lennan and other writers, where these are not mere cases of abduction. Thus, with the Kalmucks, according to Dr Clarke, the girl gallops away at full speed, pursued by her suitor, and if she does not wish to marry him she always effects her escape. This bride-racing is practised by the uncultured tribes of the Malayan Peninsula. Here, however, the chase is on foot, and generally round a circle, although sometimes in the forest; and, as Bourien (quoted by Sir John Lubbock) says, the pursuer is successful only if he "has had the good fortune to please the intended bride." A similar custom is found among the Koraks of North Eastern Asia. The ceremony takes place within a large tent containing numerous separate compartments (*pologs*) arranged in a continuous circle around its inner circumference. Mr Kennan gives[2] an amusing and instructive description of such a ceremony. The women of the encampment, armed with willows and alder rods, stationed themselves at the entrances of the pologs, the front curtains of

[1] Elphinstone 1815, p. 181.
[2] Kennan 1871, pp. 136ff.

which were thrown up.   Then at a given signal, "the bride darted suddenly into the first polog, and began a rapid flight around the tent, raising the curtains between the pologs successively, and passing under. The bridegroom instantly followed in hot pursuit, but the women who were stationed in each compartment threw every possible impediment in his way, tripping up his unwary feet, holding down the curtains to prevent his passage, and applying the willow and alder switches unmercifully to a very susceptible part of his body as he stooped to raise them. . . . With undismayed perseverance he pressed on, stumbling headlong over the outstretched feet of his female persecutors, and getting constantly entangled in the ample folds of the reindeer skin curtains which were thrown with the skill of a matador over his head and eyes.   In a moment the bride had entered the last closed polog near the door, while the unfortunate bridegroom was still struggling with his accumulated misfortunes about half way round the tent.   " I expected," says the traveller, " to see him relax his efforts, and give up the contest when the bride disappeared, and was preparing to protest strongly on his behalf against the unfairness of the trial ; but, to my surprise, he still struggled on, and with a final plunge, burst through the curtain of the last polog and rejoined his bride," who had waited for him there.   Mr Kennan adds that " the intention of the whole ceremony was evidently to give the woman an opportunity to marry the man or not, as she chose, since it was obviously impossible for him to catch her under such circumstances, unless she voluntarily waited for him in one of the pologs."

The Kamtschadales carry the same ideas into effect in a somewhat different manner.   When a young man is desirous of marrying, he offers to drudge for the relations of the girl he has chosen. She is immediately, says M. de Lesseps,[1] "enveloped in a multiplicity of garments, which conceal her to such a degree that the face itself is scarcely visible. She is not left alone a single instant, her mother and a number of old matrons accompanying her wherever she goes, sleep with her, and do not lose her from their sight upon any pretext whatever." The aim of the suitor is to touch her naked body, but her garments are so numerous and thick that his only chance of effecting his object is to tear them or pull them off. If while attempting to do this he is surprised by the female guards, they attack him, and if he resists, they scratch his face and drag him away by his hair. M. de Lesseps states that it is frequently not till after a period of two or three years that the suitor is successful in his efforts, during all which time he is the domestic slave of the family. When he has performed the touch he becomes the recognised lover of the girl, but only after her relations are satisfied by his own confession and by proof " that she was taken by surprise, and made fruitless efforts to defend herself." Professor Douglas[2] refers to the case of the Koraks in connection with his assertion that, as shown by the construction of the modern character *ch'ü*, meaning to marry ; the first form of marriage in China was by capture. Professor Douglas states that " on the evening of the marriage the Chinese bride-groom either goes himself or sends a friend to bring his bride to his house, but always after dark, as if by stealth, and the ceremony, such as it is, is performed in his house." This statement, however, does not

[1] De Lesseps 1790, II, 93.
[2] Douglas 1882, p. 69.

agree with the information given by the Rev. J. Doolittle, and it can apply only to the cases where a betrothed husband steals away the affianced girl, owing to her family improperly delaying the marriage.[1]

The practice of elopement is easily connected with the assertion by a girl of her right to have some control over the choice of a husband. It has been remarked that marriage by elopement and marriage by capture, or rather forcible marriage, differ only in the presence or absence of the woman's consent. Mr Hewitt, whose opinion this is, has shown that the former practice is very common among the Australian tribes, and he states that several examples of supposed "marriage by capture," given by Dr M'Lennan, are really cases of elopement.[2] Such is the case where capture *de facto* is said to co-exist with capture as a form, as with the Kalmucks, Kirghiz, Nogais, and Circassians, who carry off the lady by actual force of arms, if they cannot agree with her relations about the price. Elopement appears not to be at all a rare mode of obtaining a wife among the Kolarian tribes of India. With the Hos, already mentioned, it is practised for the purpose of compelling the parents to accept a smaller sum for their daughters than they would other-wise do.[3] The Khonds give the bachelor the privilege, during one of their festivals, of running away "with any unmarried girl whom he can induce to go with him, subject to a subsequent arrangement with the parents of the maiden."[4] Among the Gonds the elopement is proposed by the girl herself, but it is followed by a marriage ceremony, during which it is

---

[1] Doolittle 1868, pp. 53ff., 73.

[2] Fison and Howitt 1880, pp. 348ff.

[3] Dalton 1872, p. 193.　　　　　[4] *Ibid.*, p. 300.

the duty of the bridegroom to object to the usual ablution, and run away to be brought back again by force.[1] Elopement is not uncommon among the tribes of South Africa, and not only have Kafir girls been known to propose marriage, but they will sometimes run away with a lover.[2]

It has been shown that notwithstanding Dr M'Lennan's expression of disbelief in the existence of "maidenly coyness" among primitive peoples, the consent of the girl to be married is in many cases essential to the marriage contract, and that she has the opportunity of escaping from the proposed alliance if she objects to it. Dr Darwin carefully considered this point in connection with the subject of sexual selection,[3] and he came to the conclusion that "in utterly barbarous tribes the women have more power in choosing, rejecting, and tempting their lovers, or of afterwards changing their husbands, than might have been expected." The following examples bearing on the former part of this. conclusion may be added to those referred to by Dr Darwin. Among the North American tribes marriage is usually arranged without reference to the feelings of the persons to be united, who generally accept the choice of their parents, but this is not always so, and marriages of affection are not wanting among them.[4] Among the Abipones and the Patagonians, the purchase of a wife is cancelled if the girl refuses her consent,[5] while a Carib girl may decline to marry a man who has a kind of kinship

[1] *Ibid.*, p. 64.
[2] Shooter 1857, p. 60.
[3] Darwin 1871, II, 372.
[4] Lafitau 1724, I, 565.
[5] Peschel 1876, p. 227.

claim to her, although in this case she would lose her reputation and the benefits she might expect to gain from her own family.[1] A similar independence exists among many of the hill tribes of India. Owing to the freedom of intercourse between the young people, love matches are not uncommon among the Kolarian Santals, although it is considered more respectable if the arrangements are made by the parents or guardians without any acknowledged reference to the wishes of the engaged pair.[2] The Hos of Singbhum place so high a price on their daughters that grown-up unmarried girls remaining single are quite a special feature of their villages, notwithstanding that they flirt in the most demonstrative manner, and say frankly that they do all they can to please the young men.[3] The Garos of Assam consider it the duty of the *girls* to propose marriage.[4] It is the same with the Koch of the Himalayas, among whom the bridegroom goes to live with his wife's mother, whose orders he obeys.[5] With the polyandrous Todas a girl is allowed the privilege of refusing her consent to a proposed marriage, if after spending a day and a night with her suitor she is not satisfied with him. Even among the Dyaks of Borneo marriages are arranged between the parties after courtship, and a female may accept or reject the offer for her hand.

If the consent of the bride is an important factor in the marriage arrangement, in the cases where the ceremony of bride-racing or bride-catching is performed, no less so is it in the instances of ceremonial wife capture classed by Dr M'Lennan under the heads

---

[1] Lafitau 1724, I, 557.

[2] Dalton 1872, p. 215.

[3] *Ibid.*, p. 192.

[4] *Ibid.*, p. 64.

[5] *Ibid.*, p. 91.

of "siege or invasion of the bride's house," and "simulation of a conflict." The only difference is that where the latter forms of capture are used, the consent of the bride has already been obtained as part of the marriage-contract ; while in the other cases it has probably not even been asked, although the proposed bride generally knows that the negotiations are going on. The fact that the female is not so passive a party to the proceedings as Dr M'Lennan asserts, has been sufficiently proved, and combined with the necessity of a pre-arrangement with her relations, it renders the idea that ceremonial capture is simply in imitation of the old system of abduction extremely improbable. The improbability is increased if, as the theory supposes, the symbolical capture is essential to the validity of the marriage. The pretended abduction can hardly be accredited with a virtue which the original institution symbolised by it did not possess. The fact that women stolen or captured by tribes in the state of hostility which, according to Dr M'Lennan,[1] "is the normal state of the race in early times," were seized for the purpose of bearing children, would not sanction the theft so as to render such marriages valid in the eyes of their relations or tribesmen, whatever might be the case with the captors themselves. The real object of the latter ceremony may nevertheless be ascertained from a consideration of the effects of forcible marriage. This simple form of "marriage by capture" was largely practised by the early Arabs, among whom it originated in the old style of warfare which had for its object the procuring of captives or slaves. The capture of women for wives gave rise to what is called the "marriage of dominion," which was afterwards per-

[1] McLennan 1876, p. 108.

fected by wife-purchase.   All marriages of dominion
were regarded by the Arabs as virtual captivity, the
possession of the woman having been obtained in the
one case by force and in the other by purchase.   Dr
M'Lennan's theory would require that in the latter
case the Arabs should practise "symbolical capture,"
but there is little, if any, evidence of their doing so.
The Arabs of the Sinaitic Peninsula are, indeed, said
to have kept up "the form of capture, with a simulated resistance on the part of the bride."[1]   The
evidence of this is, however, very slight, and consists
only of the statement of Burckhardt, that it is necessary for the bridegroom to force the bride to enter his
tent, and that "the more the woman struggles, bites,
kicks, cries and strikes, the more she is applauded ever
after by her own companions."   This is an instance of
the female coyness Dr M'Lennan is sceptical of, rather
than of "marriage by capture ; " or at best it shows
the force of the feeling of etiquette, which requires a
Greenland young woman when she is asked in marriage
to profess great bashfulness, to tear her ringlets, and
finally to run away.

Dr M'Lennan lays great stress on the provision of
the Laws of Menu,[2] which permits a soldier to form
the marriage called *Racshasa*, which, he says,[3] is "the
exact prototype of the Roman and Spartan forms,
embalmed in a code of laws a thousand years before
the commencement of our era ; not as a form, but as
living substance."   In the plebeian marriages of the
Romans, when the time had arrived the bridegroom
and his friends entered the house of the bride, and
carried her off with feigned violence from the lap of

[1] Robertson Smith 1885, p. 81.
[2] Chap. III. 26, 33.   [3] McLennan 1876, p. 64.

her mother, or of her nearest female relative if her mother was dead or absent. Among the Spartans the bridegroom always carried off the bride, as Plutarch says, by violence, although the seizure was made by friendly consent between the parties concerned. Dr M'Lennan, after referring to these forms of capture, adds,[1] that " the custom is said still to prevail to a great extent among the Hindoos." It is only among the indigenous tribes that examples of the Indian practice are met with, it not being a Hindoo custom proper, although from Dr M'Lennan's statement as to the Racshasa marriage, we should by analogy expect to find the form of capture among them. As a fact, the provisions of the Laws of Menu on the subject of marriage are entirely opposed to Dr M'Lennan's theory, as expressed in a passage already quoted,[2] that among exogamous tribes, "when friendly relations came to be established between tribes and families, and their members intermarried by purchase instead of capture, the form of invasion and capture should become an essential ceremony at weddings." That the early Hindoos were exogamous appears from their code of laws,[3] on which Dr M'Lennan properly observes[4] that the rule of Menu as to the marriages of the twice-born man is just that which would enforce the ancient prejudice against the marriage of a man with a woman of his own clan, after the interfusion of the clans and their being brought under a common government by conquest or otherwise. The Hindoos, therefore, when those laws were promulgated, answered to the description of an exogamous people, among whose tribes and families friendly relations have come

[1] McLennan 1876, pp. 17ff. [2] Above, p. 402.
[3] *Menu*, III, sec. 5. [4] McLennan 1876, p. 85.

to be established, and having capture as a recognised form of " nuptial ceremony." There was more reality than ceremony, however, in the Racshasa marriage, which was " the seizure of a maiden by force from her house, while she weeps and calls for assistance, after her kinsmen and friends have been slain in battle, or wounded, and their houses broken open." This so-called marriage is evidently merely the result of the capture in warfare of a female whose defenders have been defeated ; but another provision of the Laws of Menu supposes that a girl may be made captive by her lover after a victory over her kinsmen. This is a mixture of the Racshasa marriage with the marriage of the Gandharvas, which is " the reciprocal connection of a youth and a damsel, with mutual desire . . . con-trived for the purpose of amorous embraces, and proceeding from sensual inclination." Both those marriages are permitted by law to a military man, and he alone has the privilege of the " ceremony of the Racshasas."[1] The origin of this name is doubtful, but it appears to be usually applied by Hindoo writers to non-Aryan tribes, and Dr M'Lennan suggests that the system of capture practised by the indigenous tribes " gave its designation to the exceptional, although permitted, marriage by capture among the Kshatriyas," the Hindoo military caste.[2] This ingenious surmise is probably correct, although it is possible that the Racshasas referred to in the Laws of Menu may have been Kshatriyas, or allied to them. M. L. Rousselet states that the Jats are mentioned in the Mahabharata

[1] Menu, III. sec. 24, 26, 32, 33.

[2] The Kshatriyas are mentioned in cap. III, sec. 44, and they are no doubt referred to under the phrases "Warrior," "soldier," "military man," used in other sections.

by the term *arachtra*, " those who have nothing," and
there is great reason to believe that the Jats are allied
to the Rajpoots, the modern representatives of the
Kshatriyas.[1]

Although the Racshasa "nuptial ceremony" is permitted to the military class, it is condemned as a base
marriage which produces "sons acting cruelly, speaking
falsely, abhorring the Veda, and the duties prescribed in
it," and it is said, "let mankind therefore studiously
avoid the culpable forms of marriage."[2] These culpable
marriages include, also that of the Gandharvas, that
of the Asuras, and that of the Pisáchas, of which the
last, the eighth and the basest, "is when the lover
secretly embraces the damsel, when sleeping or flushed
with strong liquor, or disordered in her intellect."
While all the other marriages are permitted, it is
expressly said[3] that "the ceremonial of Pisáchas and
Asuras must never be performed." This point will be
referred to hereafter in connection with the question as
to whether wife-purchase was practised among the early
Aryans, and we shall see that it is expressly forbidden
by the Laws of Menu.

The objection thus shewn among the early Hindoos
to wife-purchase is important, because it proves that
exogamous peoples who have marriage by capture do
not necessarily intermarry by purchase, when friendly
relations come to be established between tribes and
families. It is moreover not surprising that with the
Hindoos "the form of invasion and capture" has *not*
become an essential ceremony at weddings, although
Dr M'Lennan, as we have seen, regards the Racshasa

[1] This point has been considered by the present writer
(1886, pp. 213ff.).

[2] III. sec. 41, 42.   [3] III. sec. 25.

marriage as the exact prototype of the Roman and Spartan forms. The absence of ceremonial capture among the descendants of the Kshatriyas, who were permitted to use the Racshasa marriage, proves that there is no necessary connection between capture *de facto* and the ceremony of capture. The prohibition of wife-purchase among the Hindoos [1] moreover proves that they have not passed through the several stages required by Dr M'Lennan's theory, and it renders the exceptional Racshasa marriage useless, as evidence in favour of the theory which sees in the ceremonial capture at weddings an imitation of capture *de facto*, and which supposes the latter to have formerly prevailed among tribes who now practise marriage by purchase. The abduction allowed to the military class under certain conditions by the Laws of Menu was a relic of lawlessness, and however general the state of hostility may primitively have been, it has only a secondary bearing on the question of ceremonial capture, which has reference to the offspring of the marriage rather than to the bride herself.

That ceremonial capture has been sometimes preceded, under other social conditions, by the practice of actual abduction is not improbable, but in this case even there is not necessarily any connection between the two customs. It is said,[2] however, that when cases are met with "in which the old usage, or a remainder of it, and its symbol are found side by side, and the one, as it were, passes into the other—when, for example, in connection with marriage, either a fre-

---

[1] As to the custom of Hindoo bridegrooms, especially among the Rajpoots, requiring payments on marriage, see Browne (1857, pp. 12, 123, etc.).

[2] McLennan 1885, p. 168.

quent practice of actual capture, or of abduction without leave (which is a modification of actual capture), is found side by side with abduction by arrangement, that is, the form or symbol of capture." We have in the symbol convincing proof of the previous prevalence of actual capture. That the form of capture has been, at least in some cases, derived from the practice of actual capture may be admitted, if the old usage and its symbol, that is, abduction by arrangement, can be found, not only side by side, but "the one passing into the other." Let us see what examples of such a state of things are given by Dr M'Lennan. He infers,[1] from Nestor's account of the early Slavs, that the Polians had marriage by purchase, probably with the form of capture, and that among the other tribes wives were usually got by actual capture, and that there were in use among some of them friendly arrangements "to facilitate wiving by this method— an arrangement such as would prepare the way for capture to pass into a form." Now as to the Polians, Nestor says merely, "they had a form of marriage. The bridegroom did not himself go to fetch his bride, but some one brought her to him in the evening, and the price stipulated to be given for her was sent the next day." There is in this statement no ground for inferring the existence of a "form of capture." Indeed, the fact that the bride was not fetched from her own home is inconsistent with capture, except so far as it may be evidence that the arrangement would have been opposed by the relations of the bride, if it had not been a secret one. This, however, supposes that the bride's relations were entitled to share in the marriage price, or in other words, participate in the

[1] *Ibid.*, p. 77.

claim to the offspring of the proposed marriage, such a claim being at the base, as I have already shown, of ceremonial capture. The other Slavs are said to have obtained wives by actual capture, but they had friendly arrangements which would "prepare the way for capture to pass into a form." Those arrangements were "merry games at which they played, danced, and sang devilish songs," at the end of which "each man carried away a woman, who became his wife." This custom may be illustrated by a similar custom in use among the Santals of the present day.[1] The making of marriage arrangements is preceded by a festival, which is held annually, and lasts six days, "when all candidates for matrimony, male and female, are assembled together, and permitted to have promiscuous intercourse with each other, each lover selecting his future wife after the termination of this general carnival." In this case there is no wife capture, ceremonial or otherwise, but the necessary arrangements for marriage are made by the parents, and after the ceremony the bride is considered as separate from her clan,[2] which is a usual accompaniment of wife-purchase, of which there appears to be no trace among the Slavs other than the Polians.

Dr M‘Lennan refers[3] also to the ancient Irish, among whom abduction was a recognised custom. In the Book of Aicill, under the head of "Abduction without leave," it is said that the child of a woman who had been abducted without leave from her family, unless begotten more than a month after the abduction, belonged not to the abductor but to the mother's family. If the mother had been forcibly abducted it

[1] Above, p. 52.
[2] Hunter 1871, p. 207.
[3] McLennan 1876, p. 298.

belonged to them absolutely, and they might refuse to sell it to the abductors; but if the mother had consented to the abduction, he could force her family to sell. Where there had been an abduction without leave, the woman's family were allowed a month to bring the man to terms about her, or to reclaim her. If there was no contract, and the woman remained with her abductor longer than that period, her family lost their right to the offspring. Here we have different phases of "marriage by capture"—forcible abduction, abduction with the consent of the woman herself, and abduction without leave of her family, which, no doubt, was wanting also when the consent of the woman had not been obtained. From the reference to the consent which was necessary to take the children from the woman's family and give them to their father, it may be thought that abduction with the leave first had of the woman's family was recognised. The arrangement referred to was made, however, after the abduction, a month being fixed by custom as the term within which it ought to be come to, or the woman brought back by her family. In this case there does not appear to be any such symbolical capture, or abduction by arrangement, as Dr M'Lennan's theory requires. There was actual capture, which was afterwards compounded for, but, as the contract came after the abduction, the facts do not come within the theory according to which "the marriage is agreed upon by bargain, and the theft or abduction follows as a concerted matter of form, to make valid the marriage." It comes rather within the statement that "if there is no preceding contract, the case is one of actual abduction," an explanation which has already[1] been given of similar

---

[1] Above, p. 405.

practices common to the Scandinavians and some other European peoples.

It should be noted that in the Arab "marriage of dominion," the right of the husband was rather to the offspring of the marriage than to the woman herself, who did not change her kin on marriage.[1] The child of such a marriage belonged to the husband's tribe or family group, and marriage by capture or by purchase was always associated among the Arabs with the system of male kinship. The fact of such an association has already been considered when treating of the system of male kinship. We cannot be surprised, therefore, to find that all the peoples usually referred to as practising ceremonial capture trace descent in the male line, either alone or in combination with descent in the female line. We have instances of Dr M'Lennan's first class of cases, that of a siege or invasion of the bride's house, among European peoples —in Transylvania, France, and ancient Rome; among the Circassians, Nogais, and Kirghiz of Asia, the Indian Mussulmans, and the inland negroes of Africa. Examples of the second class, the simulated conflict, were found among European peoples in Wales, Scotland, Ireland, Scandinavia, Livonia, Lithuania, and Muscovy, and the ancient Dorians and Spartans, and among the Asiatic Mongols, Kalmucks, Afghans, and Hindoos, and the hill tribes of India. Of the third class, that of bride-racing and bride-catching, examples were met with in Europe among the Scandinavians, Germans, and Greeks; and in Asia, among the Kalmucks, Turkomans, Tunguses, Kamtschadales, and the Malays of Singapore. All those peoples have descent in the male line, and none of the tribes mentioned by

[1] Above, p. 350.

Dr M'Lennan who probably have the system of female kinship, such as the Australians, the Fuegians, the Amazon Indians, the Commen, and the Caribs of South America, have *ceremonial* capture, those peoples practising actual forcible abduction.[1] Most of the examples of "marriage by capture" given by Sir John Lubbock are also cases of forcible abduction, but where the form of capture exists it is among races having male kinship, as throughout Siberia, and with the Japanese and the Coreans, the Kafirs, the Fulahs, and the Mandingoes.

Dr M'Lennan admits[2] that the "form of capture is more distinctly marked and impressive just among those races which have male kinship." This admission is important, as it is opposed to rather than in favour of the theory that the pretended carrying off of a bride is an imitation of an earlier practice of abduction. Dr M'Lennan was, indeed, so much struck by that aspect of the question, that he says, "It might be doubted, but for the case of the Fuegians, and traces of the symbol, as if of a thing decayed, occurring in America, whether the experience of the earlier stage could generate the form." The cases here referred to as showing traces of the "symbol" are, however, examples only of forcible marriage. Indeed, they are cited[3] by Dr M'Lennan himself as "evidence of the prevalence of the practice of capturing wives *de facto*," although marriages by consent and purchase are common among the American tribes. The only apparent cases in sup-

---

[1] The association of the system of female kinship with simple capture of wives is evidence that the former was established before the latter became customary. Among the Australians, the rules of marriage are not affected by capture.
[2] McLennan 1876, p. 201. [3] *Ibid.*, pp. 46ff.

port of the view that the form of capture has been generated by the practice of abduction, are those of the Sinaitic Arabs and of the Greenlanders and the Fuegians, already mentioned. It requires considerable imagination to see in the very practical mode of obtaining a wife employed by these peoples evidence of a *form* of capture. It is not mere abduction, seeing that the consent of the relations is first obtained ; but, on the other hand, the relations do not pretend to resist the forcible seizure, which is evidently intended to overcome the real or feigned objection of the woman herself. The mere fact of the seizure being preceded by a contract with the bride's relations does not render the case one of " symbolical capture," nor is there any evidence that the abduction is really essential to the marriage, as Dr M'Lennan's theory requires, except so far as it may be necessary to obtain the bride's consent.

The form of capture as a wedding ceremonial is found in India among the hill tribes, and much light is thrown on the meaning of the ceremony by reference to the custom as observed with them. According to Colonel Dalton,[1] the bridal parties " often meet in hostile array at the entrance of the village of the bride, and a mimic fight takes place before the bridegroom's party is permitted to enter ; " a custom which is followed by some Kurmis and other Hindoo castes. Among the Khonds of Orissa the bridegroom, accompanied by a number of his friends, himself carries off the bride notwithstanding the desperate attacks of a party of young women who follow, throwing stones and bamboos at him until he reaches his own village, when they run away home screaming and laughing.[2]

[1] Dalton 1872, p. 319.
[2] Campbell, John 1861, p. 21.

Those practices are of much the same type as the Mongol ceremonial capture described by the Rev. James Gilmour, who mentions [1] that, in a case of which he was an observer, the bridegroom's party had to have a sham fight with the friends of the bride before they were allowed to enter her tent. When the marriage contract was completed the bride began to "howl most vigorously" as part of the ceremony, but, "crying and reluctant, she was dragged into the tent, and there set aside in state." The next day, the proper amount of weeping having at length been accomplished by the bride and her female friends, "a young man obeyed the command of the father, pushed aside the women, drew back the curtain, took up the bride, and carried her along under his arm as a man would carry a bundle of grass, taking care not to bump her head ornaments on the lintel of the low door, and by the help of two others, hoisted her into the saddle of a remarkably quiet horse, which stood ready to receive her." She was soon afterwards put into a cart which was driven, the bridal procession following to the bridegroom's tent, which was carefully guarded by his friends, but after a slight parley the door was opened and the bride given up.

The real meaning of the ceremonial capture is shown by a consideration of other marriage customs in use among the hill tribes of India. With many of these tribes, and with some of the Sudra castes, one of the most important of the marriage ceremonies is the applying of *sindúr* to the forehead of the bride, which consists in making a red mark between the eyes, usually with red powder. In some places, however, as in Singhbúm, among the Hos, the husband and wife

[1] Gilmour 1883, p. 258.

touch and mark each other with blood as a sign that they
have become one flesh, and Colonel Dalton supposes [1]
that this is the true origin of the "singular but very
universal" custom of *sindrahán*. Among the Dravidian Oraons the same ceremony is performed, but
with the peculiarity that the operation is carefully
screened from view, "first by cloths thrown over the
young couple, and secondly by a circle of their male
friends, some of whom hold up a screen cloth, while
others keep guard with weapons upraised, and look
very fierce, as if they had been told off to cut down
intruders, and were quite prepared to do so." [2] The
ceremony of sindrahán is thus evidently one of great
moment, and its importance consists in the consequence which flows from the husband and wife becoming one flesh. In the Singhbúm villages the same end
is attained by the bride and bridegroom drinking beer
together. By this they are made of one flesh and
become of one Kili, that is, the wife is admitted into
her husband's tribe. [3] Sir W. W. Hunter, in his very
valuable account of the aborigines of Bengal, [4] states
that one of the great ceremonies in the life of the
Santal is the union of his own tribe with another by
marriage. No man is allowed to marry a member of
his own clan, and the wife on marriage gives up her
father's clan and its gods for those of her husband.
The ceremony by which this is expressed differs among
the Santals from that adopted by the Hos. The
clothes of the bride and bridegroom are united by the
bridegroom's clansmen, "after which the girl's clans-
women bring burning charcoal, pound it with the
household pestle in token of the dissolution of the old

[1] Dalton 1872, p. 319.
[2] *Ibid.*, p. 252.
[3] *Ibid.*, p. 193.
[4] Hunter 1871, p. 207.

family ties, and extinguish it with water to signify the final separation of the bride from her clan." This separation is, in the case of the Oraons, effected, as we have seen, under the armed guard of the clansmen of the bride and bridegroom, and no doubt the sham fight which commences the marriage ceremonies is intended to show that the friends of the bride have to be satisfied before her connection with the clan can be severed. After they have made a show of opposition, the bride's clansmen express their consent by joining with the bridegroom's friends in celebrating the change which then takes place.

The essentially peaceful nature of the whole proceeding, although it expresses the objection of the clan to part with one of its members, as the struggles of the bride express her unwillingness to leave her father's family, is evidenced by the custom as observed by the Muási of Gondwáná. As the bridegroom's cavalcade approaches the bride's house, there emerges "a troop of girls all singing, headed by the mother of the bride, bearing on her head a vessel of water surmounted by a lighted chiragh (lamp). When they get near enough to the cavaliers, they pelt them with balls of boiled rice, then coyly retreat, followed of course by the young men ; but the girls make a stand at the door of the bride's house, and suffer none to enter till they have paid toll in presents to the bridesmaids."[1] This differs fundamentally from the forcible marriage, having no element of consent or agreement, which is found among the Badagas of Southern India. Sometimes rich men of this tribe employ forty or fifty Todas to go on wife-stealing expeditions, and they carry off by force the wives of other Badagas.[2]

[1] Dalton 1872, p. 233.
[2] Shortt 1868, p. 75.

The dissolution of old family ties on marriage, and the making of the husband and wife of one flesh, as practised by the hill tribes of India, is accompanied by the important result that all the offspring of the marriage belong to their father's clan. This agrees with the fact previously mentioned, that nearly all the peoples who have ceremonial capture in connection with marriage trace descent in the male line. We cannot doubt, therefore, that the ceremony has relation to the change which then takes place in the position of the bride, and that it is intended to denote that her family and clan have ceased to have any claim to her or her offspring. Where there is a bride-chase, either alone or in connection with a sham fight, the consent of the female on whose behalf the marital engagement has been entered into is shown by the capture which follows. By the sham conflict the consent also of the friends of the bride to the marriage and its consequences is evidenced. What is equally essential, however, the marriage becomes a matter of public notoriety.[1] This is an important consideration among uncultured peoples who have no written records; and in the case of the sham fight especially, not only is the marriage made

[1] The view expressed in the text is confirmed indirectly by a statement of the Rev. J. Mackenzie in relation to marriages among certain South African tribes. He says: "In Bechuana-land the cattle paid by the bridegroom under native law to the bride's father was the only way in olden times of establishing the validity of the marriage and the legitimacy of the children. Without the payment of the cattle the father could not establish before natives that the children were his. But Christian natives were getting accustomed to the marriage register in the native church as a still better proof of the marriage, of the consent of the father-in-law and other relatives, and of the legitimacy of the children" (Mackenzie 1887, p. 94).

public, but it is impressed effectually on the memories of those concerned in the proceedings. Nor is the general conclusion affected by the consideration that ceremonial capture is found among peoples having kinship in the female line. With the Gáros[1] of North-Eastern India, the initiation in marriage is taken, not by the bridegroom or his friends, but by the bride. A woman selects the man whom she would like to marry, and if he is agreeable, the approval of their parents is sought. Should they object, they are beaten until they give the desired consent. The bride and her friends then proceed to the house of the intended husband to secure him. He pretends to run away, but he is quickly caught, and in spite of his resistance is married " amidst lamentations and counterfeit grief both on his part and that of his parents." The peculiarity of this form of capture is accounted for by the fact that the Gáros have the system of descent in the female line, as opposed to the male kinship associated with the usual phases of ceremonial capture. The Gáro villages are divided into máháris, or motherhoods, particular máháris being especially connected with and inter-marrying with each other, and the offspring of a marriage belonging to the máhári of their mother. The fact that it is the bridegroom and not the bride who is captured, furnishes a strong argument in support of the explanation given above of ceremonial capture in marriage ; seeing that there is no evidence of the former general abduction of men for husbands, and systematic " capture " of bridegrooms cannot therefore have originated in the institution of an earlier practice of abduction.

The following general conclusions appear to be

[1] Rowney 1882, p. 192.

warranted by the facts now known as to "marriage by capture" of females :—

(1.) In all ages of the world women have been the objects of capture by peoples of a low degree of culture, either for slaves or for wives (child-bearing).

(2.) Such capture is without the consent of the female herself, or of her relations.

(3.) The "capture" in use among many peoples as part of the marriage ceremony, may have reference to the consent of the female herself, or of her relations.

(4.) Where the "capture" has reference to the consent of the female, she can avail herself of the opportunity of refusing it, or she must publicly acknowledge it.

(5.) Where the "capture" has reference to the consent of the relations of the female, they publicly ratify the contract of marriage, and accept its consequences —the loss to their kindred group of the offspring of the marriage, who, in pursuance of the rule of descent in the male line, are of kin to and form part of the husband's family group.

CHAPTER XII.

MONOGAMY.

In the chapter on monandry we have treated of the imperfect system of marriage, which, while permitting a man to marry again when his first wife is childless, either after or without divorcing her, or to take secondary wives or concubines with or without the consent of the first wife, refuses to allow a woman to have at one time more than one husband, or to receive the attentions of other men. This is the social condition referred to by Dr Morgan in relation to the Homeric Greeks, when he says[1] that the "usages and customs on the part of unmarried as well as married men, cited approvingly by the great poet of the period, and sustained by public sentiment, tend to show that whatever of monogamy existed, was through an enforced restraint upon wives, while their husbands were not monogamists in the preponderating number of cases." Mr Morgan remarks further,[2] that "from first to last among the Greeks there was a principle of egotism or studied selfishness at work among the males, tending to lessen the appreciation of women, scarcely found among savages." Not that woman was treated with cruelty, nor with discourtesy within the range of their permitted privileges, "but their education was superficial, intercourse with the opposite sex was denied them, and their inferiority was inculcated as a principle,

[1] Morgan 1877, p. 473.   [2] *Ibid.*, p. 474.

until it came to be accepted as a fact by the women themselves."

There is one feature of the inferiority assigned to women among monandrous peoples which should not be lost sight of, as it has a bearing on the development of true monogamy. Among uncultured races, on the death of a woman's husband she generally passes to the person who succeeds him as head of the family group, not being her own son. The custom of the Levirate was of a different nature, as there the widow was taken by the nearest kinsman of her deceased husband for the purpose of raising up seed to the dead man. Prof. Hearn observes that the marriage of the heir with the widow to raise up male issue for the Aryan household did not differ in principle from the Levir's commission. He says,[1] " The heir took the inheritance as it stood, with all its advantages and all its incumbrances. His duty was to provide the house with a son, who should have the right to perform the *sacra* and the means of performing them. Whether the woman was maid or widow was not material. In the one case by right of selection, in the other case by right of birth. She was the proper mother of the desired son." Such may have been the rule among the primitive Aryans, but the provisions of the laws of Menu, referred to by M. de Coulanges,[2] as sanctioning it, apply only to the commercial classes.[3] It is expressly said, " Such a commission to a brother or other near kinsman is nowhere mentioned in the nuptial texts of the Veda ; nor is the marriage of a widow ever named in the laws concerning marriage." The practice is declared, moreover, to be fit only for cattle.[4]

[1] Hearn 1879, p. 161.   [2] Fustel de Coulanges 1876, p. 53.
[3] *Menu*, IX. 59.   [4] *Menu*, IX. 65, 66.

Only when a man dies after troth verbally plighted, but before consummation, does the code of Menu allow the husband's brother to take the betrothed damsel to wife, and then he is to approach her only "once in each proper season, and until issue be had."[1]

The point to be considered, however, is the custom of temporarily or permanently prohibiting the second marriage of a woman on the death of her husband. Some of the American tribes compel widows to mourn their husband's deaths, and to devote themselves to a life of austerity and chastity for several years.[2] The cruelties inflicted on the New Caledonian widow, and the hardship she endures during the three years succeeding her husband's death, are so great, that women who have married again often commit suicide in the event of the second husband's death, rather than undergo them a second time.[3] The old Peruvians, with many peoples of Asia and Africa, effectually prevented the remarriage of the wives of dead men by killing them and burying them in their husband's graves. This was doubtless on the same principle as that which leads the savage to desire to be accompanied into the other world by some of his followers or slaves. On the death of the mother of Tchaka, the noted Zulu chief, ten young girls were buried alive in her grave.[4] So also in Japan, formerly servants were buried alive in their master's tomb.[5] Children of both sexes were killed on the burial of a Mongol king, and placed in

[1] *Menu*, IX. 69, 70.
[2] Cox 1883, II, 327; cf. Alexander 1779, II, 296.
[3] Kane 1859; Greenwood 1865, p. 373.
[4] Wood 1868–70, I, 72.
[5] Busk 1841, p. 196.

the grave around the corpse, that they might serve him in the future life.[1] The Hindoo custom of Sati, or "devoted wife," which required a wife to allow herself to be burnt on her dead husband's funeral pyre, is supposed[2] to have been borrowed from the Scythians, among whom, according to Herodotus,[3] one of the king's concubines was strangled and buried in his tomb. Some of the Thracians, who were an allied people, appear to have more nearly resembled in their funeral rites the Hindoo practice. Herodotus says,[4] that when any man dies, " a great contest arises among the wives, and violent disputes among their friends, on this point, which of them was most loved by the husband. She who is adjudged to have been so, and is so honoured, having been extolled both by men and women, is slain on the tomb by her own nearest relative, and when slain, is buried with her husband ; the others deem this a great misfortune, for this is the utmost disgrace to them." The Hindoo widow was also supposed to die by choice, and to survive her husband was considered a great disgrace.

The practice of Sati was most probably brought into India by invaders from Central Asia, and it must have been introduced since the compilation of the " Laws of Menu," which do not allude to it. It is evident, however, from several provisions of these Laws, that although the widow at that period did not die with her husband, a virtuous wife was not allowed to marry again.[5] The husband and the son of a twice-married

---

[1] Huc 1855, I, 80.

[2] Monier-Williams 1876, p. 258n.

[3] Bk. IV. 71.   [4] Bk. V. 5.

[5] V. 162. The later *Institutes of Nárada* (Jolly 1876) give five cases in which a woman may take another husband (XII. 97).

woman are classed among the persons who are to be avoided by an exalted and learned priest at a *srâddha* to the gods and to ancestors.[1] The widow who, from a wish to bear children, marries again, " brings disgrace on herself here below, and shall be excluded from the seat of her lord ; " while " a virtuous wife ascends to heaven, though she have no child, if, after the decease of her lord, she devote herself to pious austerity." [2] This rule appears to have been strictly observed in India, where it was usual for a widow who was not permitted to die with her husband, to devote herself to a life of charity and penance, sitting by the roadside to supply travellers with boiled rice and beans, or with fire to enable them to ignite their tobacco.[3] The Chinese entertain much the same view in relation to the marriage of widows as the Hindoos. They consider it a disgrace to a family for one of its sons to marry a widow, " as well as a disgraceful or shameful step on the part of the widow to consent to marry again." This step would bring dishonour on the families with which she was connected, and especially upon the memory of her deceased husband.[4] In China, moreover, widows impelled by attachment, poverty, or the prospect of unkind treatment, sometimes resolve not to survive their husbands, and they accordingly commit suicide by starving themselves to death, drowning, or by taking poison.[5] In some parts, widows or betrothed girls whose intended husbands have died, hang themselves in public, after giving

[1] *Menu*, III. 155, 166, 167.   [2] *Menu*, V. 160, 161.

[3] Tavernier 1889, pp. 97, 169.

[4] Doolittle 1868, p. 70. Widows are sometimes purchased by families who cannot afford to buy a girl of good character for a son. The wife of a living man may be acquired for that purpose.   [5] *Ibid.*, pp. 77ff

notice of their intention, so that any one who wishes
to do so may witness the act.   Women and girls who
thus commit suicide may have their names recorded
on the large general tablets erected in the temple they
have previously visited, or they may have a special
tablet placed there on payment of a sum of money to
the institution.   Incense and candles are burned at
stated periods in memory of those " virtuous and filial
women."   Moreover, honorary tablets or portals are
sometimes erected with the permission of the Emperor
in honour of virtuous widows " who have obeyed with
filial devotion the parents of their husbands."   The
Chinese sometimes show their appreciation of the
merits of widowhood by establishing societies for the
relief of indigent and virtuous widows.[1]

Among the early Hebrews, widows who were not
subject to the law of the Levirate were allowed to
have a second husband.   This may be inferred from
the Mosaic regulation that a priest was to marry a
virgin and not a widow, or one divorced, a polluted
woman, or a harlot.[2]   The classing of these women
together shows, however, in what light widows were
regarded, and we may judge from the numerous
passages in the Old Testament where the oppression
of widows is complained of or forbidden, that their lot
cannot have been a very happy one among the
Hebrews.[3]   Their position was less unfavourable
among the early Aryans.   This appears from the fact
that Zoroaster required that on a man's death the
" full subsistence " of his widow should be provided

---

[1] *Ibid.*, p. 475.   [2] Lev. 21 : 14.

[3] One of the acts forbidden in the religious ritual of the
ancient Egyptians is vexing the widow (Fontane 1882, p.
417).

for.[1] According to the Vedas, the brother of the dead Arya is to be the protector of his widow.[2]

The ideas entertained by the classical peoples of antiquity on the remarriage of widows resembled that of the early Aryans generally. Among the Romans a woman who had been married to only one husband, or who had continued in widowhood after her husband's death, was held in particular respect. The phrase *univira* is used in ancient inscriptions as a term of honour. Such women who married a second time were not allowed to officiate at the annual rites of Female Fortune.[3] As to the ancient Greeks, Dr Alexander remarks[4] that their history has "transmitted to posterity, with some degree of infamy, the name of her who first ventured on a second marriage," Gorgophona, the supposed daughter of Perseus and Andromeda. The practice, though soon afterwards followed by others, was long the subject of public odium ; "for during a great part of the heroic age, widows who remarried were considered as having offended against public decency ; a custom to which Virgil plainly alludes, when he describes the conflict in the heart of Dido, between her love for Æneas and fear of wounding her honour by a second marriage."

The sense of self-respect which leads the relatives of a deceased husband in China to provide wholly or partially for his widow that she may not marry again,[5] is in the case of Dido transferred to the woman

---

[1] Fontane 1881*b*, p. 276.

[2] Fontane 1881*a*, p. 65.

[3] Adam 1791, p. 408. Such second marriages were among the Germans forbidden by law (Tacitus, *Germania*, 19).

[4] Alexander 1779, II, 292.

[5] Doolittle 1868, p. 71.

herself. The individual immediately concerned has come to consider remarriage dishonourable. Nor was such a feeling restricted to the second marriages of women. Such marriages would seem to have been disapproved of by the Greeks for men also under some circumstances, as appears from the fact that " Charonides excluded all those from the public councils of the State who had children, and married a second wife. It is impossible (said he) that a man can advise well for his country, who does not consult the good of his own family : he whose first marriage has been happy, ought to rest satisfied with that happiness ; if unhappy, he must be out of his senses to risk being so again." [1] If men could be restricted by a sense of propriety from marrying again on the death of their first wives,[2] they might no less be restricted from marrying a second wife in the lifetime of the first one. It is doubtful, however, whether the recognition of the impropriety of the act could become generally recognised where the conditions of the monandrous family exist. A people who practise wife-purchase, and allow an almost unrestricted power of divorce to husbands, cannot be expected to attain to the stage of pure monogamy. This can be reached only when women have ceased to be sold by their relations into the power of a husband, and when the wife has come to be recognised as on an equality with her husband, not only in the household, but before the

[1] Alexander 1779, I, 292.

[2] In Cambodia, a man who has lost his first wife ought, if he wishes to be held in high consideration, not to remarry, that is, a woman of the same rank ; and he would be still more highly regarded if he donned the religious habit (Moura 1882–83, I, 334).

law. Dr Morgan remarks,[1] in relation to the Greeks,
"The wife was not the companion and the equal of her
husband, but stood to him in the relation of a daughter;
thus denying the fundamental principle of monogamy
as the institution in its highest form must be understood. The wife is necessarily the equal of her husband in dignity, in personal rights, and in social
position." Elsewhere[2] the same writer says, that while
the monogamian family improved with human progress,
"it fell short of its true ideal in the classical period.
Its highest known perfection, at least, was not attained
until modern times." Dr Morgan does not, however,
account for this fact, and an explanation of it was
hardly possible on the lines of his argument. In a
former chapter the insufficiency was shown of his
explanation of the origin of monogamy as due to the
growth of property, and the desire for its transmission
to "the actual progeny of the married pair." These
ideas alone would not have led to the establishment of
monandry, and still less could they have formed a
sufficient basis for the higher phase of marriage exhibited in monogamy, which forbids a man, no less
than his wife, to form a second sexual union during
the existence of their marriage.

The ideas as to the perpetuation of the family entertained by the Chinese, have little reference to the
transmission of property. Sons are desired, not to
retain wealth in the family, but to ensure that the
spirit of their deceased father shall reach in safety the
place where the ancestral spirits dwell, and that the
necessary offerings shall afterwards be made to him
among the manes of his ancestors. The ancient
Egyptians entertained similar ideas. The Chinese

[1] Morgan 1877, p. 475.   [2] *Ibid.*, p. 480.

think that a man has three souls or spirits, of which one resides in the ancestral tablet representing the deceased.[1] That notion answers to the belief of the ancient Egyptians, that there are three principles enclosed within the material body—the soul, *ba*, which is the envelop of the intelligence ; *khou*, the double or immaterial body ; *ka*, which is the covering of the soul.[2] The Chinese belief that one of the three spirits of the deceased resides in the ancestral tablet, agrees with the Egyptian idea that the *ka* or double took up its abode, after the destruction of the body, in one of the statues provided for it, and enclosed with the mummified body in the tomb.[3] Moreover, " the soul enveloped in the *ka*, which formed for it a subtle body, often returned, in the course of its long infernal wanderings, and of the trials which marked them, to repose in the tomb and regain its powers by refreshing itself with the offerings that were deposited at regular intervals, while drinking the holy water of the Nile."[4] It is evident how important to the welfare of the departed must have been the due observance of the funeral rites and the subsequent offerings made at the tomb. The Egyptians, like the Chinese, had great reverence for the dead, and each family had yearly a special fête known as the " reunion of the relations of the deceased," at which offerings were made at the *mastaba* or tomb, and the visitors spoke to the deceased, and burnt incense before his statue.[5]

Ideas similar to those entertained by the Chinese and the ancient Egyptians are found, on examination, to underlie the marriage system of the early Aryan

---

[1] Doolittle 1868, pp. 135, 158.
[2] Lenormant 1881–88, III, 228.
[3] *Ibid.*, III, 237.   [4] *Ibid.*, III, 241.   [5] *Ibid.*, III, 133, 144.

peoples. As to the Iranians, the union of men and women is declared in the Vendidad to be the act most agreeable to Ormuzd. Marriage is, however, enjoined by Zoroaster merely for the development and the greatness of the nation. Hence the ceremony of marriage is not an essentially religious rite. But the act of consummation ought to be sanctified, and the faithful Mazdian was to address a prayer to God that he would bless it.[1] He did not, however, desire offspring to be a source of wealth, or merely for the sake of the present life. The Mazdian, in praying to Ormuzd, asked for "children renowned by merit, who will be chiefs in the assemblies, who will enable me to gain paradise, who will thus deliver me from oppression, I who wish good with intelligence. Cause my soul to be eternally happy." Moreover, the Mazdian could even after death escape from punishment for sin by the prayers and good works of the living, provided that the souls to be delivered from hell repent of the faults they had committed in life. But "the prayer for the dead," which was offered during five days of each year, had virtue only when it was said by a relation of the condemned soul. Children prayed for their father and their mother, parents for their children, the brother prayed for his sister, and the sister for her brother; grandchildren for their grandparents, and grandparents for their grandchildren. Relations to the fourth degree could thus succour each other, and even the servant and the son of the servant could deliver by their prayers the soul of their master or mistress.[2] We have here the influence of the same idea as that associated with the possession of a son among the Chinese and Egyptians—the securing of happiness in

[1] Fontane 1881b, pp. 108, 113.　　[2] Ibid., p. 209.

the future life. Instead of sacrifices and offerings, however, the means employed by the Mazdians was prayer,[1] and the 12th fargard of the Vendidad fixes the number of prayers which ought to be said after the death of the Mazdian by each of his relations.[2] This answers to the " degrees of assistance and friendship" which the members of a family owed to each other, and which, as between father and son, was a thousand degrees.[3] The Iranians regarded prayer as of wonderful efficacy when said in the proper spirit, and the prayers of a son must have been looked forward to by the Mazdian as of the greatest importance in connection with his own condition after death.

Marriage was looked upon by the Vedic Aryas in much the same light as by the Iranians. The family resulted from the union of a man and a woman, who were husband and wife, to become father and mother. The husband, as the head of the family, was called *pati*, master, but he was also *pitri*, as the nourisher of his wife and children. The wife was *mâtri*, the distributor, and was also called *dam*, which is a word of commandment, but used with reference only to the woman's children and servants, and not to her husband. The son was *suta* and *sunu*, the " begotten " and the " disciple " of his father. Through the son the family was perpetuated, and he is always first mentioned with his father in the hymns to the guardian deities, the mother coming next.[4] The daughter appears to be forgotten ; but when a wife became the mother of a son she was said to be deserving of homage, and she had the privilege of partaking with her husband the

[1] *Ibid.*, p. 171.   [2] *Ibid.*, p. 104.
[3] *Ibid.*, p. 292.
[4] Fontane 1881*a*, p. 58.

honour of joining in sacrifice.[1] The son loves and respects his father, whom he approaches with the same gesture as the divinity is saluted with before the altar, and addresses him in the tone of prayer.[2]

M. Fustel de Coulanges, in his admirable work, remarks[3] that "the Hindoo as the Greek regarded the dead as divine beings who enjoyed a happy existence. But their happiness depended on a condition; it was necessary that the offerings should be regularly made to them by the living. If these ceased to accomplish the *srâddha* for a dead person, the soul of the deceased left his peaceful dwelling, and became a wandering soul which tormented the living; so that if the manes were truly gods, it was only because the living honoured them with worship." This worship of the dead appears to have been of the greatest antiquity, and it was so closely connected with the worship of the hearth that they made but one cultus. M. de Coulanges supposes[4] that "the domestic hearth has been in its origin only the symbol of the worship of the dead, that under the stone of the hearth an ancestor reposed, that the fire was there lighted to honour him, and that this fire seemed to maintain the life in him or represented his watchful soul." This is only a conjecture, but strong evidence has been furnished by Prof. Hearn in proof of the early worship of the hearth and its connection with the worship of deceased ancestors.[5] This opinion is confirmed by the fact that each family had its own sacred fire, which represented the ancestors, and which had nothing in common with the fire on the hearth of

[1] *Ibid.*, p. 62.

[2] As with the Iranians, prayer was regarded as all powerful (*Ibid.*, p. 187).

[3] Fustel de Coulanges 1876, p. 17.

[4] *Ibid.*, p. 30. [5] Hearn 1879, pp. 50ff.

a neighbouring family.[1]   M. de Coulanges points out
that the offerings to the dead could be made only by
male descendants.   It was the duty of the son to make
the libations and sacrifices to the manes of his father
and of all his ancestors ; and if " the sacrifices were
always accomplished according to the rites, if the food
was placed on the tomb on the appointed days, then
the ancestor became a protecting deity," but if they
were neglected the dead were caused to succumb, and
their happiness was destroyed.[2]   The birth of a son
was then all important to the Hindoo, who becomes
perfect only " when he consists of (three persons
united) his wife, himself, and his son " ;[3] and who is
said by the birth of his eldest son to discharge his debt
to his progenitors and to attain immortality.[4]   The
eldest son is therefore said to be begotten from a sense
of duty, an idea which must have been unknown to
the Greeks if Mr Morgan's opinion that they married
for the purpose of transmitting property to their own
lawful offspring is correct.

What has been said above in relation to the Aryas
of India is applicable in great measure to the early
Greeks and Romans.   Isaios said, " No man who knows
he must die can have so little regard for himself as to
leave his family without descendants, for then there
would be no one to render him the worship due to the
dead.[5]   With a people entertaining such ideas, marriage would be obligatory.   As pointed out by M. de
Coulanges,[6] " Celibacy is a crime in the eyes of a religion which considered the continuity of the family the

---

[1] Fustel de Coulanges 1876, p. 35. The Vedas teach that the
sacred fire is the cause of male posterity (p. 37).
[2] Fustel de Coulanges 1876, p. 33.   [3] *Menu*, IX. 45.
[4] *Menu*, IX. 106, 107.   [5] Quoted by Hearn (1879, p. 71).
[6] Fustel de Coulanges 1876, p. 108.

first and holiest of duties. But the union it prescribes can be accomplished only in the presence of the domestic divinities; it is the religious, sacred, and indissoluble union of husband and wife." To say, therefore, that with the Greeks the chief object of marriage was the procreation of children in lawful wedlock is only half the truth. Becker indeed affirms that marriage in reference to the procreation of children was considered by the Greeks a necessity, "enforced by their duty to the gods, to the state, and to their ancestors," from which Dr Morgan infers[1] that marriage was not grounded upon sentiment, but upon necessity and duty. Whatever may have been the case with the later Greeks, the absence of sentiment can hardly be affirmed in relation to the married life of those of the Homeric age. Mr Gladstone remarks[2] that the general tone of the intercourse between husband and wife during that period is "thoroughly natural: full of warmth, dignity, reciprocal deference, and substantial if not conventual delicacy. . . . The fulness of moral and intelligent being is alike complete, and alike acknowledged, on the one side and the other. Nor is this description confined to the scenes properly Hellenic. Of rude manners to a woman there is not a real trace in the poems. And to this circumstance we may add its true correlative, that the women of Homer are truly and profoundly feminine. As to the intensity of conjugal love, it has never passed the climax which it reaches in Odysseus and Penelope."

The monogamous alliances of the early Aryans, as of the ancient Egyptians, differ essentially from the phase of marriage to which the term *monandry* is

[1] Morgan 1877, p. 476.
[2] Gladstone 1869, p. 411.

applied. There appears to have been an absence in
the former of actual wife purchase, notwithstanding
the full recognition of male kinship[1] based on the
transfer of the right to offspring from the family of the
mother to the father. The father disposes of his
daughter, and the brother of his sister, in marriage,
but in the sacred books of the Iranians nothing is said
as to a dowry,[2] nor of the giving to the wife's father
or relations of presents which might represent the
bride-price. The code of Menu, moreover, expressly
affirms[3] that no father who knows the law should
receive a gratuity, however small, for giving his
daughter in marriage, since the taking by a father of
a gratuity is an "actual sale" of the daughter. The
giving of a bull and a cow in the nuptial ceremony of
the Rishis is referred to, but it is declared not to be a
bribe to the father. The sale of the daughter is supposed, however, to be referred to in the marriage
named Asura,[4] where the bridegroom, "having given
as much wealth as he can afford to the father and
paternal kinsmen, and to the damsel herself, takes her
voluntarily as his bride." The code of Menu expressly declares this marriage to be illegal, and classes
it with the sinful marriage Pisácha, although it states
that by some it was considered lawful for a merchant
and servile man.[5]   Dr M'Lennan refers to Asura
practice as evidence that marriage among the early
Hindoos proceeded upon contract. He argues further
that the Hindoos were exogamous, and that "among
early exogamous peoples, who had got beyond capture,
purchase was the only way of getting a wife."[6] This

---

[1] Above, p. 382.   [2] Fontane 1881b, p. 109.
[3] III. 51, 53.   [4] III. 31.   [5] III. 23, 25.
[6] McLennan 1885, p. 289.

general statement is of little value apart from illustrative examples, as so much depends on the views entertained as to exogamy and capture in relation to marriage. Dr M'Lennan affirms, however, that it was a custom, "coming down from very early times, that, at the time of marriage, the bridegroom should make a gift—and a very substantial one—to the bride's father," which, however, it was the duty of the father to return. Dr M'Lennan assumes that there was a time when he did not return the gift; but it is declared in Menu that "even in former creations" the virtuous did not approve "the tacit sale of a daughter for a price, under the name of a nuptial gratuity."[1] The facts may perhaps be explained by reference to Toda practice, which we shall be justified in citing, as the ancestors of this Dravidian people were probably comprehended among the aboriginal Asuras of the Vedic writers."[2] On betrothal, the young man offers a gift of buffaloes for the girl he desires to have for wife, and if the number is satisfactory, her father or other male protector promises an equivalent present in exchange. Colonel Marshall observes[3] that the transaction "is not the payment so much as the exchange of dowries," and it is a security for good behaviour rather than a case of wife-purchase. If the wife should leave her husband he would claim from her father restitution of the dowry he had paid, and if he discarded his wife her father would do the same thing, or if the marriage was cancelled owing to the husband not having fulfilled his part of the contract, he would be fined a buffalo or two.[4]

[1] IX. 98, 100.　　　　　　　　[2] Wheeler 1867, I, 106.
[3] Marshall 1873, p. 211.
[4] *Ibid.*, p. 217.

It is possible that to the primitive exchange of dowries. rather than to the bride-price of Sir Henry Maine,[1] we may trace the Stridhan or "woman's property" of Hindoo law, which consisted at first of all property conferred on the wife by the husband "at the nuptial fire," although afterwards it came to include property assigned to the wife at the marriage by her own family, the dowry of Roman law, and finally all the property of a married woman. With the early Greeks the so-called bride-price consisted of presents to the bride's father.[2] Instead of receiving presents on giving their daughters in marriage, the Greeks came in time to supply them with a dowry. Girls without dowries were neglected, and it appears from a pleading of Demosthenes that at Athens the State provided a dowry for those who through poverty and plainness would otherwise have remained unmarried.[3] It has been said that in Greece and Rome a young girl without dowry was permitted to obtain one by prostitution of her person,[4] but it must be doubted whether this was not a very exceptional thing. The dowry paid by the bride's father was at first constituted by securities given in the presence of witnesses, then by a public action, and it was secured on the property of the husband. Its payment was introduced to secure independence to wives, and through it a daughter, instead of being in the hand or power of her husband, continued a member of her father's *familia,* and inherited from him.[5] When the

[1] Maine 1875, p. 324.   [2] Duruy 1886–89, I, 164.
[3] Ménard 1880–83, II, 67.
[4] Above, p. 88.
[5] If a daughter was married when she inherited from her father, the marriage was cancelled.

marriage was *sine conventione,* the children belonged to the husband, although the wife retained her original familia, and they were regarded as being on the same footing as the servile members of the family group.

The authority of a man over his wife when she was in the hand of her husband, was such that, among the Romans at least, she could be put to death for adultery, and even for drunkenness. The husband's power was shown also in connection with the practice of divorce. A wife could be put away legally not only for adultery or for poisoning her children, but also for counterfeiting the keys entrusted to her,[1] or drinking wine without her husband's knowledge. Adultery was rare probably in the early period of Roman history, when, although manners were rude, the people "elevated altars to Modesty, treated matrons with a profound respect, and regarded with horror every blow to the sanctity of marriage."[2] It is a curious fact that it was five hundred years before a case of divorce occurred at Rome. Probably, however, this refers to a divorce from the religious marriage by *confarreatio,* which could be dissolved only by a ceremony equally formal with that by which it had been contracted. Where a man and woman had become united by the form of marriage known as *coemptio,* or mutual purchase, or were husband and wife by *usucapio,* or cohabitation for a year without the *usus* having been broken by the wife absenting herself for three nights, the wife could be divorced without much difficulty.[3] The first re-

[1] The keys were placed in the hands of the wife immediately after she was carried into the house by her husband (Ménard 1880–83, II, 151).

[2] Daremberg and Saglio 1877–1919, p. 85, art. "Adult."

[3] Fustel de Coulanges 1876, p. 48.

corded case of divorce at Rome was that of Carvilius
Ruga, who put away his wife because she had not
borne him children. He tenderly loved her, but he
thought he was bound to sacrifice his love to religion,
as he had sworn (in the formula of marriage) that he
took her to wife that she might have children. M. de
Coulanges suggests[1] the possibility that with the
ancients divorce was a duty in such a case, although
this is not proved by any formal text, and he refers to
the fact that, according to Herodotus, two kings of
Sparta were compelled to repudiate their wives on
account of sterility, and also to the provision of the
Code of Menu,[2] which allowed a barren wife to be
superseded by another in the eighth year. The power
of a wife to leave her husband was anciently very
slight. If he was absent from her for a certain time,
she was at liberty to marry again, but it was not until
the later period of the republic that women exercised
the same right of divorce as their husbands. Afterwards, however, women often deserted their husbands,
and some women exercised this right so freely that
Seneca said they reckoned their years, not from the
number of Consuls, but from the number of their
husbands.[3]

It is probable that divorce was not very usual among
the Greeks. Adultery even was not an unpardonable
offence, and a woman was never severely punished for
it. The guilty woman was only declared infamous ;
she could not carry certain ornaments, nor assist at
public sacrifices. If she did not observe these pro-

[1] *Ibid.*, p. 53.
[2] IX. 81. This provision applies, however, only to the commercial and servile classes.
[3] Adams 1791, p. 407.

hibitions her ornaments might be snatched away, her clothes torn, and she could even be struck but not wounded.[1] M. Victor Duruy remarks that "Clytemnestra, Antea, Phedra, Alcmena, and all the wives carried off or seduced by heroes and gods, show the indulgence of the men of that time for the foibles they had so often provoked." In the same spirit Mr Gladstone admits[2] that the indignation of the Greeks against Paris was as the effeminate coward rather than as the ravisher, and he adds that the shame of the abduction lay in the fact that Paris was the guest of Menelaus. Probably the fact that, although polygyny was forbidden, concubinage was permitted, may partly account for the infrequency of divorce among the early Greeks. It betokens a certain laxity in sexual manners, which is evidenced, moreover, by the fact that cohabitation before marriage was not considered improper,[3] and that bastards had a right to share in the paternal estate, although they took a smaller portion than the legitimate children.[4] The want of chastity in a daughter was punished with great severity by her father, when discovered, but it is significant that "furtive pregnancy of young women (which is often laid to the account of a god) is a frequently recurring incident in the legendary stories." Prolonged absence of a wife, although she had become the wife of another man, was not considered a bar to her resuming her original domestic position, showing the continuance of the proprietary right, the invasion of which, even

---

[1] Duruy 1886–89, I, 166. [2] Gladstone 1869, p. 401.
[3] *Ibid.*, p. 405.
[4] Grote 1846–56, I, p. 476. M. Ménard states, however, that the law did not recognise children by concubines (1880–3, II, 66).

in the Homeric age, was compounded for by payment of a fine.[1] The Greek wife was a citizen, she was protected by the law, and enjoyed all civil rights. Demosthenes in his speech before the judges against Neæra, who, although a foreigner and a dissolute woman, had married an Athenian, says,[2] "Now whatever may be the poverty of the poor virgin, the law provides her a sufficient dowry, notwithstanding she may not have received from nature an agreeable face. But if you outrage this law, if you weaken it by the acquital of Neæra, the infamy of prostitutes will mark the foreheads of the daughters of your fellow-citizens who, through want of dowry, cannot be married ; and the courtesan will enjoy all the privileges of the honest woman ; freedom, that is, to surround herself with a family, to appear at the initiations and at the sacrifices, and to partake of all civil rights."

It is evident that the position of woman socially, and in relation to the question of divorce, was higher among the early Aryans than with the Chinese and other monandrous peoples.   A Vedic hymn says, "Women deprived of the tutelage of their brothers, like wives separated from their husbands, resemble unjust and impious Aryas who live without sacrificing to the gods ; they can bring forth only darkness."[3] From this hymn we may judge that separation between man and wife was not regarded with favour, although the Aryan wife was sometimes repudiated and abandoned.   It is doubtful whether a wife could be put away even owing to her being childless.   This would not be done among the Iranians, at least, as,

[1] Gladstone 1869, pp. 407, 411.
[2] Quoted by M. Ménard 1880–83, II, 66.
[3] Fontane 1881a, p. 63.

according to the teaching of the Persian lawgiver, when the Mazdian sees his wife and fields struck with sterility, it is a sign that he is in a state of sin.[1] When marriage is based on a sentiment of affection, and is consecrated by religion, it is not surprising that husband and wife live together on a footing of equality, and that the one-sided monandry of the Turanian peoples gives place to the more elevated phase of marriage, in which the man and woman are united by a spiritual as well as a physical tie, and which is for both parties a life-long bond. It is very improbable that such a result could have been attained without the influence of religious teaching. We have seen that it was the religion of the hearth and of ancestors which united the members of the ancient Aryan family, and as marriage was the mode pointed out by nature for providing from time to time for a succession of individuals to perform the rites of that religion, marriage itself was regarded as sacred.

M. de Coulanges affirms[2] that marriage was established by the domestic religion, and it was so in the sense that its ultimate object was to perpetuate the religion which sanctioned it. He points out that marriage had other important religious consequences. All the individuals constituting the family were admitted to the rites of domestic worship, and only those individuals. On marriage the wife was to abandon her father's hearth to go and worship before that of another family. On the other hand, when a man married he had to introduce a stranger to his hearth, with whom he would have to perform the mysterious ceremonies of its worship, and to whom he would have to reveal the rites and the formulas which were the

[1] Fontane 1881b, p. 211. [2] Fustel de Coulanges 1876, p. 41.

inheritance of his family. We thus see how important marriage must have been in the eyes of the Aryans, and how necessary it was that it should be sanctioned by religion. Its nature was so well recognised by the ancients that it was designated by the word τελος, which signified "*sacred ceremony*," "as though marriage had been formerly the sacred ceremony *par excellence*."[1] The ceremonies of marriage terminated with the bride-groom and bride eating together a cake or some bread at the husband's hearth, "in the midst of the recita-tion of prayers, and in the presence of and under the eyes of the domestic divinities," and from that moment they are associated in the same worship. The dissolu-tion of such a marriage was almost impossible, and a new religious ceremony was necessary for the purpose. The effect of the *confarreatio* could only be destroyed by the *diffarreatio*, in which the wife renounced the worship and the gods of her husband, and then the religious tie being broken, the marriage was at an end.[2] M. de Coulanges may well suggest that with such ceremonies it was scarcely possible that a husband should have more than one wife at a time. It is not surprising, indeed, that it came to be looked upon as dishonourable for a man to marry again, even on the death of his wife.

The sacredness of marriage and the domestic worship from which its character was derived were known to the common ancestors of all the Aryan nations. There was another belief which influenced their conduct very greatly, and which probably had much to do with the development of systematic monogamy. Reference was made in a former chapter[3] to the doctrine of emana-tions as being essential to Chinese philosophy. This

[1] *Ibid.*, p. 43.   [2] *Ibid.*, p. 48.   [3] Above, p. 234.

doctrine, with that of the descent and ascent of souls springing from it,[1] was widely spread in the ancient world, and it was connected with the old religion of nature which the Iranians shared with the Aryas of India, and on which Zoroaster based his religious teaching.[2] In the philosophic speculations of the Scythic Magi it was held that all life is derived from the principle of heat which pervades the universe, and the soul was therefore regarded as a small portion of the immortal fire, or an emanation from the universal soul. When the soul was seduced by the fatal attractions of matter, it was said to have *fallen into the paths of generation.*[3] In pursuance of this doctrine, birth was looked upon, if not as an evil, yet as the source of evil. The association of the human soul with a material body was considered a mark of degradation, and a proof of spiritual impurity. Until the soul is purified, and thus enabled to ascend again to the regions from which it has descended, it is doomed to wander through a series of material transformations, and the chief aim of all the great religious systems of antiquity was to provide a means of escaping from the dreaded cycle of material existence.[4] The followers of Zoroaster sought to attain that end by holiness of conduct in this present life. The importance of purity forms the central idea of the Avesta, and its moral teaching is embodied in the dogma that three degrees of purity are required as the evidence of

[1] These doctrines are fully considered in Wake 1878, II, ch. 3.
[2] Geiger 1885, p. 24.
[3] Wake 1878, II, 184.
[4] *Ibid.*, II, 348.

salvation,—purity of thought, purity of word, and purity of action.[1]

It is in the application of these ideas to marriage that we have the real origin of the monogamous family, which has become firmly established under the influence of Christian teaching.   It would not be surprising if those ideas led to a declaration that a state of marriage is one of impurity, and therefore not to be entered into at all.   Indeed such a doctrine as this was anciently held by some sects.   The Gnostics sought to perpetuate in Christianity certain doctrines based on the existence in the universe of two principles opposed to each other, answering to light and darkness, embodied in the religious system of Zoroaster.   Satur- ninus, one of the earliest and most celebrated of the Gnostics, taught[2] that marriage having been instituted by the powers of darkness, for the purpose of per- petuating the race of their partisans, it was the duty of men endowed with a ray of the divine light to prevent both the diffusion of this germ of celestial life and the propagation of so imperfect an order of things. The Essenes of Palestine appear to have entertained similar ideas based on the doctrine of the descent and ascent of souls.   They considered the body as en- chaining the soul, which was originally pure and formed of the finest ether, but that on death the soul rises heavenward, while the material body perishes. Consistently with these opinions, the sect did not allow marriage, or if it was allowed by some of them, it was only for the sake of raising children.[3]   In the apoch-

[1] *Ibid.*, II, 316.

[2] Matter 1828, I, 290.

[3] Wake 1878, II, 355; cf. the works of Philo Judaeus (trans. Yonge 1854–55, IV, 221).

ryphal Hebrew book of the Wisdom of Solomon, chapter iii., we read, "Blessed is the barren that is undefiled, which hath not known the sinful bed : she shall have fruit in the visitation of souls. And blessed is the eunuch which with his hands hath wrought no iniquity, nor imagined things against God : for unto him shall be given the special gift of faith, and an entrance in the temple of the Lord more acceptable to his mind." Again, in chapter iv. : "Better is it to have no children, and to have virtue : for the memorial thereof is immortal . . . it weareth a crown and triumpheth for ever, having gotten the victory, striving for undefiled rewards." We are reminded by this passage of the one hundred and forty-four thousand seen by St John on Mount Sion with the Lamb, who were the first fruits of those who were redeemed among men, and who had not been defiled with women. Of them it is said, " In their mouth was found no guile : for they are without fault before the throne of God."[1] These ideas agree with those entertained by the Essenes, and they may be traced to the same source as that which gave to the Zend Avesta its idea of spiritual purity which was reproduced in the Christian system of morals.

Although St Paul allowed marriage he appears to have regarded it as not so high a state as that of virginity. The superiority of virginity was afterwards zealously enforced by Jerome[2] and other Christian fathers, and it led Origen, acting on the saying of Jesus, "There are eunuchs which make themselves eunuchs for the kingdom of heaven's sake,"[3] to make

[1] Rev. 14 : 1 *et seq.*
[2] Marriage had in the eyes of Jerome one virtue—it produced virgins. [3] Matt. 19 : 12.

an eunuch of himself; although he afterwards repented
of the act, as being too literal an interpretation of the
passage.[1] The words of Jesus cannot be taken as a
command, and probably they are intended rather to
draw a contrast between the physical act and the self-
control exercised by those who wish to obtain the
same end, through a conviction of the sinfulness of
gratifying the carnal desires. St Paul taught that the
body is the temple of the Holy Ghost, and ought,
therefore, to be kept holy, and his commendation of
the unmarried state was sure to lead to the extrava-
gances of a later age. The permission to marry,
given[2] to those who could not contain, was not always
continued by Paul's successors. Many of these took
the virgin Christ as their example, while boldly
declaring that, as the church was the bride of Christ,
every member of the church was spiritually espoused
to him. Carnal marriage thus became spiritual
adultery, and so strongly developed in the fourth
century was the feeling in favour of a celibate life,
that not only did husbands and wives mutually release
each other from the duties of the married state, but
female saints gloried that, although married, they had
retained their virginity. Mr Lecky does not scruple
to affirm that the cardinal virtue of the religious type
to which the writers of the fourth and fifth centuries
continually referred was chastity—"the absolute suppression of the whole sensual side of our nature."[3]
Gibbon lays especial stress on the importance attached

---

[1] Smith, W. 1877–87, IV, art. "Origen" (p. 98). For an
account of the Scoptsis, a modern Russian sect, who act on a
literal rendering of Matthew, see Kopernicky and Davis
(1870).

[2] 1 Cor. 7 : 1 *et seq.*, 25 *et seq.*

[3] Lecky 1869, II, 130.

to that virtue by the fathers. He says,[1] " The chaste severity of the fathers, in whatever related to the commerce of the two sexes, flowed from the same principle—their abhorrence of every enjoyment which might gratify the sensual, and degrade the spiritual nature of man. It was their favourite opinion that if Adam had preserved his obedience to the Creator, he would have lived for ever in a state of virgin purity, and that some harmless mode of vegetation might have peopled Paradise with a race of innocent and immortal beings. The use of marriage was permitted only to his fallen posterity as a necessary expedient to continue the human species, and as a restraint, however imperfect, on the natural licentiousness of desire. The hesitation of the orthodox casuists on this interesting subject betrays the perplexity of men unwilling to approve an institution which they were compelled to tolerate." Marriage when once formed was declared to be indissoluble, and " the practice of second nuptials was branded with the name of a legal adultery. . . . Since desire was imputed as a crime, and marriage was tolerated as a defect, it was consistent with the same principles to consider a state of celibacy as the nearest approach to the divine perfection. It was with the utmost difficulty that ancient Rome could support the institution of the vestals, but the primitive church was filled with a great number of persons of either sex who had devoted themselves to a profession of perpetual chastity."

Certain practices referred to by Gibbon were clearly governed by an exaggerated view of the requirements of a state of absolute purity, but the principle itself was not merely consistent with the fundamental idea

[1] Gibbon 1776–88, II, 186.

of Pauline Christianity." It was in reality essential
to it, seeing that the teaching of St Paul is based on
the supposed sinfulness of man arising from the "fall"
of Adam. The idea, embodied in the Jehovistic
legend, that the Creator originally intended the first
man and woman to be the sole occupants of Eden,
assumes that they were to remain in a state of
virginity, and it is directly connected with and based
upon the ancient dogma of the impurity of matter, and
was probably an esoteric doctrine known to the early
Hebrews.[1] In one of the creation legends given in
the book of Genesis, however, the practice of monogamy is distinctly enforced. It is said that "a man
shall leave his father and mother and shall cleave unto
his wife, and they shall be one flesh." This command
is usually regarded as proving that monogamy was
the primitive law of marriage, and it is inferred that
all the other phases of marriage, which are described
in the preceding pages, are marks of degradation
resulting from the fall of Adamic man. In reply, it
may be observed, in the first place, that the law of
monogamy is contrary to the practice of the Hebrew
patriarchs or kings, and so inconsistent with the
legend of the fall, that we must suppose the passage
quoted to be a mere gloss on the earlier account of the
creation of woman out of the side of man. The
earliest tradition of the Hebrew Scriptures is that
preserved by the Elohistic writer, who says, "God

---

[1] This opinion is consistent with the conclusion that, if the
legends of the Avesta were not borrowed from the Persians
by the Jews during their captivity — a view which is said to
be opposed by the archaic character of the Hebrew of the
first three chapters of *Genesis* — "the real contact point between them and the Jewish history must be found in pre-
Mosaic times, in the days of the early patriarchs" (*"The
Speaker's Commentary,"* 1871–88, I, 49).

created man in his own image, in the image of God created he him ; male and female, created he them. And God blessed them : and God said unto them, Be fruitful, and multiply and replenish the earth." Here no law of marriage is expressed, unless it is in the command, given also to the fishes and birds, to "be fruitful and multiply." It should be noticed, moreover, that in the continuation of the Elohistic narrative, nothing is said about marriage, but merely that "in the day that God created man, in the likeness of God made he him ; male and female created he them ; and blessed them, and called their name Adam (man)." [1] This is not consistent with the legend of the creation of Eve, which, judging from the succeeding catastrophe, was connected with the doctrines of "emanations" and of the descent and ascent of souls, and it cannot be regarded as giving any express sanction to monogamy, which probably was first instituted as a system among the primitive people who developed those doctrines, and under the influence of religious teaching such as that ascribed to Zoroaster.

It is possible, of course, that monogamy was the law of marriage among an ancient race from which both the Hebrews and the Iranians were descended, that is, the people of whom Noah was the eponymous ancestor. [2] This would carry back the institution of that phase of marriage to a much more distant period than is allowed by Dr Morgan and other writers. At the same time, the mere fact that the common ancestor of the Semitic and Japhetic, and also the Hamitic races, was a mono-

---

[1] Gen. 5 : 1, 2.

[2] Noah and his three sons are spoken of as having each only one wife (Gen. 7 : 13).

gamist, would not be proof that monogamy was customary among the primeval races of mankind, not
even if by Japhet we are to understand, as M. Lenor-
mont suggests,[1] "the chief of the race *par excellence.*"
The distinguished French writer points out that neither
the Turanians nor the Negroes appear among the
descendants of Noah, mentioned in Genesis, and those
races can claim not only a greater antiquity than the
other races named, but also, as to the Turanians at least,
an earlier civilisation. Moreover, they are without any
such traditions of the great deluge, as are said to have
been preserved by the Aryan, Semitic, and Hamitic
races.[2] It is, however, among the yellow and dark
races that we meet with the earliest types of marriage,
and we must presume that they perpetuated customs
which had been in use among their ancestors from a
distant antiquity. When the first Iranian empire was
founded, the legendary Djemschid is said to have
driven southward a race of men described as being
"black, with elephant's ears,"[3] and this race was probably the same as that which the Vedic Aryans met
with when they first invaded India. That polyandry
was then practised by this race, as it has been among
the yellow Tibetans, from time immemorial, is very
probable. We may justly infer from the statement in
Genesis that the descendants of Cain knew not Jehovah,
that the Cainite Turanians did not act in accordance
with the laws of conduct, in relation to marriage
especially, which governed the social life of the
descendants of Noah, or, which may be taken as the
same thing, those of Seth. We may presume, there-

[1] Lenormant 1881–88, I, 114.
[2] *Ibid.*, I, 91.
[3] Fontane 1881*b*, p. 236.

fore, that mankind has progressed upwards from a state of group-marriage, through polyandry and polygyny, to the monandry which was developed by the more cultured races before they left the common home, to give place finally to the monogamy of the descendants of Japhet. The Japhetic culture was not only morally the most advanced, but it was the latest to be developed, and its marriage system was no doubt that which in one of the legends of Genesis is said to have been instituted when the Adamic race first came into being.

Reference must be made to the system of relationships employed by the peoples among whom marriage is of the monogamous type. We have seen [1] that the Turanians, who prefer male kinship to female kinship for the purposes of descent, make use of the classificatory system, in which persons related by blood are placed in certain general classes, not according to their relationship to a particular individual, but according to the generation or grade to which they belong. With the rise of monandrous marriages, however, a new system was developed. In this every relationship is specific, and it is in use among the peoples belonging to the Arabian, Aryan, and Semitic stocks. Dr Morgan gives [2] reasons for believing that the ancestors of these races formerly possessed the Turanian classificatory system, and he supposes that when the monogamian family became generally established, they " fell back upon the old descriptive form, always in use under the Turanian system, and allowed the previous one to die out as useless and untrue to descents." This is, however, hardly a correct statement of the change. It has been shown at a preceding page [3] that, although under

[1] Above, p. 398.　　　　　　　[2] Morgan 1877, p. 481.
[3] Above, p. 254.

the classificatory system, *kinship* was preferably traced
for certain purposes through the female or the male
line, yet that simple relationship, in both lines, was
fully recognised. The same relationships as those of
the descriptive system are admitted, but they are
identified in a different manner, as in the one case the
individuals belonging to a group of persons are
specified, while in the other case only the group itself
is pointed out. The nature of the descriptive system
is shown by Dr Morgan's remark that originally it
" described the persons by means of the primary terms,
or a combination of them, as brother's son for nephew,
father's brother for uncle, and father's brother's son for
cousin." The Roman civilisation introduced a new
method of description " to perfect the framework of a
code of descents," and that method was adopted by
the Aryan nations, among whom the Roman influence
extended. Dr Morgan explains[1] that the additions
consisted chiefly " in distinguishing the relationships
of uncle and aunt on the father's side from those on
the mother's side, with the invention of terms to
express these relationships in the concrete ; and in
creating a term for grandfather to be used as the correlative of *nepos*. With these terms and the primary,
in connection with suitable augments, they were enabled
to systematise the relationships in the lineal and in
the first five collateral lines, which included the body
of the kindred of every individual."[2]

[1] Morgan 1877, p. 485.

[2] It is remarkable that the Chinese, who use the Turanian
classificatory system of relationships, have invented a plan
for "the separation of the several lines and branches of lines
from each other, and for the specialisation of the relationships of every kinsman to the central *Ego*," which is second
only to the Roman form (Morgan, 1871, p. 414).

The practical effect of the development of this "descriptive" system of relationships is that *kinship*, instead of being restricted to either the male or the female line to the exclusion of the other, is traced through both lines alike. A man's kinsmen, therefore, include the ancestors of his father and of his mother, and the descendants of both of them. There is here no such distinction between relationship and kinship as exists where descent is traced in only one line. In the descriptive system kinship is co-extensive with relationship under the classificatory system, and logically the natural restraints on intermarriage ought to be equally extended. We have seen[1] that where kinship through the father is preferred, all persons who bear the father's family name are debarred from inter-marriage, and where kinship is traced through the mother only the persons forbidden to intermarry are those who belong to her family. With kinship traced through both the male and the female lines, therefore, all the members of both the father's and the mother's family groups should be prohibited from forming marital alliances among themselves. It is not so in reality, however, and the very extension of the idea of kinship has much limited the range within which the prejudice against the intermarriage of consanguinei is operative. With some primitive peoples who disallow the intermarriage of persons akin by virtue of the rule of descent in the female line, marriage is also pro-hibited between persons who are closely related by the male line as well. Where the descriptive system of relationships is established, however, all persons who are lineally related are forbidden to intermarry, and also those who are collaterally related within three

[1] Above, p. 295.

degrees of the Civil Law; but persons related in the
fourth or any higher degree, on either the father's or
mother's side, may intermarry.   Thus, as first cousins
are related in the fourth degree they may intermarry,
as well as nephew and great aunt or niece and great
uncle, but not uncle and niece or aunt and nephew,
who are related only in the third degree.

The prohibited degrees have, however, received
under the influence of Christian teaching an extension
far beyond what is known to the more primitive
systems of marriage.   Not only is consanguinity a bar
to marriage, but so also is affinity in the same degrees.
The rule as to affinity is based on the idea that husband
and wife are one flesh, and it supposes a man to be
related to all the consanguinei of his wife, who on her
part is related to all the consanguinei of her husband.
As expressed in the Table of Kindred and Affinity,
which is recognised by English Law, a man cannot
marry the sister, aunt, or niece of his deceased wife,
and a woman cannot marry her deceased husband's
brother, uncle, or nephew.   This result is in accordance
with the spirit of the higher law of marriage which
finds expression in Christian morals, and it would be
accepted by those who look upon a second marriage as
a sign of spiritual inferiority, although not contrary to
the law of marriage as exhibited in practice among
primitive peoples.

In conclusion, let us see how we are to explain the
divergence between the advanced ideas on the subject
of marriage expressed in the legendary history of the
creation of Eve and those entertained by the Hebrew
Patriarchs.   The actual difference between them is
well shown by a comparison of the earlier and later
opinions on that subject.   These show a most complete

contrast. According to the Christian notion of sexual morality as finally developed, marriage is not only a sacred state, but its contraction is in most cases a sacred duty. With the early Hebrews, on the other hand, marriage was not considered a sacred state, and although it was considered a duty, yet the obligation originated in a different idea from that which affected the Christian mind. The Christian motive to marriage is found in the saying of St Paul, " It is better to marry than to burn." The Hebrew motive sprang from the ardent desire for children, which is so characteristic of Eastern peoples. This motive, having no relation to purity of life except so far as, according to the teachings of the later Hebrew writers, the duty of a man towards his wife was concerned, was quite consistent with recognised concubinage. With Christianity it was just the contrary. The motive here was individual purity, both of body and of mind, which was thought to be materialised or debased by sexual indulgence ; and it was for the preservation in some measure of this purity that marriage was allowed when it was found that the power of leading a strictly celibate life was not the gift of every man. Hence arises the sacredness of marriage, which is viewed by early Christianity not so much as the indissoluble union of man and woman—although this was insisted on except in the case of the woman's infidelity—or as having for its object the increase of the family or the perpetuation of mankind, but as the means by which the human soul is preserved in a state of comparative purity.

Marriage required, in the view of the early Christians, an excuse arising from the imperfection or weakness of man's material nature, and the author of the first epistle to Timothy (iv. 3) condemns those who forbid to marry. A second marriage was, however, regarded as evidence of a degenerate state. Thus, when speaking of widows, it is said[1] that a true widow "hath her hope set on God, and continueth in supplications and prayers night and day," and a widow is not to be taken into the number of those relieved by the church (v. 16), unless, among other qualifications, she has been the wife of one man (v. 9). The younger widows are to be refused, "for when they have waxed wanton against Christ, they desire to marry, having condemnation, because they have rejected their first faith" (v. 11, 12), and hence they are enjoined to marry and bear children (v. 14). Elsewhere,[2] St Paul says a woman may on her husband's death marry whom she will, but that "she is happier if she abide as she is." Nor was the second marriage of a man more agreeable to primitive Christian feeling than that of a woman. The bishop and the deacons were to be the husbands of one wife, from which we may infer that those who remarried were not esteemed sufficiently holy to be capable of filling those offices. The use of marriage was, moreover, restricted to this present life, there being no occasion for it after the soul has escaped from its material covering. Hence Jesus, while saying that the sons of this age marry and are given in marriage, is reported to have asserted[3] that they who were accounted worthy to attain to the resurrection of the dead neither marry nor are given in marriage, a state which he considered preferable even for this life, if we may judge from his reference to "eunuchs for the kingdom

---

[1] I Tim. 5 : 5.　　[2] I Cor. 7 : 39, 40.　　[3] Luke 20 : 34 *et seq.*

of heaven's sake." St Paul was evidently of the same opinion when he wrote[1] that "it is good for a man not to touch a woman," although he affirms (v. 25) that he had no commandment of the Lord concerning virgins. The condition which recommends itself to the apostles was that referred to by St Paul when he said,[2] "Have we no right to lead about a wife that is a believer, even as the rest of the apostles, and the brethren of the Lord, and Cephas?" This cannot have been a state of marriage, as the apostle elsewhere (vii. 8) makes known that he was unmarried. It evidently refers to such a custom as that related in connection with Jesus himself.[3] At the crucifixion, beholding from afar, were many women, "which had followed Jesus from Galilee, ministering unto him." That which an apostle might find conducive to his spiritual welfare is not fitted, however, for those on the natural plane. For mankind in general the law of marriage is still expressed in the words,[4] "A man shall leave his father and mother, and shall cleave to his wife; and the twain shall become one flesh," and no advance can be made beyond this monogamy so long as marriage is practised.

In the eyes of the founders of Christianity, however, although marriage was a sacred bond when entered into, virginity was a higher state. This view is confirmed by the reply of Jesus to the Sadducees who asked him,[5] "Whose wife at the resurrection would the woman be who married seven brothers in succession?" The object of the inquiry was to throw ridicule on the doctrine of the resurrection, but Jesus met the objec-

---

[1] 1 Cor. 7 : 1 ; and see 5 : 7–9 and 32–34.
[2] 1 Cor. 9 : 5. [3] Matt. 27 : 55 ; see Luke 8 : 2, 3.
[4] Mark 10 : 7–9 ; Gen. 2 : 24. [5] Matt. 22 : 24 *et seq.*

tion by the reply, "In the resurrection they neither marry, nor are given in marriage, but are as angels in heaven." The teaching of Jesus in relation to the kingdom of heaven, not only as a present power, but as being in the heart, renders it probable that he would regard virginity as the proper condition for its members on earth. It is observable he makes no reference to a wife when he says,[1] "There is no man that hath left house, or brethren, or sisters, or mother, or father, or children, or lands for my sake, and for the gospel's sake, but he shall receive an hundredfold now in this time, houses, and brethren, and sisters, and mothers, and children, and lands, with persecutions, and in the world to come eternal life." The spiritual nature of the hundredfold recompense precludes the mention of "wife." That the recompense is spiritual is proved by the conduct of Jesus in regard to his own mother and brethren. When these came to seek him,[2] he said to those who told him, "Who is my mother and my brethren?" And, looking round on them which sat round about him, he added, "Behold my mother and my brethren! For whosoever shall do the will of God, the same is my brother, and sister, and mother." If these natural ties are so little thought of, the marriage relation from which they spring must have been as little regarded. This feeling, which is deeply rooted in the human heart, was at one time widely spread not only among Christians but also among the followers of Gautama Buddha, and it has still great influence over the minds of those who think more highly of a future life than of the present. The objection to "marriage" is not restricted merely to those who regard the activity of the sexual instinct as

[1] Mark 10: 29, 30. [2] Mark 3: 32 et seq.

inconsistent with religious devotion. Marriage has its intellectual opponents also, and it is quite possible that in some future age the life of virginity may come to be considered the condition proper to those who are morally or intellectually in advance of their fellows, and that to which the human race is slowly but surely tending.

Note to Page 109

*[Wake's scheme is more economically represented in the modern form:

$$\begin{bmatrix} \text{Muri} & = & \text{Kumbo} \\ \text{Kubi} & = & \text{Ipai} \end{bmatrix}$$

in which the equation signs stand for marriage and the vertical lines for descent.—R.N.]

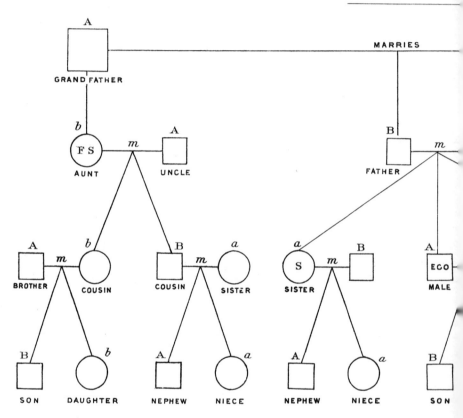

MARRIES

GRANDFATHER

b FS AUNT — *m* — A UNCLE

B FATHER — *m*

A BROTHER — *m* — *b* COUSIN

B COUSIN — *m* — *a* SISTER

a S SISTER — *m* — B

A EGO MALE

B SON

b DAUGHTER

A NEPHEW

a NIECE

A NEPHEW

a NIECE

B SON

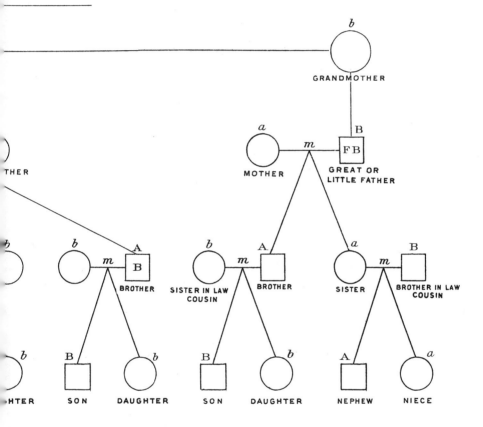

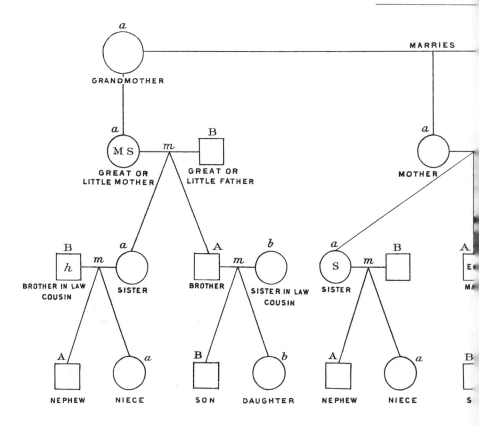

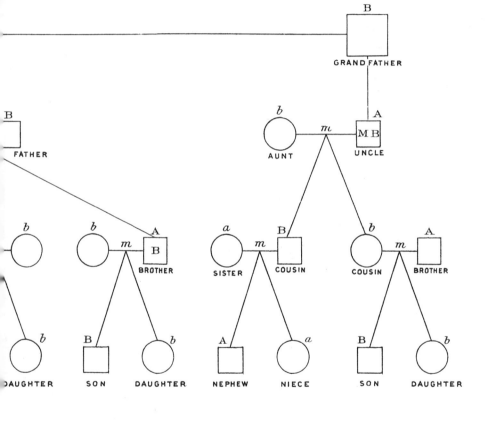

BIBLIOGRAPHY OF WORKS CITED

Adam, Alexander
    1791   *Roman Antiquities: Or, A Description of the Manners and Customs of the Romans.* Edinburgh.

Alexander, William
    1779   *The History of Women, from the Earliest Antiquity to the Present Time, Giving Some Account of Almost Every Interesting Particular Concerning That Sex among All Nations.* 2 vols. London.

Bachofen, J. J.
    1861   *Das Mutterrecht.* Stuttgart.

Baecker, Louis de
    1874   *L'Archipel indien.* Paris.

Bailey, John
    1863   "An Account of the Wild Tribe of the Veddahs of Ceylon; Their Habits, Manners, and Superstitions." *Transactions of the Ethnological Society of London,* N.S., 2:278–320.

Bancroft, H. H.
    1875   *The Native Races of the Pacific States of North America.* 5 vols. New York.

Barrow, John
    1806   *Travels into the Interior of South Africa.* London.

Bates, H. W. (ed.)
    [1870–76]   *Illustrated Travels: A Record of Discovery, Geography, and Adventure.* 6 vols. London. [Dates of publication from catalogue of the Bodleian Library. British Museum catalogue has 1869–75.]

Becker, Wilheld Adolph
    1845   *Charicles: Or, Illustrations of the Private Life of the Ancient Greeks.* Translated by Frederick Metcalfe. London.

Belcher, Edward
    1867 "Notes on the Andaman Islanders." *Transactions of the Ethnological Society of London*, N.S., 5 : 40–49.

Bonwick, James
    1870 *Daily Life and Origin of the Tasmanians*. London.

Bosman, Willem
    1721 *A New and Accurate Description of the Coast of Guinea*. 2d ed. London.

Bowdich, T. E.
    1819 *Mission from Cape Coast Castle to Ashantee*. London.

Bowring, John
    1857 *The Kingdom and People of Siam*. 2 vols. London.

Brand, John
    1877 *Popular Antiquities of Great Britain*. London.

Brett, W. H.
    1868 *The Indian Tribes of Guiana: Their Condition and Habits*. London.

Brinton, Daniel
    1882 *American Hero-Myths: A Study in the Native Religions of the Western Continent*. Philadelphia.

Brook, Charles
    1866 *Ten Years in Sarawak*. 2 vols. London.

Browne, John Cave
    1857 *Indian Infanticide, Its Origin, Progress, and Suppression*. London.

Bruce, James
    1813 *Travels to Discover the Source of the Nile*. 3d ed. 8 vols. Edinburgh.

Bühler, G. (trans.)
    1886 *The Laws of Manu*. ("Sacred Books of the East," Vol. XXV.) Oxford.

[Burton, R. F.]
    1863 *Wanderings in West Africa*. 2 vols. London.

Busk, W. (ed.)
    1841 *Manners and Customs of the Japanese, in the Nineteenth Century*. London.

Campbell, James
    1870 "Polygamy: its Influence on Sex and Population." *Journal*

of Anthropology, 2 : 192–7.

Campbell, John

1861   *Narrative of Major-General J. Campbell of his Operations in the Hill Tracts of Orissa, for the Suppression of Human Sacrifice and Female Infanticide.* [Printed for private circulation.] London.

Carver, Jonathan

1778   *Travels through the Interior Parts of North America.* London.

Castren, Mathias Alexander

1856   *Reiseberichte und Briefe aus den Jahren 1845–49.* St. Petersburg.

Catlin, George

1876   *Illustrations of the Manners, Customs and Condition of the North American Indians.* 2 vols. London.

Chaillu, P. B. du

1861   *Explorations and Adventures in Equatorial Africa.* London.

Chalmers, James

1887   *Pioneering in New Guinea.* London.

Charnay, D.

[1870]   ''A Bird's-eye View of Madagascar.'' (In Bates 1870–76, I, 49–57).

Codrington, R. H.

1881   ''Religious Beliefs and Practices in Melanesia.'' *Journal of the Anthropological Institute* 10 : 261–315.

Conder, C. R.

1887   ''The Present Condition of the Native Tribes of Bechuanaland.'' *Journal of the Anthropological Institute* 16 : 76–92.

Cook, James

1784   *A Voyage to the Pacific Ocean, Undertaken . . . in the Years 1776 . . . etc.* London.

Cox, Ross

1883   *Adventures on the Columbia River.* 2 vols. London.

Cranz, David

1767   *The History of Greenland.* 2 vols. London.

Cruickshank, Brodie

1835   *Eighteen Years on the Gold Coast of Africa.* 2 vols. London.

Dalton, Edward Tuite
    1872   *Descriptive Ethnology of Bengal.* Calcutta.
Daremberg, C. V., and Saglio, E.
    1877–1919 *Dictionnaire des antiquités grecques et romaines.* 5 vols.
        Paris.
Darwin, Charles Robert
    1871   *The Descent of Man.* 2 vols. London.
Dawson, James
    1881   *Australian Aborigines.* Melbourne.
De Quincey, Thomas
    1854   *Autobiographic Sketches.* ("Selections Grave and Gay,"
        Vol. II.) Edinburgh.
Dobrizhoffer, Martinus
    1822   *An Account of the Abipones, an Equestrian People of Para-*
        guay. 3 vols. London.
Doolittle, Justus
    1868   *Social Life of the Chinese.* New York.
Douglas, Robert K.
    1882   *China.* London.
Drew, Frederic
    1875   *The Jummoo and Kashmir Territories.* London.
Dufour, Pierre
    1851–61 *Histoire de la prostitution chez tous les peuples du monde*
        6 vols. Bruxelles.
Du Halde, Jean-Baptiste
    1735   *Description . . . de l'empire de la Chine.* 4 vols. Paris.
Duncan, Jonathan
    1798   "Historical Remarks on the Coast of Malabar." *Asiatick*
        Researches 5 : 1–36.
Duncan, Peter Martin (ed.)
    [1876–82] *Cassell's Natural History.* London.
Durand, J. B. L.
    1806   *A Voyage to Senegal.* ("Collection of Modern Voyages and
        Travels," Vol. IV.) London.
Duruy, Victor
    1886–89 *Histoire des Grecs.* 3 vols. Paris.

Edkins, Joseph
  1859 *The Religious Condition of the Chinese.* London.
Ellis, William
  1832–34 *Polynesian Researches.* 2d ed. 4 vols. London.
  1838 *History of Madagascar.* 2 vols. London.
Elphinstone, Mountstuart
  1815 *An Account of the Kingdom of Caubul.* London.
Faidherbe, Léon
  1874 *Instructions sur l'anthropologie de l'Algérie.* Paris.
Fenton, John
  1880 *Early Hebrew Life: A Study in Sociology.* London.
Fison, Lorimer
  1881 "Notes on Fijian Burial Customs." *Journal of the Anthropological Institute* 10: 137–49.
Fison, Lorimer, and Howitt, A. W.
  1880 *Kamilaroi and Kurnai.* Melbourne.
Fitzroy, Robert
  1839 *Narrative of the Surveying Voyages of His Majesty's Ships "Adventure" and "Beagle."* 3 vols. London.
Fontane, Marius
  1881a *L'Inde védique.* (Histoire universelle, Vol. I.) Paris.
  1881b *Les Iraniens.* (Histoire universelle, Vol. II.) Paris.
  1882 *Les Egyptes.* (Histoire universelle, Vol. III.) Paris.
Forbes, David
  1870 "On the Aymara Indians of Bolivia and Peru." *Journal of the Ethnological Society of London,* N.S. 2: 193–305.
Fornander, Abraham
  1878 *An Account of the Polynesian Race.* 3 vols. London.
Forster, Johann Rheinhold
  1778 *Observations Made during a Voyage around the World.* London.
Frazer, J. G.
  1887 *Totemism.* Edinburgh.
Fustel de Coulanges, N. D.
  1876 *La Cité antique.* 6th ed. Paris.
Gason, S.
  1879 "The Dieyerie Tribe of Australian Aborigines." in *The*

Native Tribes of South Australia, edited by J. D. Woods, pp. 253–306. Adelaide.

Geiger, Wilhelm
    1885   *Civilisation of the Eastern Irānians in Ancient Times.* 2 vols. London.

Gibbon, Edward
    1776–88 *The History of the Decline and Fall of the Roman Empire.* 6 vols. London.

Gill, W. Wyatt
    1876   *Life in the Southern Isles.* London.

Gilmour, James
    [1883] *Among the Mongols.* London.

Giraud-Teulon, Alexis
    1867   *Etudes sur les sociétés anciennes: La Mère chez certains peuples de l'antiquité.* Paris.

Gladstone, William Ewart
    1869   *Juventus Mundi: The Gods and Men of the Heroic Age.* London.

Gravier, Gabriel
    1881   *Etude sur le sauvage du Brésil.* Paris.

Gray, J. H.
    1878   *China.* 2 vols. London.

Greenwood, James
    1865   *Savage Habits and Customs.* (Curiosities of Savage Life, Second Series, Vol. II.) 3d ed. 2 vols. London.

Grey, George
    1841   *Journals of Two Expeditions of Discovery in North-West and Western Australia.* 2 vols. London.

Grote, George
    1846–56 *A History of Greece.* 12 vols. London.
    1865   *Plato, and the Other Companions of Sokrates.* 3 vols. London.

Grout, Josiah
    [1864?] *Zulu-Land.* Philadelphia.

Gubernatis, Angelo de
    1872   *Zoological Mythology: The Legends of Animals.* 2 vols. London.

Hall, Charles Francis
    1864   *Life with the Esquimaux.* 2 vols. London.

Hart, Robert
  1871 "Table of Consanguinity and Affinity of the Chinese, in the Mandarin Dialect." (In Morgan 1871, pp. 432–7).
Hearn, W. E.
  1879 *The Aryan Household*. London.
Henry, B. C.
  1886 *Ling-Nam: Interior Views of South China*. London.
Herodotus
  1849 *Herodotus, Literally Translated by H. Cary*. London.
Hickson, S. J.
  1887 "Notes on the Sengirese." *Journal of the Anthropological Institute* 16 : 136–43.
Home, Henry (Lord Kames)
  1819 *Sketches of the History of Man*. New ed. 3 vols. Glasgow.
Howitt, A. W.
  1883 "Notes on the Australian Class Systems." *Journal of the Anthropological Institute* 12 : 496–510.
  1884 "Remarks on the Class Systems Collected by Mr. Palmer." *Journal of the Anthropological Institute* 13 : 335–46.
  1885 "Australian Group Relations." *Report of the Regents of the Smithsonian Institution, 1883*, pp. 797–824. Washington.
Howitt, A. W., and Fison, Lorimer
  1883 "From Mother-Right to Father-Right." *Journal of the Anthropological Institute* 12 : 30–46.
  1885 "On the Deme and the Horde." *Journal of the Anthropological Institute* 14 : 142–68.
Huc, Evariste Régis
  [1851] *Travels in Tartary, Thibet, and China*, translated by W. Hazlitt. London.
  1855 *The Chinese Empire*. 2 vols. London.
Humbert, Aimé
  1870 *Le Japon illustré*. 2 vols. Paris.
Hunter, W. W.
  1871 *The Annals of Rural Bengal*. London.
  1881 *The Imperial Gazetteer of India*. 9 vols. London.
Jarves, James Jackson
  1843 *History of the Hawaiian or Sandwich Islands*. Boston, Mass.

Jolly, Julius Ernst (trans.)
  1876 *Náradíya Dharmaśastra: Or, The Institutes of Nárada.*
        London.
Kane, Paul
  1859 *Wanderings of an Artist among the Indians of North Amer-*
        ica. London.
Kay, Stephen
  1833 *Travels and Researches in Caffraria.* London.
Kennan, George
  1871 *Tent Life in Siberia.* London.
Kolben, Peter
  1731 *The Present State of the Cape of Good-Hope: Or, A Particu-*
        lar Account of the Several Nations of the Hottentots. 2 vols.
        London.
Kopernicky, Isidore, and Davis, J. Barnard
  1870 "On the Strange Peculiarities Observed by a Religious Sect
        of Moscovites, Called Scoptsis." *Journal of Anthropology*
        1 : cxxi–cxxxv.
Lafitau, Joseph François
  1724 *Moeurs des sauvages amériquains comparées aux moeurs*
        des premiers temps. 2 vols. Paris. [Quarto. There is another
        issue of this work, brought out by the same publishers and
        also dated 1724, in four octavo volumes.]
Lahontan, Louis Armand de Lom d'Arce, Baron de
  1728 *Mémoires de l'Amérique septentrionale.* (Nouveaux Voy-
        ages de Mr. le Baron de Lahontan, dans l'Amérique sep-
        tentrionale . . ., Tome 2.) Amsterdam.
Lane, Edward William
  1836 *An Account of the Manners and Customs of the Modern*
        Egyptians. 2 vols. London.
Lang, Andrew
  1884 *Custom and Myth.* London.
Lasso de la Vega, Garcia
  1715 *Histoire des Yncas, rois due Pérou.* Translated from the
        Spanish by J. Baudoin. 2 vols. Paris.
  1869–71 *First Part of the Royal Commentaries of the Yncas.*
        Translated by C. R. Markham. 2 vols. London.

Lecky, W. E. H.

    1869   *History of European Morals from Augustus to Charlemagne.* 2 vols. London.

Legge, James

    1869   *The Life and Teachings of Confucius.* (The Chinese Classics, Vol. I.) 3d ed. London.

Lenormant, François

    [1878]   *Chaldean Magic: Its Origin and Development.* Translated by W. R. C[ooper]. London.

    1881–88   *Histoire ancienne de l'Orient.* 9th ed. 6 vols. Paris.

Lesseps, J.-B.B. de

    1790   *Travels in Kamtschatka.* 2 vols. London.

Letourneau, C. J. M.

    1876   *La Sociologie d'après l'ethnographie.* Paris.

Lewin, Thomas H.

    1870   *The Wild Races of South-Eastern India.* London.

Lubbock, John

    1875   *The Origin of Civilisation and the Primitive Condition of Man.* 3d ed. London.

    1885   "On Customs of Marriage and Systems of Relationship among the Australians." *Journal of the Anthropological Institute* 14: 292–300.

Mackenzie, J.

    1887   "Discussion" of Conder 1887. *Journal of the Anthropological Institute* 16: 94–5.

McLennan, J. F.

    1866   "Bride-Catching." *The Argosy* 2, No. 7: 31–42.

    1869–70   "The Worship of Animals and Plants." *Fortnightly Review, N. S.* 6: 407–27, 562–82; 7: 194–216. [Reprinted in *Studies in Ancient History, The Second Series,* edited by Eleonora A. McLennan and Arthur Platt (London, 1896), pp. 491–569.]

    1876   *Studies in Ancient History: Comprising a Reprint of Primitive Marriage, An Inquiry into the Origin of the Form of Capture in Marriage Ceremonies.* London.

    1885   *The Patriarchal Theory.* Based on the papers of the late

J. F. McL., edited and completed by Donald McLennan. London.

Maharajas, The

1861   [A series of extracts from Indian newspapers on the Mahārā-jas.] Bombay.

Maine, H. J. S.

1871   *Village-Communities in the East and West.* London.

1875   *Lectures on the Early History of Institutions.* London.

Mallet, Paul Henri

1770   *Northern Antiquities: Or, a Description of the Manners, Customs, Religion and Laws of the Ancient Danes, and other Northern Nations.* Translated by T. Percy. 2 vols. London.

Man, E. H.

1883   "On the Aboriginal Inhabitants of the Andaman Islands, Part II." *Journal of the Anthropological Institute* 12 : 117–75.

Mariner, William

1817   *An Account of the Natives of the Tonga Islands.* 2 vols. London.

Marsden, William

1811   *The History of Sumatra.* 3d ed. London.

Marshall, William Elliot

1873   *A Phrenologist among the Todas.* London.

Maspero, Gaston

1886   *Histoire ancienne des peuples de l'Orient.* 4th ed. Paris.

Massey, Gerald

1883   *The Natural Genesis.* (A Book of the Beginnings, Part 2.) London.

Matter, A. Jacques

1828   *Histoire critique du gnosticisme.* 2 vols. Paris.

Meadows, Thomas Taylor

1856   *The Chinese and Their Rebellions.* London.

Ménard, René

1880–83 *La vie privée des anciens.* 4 vols. Paris.

Meyners d'Estrey des Frasmes, G. H. J.

1881   *La Papouasie ou Nouvelle Guinée occidentale.* Paris.

Mitford, A. B. F.

1871   *Tales of Old Japan.* 2 vols. London.

Moffat, Robert
1842 *Missionary Labours and Scenes in Southern Africa.* London.
Monier-Williams, Monier
1876 *Indian Wisdom.* 3d ed. London.
Morgan, Lewis H.
1871 *Systems of Consanguinity and Affinity of the Human Family.* (Smithsonian Contributions to Knowledge, 218.) Washington.
1877 *Ancient Society: Or, Researches in the Lines of Human Progress from Savagery, through Barbarism to Civilization.* London.
Moura, J.
1882–83 *Le Royaume du Cambodge.* 2 vols. Paris.
Müller, Friedrich Max
1868 *Chips from a German Workshop.* 2d ed. 2 vols. London.
Musters, G. C.
1871 *At Home with the Patagonians.* London.
Peschel, Oscar
1876 *The Races of Man and their Geographical Distribution.* London.
Pétis de la Croix, François (*the elder*)
1722 *The History of Genghizcan the Great.* London.
Philo Judaeus
1854–55 *The Works of Philo Judaeus.* Translated by C. D. Yonge. 4 vols. London.
Poole, Francis
1872 *Queen Charlotte Islands.* London.
Popular Encyclopaedia, The
1841 [First edition; many subsequent editions.] London.
Pratt, George
1878 *A Grammar and Dictionary of the Samoan Language.* London.
Prichard, J. C.
1836–47 *Researches into the Physical History of Mankind.* 3d ed. 5 vols. London.
Pritchard, W. T.
1865 "Viti, and its Inhabitants." *Memoirs of the Anthropological Society of London* 1: 195–209.

1866   *Polynesian Reminiscences.* London.
Prjévalskii, N. M.
   1880   *Mongolie et pays des Tangoutes.* Paris.
Reade, William Winwood
   1874   *The Martyrdom of Man.* London.
Reclus, Elisée
   1876–94 *Nouvelle Géographie universelle: la terre et les hommes.*
         19 vols. Paris.
   1885   *Les Primitifs.* 2d ed. Paris.
Rémusat, J. P. B.
   1829   *Nouveaux Mélanges asiatiques.* 2 vols. Paris.
Renouard de Sainte-Croix, C.L.F.F.
   1812   *Ta-Tsing-Leu-Lée: ou, les lois fondamentales du code pénal
         de la Chine.* [n.p.]
Ridley, William
   1875   *Kamilaroi, Dippil, and Turrubul: Languages spoken by
         Australian Aborigines.* 2d ed. Sydney.
Robertson Smith, William
   1885   *Kinship and Marriage in Early Arabia.* London.
Rowney, Horatio Bickerstaffe
   1822   *The Wild Tribes of India.* London.
Sanderson, John
   1879   "Polygamous Marriages among the Kafirs of Natal and
         Countries Around." *Journal of the Anthropological Insti-
         tute* 8: 254–60.
Sangermano, Vincentius
   1833   *A Description of the Burmese Empire.* London.
Seemann, Berthold Carl
   1862   *Viti: An Account of a Government Mission to the Vitian or
         Fijian Islands in the Years 1860–61.* Cambridge.
Shooter, Joseph
   1857   *The Kafirs of Natal and the Zulu Country.* London.
Shortt, John
   1868   *An Account of the Tribes of the Neilgherries.* Madras.
   1869   "On the Wild Tribes of Southern India." *Transactions of
         the Ethnological Society, N.S.* 7: 186–94.
   1870   "The Bayadère: Or, Dancing Girls of Southern India."
         Memoirs of the Anthropological Society of London 3: 182–94.

Sibree, James
[1870] *Madagascar and its People.* London.
1880 "Relationships and Names Used for Them among the Peoples of Madagascar, Chiefly the Hovas; Together with Observations upon Marriage Customs and Morals among the Malagasy." *Journal of the Anthropological Institute* 9 : 35–49.

Smith, John
1616 *A Description of New England.* London. In *A General Collection of the Best and Most Interesting Voyages and Travels in all Parts of the World,* edited by John Pinkerton. London, 1808–14. Vol. XIII.)

Smith, Reginald Bosworth
1876 *Mohammed and Mohammedanism.* 2d ed. London.

Smith, William (ed.)
1842 *A Dictionary of Greek and Roman Antiquities.* London.
1877–87 *A Dictionary of Christian Biography.* 4 vols. London.

"*Speaker's Commentary, The*"
1871–88 *The Holy Bible according to the Authorized Version, A.D. 1611, with an Explanatory and Critical Commentary. . . .* 12 vols. London. [Written at the suggestion of J. E. Denison, Speaker of the House of Commons, and commonly referred to after this circumstance.]

Speke, John Hanning
1863 *Journal of the Discovery of the Nile.* Edinburgh.

Spencer, Herbert
1874 *Descriptive Sociology, No. 3: Types of Lowest Races.* London.
1875 *Descriptive Sociology, No. 4: African Races.* London.
1876–96 *Principles of Sociology.* (*A System of Synthetic Philosophy,* vols. VI–VIII.) 3 vols. London.

Spix, J. B. von, and Martius, C. F. P. von.
1824 *Travels in Brazil in the Years 1817–1820.* 2 vols. London.

Staunton, G. T. (trans.)
1810 *Ta Tsing Leu Lee: Being the Fundamental Laws . . . of China.* London.

Sutherland, J. C. C. (trans.)
1865 *The Dattaka-Mímánsá and Dattaka-Chandriká.* Madras.

Tavernier, J.-B.
 1889   *Travels in India.* 2 vols. London
Taylor, Richard
 1870   *Te Ika a Maui: Or, New Zealand and its Inhabitants.* 2d ed.
        London.
Thompson, George
 1827   *Travels and Adventures in Southern Africa.* 2 vols. London.
Turner, George
 1861   *Nineteen Years in Polynesia.* London.
Turner, Samuel
 1800   *An Account of an Embassy to the Court of the Teshoo
        Lama, in Tibet.* London.
Tylor, E. B.
 1865   *Researches into the Early History of Mankind.* London.
        [Edited and abridged with an introduction by Paul Bohan-
        nan. Chicago: University of Chicago Press, 1964.]
 1871   *Primitive Culture.* 2 vols. London.
Ujfalvy, K. J. de
 1880   *Expédition scientifique française en Russie, etc., Vol. III:
        Les Bachkirs, les Vêpses, et les antiquités finno-ongriennes
        et altaïques. . . .* Paris.
Vambery, Armin
 1864   *Travels in Central Asia.* London.
Wake, Charles Staniland
 1868   *Chapters on Man.* London.
 1873   ''Man and the Ape.'' *Journal of the Anthropological In-
        stitute* 2 : 315–28.
 1878   *The Evolution of Morality, Being a History of the Develop-
        ment of Moral Culture.* 2 Vols. London.
 1879   ''The Origin of the Classificatory System of Relationships.''
        Journal of the Anthropological Institute 8 : 144–79.
 1884   ''The Nature and Origin of Group Marriage.'' *Journal of
        the Anthropological Institute* 13 : 151–61.
 1886   ''Les Cambodgiens et leur origine.'' *Revue d'anthropologie,*
        3ᵉ série 1 : 204–25.
 1888a *Serpent-Worship, and Other Essays, with a Chapter on
        Totemism.* London.

1888b "The Primitive Human Horde." *Journal of the Anthropological Institute* 17: 276–82.

Weill, Emmanuel
    1874   *La Femme juive: sa condition légale d'après la Bible et le Talmud.* Paris.

Wheeler, James Talboys
    1867   *The History of India from the Earliest Ages.* London.

Wilkes, C.
    1849   *Narrative of the United States Exploring Expedition, 1838–42.* 5 vols. Philadelphia.

Wilkinson, John Gardner
    1837–41 *Manners and Customs of the Ancient Egyptians.* 3 vols. London.

Wilson, Andrew
    1875   *The Abode of Snow: Observations on a Journey from Chinese Tibet to the Indian Caucasus, through the Upper Valleys of the Himalayas.* Edinburgh and London.

Winterbottom, Thomas
    1803   *An Account of the Native Africans in the Neighbourhood of Sierra Leone.* 2 vols. London.

Wood, John George
    1868–70 *The Natural History of Man, Being an Account of the Manners and Customs of the Uncivilized Races of Men.* 2 vols. London.

Woods, J. D. (ed.)
    1879   *The Native Tribes of South Australia.* Adelaide.

Zeen-ud-Deen
    1833   *Tohfut-ul-Mujahideen,* translated by M. J. Rowlandson. London.

INDEX

Abipones, 263, 264, 415

Abors, 79, 188–89, 209

Abyssinia, 83

Acca Laurentia, 88

Accessory spouses, 84, 115 ff.

'Acîca (sacrifice), 395–96

Adam, 463–65

Adelaide, 211

Adoption, 34 n. 2, 327 ff.

Adultery: among Greeks, 454; among Romans, 453

Affinity and kinship, 470

Afghans, 218, 411, 426

Africa, 214, 215, 222, 251, 271

African races: condition of women among, 214; polygyny of, 190

Agnation among Aryan nations, 359 ff., 384

Ahitas, 409

Ahts, 65

Adolingas, 120, 295

Aleuts, 59 n. 5

Alexander, W., 441

Algonkins, 132, 182, 322 n. 4

Alliance, 390

Amazon Indians, 427

Ambel ana (ambil anak), 292

American aborigines: condition of women among, 216; early betrothals among, 79; individual marriage among, 249; influence of maternal uncle among, 80; pairing family of, 131, 249; polygyny of, 181, 201; prohibited marriages among, 59; sexual hospitality among, 83; social arrangements of, 301; totemic system of, 308 ff., 322; wife purchase among, 389

Ancestors: offerings to manes of, 443; worship of, among early Aryans, 447, and female kinship, 313, in primitive family, 384, and totemism, 316

Ancestral tablet, worship of, 231, 234

Andaman Islanders, marriage among, 59, 95

Ani, 203

Animals, as totems, 314 ff.

Aphrodite, 16

Arab *hayy*, comparison of, with gens, 307

Arabia Felix, 164

Arabs, 95, 154, 148, 150, 152, 161, 164, 168, 171, 175 n. 2, 177, 196, 197, 210, 215, 228, 271, 299–301, 307, 308, 312, 328, 343, 349, 392, 394, 405, 417–18, 426, 428, 467; ideas of, on fatherhood, 177, 392, 395

Arabs, early: eating together a bond of union among, 394; kindred group of, 307; kinship through females among, 394; law of marriage among, 349; marriage by capture among, 350, 417; marriage of dominion among, 350, 417; polyandry among, 145 ff., 164 ff., 393; prohibited marriages among, 61; rite of *acîca* among, 395; social arrangements of, 299; temporary marriages of, 95 ff., 144 ff.; use of totems by, 308, 317; wife purchase among, 350, 393

Arawaks, 264

Areoi festivals: licentiousness at, 40; institution, nature of, 138

Areois and Nairs compared, 140

Arjuna, 160

Armenia, ancient, sacred prostitution in, 87

497